INTRODUCTION TO CORPORATE AND PERSONAL INSOLVENCY LAW

by
FIONA TOLMIE, LL.M.
Senior Lecturer in Law
Kingston University

LONDON
SWEET & MAXWELL
1998

Published in 1998 by
Sweet & Maxwell Limited
100 Avenue Road,
Swiss Cottage,
London NW3 3PF

Typeset by Interactive Sciences Ltd, Gloucester
Printed and bound in Great Britain by Clays Ltd, St Ives plc

No natural forests were destroyed to make this product, only farmed timber was used and re-planted.

ISBN 0 421 59850 6

A CIP catalogue record for this book is available from The British Library.

PREFACE

This is the book for which the third year Law and Law and Accounting students to whom I teach an option on insolvency law have been asking: a book on both corporate and personal insolvency within their price range. The fact that no such book appears to exist is probably due to the fact that insolvency law has tended to be studied on university courses in the context of company law (in the case of corporate insolvency) and, to a lesser extent, personal property law (in the case of bankruptcy). This reflects the fact that for much of their history the two strands of corporate and personal insolvency law have developed separately; even now, each aspect is dealt with by distinct sections of the insolvency legislation. It also reflects the fact that it is only very recently that insolvency law has begun to be seen as a subject in its own right. It is a great pity that insolvency law as such does not feature in the curriculum of more law schools; this may well be due to the apparently prevalent view that insolvency law is largely concerned with tedious procedural rules and lacks intellectual and conceptual content. Nothing could be further from the truth and, as a final year subject, it provides an ideal opportunity to revise and consider the interaction of numerous areas of the law previously studied in isolation. Insolvency law may be considered as an octopus amongst the categories into which the law is divided; its tentacles spread into many other areas. Readers of this text will come across aspects of the law relating to real and personal property, companies and partnerships, contract, civil litigation, employment, family breakdown, trusts, crime and conflict of laws. It has frequently been a situation of insolvency which has been the dynamic for the development of rules of property law since it is when a debtor has insufficient resources to meet all claims that the question of the ownership of assets associated with him or her becomes most pressing.

Insolvency law is a particularly appropriate topic of study for students on cross-disciplinary law and business (particularly accountancy) courses and for that reason this book does not assume much prior knowledge of property law and attempts to provide an introduction to the necessary concepts.

The intention of the book as a whole is merely to provide an introduction to both the current legal rules and the underlying issues of this vast, sprawling and rapidly developing subject and, in that sense, it is not the escape route from the library for which my students have been wishing. It aims to provide a basic framework of knowledge together with references both to the work of those who have written with authority in greater depth and to sources for updating the law which is constantly changing; in the final weeks of preparing this manuscript it seemed that insolvency cases were being reported almost every other day. Students using this book will find numerous signposts to the works of Professors Fletcher, Goode, Rajak, Ziegal and others referred to in the footnotes. They will also need to consult the law reports (particularly the specialised company law reports), and the periodicals, particularly *Tolley's Insolvency Law and Practice*, the *Company Lawyer* and the *Journal of Business Law*. The Internet is also likely to prove helpful in keeping up to date; Department of Trade and Industry press releases, information from the Insolvency Service and *Hansard* can be accessed via http://www.open.gov.uk. The U.K. bankruptcy and insolvency website at http://www.insolvency.co.uk may also be of assistance. The manuscript for the book was delivered at the end of 1997, but I have attempted at proof stage to bring the law up to date as at Easter 1998.

I have decided to use the masculine pronoun throughout the book since this seemed the least cumbersome of the various available options for dealing with the difficulty that any particular individual might be either male or female; in statistical terms, where the reference is to either an insolvency practitioner or an insolvent, it is also likely to be the correct pronoun. Regrettably, women are in fact very poorly represented amongst insolvency practitioners, particularly at a senior level. A survey of members by the Society of Practitioners of Insolvency in 1997 revealed that the proportion of female members in the various regions varied between 11 per cent and 22 per cent; of all female members 28 per cent are partners or principals, whereas 55 per cent of male members were partners or principals. Happily, from the female point of view, another recent survey carried out by the Society of Practitioners of Insolvency showed that women are also far less likely than men to be undischarged bankrupts; this was demonstrated by the fact that five out of every six personal insolvency victims were men despite the fact that women currently make up one in four of those running businesses. Furthermore, the women owed less on average than the men.

Finally, I must apologise to Andrew, Isabel and Tom for the effect which writing this book had on family life in the latter part of 1997 and I thank them for their forbearance.

Fiona Tolmie
Kingston Law School
June 1998

TABLE OF CONTENTS

PART VI: AN INTRODUCTION TO ISSUES OF CROSS-BORDER INSOLVENCY

TABLE OF CASES

TABLE OF STATUTES

TABLE OF STATUTORY INSTRUMENTS

PART I

GENERAL INTRODUCTION

CHAPTER 1

INTRODUCTION

1. Introduction to insolvency law

Insolvency can be defined broadly as the inability to meet one's debts either because of a lack of available cash at the relevant time[1] or, more fundamentally, because total liabilities exceed the assets which can be made available to meet them. Insolvency is something which will have to be dealt with by any society which recognises the use of credit; as soon as society provides the ability to commit to the future performance of an obligation, it provides the chance that performance will not be possible at that future time. Even if society could prevent the voluntary incurring of future obligations there would still be imposed obligations such as tort damages and tax which some might find impossible to meet.

As the Cork Committee[2] recognised: "the roots of insolvency law are embedded deep in our legal, social and economic history. It has always been recognised that the topic is one which touches on most aspects of commercial law, in the sense that there is always a risk that all mercantile contracts may at one time or another fall to be investigated by the Bankruptcy Courts."[3]

The Cork Report further observed[4] that "the law of insolvency takes the form of a compact to which there are three parties: the debtor, his creditors and society". Any system which is to cope with the consequences of an insolvency has to bear in mind the interests of these three parties. The debtor is concerned to be relieved from the harassment of his creditors and to be able to make a fresh start, preferably without having to undergo the rigours of a formal insolvency regime. The creditors want to recoup as much as possible of what they are owed and

---

[1] This is often referred to as a cash-flow or liquidity problem.
[2] Report of the Review Committee on Insolvency Law and Practice (1982) Cmnd 8558, hereinafter "the Cork Report". See Chap. 5.4 for an explanation of the importance of this Report in shaping current insolvency legislation.
[3] At para. 30.
[4] At para. 192.

will be concerned about the division between themselves of the available assets. This question of the distribution of the insolvent's assets clearly raises fundamental issues of priority as between the various creditors and also, in the case of an individual insolvent, of the conflict between the debtor's dependants and his creditors. Society as a whole is concerned that commercial morality should be maintained; the system should not favour the debtor to such an extent that there is no incentive for debtors to meet their obligations. Insolvency law has always had to grapple with the question of the extent to which those unable to pay their debts should be treated as culpable or as merely unfortunate.

The balance between the interests of these three parties is a fundamental issue of policy. Where the insolvent is an individual, it is clear that rehabilitation of the debtor must be an aim of the law although there is scope for debate about the extent to which the creditors must lose out in order to leave the debtor with sufficient assets to achieve that aim. In the case of a corporate debtor, there is not the same unarguable need to achieve a rescue of either the legal person or the business entity; this is demonstrated by a comparison of the differing degrees to which the "rescue culture" has become embedded in insolvency laws throughout the world. In the United States, for example, the balance is in favour of the debtor at the expense of the creditors whereas in the United Kingdom the converse is the case.

The Cork Committee stated[5] the following extensive list of the aims of a good modern insolvency law:

(a) to recognise that the world in which we live and the creation of wealth depend upon a system founded on credit[6] and that such a system requires, as a correlative, an insolvency procedure to cope with its casualties;

(b) to diagnose and treat an imminent insolvency at an early rather than a late stage[7];

(c) to relieve and protect where necessary the insolvent, and in particular the individual insolvent, from any harassment and undue demands by his creditors,[8] whilst taking into consideration the rights which the insolvent (and where an individual, his family[9]) should legitimately continue to enjoy; at the same

---

[5] At para. 198.
[6] This is considered further in Chap. 2, below.
[7] Part II, below, is concerned with "rescue" procedures.
[8] See Chaps 9.3 and 10.4 for the circumstances in which a debtor may be protected from creditors in the course of a "rescue". See Chap. 25.2 for the stay on proceedings brought about by a liquidation or bankruptcy.
[9] See Chap. 27.3 on the bankrupt's home, Chap. 27.5 on the bankrupt's income and Chap. 33 on pensions.

time, to have regard to the rights of creditors whose own position may be at risk because of the insolvency;

(d) to prevent conflicts between individual creditors[10];

(e) to realise the assets of the insolvent which should properly be taken to satisfy his debts, with the minimum of delay and expense[11];

(f) to distribute the proceeds of the realisations amongst the creditors in a fair and equitable manner, with the minimum of delay and expense[12];

(g) to ensure that the processes of realisation and distribution are administered in an honest and competent manner[13];

(h) to ascertain the causes of the insolvent's failure and, if and so far as his conduct or, in the case of a company, the conduct of its officers or agents, merits criticism or punishment, to decide what measures, if any, require to be taken against him or his associates, or such officers or agents[14];

(i) to recognise that the effects of insolvency are not limited to the private interests of the insolvent and his creditors, but that other interests of society or other groups in society are vitally affected by the insolvency and its outcome, and to ensure that these public interests are recognised and safeguarded[15];

(j) to provide means for the preservation of viable commercial enterprises capable of making a useful contribution to the economic life of the country[16];

(k) to devise a framework of law for the governing of insolvency matters which commands universal respect and observance, and yet is sufficiently flexible to adapt to and deal with the rapidly changing conditions of our modern world;

(l) to ensure due recognition and respect abroad for English insolvency proceedings.[17]"

There are those who would argue that such an ambitious list is doomed to failure and that insolvency law should restrict itself to dealing with

---

[10] See Pt. V generally on the battle between the creditors.
[11] See Chaps 26–29.
[12] See Chap. 35.
[13] See Chap. 20 on the control of the insolvency system.
[14] See Chap. 21 on investigation of the insolvent and Chap. 22 on criminal offences.
[15] See Pt. IV generally.
[16] See Chaps 10–12.
[17] See Chap. 36.

the distribution of the assets of an insolvent. This is a debate which has largely taken place between American academics, with Professor Jackson[18] as a leading proponent of the more restrictive view and Professor Warren[19] advancing the case of those with other interests. Professor Jackson, who sees the purpose of insolvency law as debt collection, argues that the purpose of insolvency law is the co-ordination of the claims of creditors in order to enhance the value of the debtor's assets for all claimants. He says that insolvency law should guarantee the claimants in total at least as much as they would in total have received by individual enforcement of their claims: this has been described as the "common pool" philosophy. Professor Warren, on the other hand, advances the case for consideration of wider interests including those of employees, suppliers, customers, neighbours and government. She argues that the purpose of insolvency law is to provide a forum in which all interests can be heard. Professor Goode summarises and considers the debate from this side of the Atlantic in the second edition of his *Principles of Corporate Insolvency*.[20]

2. Introduction to this text

The rest of Part I considers the nature and role of credit in society and identifies the different categories of debtor and some of the reasons for their indebtedness. It explains the methods of debt enforcement available where there is no formal insolvency regime in existence. A brief outline of the history of English insolvency law, which goes back to Tudor times, is given since the current state of the law, particularly the separate treatment of personal and corporate insolvent, can only be fully understood in the light of this history. The historical outline concludes with a summary of the currently available insolvency regimes and the insolvency jurisdiction of the courts.

Part II considers the methods by which a debtor who is in fact insolvent, or nearly so, can attempt to avoid bankruptcy or liquidation. Part III considers the process and implications of subjection to either

---

[18] Jackson, *The Logic and Limits of Bankruptcy Law*; Jackson 91 Yale L.J. 857; Baird and Jackson 51 Univ. of Chicago L. Rev. 97 (1984); Baird and Jackson 55 Univ. of Chicago L. Rev. 738 (1988); Jackson 14 Journal of Legal Studies 73 (1985).

[19] 54 Univ. of Chicago L. Rev. 775 (1987) and see Professor Baird's reply, *ibid.*, 815.

[20] At p.35 *et seq.* He finds Professor Warren convincing and Professor Jackson's arguments ultimately unpersuasive. For another synopsis and discussion see Flessner, Ziegel (ed.) *Current Developments in International and Comparative Corporate Insolvency Law*, Chap. 2.

bankruptcy or liquidation. Part IV concentrates on the aspects of insolvency law intended to maintain public confidence in the legal framework governing the workings of the economy. Part V turns to the aspect which many would consider the core of insolvency law: the battle for the assets between the creditors. Part VI is an introduction to the problems of cross-border insolvency.

CHAPTER 2

CREDIT

1. Introduction

This chapter examines the role of credit in society. It goes on to provide a brief introduction to the mechanics of credit provision and then considers the ways in which a creditor can seek to enhance his chances of repayment by taking security.

2. The role of credit in society[1]

Credit was described as "the lifeblood of the modern industrialised economy" and "the cornerstone of the trading community" by the Cork Report.[2] The credit industry enables those who have money lying idle to make it available, in return for payment, to those who have a need for it. Businesses have always sought to raise capital in order to finance the production of the goods or services which will earn them profits; the ability to borrow that capital enables the business to grow faster than if it were solely dependant on the input from the owners' resources. As the scale of production increased with the Industrial Revolution so did the need for capital. The nineteenth century saw great developments in the means by which such finance could be supplied[3]; this included an increase in the financing of commerce and industry by way of secured loans.

Credit will often be provided on a long-term basis by investors and banks but businesses will also seek to obtain a delay in the time at which they need to make payments in respect of current liabilities. Short-term creditors are likely to include employees, who will usually be paid in arrears, and suppliers, who will often supply on credit terms. Many suppliers find themselves providing credit without their consent when

---

[1] See, generally, the Report of the Crowther Committee on Consumer Credit (Cmnd. 4596, 1971); Berthoud and Kempson, *Credit and Debt: The PSI Report* (1992); Ramsey, *Debtors and Creditors*, Howell et al., *Aspects of Credit and Debt*.

[2] At para. 10.

[3] See the description in Chap. 3.4 of the development of the limited liability company.

their customers fail to pay them within the agreed period and the question of the extent to which legislation can assist such involuntary creditors has become a live one, recently.[4]

Consumer credit is largely a phenomenon of the twentieth century. Attitudes towards credit were coloured for a long time by medieval Church teaching that all usury (*i.e.* lending at interest) was sinful.[5] Although borrowing was permitted, albeit with tight restrictions on rates of interest, from the mid-sixteenth century, the view that it was immoral for non-business people to take credit remained strong. Providers of consumer credit supplying goods under some of the early hire-purchase agreements of the nineteenth century would advertise that the goods would be delivered in plain vans so that the neighbours would remain in ignorance of the source of the goods. Attitudes to consumer credit still appear ambivalent. Surveys carried out in 1979 and 1989 discovered that even now only a minority are prepared to declare themselves positively in favour of the use of credit[6]; the majority said either that it was never a good thing or should be used only as a last resort.[7]

The twentieth century has seen a great change in the availability of consumer credit (particularly with the lifting of government controls on the provision of credit during the 1980s) and the numbers of people willing to use it, whether or not they approve of it.[8] During the nineteenth century the available forms of credit were mainly used by those in need as a method of obtaining money to pay for necessities. The use of credit to obtain goods in advance of being able to afford them has only recently become commonplace. The initial development of the hire purchase transaction[9] in the nineteenth century provided a means of financing the increasing twentieth-century demand for cars. The use of credit has spread to the acquisition of many other consumer durables.

---

[4] The government is proposing to introduce statutory interest on outstanding debts owed to small businesses: the Late Payment of Commercial Debts (Interest) Bill is expected to become law during 1998. Consultation produced a mixed response to the proposal with some opposition on the grounds that small businesses are often themselves late payers and that they will be reluctant to demand interest from large, important clients. See DTI Press Release July 28, 1997 and March 10, 1998 and NatWest Bank Survey December 8, 1997.

[5] Simpson, *A History of the Common Law of Contract*, pp. 510–518; Cornish and Clark, *Law and Society in England*, pp. 226 *et seq.*

[6] Berthoud and Kempson, *Credit and Debt*.

[7] Younger people were more likely to think credit was a good thing which may reflect a generational shift in attitudes. Amongst younger people, those with above average incomes were more likely to favour credit; this probably reflects a realisation of the greater risk of default amongst those with lower incomes.

[8] In 1979, only 11% of credit commitments were held by people who thought that credit was never a good thing; by 1989 this proportion had nearly doubled to 21% (Berthoud and Kempson, *Credit and Debt*).

[9] Used initially in relation to furniture, pianos and sewing machines.

The spread of home ownership has been accompanied by widespread mortgage borrowing. Cash dealings are increasingly being replaced by credit transactions with the proliferation of credit cards.

The Crowther Committee, which was appointed to carry out a wide ranging review of consumer credit and reported in 1971[10], concluded that consumer credit offered advantages to the individual which were both monetary and non-monetary and, therefore, it could be argued that consumer credit contributed to a better allocation of resources by increasing both consumer satisfaction and economic efficiency. Amongst the identified advantages were that consumers could enjoy capital goods[11] sooner than would otherwise be possible and, in inflationary times, possibly more cheaply; some consumers found it easier to borrow and pay back rather than save up; there could be practical convenience in using credit, and it made it possible to bridge the gap between income and spending in intervals between receipt of income. The Committee concluded that a rational consumer would increase his use of consumer credit, within the constraints imposed upon him by his income and his net worth, up to the point where his additional satisfaction from the goods and services thus acquired is equal to the additional cost of credit incurred in purchasing them. Indeed, it concluded that it was probable that insufficient use was being made of consumer credit; this seems less likely to be the case now given the subsequent continuing large increase in the use of consumer credit. The Crowther Committee found that in 1969 only 20 per cent of people used any source of credit. Berthoud and Kempson[12] carrying out research in 1989 found that 75 per cent of households had access to credit facilities and that 60 per cent were actively using those facilities. They also noted a striking increase in the number of people with multiple credit commitments.

The concomitant to the expansion of consumer credit has been the extension of the business of the banks from their traditional role of lending to commerce and industry into the personal lending market. Finance houses have come into being with the role of financing the provision of credit by retailers to their customers. Although bank loans are still the largest form of consumer credit, these are declining in importance as credit card lending continues to expand: bank loans

---

[10] Cmnd. 4596.

[11] Crowther pointed out that borrowing for the purpose of acquiring equipment such as a washing machine was justifiable on the same grounds as that for borrowing to buy a house since in both cases the purchaser is acquiring property which render services and give satisfaction over a period.

[12] *Credit and Debt: The PSI Report* (1992).

formed 56 per cent of total consumer credit, excluding mortgage borrowing, in 1995 and bank credit card lending had risen from nearly 12 per cent of consumer credit in 1981 to 21 per cent in 1995.[13]

The Cork Committee pointed out[14] that the foundation of the whole credit world and maintenance of respect for the legal structure surrounding it rests upon a belief in the sanctity of contract; such a belief required that a failure to repay result in the application of an effective form of sanction against the dishonest or reckless insolvent. At the same time, it had to be recognised that some debtors were in difficulty through misfortune rather than dishonesty. In considering where to strike the balance between creditor and debtor "it must be remembered that it is the creditor who possesses the capital—which, in the aggregate, is the capital of society as a whole—to which the debtor seeks access for purposes beneficial first to himself, secondly to the creditor in providing him with a market for his capital and, thirdly, to society as a whole".

3. Mechanisms for the provision of credit and the taking of security[15]

a) Introduction

There are two basic mechanisms of credit provision recognised by the law: sales credit and loan credit.

Sales credit arises where the creditor leaves the price for goods or services outstanding but charges more (either expressly to the debtor or by raising the price of the goods to all customers) to cover the risk. The seller will also consider that the risk of default is offset by the greater volume of sales. Some forms of sales credit leave the seller with a proprietary claim to the goods being sold until payment has been received in full.

Loan credit consists of the lending of a sum of money in return for an agreement to return the money and to pay interest on the loan. The creditor is putting his money to work and the rate of interest which he charges will be high enough to compensate him for the risk that some of those to whom he lends will default. Those who present a greater risk of default are likely to be charged a higher rate of interest.[16] In many

---

[13] *Social Trends* (1997). Credit card expenditure in 1995 amounted to £41.2 billion; there were nearly 30 million credit cards in issue at the end of 1995.

[14] para. 21.

[15] See, generally, Goode, *Legal Problems of Credit and Security* (2nd ed.) and Pts IV and V of *Commercial Law* (2nd ed.).

[16] This has the effect that those most in need of credit may have to pay higher than average interest charges. See Howells *et al.*, *Aspects of Credit and Debt*, Chap. 2 for a discussion of the provision of credit to the less well-off which includes consideration of credit unions and social lending.

cases the lender will also seek security either by way of guarantee or by taking a charge over property of the debtor. Where additional security is taken, the interest rate should be lower to reflect the lower risk.[17]

b) Forms of sale credit[18]

It should be noted that the creditor is frequently not the apparent supplier of the goods but a finance house to whom the apparent supplier has either sold the goods or assigned the debts. In the former case the contract of sale will be between the finance house and the customer.[19]

A credit sale will involve the seller transferring possession and ownership of the goods but leaving the price outstanding for a period. If the buyer defaults, the seller will have a purely personal remedy against him.

In a conditional sale, the seller transfers possession but retains ownership of the goods until the price has been paid. In case of default, the seller will have the right to reclaim the goods unless a third party has acquired a good title to them. The purchaser will be a "buyer in possession" for the purpose of the Factors Act 1889 and section 25 of the Sale of Goods Act 1979[20] able to confer good title on innocent third parties.

In a contract of hire purchase, the supplier puts the customer in possession of goods in return for a deposit and an agreement that periodic rental payments will be made over a specified period. The contract will provide an option for the customer to acquire ownership of the goods at the end of the rental period. In the case of default, the supplier will be able to repossess the goods.[21]

c) Loan credit

This category includes building society mortgage advances, bank loans and overdrafts and payments to suppliers under credit card arrangements. A distinction may be made between transactions for a fixed

---

[17] This is the theory but there are those who argue that the interest rate will be what the market will bear without much relationship to the risk undertaken.

[18] See, generally, Goode, *Commercial Law* (2nd ed.); Sealey & Hooley, *Cases and Materials in Commercial Law*; Atiyah, *Sale of Goods* (9th ed.). Chap. 28, below, contains a more detailed consideration of retention of title clauses.

[19] The Consumer Credit Act 1974, s.56 provides that the finance house will be treated as having made the negotiating statements made by the retailer. Where the arrangement is not a consumer credit agreement, the purchaser will still have to rely on the collateral contract device established in *Andrews v. Hopkinson* [1957] 1 Q.B. 229.

[20] Unless the agreement is a consumer credit agreement within the Consumer Credit Act 1974: Sale of Goods Act 1979, s.25(2).

[21] Subject to the restrictions contained in ss90 and 92 of the Consumer Credit Act 1974.

amount of credit such as bank loans and transactions which provide the debtor with a facility on which he can draw from time to time. Obvious examples of this latter type are bank overdrafts and credit card agreements; these are described as running account credit or revolving credit. Drawings may be made from time to time up to a specified level of credit; repayments into the account will restore, to that extent, the amount of credit available.

Creditors making loans will often seek to protect their position in the event of the debtor's default by taking security over assets of either the debtor or a third party or by seeking a guarantee from a third party. A creditor who is able to monitor closely the situation of the debtor may not feel the need to take security. Costs of monitoring are likely to increase the cost of the credit and the debtor may prefer to offer security in return for a lower rate of interest.

4. Consensual security[22]

a) Security over assets

There are four kinds of consensual security over assets known to English law: the pledge, the contractual lien, the equitable charge and the mortgage.[23]

The earliest forms of security required that the lender be given possession of (but no ownership interest in) assets belonging to the borrower. A pledge of the property will give the pledgee an implied right to sell the property in the event of the debtor's default and to repay himself out of the proceeds. A contractual lien allows the creditor to retain goods which have been delivered to him for some purpose other than security; any power of sale would have to be express rather than implied. Possessory security tends to be inefficient; it is a nuisance for the creditor to have to hold the asset and loss of its possession may deprive the debtor of the ability to use it to generate income. Possessory security rights require no registration since the fact that the borrower is out of possession is sufficient notice to third parties that the borrower is not free to dispose of the property.

A mortgage is the converse of a pledge; it involves the debtor retaining possession of the property but transferring ownership of it to the creditor on condition that the asset be reconveyed when the debt is

---

[22] See Goode, above, n.15. In relation to company charges, see Gough, *Company Charges* (2nd ed.).
[23] See *Re Coslett (Contractors) Ltd* [1997] 4 All E.R. 115 at 126.

paid. A non-possessory mortgage of land became possible by the sixteenth century but it was not until the enactment of the Bills of Sale Act
1854 that it became possible to grant a chattel mortgage: before this the
continuation in possession was regarded as almost conclusive evidence
of an intent to defraud creditors. The Bills of Sale legislation provided
for the registration of non-possessory chattel mortgages in writing so the
courts accepted properly registered bills of sale as non-fraudulent. It is
no longer[24] possible to grant a mortgage of land in this way; such a
mortgage has to take effect as a charge by way of legal mortgage or as
a lease for a term of years absolute.

A charge involves the transfer of neither possession nor ownership; it
consists of an appropriation of specified property of the debtor to
payment of the debt. The creditor will usually enforce the charge by
obtaining the appointment of a receiver. A charge can exist only in
equity[25] or by statute. A charge may be fixed, in which case it will attach
to specific assets, or floating, in which case it will hover over a class of
assets until it crystallises at which point it will attach to the assets which
the class contains at that time.[26] Once a charge attaches to a specific
asset, the chargor cannot dispose of the asset free of the charge without
the chargee's consent. The provisions of the Bills of Sale legislation
which require specific details of all assets caught by the security make
it impossible for an individual to give a floating charge. The Bills of
Sale legislation does not apply to companies who are, therefore, able to
give valid floating security over the entirety of their undertaking. The
only individuals able to give floating security are farmers who can give
agricultural charges.[27]

Most forms of mortgage or charge require registration in order to bind
third parties to whom the secured property may be transferred. A
number of different public registers are maintained for this purpose; for
example, there are registers for mortgages and charges over land, ships
and aircraft, for bills of sale and for charges granted by companies.

b) Personal security: the guarantee[28]

A guarantee is an undertaking to answer for the default of another either
by way of personal commitment or by the provision of real security or

---

[24] Since the Law of Property Act 1925.
[25] Since it requires neither conveyance nor assignment, it can only be given validity by the
equitable notion that that which is agreed to be done shall be treated as having been
done.
[26] The nature of the floating charge is considered further in Chap. 29.
[27] Under the Agricultural Credits Act 1928.
[28] See Goode, *Commercial Law* (2nd ed.), Chap. 30.

both. A guarantee is typically a unilateral contract under which the guarantor promises to provide the guarantee if the bank provides the credit but where the bank makes no promise to do so. A guarantee must be evidenced in writing.[29]

A guarantor can only be sued if the principal debtor defaults and the guarantor's obligation is enforceable only to the same extent as that of the debtor.[30] A guarantor will be discharged by an event which extinguishes the principal debtor's liability. In the absence of clear words to the contrary, the guarantor will be liable to the damages for which the principal debtor would be liable on failure to pay.[31]

A guarantor has an implied contractual right to be indemnified by a debtor at whose request the guarantee has been given. A guarantor who discharges the debt he has guaranteed is entitled to be subrogated to the creditor's rights against the debtor, including right to enforce security. If the guarantor's rights against the debtor are adversely affected by the creditor's conduct the guarantor will usually be discharged from his obligations.

Lenders will frequently seek a guarantee of the borrower's obligations from a third party. Groups of companies often provide cross-guarantees of each other's indebtedness. Directors of small companies may be asked to guarantee the company's obligations.

5. The distinction between a secured loan and sale credit[32]

Sale credit has always been regarded by the law as distinct from loan credit and has been the subject of different common law rules. For example, until the passing of the Consumer Credit Act 1974 which equates the two forms of credit with regard to transactions below a certain limit entered into by individuals, the legislation regulating money lending did not apply to forms of sale credit. A major consequence of this distinct treatment is that retention of title under sale credit is not regarded as a security interest for the purposes of registration. It is also possible to raise finance whilst strictly avoiding becoming

---

[29] This is one of the few remaining provisions of the Statute of Frauds 1677, s.4. If it secures a regulated agreement under the Consumer Credit Act 1974 it must actually be in writing.

[30] This may be contrasted with an indemnity which is a primary obligation with an existence independent of the contract between the lender and the principal debtor.

[31] *Moschi v. Lep Air Services Ltd* [1973] A.C. 331.

[32] See, generally, Diamond, *Review of security interests in property* (DTI 1988). Amongst the many articles on this topic and the need for reform are Goode (1984) 100 L.Q.R. 234, Diamond (1989) 42 C.L.P. 231, Lawson [1989] J.B.L. 287, Bridge [1992] J.B.L. 1, Ziegel [1995] C.L.J. 430.

party to a loan. There are situations in which someone in need of credit may be restricted, by statute or otherwise, from taking a loan; this restriction would not prevent the achievement of the same end through the mechanism of sale credit.[33] Businesses may also seek to structure their acquisition of finance in the way most favourable to their accounting records; increasingly, however, accountants are being required to have regard to the economic rather than the legal substance of transactions.

The courts have frequently been faced with the need to decide whether a particular transaction is a loan with security or is an example of sale credit, generally in connection with the question of whether registration was necessary for the validity of the transaction. The Court of Appeal in *Welsh Development Agency v. Export Finance Co. Ltd*[34] held that the court must look at the legal substance of a transaction and not at the labels which the parties have chosen to put on it. The court is not, however, to look beyond the legal form of the transaction to its economic effect. The court may decide that the transaction is not what it purports to be because it is a sham intended to mask the true agreement of the parties. Where the agreement is not a sham, it may still fail to fall into the legal category into which the parties have sought to put it because its provisions are inconsistent with the legal nature of such a transaction.

The courts have found it difficult to arrive at any precise distinction between transactions of sale and transactions by way of security. Romer L.J. set out what he regarded as the essential differences between a sale and a mortgage or charge in *Re George Inglefield Ltd*.[35] First, in a transaction of sale the vendor is not entitled to get back the subject-matter of the sale by returning to the purchaser the money which has passed between them. A mortgagor, on the other hand, is entitled until foreclosure to get back the subject-matter of the mortgage by returning the money. Secondly, if the mortgagee sells the subject-matter of the mortgage for a sum more than sufficient to repay him, he must account to the mortgagor whereas a purchaser may keep the profit on a sub-sale. Thirdly, if the mortgagee sells the property for less than the amount needed to repay him, he may still claim the balance from the mortgagor whereas if a purchaser resells for less than he paid he cannot recoup the

---

[33] See, for example, the background to the case of *Darlington B.C. v. Wiltshier Northern* [1995] 3 All E.R. 895, where the council needed finance to build a recreation centre but was subject to government borrowing restrictions. Instead of lending the authority the money needed to pay the builders, the bank contracted with the builders and subsequently sold the benefit of the contract to the council.

[34] [1992] B.C.C. 270.

[35] [1933] Ch. 1.

loss from his vendor. A transaction need not, however, bear all three indicia to fall into a particular category. Dillon L.J. in *Welsh Development Agency v. Export Finance Co. Ltd* said that: "In my judgment there is no one clear touchstone by which it can necessarily and inevitably be said that a document which is not a sham and which is expressed as an agreement for sale must necessarily, as a matter of law, amount to no more than the creation of a mortgage or charge on the property expressed to be sold".

The agreement in the *Welsh Development* case was an example of the type of transaction which sits very close to the borderline between sale and security. A company whose business involved the sale of computer disks to overseas buyers raised finance by selling the disks to Export Finance Co. ("Exfinco") before selling them, as agent for Exfinco, to the overseas buyers. Exfinco would pay the company 90 per cent of the price payable by the overseas buyer, less a discount fixed at the time of the transaction, which was to be adjusted later by reference to the time which it took all overseas buyers to pay what they owed. The agreement also provided that on giving three months' notice the company would be liable to pay to Exfinco a sum equal to all amounts owed by overseas buyers and thereupon all rights in the goods and the debts of the overseas buyers would be relinquished in favour of the company. The company had also given a floating charge over all its assets to the Welsh Development Agency who claimed that Exfinco's interest in the disks only amounted to a charge, which was void for non-registration, to secure the money it had advanced to the company. They argued that the discount was really an interest payment and that there was a right of redemption. The Court of Appeal held that none of the features which the Welsh Development Agency relied on was necessarily inconsistent with a contract of sale although they would more usually be found in a contract to lend money. At the same time, it was plainly intended that Exfinco would have the rights and remedies of a seller of goods against the overseas buyers should it find it necessary to exercise them. The description of the transaction as a sale, although not conclusive, could not be ignored.

There is considerable criticism of the artificiality of the distinctions which the courts are forced to make and which would in most cases be unnecessary if the legal consequences of the transactions were determined by their purpose rather than by their form.

CHAPTER 3

THE DEBTORS

1. Introduction

This chapter considers the categories of debtor who may become insolvent and some of the common reasons for debtors becoming insolvent. It also explains how individuals may seek the protection of limited liability by conducting their business through the medium of a limited liability company.

2. Individuals

a) Insolvent individuals

Insolvent individuals can be divided into three groups: consumer debtors, sole traders and those who have given personal guarantees of the obligations of insolvent company.[1]

b) Consumer debtors

Consumer debtors are those individuals who have incurred non-business debts. These will include mortgage repayments, credit card repayments, amounts outstanding under hire purchase and other credit sales, bank loans and overdrafts. Most consumer debt is repaid without difficulty but some debtors find themselves unable to meet the required repayments. Failure to pay national and local tax bills and to meet amounts owing to the utilities often give rise to outstanding debt.

Various studies have been carried out to identify the reasons for consumer over-indebtedness.[2] The conclusions are that inability to pay may be the result of straightforward over-commitment and failure in budgeting but that it seems often to be triggered by some unforeseen

---

[1] A survey by the Society of Practitioners of Insolvency (published July 1997) found that 14% of non-business individual insolvencies resulted from the giving of guarantees.
[2] see Berthoud and Kempson, *Credit and Debt: The PSI Report* (1992).

event such as illness or redundancy which prevents the debtor from earning what he had expected. Family breakdown is a factor in a substantial number of insolvencies.[3]

Inability to meet debts is often associated with low income.[4] Low income households tend to use credit less than affluent households; they have more restricted access to credit and it will usually be more expensive than the credit available to the more affluent. It tends to be used for the traditional reason of necessity rather than for obtaining goods earlier than could otherwise be the case. This group of debtors tends not to fall within the scope of insolvency law since there are rarely sufficient assets to make it worthwhile for a creditor to take action and the debtors themselves cannot afford to do so; they are likely to remain under the burden of debt permanently.[5]

Both the Cork and Crowther Committees recognised the need for rational and informed decision-making by consumers in order to avoid overcommitment. The recommendations of the Crowther Committee led to the enactment of the Consumer Credit Act 1974 whose contents include rules on the uniform calculation and advertising of the cost of credit, the information to be contained in the documentation and provisions intended to prevent high pressure selling. The Cork Committee said[6] that, apart from these measures, the only protection afforded an individual was his "own innate sense of honesty and prudence" and went on to observe that it was regrettable that the educational system did not do more to provide basic training in the handling of credit.

Some commentators have focused on the actions of creditors who may have encouraged over-borrowing, levied excessive charges or made arrangements for collecting payments which encourage default.

Gordon Borrie, at one time Director General of Fair Trading with responsibility for keeping developments relating to credit under review, has said[7] that the available evidence suggests that many borrowers lack

---

[3] In 1995, credit card debts lay behind more than a quarter of the personal insolvencies surveyed and divorce and child maintenance accounted for a further 10%: survey by Society of Practitioners in Insolvency, May 1996.

[4] Berthoud and Kempson, *Credit and Debt: The PSI Report* (1992) found evidence that households on low incomes were the most likely to be in arrears with credit repayments. The 1997 Survey by the Society of Practitioners of Insolvency found an average income of insolvent individuals of £21,400 in a survey which included people at all income levels from state benefit to several hundred thousand pounds in some cases. The survey was based on over 1800 cases of insolvency encountered by members of the Society during 1996; it is unlikely that many of those on low incomes will consult insolvency practitioners about their financial problems or have insolvency practitioners appointed as trustees in bankruptcy.

[5] See Ford and Wilson, *Insolvency Law: Theory and Practice* (ed. Rajak), Chap. 6.

[6] At para. 15.

[7] Chap. 3, Howells *et al.* (eds) *Aspects of Credit and Debt*.

the knowledge and skills to make sound credit decisions. He suggested that lenders had a responsibility to exercise caution and restraint in their marketing, their credit-granting criteria and practices and in their duty to help borrowers understand the commitment being undertaken.

c) Sole traders

Sole trader is the term used for an individual who is in business by himself. He will be personally liable, without limit, for the liabilities of that business.

d) Guarantors of insolvent companies

Individuals who have guaranteed the liabilities of an insolvent company will have unlimited liability to the extent of the amount guaranteed.

3. Partnerships[8]

Partnership is the relationship between two or more persons carrying on business in common with a view to profit. The relationship between the partners is governed by contract and agency law, codified to a great extent in the Partnership Act 1890. Partnerships are usually professional practices; it is unusual nowadays for a partnership to be formed to carry on a commercial activity.[9] In England and Wales a partnership is not a separate legal entity although procedural rules allow litigation to be brought by and against the partners in the firm name. Property brought into the partnership stock or acquired on account of the firm or for the purposes and in the course of the partnership business will be partnership property to be held and applied by the partners exclusively for the purposes of the partnership and in accordance with the partnership agreement.[10] The issue of whether particular property is partnership property or the property of an individual partner will be of great importance as between the creditors of the firm and the creditors of the individual partners in the event of insolvency.

In most cases, partners will be jointly liable without limit for the debts of the partnership.[11] A joint obligation is one owed by two or more persons together so that anyone bringing a claim to enforce the obligation must sue them all. Where the obligation is joint and several, the

---

[8] See, generally, Morse, *Partnership Law* (3rd ed.).
[9] See Cork Report, para. 1671.
[10] Partnership Act 1890, s.20(1).
[11] *ibid.* ss5–18 set out the circumstances in which partners will become liable to persons dealing with the firm. These rules are based on normal agency principles.

claimant may choose to sue them all together or one or more of them individually; partners are severally as well as jointly liable for loss or injury caused to a third party by wrongful acts or omissions of the firm or by its misapplication of funds.[12]

Section 17 of the Partnership Act 1890 provides that a person who is admitted as a partner into an existing firm does not thereby become liable to the creditors of the firm for anything done before he became a partner and that a partner who leaves the firm does not thereby cease to be liable for partnership debts or obligations incurred before his retirement unless there is an agreement to the contrary between the retiring partner, the newly constituted firm and the creditors. A retiring partner will continue to incur liability for the debts of the partnership to those who have not been notified of the retirement; those who have previously dealt with the business should be given actual notice but a notice in the *London Gazette* will be treated as sufficient notice to those who have not previously dealt with the firm. It is common for retiring partners to be given an indemnity by the continuing partners against continuing liability but an agreement which does not involve the creditors will only protect the ex-partners if the continuing partners remain solvent.

It is possible for one partner to go bankrupt in relation to his personal affairs without the partnership business being treated as insolvent although the bankruptcy will be treated as dissolving the partnership unless there has been agreement to the contrary.[13] Equally, the partnership business may be incapable of meeting its debts but some or all of the partners may still be solvent.

The current law relating to insolvent partnerships is contained in the Insolvent Partnerships Order 1994 made under section 420 of the Insolvency Act 1986. Since 1986 it has been possible for a partnership to be wound up as if it were a company; this has led to partners becoming liable to many of the sanctions available against directors.

Under the Limited Partnerships Act 1907 partners not involved in the management of the business can enjoy limited liability but this provision is little used because it is usually preferable to set up a limited liability company. The Limited Partnerships Act 1907 does not, in any event, assist those who wish to be active in the management of the business. Many professional bodies did not permit their members to operate through limited liability companies until relatively recently; some still do not. Many existing professional partnerships do not wish to incur the tax costs and loss of privacy involved in incorporation but have become increasingly outspoken about what they perceive as the

---

[12] Partnership Act 1890, s.12.
[13] *ibid.* s.33.

unfair exposure of their businesses to limited liability. The Department of Trade and Industry has produced a consultation paper[14] on the possibility of making a limited liability partnership available to professionals and the Law Commission has been asked to carry out a general review of the law of partnership, including a consideration of how such a structure might be made more widely available.[15]

4. Limited liability companies[16]

Many businesses are run through the medium of a company and by far the most numerous form of company is the company registered with limited liability under the provisions of the Companies Act 1985. Those wishing to bring a company into being have merely to register the necessary documents with and pay the requisite fee to the Registrar of Companies; it only requires one person to undertake to become a member of a company. Once the certificate of incorporation is issued, the company is recognised by law as being a person separate from any other person involved with it.

Although a company is recognised as a person in the eyes of the law, it is an intangible person incapable of any physical activity; it will act (honestly or dishonestly, competently or incompetently) through the agency of human people. The company's everyday affairs will be controlled by its board of directors, some of whom may also have contracts of employment with the company (in which case they are referred to as executive directors).[17] Some of the more important decisions (including the appointment of directors) are reserved for the members and shareholders of the company.

The company will need assets with which to run a business and it may issue shares in return for money or assets and borrow money from banks and other lenders. Shares will give the shareholders rights of participation in the governance of the company and in the profits made by the business and the right to a return of the capital on a solvent winding up of the company. Lenders will be promised annual interest (which will not be dependant on the company making a profit) and may demand

---

[14] URN 97/597 in February 1997.
[15] See Freedman and Finch [1997] J.B.L. 387.
[16] See, generally, company law textbooks such as Davies, *Gower's Principles of Modern Company Law* and Farrar, Furey and Hannigan, *Farrar's Company Law*. For a less traditional approach see Cheffins, *Theory, Structure and Operation of Companies*.
[17] Other terminology which will be met in connection with directors are the "*de facto* director" who, unlike the "*de iure* director" has not been formally appointed to the office of director which he appears to be occupying, and the "shadow director" who is able to control the decision-making of the actual directors and who may or may not be visible to the outside world.

either real security or personal guarantees of repayment. Loans to companies are evidenced by documents described as debentures and the lenders are often referred to as debenture holders.[18] Those who have lent money to the company will be entitled to claim with the other creditors in an insolvent winding up of the company whilst the shareholders will only have a claim once all the creditors have been repaid in full. There may be hierarchies of both lenders and shareholders. Those lenders with prior claim to repayment are often referred to as having senior debt whilst the debt which is subordinated to the senior debt is described as junior.

Contracts entered into by the directors and employees in relation to the business will be entered into by them on behalf of the company and it is the company, and no-one else (unless guarantees have been taken), who will be liable on those contracts. The term "limited liability company" is a misleading one since it is not the company whose liability is limited but that of the shareholders whose liability is limited to the amount that they have agreed to pay for their shares. In return for the privilege of limited liability, companies have to make public information about their financial state which businesses run by those with unlimited liability may keep secret. Company law contains various rules on the maintenance of share capital designed to prevent the return to the shareholders of their contribution (or their release from the obligation to make such contribution) whilst the company is a going concern; for example, shareholders may only be paid dividends from profit made by the company. Nothing, however, can prevent the company from dissipating the assets in the course of unsuccessful trading.

Limited liability is not a necessary concomitant of incorporation.[19] When the registered company was introduced by the Joint Stock Companies Act 1844, limited liability was excluded from its provisions; personal liability of members was retained although creditors would have to proceed first against the assets of the company. Limited liability was finally introduced, after much debate[20] in 1855, with a number of safeguards, including a minimum capital requirement. These safeguards were removed by the Joint Stock Companies Act 1856, which reflected

---

[18] The term is usually understood to mean those who are secured creditors of the company but strictly it refers to anyone who has lent money to the company.

[19] See *Hicks* [1997] J.B.L. 306 for the suggestion that small businesses do not incorporate for the protection of limited liability and that there is a need for an unlimited corporate form to meet the needs of small businesses.

[20] see Paul L. Davies, *Gower's Principles of Modern Company Law* (6th ed.) pp. 40 *et seq.* and the extensive references therein.

the laissez-faire view that those who dealt with companies, knowing them to be limited, knew what risks they were running. One of the main arguments of the pro-limited liability lobby was that, in the absence of limited liability, businesses would have developed a practice of contracting with limited liability; this was simply a more efficient method of achieving the same end.[21]

Running a business through a company, therefore, allows the insulation from its liabilities of those human beings who are instrumental in running its affairs. Since there is no need to have more than one member, a sole trader may incorporate his existing business by transferring it to a company, of which he is the sole director, in return for shares in the company; the liabilities of the business will in future belong to the company and his personal assets will be protected from attack. It is likely, however, that those extending any substantial amount of credit to the company will seek personal guarantee of repayment from the directors so that there would still be personal liability on the failure of the business. There is still considerable scope for individuals responsible for the running of an incorporated business to incur liabilities on its behalf which it is unable to meet and which it will be wound up without having met. Meanwhile, the individuals move on, personal wealth unscathed, to the next company; this is the so-called "Phoenix syndrome". The Cork Committee recognised this as one of the main problems with which the law of insolvency had to be seen to be dealing.

The Insolvency Act 1986 contains provisions under which directors of a company who allow it to continue trading after they should have realised that it could not avoid insolvent liquidation will be liable for the further loss caused to creditors.[22] Under the Company Directors Disqualification Act 1986, directors whose conduct in relation to an insolvent company shows them to be unfit to be concerned in the management of a company will be disqualified for a period of years from being a director.[23] The legislation employs the concept of the "shadow director"[24] to prevent those who are in fact running a company from insulating themselves from exposure to these risks by not formally holding the office of director.

---

[21] This is similar to the argument in favour of recognition of the rights of secured creditors in an insolvency discussed later in the text. See Cheffins, *Company Law: Theory, Structure and Operation*, Chap. 11.1 for a contemporary debate, with extensive references, on the merits of limited liability.

[22] See Chap. 31.

[23] See Chap. 23.

[24] Insolvency Act, s.251 and Company Directors Disqualification Act 1986, s.22(5).

5. Reasons for business failure

Various studies have been undertaken into the reasons for the financial failure of businesses and some academic writers have produced formulae designed to identify those businesses at risk of insolvency.[25]

Other less scientific approaches to this question are perhaps easier to comprehend. There seems to be a consensus[26] that most failures are the result of bad management although in a small minority of cases the business has been the victim of bad luck such that even the most competent of management could not have survived.[27] Another frequent problem is inadequate or inappropriate initial capitalisation of the business. Lingard identifies three areas as being of particular importance: inefficient production (which includes technical problems; inefficient procedures; poor labour relations; poor stock control and overstaffing); lack of skilful marketing and absence of stringent financial control. Argenti also focuses on the lack of adequate accounting information whilst also identifying structural defects (such as one-man rule, an unbalanced top team, a lack of management depth and a weak finance function). The Cork Committee observed[28] that in all insolvencies of substance, a crucial element contributing to the collapse is the wilful, or at least grossly negligent, failure of the insolvent to have kept proper books of account, or a refusal to inspect them or to believe what they reveal or what he is told about them. Proper accounting systems will provide for accurate cash flow forecasts and project projections, adequate provision for contingencies, accurate and up to date costing systems, proper systems of credit control and checks against theft and other fraud.

The Society of Practitioners of Insolvency's 6th survey of corporate insolvencies published in 1996 identified "management failure" as the primary factor in 44 per cent of cases surveyed and "loss of market" as the primary factor in 31 per cent of cases. The most common management failing was allowing profit margins to be eroded; other failings included over-optimism and over-gearing (that is, borrowing too much). A lack of management information was relevant in 29 per cent of cases.

---

[25] See Cooke and Hicks [1993] J.B.L. 338, Hamilton *et al.* 13 I.L.&P. 78; Belcher A., *Corporate Rescue*.
[26] See J. Argenti, *Corporate Collapse*; J. Lingard, *Corporate Rescue and Insolvencies* (2nd ed.), Chap. 1.
[27] Obviously, competent management will succeed in riding out unforeseen events which completely defeat less competently managed businesses.
[28] At para. 217.

The 7th Corporate Insolvency Survey, covering the year to July 1997, showed financial failure factors (in particular, cash flow management) as being the most significant amongst the more preventable causes of insolvency. The Society published its 6th survey on Personal Insolvency in 1997 and this identified the principal reasons for the business failure of individuals as loss of market (23 per cent), failure to pay tax or VAT (22 per cent), lack of working capital or cash flow problems (16 per cent), management failure (15 per cent) and bad debts (10 per cent).

CHAPTER 4

ENFORCEMENT OF DEBT

1. Introduction

The creditors of a debtor who has not yet been made formally insolvent will take individual action to recover the outstanding amounts; each creditor is entitled to attempt to obtain all of what is owing even though this would leave insufficient to cover the other debts.

The rights of the creditor may be personal (*"in personam"*) against the debtor or, in some circumstances, real (*"in rem"*) against the assets in the possession of the debtor. Real rights may arise from contract or by operation of law; for example, an unpaid landlord has the right to exercise the ancient common law remedy of distress over goods on the debtor's premises. Some creditors have other self-help measures available which may assist them in persuading their debtor to pay; utility companies, for example, may be able to disconnect supplies which is likely to persuade any debtor who can do so to meet arrears.

A creditor who is not in a position to exercise self-help over assets of the debtor and who cannot persuade the debtor to pay[1] will have to take court action to obtain judgment for the debt.[2] Obtaining a judgment does not of itself ensure payment of what is owing; the mechanics of enforcing such a judgment are considered later in this Chapter. The sensible creditor will have ascertained that there will be assets available to meet a successful claim and may seek to obtain one of the various procedural securities available; these include an order for the payment into court of money[3] and the appointment of a receiver of property by the court. Alternatively, but less securely because giving a purely personal right against the debtor, the creditor may seek a *Mareva* injunction freezing

---

[1] The persuasion will often come from commercial debt collection agencies to whom the debts have been passed. Harassment of debtors is a criminal offence punishable by a fine.

[2] Ford, *Consuming Credit: Debt and Poverty in the U.K.* at p. 89 argues that the judicial debt recovery process is too weighted in favour of the creditor.

[3] Under RSC, Ord. 14, r. 4(3) or CCR, Ord. 9, r. 14 (in fulfilment of a condition of leave to defend), RSC, Ord. 22, r. 1 or CCR, Ord. 11, r. 1 (payment into court) or in compliance with an order for security for costs (RSC, Ord. 23 or CCR, Ord.13, r. 8 or by statute).

the assets of the debtor; this is appropriate where the creditor fears the removal of the assets from the jurisdiction.

2. Enforcement of security[4]

a) General

A creditor may have security rights either because he has entered into a contract to that effect[5] or because of some principle of law. The main categories of real rights arising by operation of law which may avoid the creditor having to take personal action against the debtor are[6] the lien,[7] the statutory charge, non-contractual rights of set-off and the equitable right to trace. Receivership as a method of enforcing a mortgage or charge is considered in greater detail in Chapter 6, below.

b) The remedies of a mortgagee[8]

A mortgagee[9] may have the right to go into possession of the property, the right to appoint a receiver of the income of the property, the right to sell the property and the right to foreclose (which is exercised very rarely).

A mortgagee who goes into possession becomes subject to strict liabilities which, where the mortgagee's concern is to obtain the income from the property, make going into possession a less attractive option than appointing a receiver of the income. The right to possession will usually only be exercised in order to obtain vacant possession by a mortgagee intending to exercise a right to sell the property. The High Court has an equitable jurisdiction to stay possession proceedings[10] which is exercised sparingly.[11] Statutory relief is provided by section 36 of the Administration of Justice Act 1970 in respect of "dwelling

---

[4] See, generally, Goode, *Legal Problems of Credit and Security* (2nd ed.).
[5] See Chap. 2.
[6] See Goode, *Commercial Law* (2nd ed.) p. 668 *et seq.*
[7] Including the statutory lien conferred by section 41 of the Sale of Goods Act 1979 on the unpaid seller of goods.
[8] See Gray, *Elements of Land Law*, Chap. 20.
[9] Including a holder of a mortgage by way of legal charge.
[10] A court order is not necessary to go into possession if this can be done without committing a breach of the peace or making a violent entry unless the right is restricted by statute. A court order is necessary to enforce a right to possession of land under a mortgage securing an agreement regulated by the Consumer Credit Act 1974.
[11] *Birmingham Citizens Permanent Building Society v. Caunt* [1962] Ch. 883.

houses" where there appears to be a realistic possibility that the mortgagor may remedy his default within a reasonable period of time.[12] One of the main difficulties is that defendants often fail to communicate with the court or attend the hearing, thus depriving the court of the ability to exercise its discretionary powers.

A mortgagee must take reasonable care to obtain the proper market value for the property although the timing of the sale is entirely a matter for him.[13]

c) Charge

Documents conferring charges will usually confer an express right on the chargee to possession and sale of the encumbered property in the event of default. Such powers will often be conferred impliedly or by statute[14] but, in the absence of an express provision, an equitable chargee will need court consent for possession and, unless the charge was under seal, to sell or appoint a receiver. A chargee of land by way of legal mortgage has the same rights and remedies as a legal mortgagee.[15]

d) Pledge

A pledgee will have a right to sell the pledged goods.

e) Contractual lien

The holder of a lien has the right to detain the goods until the debt is paid. There may also be contractual right of sale in which case the security will be tantamount to a pledge except that the lienee will have been in possession of the goods before the security rights came into existence.

---

[12] The standard period of reasonable period is between two and four years but in *Cheltenham and Gloucester Building Society v. Norgan* [1996] 1 W.L.R. 343 it was held that a reasonable period could be the full term of the mortgage providing there was sufficient equity to protect the lender's eventual entitlement to repayment in full and a reasonable prospect of the borrower being able to pay off the arrears in full by that time as well.

[13] *Cuckmere Brick Co Ltd v. Mutual Finance Ltd* [1971] 2 All E.R. 633, *Palk v. Mortgage Services Funding plc* [1993] 2 All E.R. 481, *AIB Finance v. Debtors* [1997] 4 All E.R. 677 and *The Times*, March 11, 1998, CA.

[14] See Law of Property Act 1925, ss101, 109 where the charge is contained in a deed.

[15] Law of Property Act 1925, s.87(1).

3. Distress[16]

This is a self-help remedy[17] entitling landlords in certain circumstances to seize property found on the premises and to recoup any arrears of rent from the proceeds of sale. Landlords see distress as an easier remedy than forfeiture of the lease, a right which is qualified by the court's discretion to grant relief and which also carries the risk that the landlord may be left with empty premises and no rent. Distress may also be used as a bargaining ploy to achieve payment of the arrears or surrender of the lease.

The right to distrain arises as soon as the tenant is in arrears with the rent. The process of distraint is governed by complex and often obscure ancient rules, including, for example, a prohibition on the levy of distress on Sundays or between sunset or sunrise. Distress consists of entry (not by force) onto the demised premises, seizure (by identifying the goods to be taken) and impounding (by transferring them to the landlord's control). Goods may be transferred to the physical control of the landlord or the landlord may take walking possession of the goods by leaving them in the tenant's possession on the tenant undertaking not to disturb or dispose of them. The landlord will generally have the power to sell the goods after five days from the time of impounding.

Any goods may be seized apart from those in the category of privileged goods under common law or statute; it can be difficult to determine which goods fall into this category. Goods immune from distress include clothes and bedding to a value of £100, tools of trade to a value of £150, perishable foods, tenant's fixtures, the property of lodgers and things in actual use. Where the goods of a third party have been seized, the true owner may reclaim his property by serving a statutory declaration under the Law of Distress Amendment Act 1908. Anyone with a prior claim to the goods at the time of the levy will be protected; the exception is that the landlord will have priority in respect of arrears of rent for up to 12 months over an execution creditor.

The Law Commission has recommended the abolition of distress: "We see distress for rent as wrong in principle because it offers an extra-judicial debt enforcement remedy in circumstances which are, because

---

[16] See Gray, *Elements of Land Law* (2nd ed.) pp. 839 *et seq.*, McLoughlin, *Commercial Leases and Insolvency*, Law Commission Working Paper No. 97, May 1986, Law Commission, Landlord and Tenant: Distress for Rent: Law Com. No. 194, February 4, 1991. A. Clarke (1992) 45 C.L.P. 81.

[17] Leave of the court will be required in some circumstances (protected or statutory tenancies under Rent Act 1977 or assured tenancies within Housing Act 1988, protected occupancy or statutory tenancy within Rent (Agriculture) Act 1976) and corporate landlords will have to use a certificated bailiff who will have to comply with additional rules.

of its intrinsic nature, the way in which it arises and the manner of its exercise, unjust to the debtors, to other creditors and to third parties."

Remedies referred to as distress have been introduced by statute for the recovery of rates, taxes and certain fines imposed by magistrates' courts.

4. Enforcement of a judgment debt against a solvent debtor

The court may make an order allowing the judgment debtor to pay by instalments.[18] If the debtor still refuses to pay pursuant to the judgment, the creditor may then proceed to enforce judgment in one of the following ways. The debtor may be called for an examination as to his means before an officer of the court[19] thus allowing the creditor to inquire into the debtor's financial position and choose the most effective method of enforcing the judgment. Failure to comply may lead to the committal of the debtor for contempt of court.

The creditor will have the choice of the following methods of enforcement:

a) Execution

Execution against chattels pursuant to a writ of *fieri facias (fi. fa.)* in the High Court or warrant of execution in the county court which allows the judgment creditor to obtain the seizure and sale of chattels owned by the debtor so as to satisfy the judgment.[20] County court judgments over £1,000 may be transferred to the High Court for enforcement; judgments over £5,000 must be so transferred. Judgment creditors may wish to have the judgment enforced by the High Court sheriffs since it tends to be thought that they are more effective than the county court bailiffs. A further advantage of transferring the judgment is that, in the High Court, interest will be recoverable from the date of the certificate of judgment.

Certain goods are exempt from seizure under section 15 of the Courts and Legal Services Act 1990:

---

[18] The High Court has power on the application of the defendant to stay execution of the judgment provided debtor pays by such instalments as the court deems appropriate: Execution Act 1844, s.61; RSC, Ord. 47, r. 1. The county court has express power to make an instalment order on application of either party under County Courts Act 1984, s.71(1).

[19] RSC, Ord. 48, r. 1; CCR, Ord. 25, r. 3.

[20] see Millett L.J. in *Re a Debtor (No. 340 of 1992)* [1996] 2 All E.R. 211 for recent consideration of execution against chattels under the writ of *fi. fa.*

(i) such tools, books, vehicles and other items of equipment as are necessary to the defendant for use personally in his job or business

(ii) such clothing, bedding, furniture, household equipment and provisions as are necessary for satisfying the basic domestic needs of the defendant and his family.

It will often be the case that there are no goods worth seizing on the premises or that goods apparently belonging to the debtor are discovered to belong to a third party.

b) Charging order

A charging order allows the imposition of a charge on any freehold or leasehold land owned by a judgment debtor so as to provide security for payment of the judgment debt. In the first instance an order nisi will be made on the *ex parte* application of the creditor, possibly accompanied by an injunction restraining dealings with the land. At a subsequent hearing, the court will decide whether to make the order absolute or discharge it. Section 1(5) of the Charging Orders Act 1979 provides that the court should consider all the circumstances of the case and, in particular, any evidence before it as to the personal circumstances of the debtor and as to whether any other creditor of the debtor would be likely to be unduly prejudiced by the making of the order. The court will take into account the possibility of jeopardising an arrangement between debtor and creditors generally.[21] If the creditor wishes to enforce the charge he must apply for an order for sale as if he was a mortgagee of the land. The court has wide powers under section 36(2) of the Administration of Justice Act 1970 to adjourn the proceedings or stay or suspend its order if it seems likely that the debtor will pay the secured debt within a reasonable time.

c) Garnishee order

A garnishee order will be appropriate where the creditor knows that the judgment debtor has debts owing to him which could instead be paid to the creditor. The most common form of debt garnished is money standing to the credit of a debtor in a bank account. The creditor applies *ex parte* by affidavit for a garnishee order nisi; this avoids the debtor being given notice of proceedings and frustrating them by obtaining immediate payment of the debt to himself. There will then be a hearing at which the court will decide whether or not to make the order absolute;

---

[21] *Rainbow v. Moorgate Properties Ltd* [1975] 2 All E.R. 821.

the order will be made absolute unless the court finds that the garnishee is not indebted to the debtor or that someone else has a prior claim to the money.

d) Attachment of Earnings Order

An attachment of earnings order will be appropriate where the judgment debtor has regular employment but no substantial assets. The order can only be made by the debtor's local county court but that court has power to enforce judgments made by the High Court or by other county courts. The two pre-conditions to such an order are that the debtor has defaulted in one or more instalments under a judgment ordered to be paid by instalments and that the debtor is in employment. The debtor will have to submit a statement of means and will be told that it is possible to apply for a suspended order under which, provided he makes regular payments, his employers will not be contacted. The court will determine both a normal deduction rate and a protected earnings rate, the latter being a minimum sum necessary to provide for the debtor and his dependants below which the debtor's earnings may not be reduced by the order. The order will be addressed to the debtor's employer and requires them on penalty of a fine to take all reasonable steps to ensure that the appropriate deduction is made from the debtor's wages and paid to the court.

CHAPTER 5

HISTORY OF INSOLVENCY LAW[1]

1. Introduction

English law has developed parallel systems for dealing with insolvent individuals and insolvent companies; the current regimes are outlined at the end of this explanation of their historical development. Business insolvency is largely dealt with by the corporate insolvency system[2] rather than by the personal insolvency system; this mirrors the separate provisions of earlier times for insolvent traders (called bankruptcy law) and for other insolvent individuals (called insolvency law).

Modern insolvency law has regard to, first, the interests of the creditor in obtaining as far as possible what is due to him; secondly, the interests of the debtor in providing for his relief from harassment and his rehabilitation; and, thirdly, the public interest in ensuring that insolvencies are investigated and that the dishonest and reckless debtor is punished. These three elements entered English insolvency law at very different stages in its development.[3]

2. History of bankruptcy law

Bankruptcy law originally derives from the Law Merchant, a medieval body of law of common European usage whose origins could be traced back to Roman law[4] via the mercantile laws of Italy. The word "bankruptcy" originates from "banca rupta" which described the medieval custom in the Italian city states of breaking the benches of bankers and tradesmen who absconded with the property of their creditors. The first

---

[1] Cork Chap. 2; Cornish and Clark, *Law and Society in England* Pt. 2, Chap. 1; W. S. Holdsworth, *A History of English Law*, Vol. 8, p. 229 *et seq.*; Fletcher, *Law of Insolvency*; V. Markham Lester, *Victorian Insolvency*.

[2] Although some insolvent businesses will be owned by individuals and subject to bankruptcy law. Insolvent partnerships can be wound up in the same way as companies.

[3] See Cornish and Clark, above, p. 231.

[4] *Cessio bonorum* (the assignment of property for the benefit of creditors), *distractio bonorum* (the forced liquidation of assets), *remissio* and *dilatio* (compositions with creditors).

measures of collective insolvency law were introduced into English law by statute in Tudor times. Prior to this, creditors pursued their individual actions against either the property or[5] the person of the debtor. The creditor chose either to seize the assets of the debtor or to have the debtor summarily arrested and thrown into prison until he paid the debt.[6] Debtors developed methods of avoiding imprisonment; these included flight from the kingdom and, since entry into someone's house for the purpose of executing civil process was forbidden, "keeping house".

The Tudor legislation was prompted by problems caused by debtors avoiding making either person or property available to the creditors. English merchants were beginning to complain that English law was lagging behind that of other mercantile communities.[7] The Act of 1542 was described as "an act against such persons as do make bankrupts" and its preamble explained the reason for its enactment: "whereas diverse and sundry persons, craftily obtaining into their hands great substance of other men's goods, do suddenly flee to parts unknown, or keep their houses, not minding to pay or restore to any of their creditors their debts and duties, but at their own wills and pleasures consume the substance obtained by credit of other men, for their own pleasure and delicate living, against all reason, equity and good conscience".

The 1542 Act provided for the sale and rateable distribution amongst creditors of the "offender's" property; this was the introduction of the *pari passu* principle into English law although the focus of the legislation was more on the collection of the debtor's assets than on their distribution. In 1570 the 1542 Act was replaced by a more comprehensive statute which was itself amended and enlarged by statutes of 1604 and 1623. The legislation authorised the Lord Chancellor and the Commissioners in Bankruptcy appointed by him to summon the bankrupt before them, on the petition of a creditor, examine him on oath and if necessary imprison him until he forfeited his possessions. For such a commission to issue, the debtor had to be shown to have committed an act of bankruptcy; the list of acts of bankruptcy was extended over the years to cover most acts and states of affairs capable of indicating a state of inability to pay debts.[8] The 1570 Act included provisions for the

---

[5] Since the late 13th century.
[6] See generally Cohen, "The History of Imprisonment for Debt and its relation to the development of discharge in bankruptcy" in The Journal of Legal History Vol. 3, No. 2—Sept. 1982.
[7] See Holdsworth, above, n. 1 above.
[8] These remained a necessary prerequisite for a bankruptcy order until 1986; see Chap. 14.1 below.

setting aside of fraudulent conveyances.[9] It was this Act which limited the scope of the bankruptcy laws to traders and merchants, persons who earned their living by "buying and selling", probably because it was this category of people who were most likely to have incurred credit and whose assets were of a nature that made it relatively easy to abscond with them. At this stage, the distribution of the bankrupt's assets did not release him from liability for any amount still outstanding.

Discharge was first introduced in 1705, probably in an attempt to persuade insolvent debtors to co-operate with the bankruptcy process.[10] This concession was almost immediately restricted with the requirement in 1706 of the approval of four-fifths of the creditors, the commissioners and the Lord Chancellor for discharge. The requirement of creditor approval for discharge was not abolished until 1842 and gave undue power to vindictive minority creditors. In 1842 the power to grant discharge was given to the court; there followed a period in which Parliament tried to distinguish those who should be granted discharge from those who did not deserve it.[11]

Since the bankruptcy legislation was at this time confined to traders who earned their living by buying and selling,[12] it became a privilege to be a trader with this possibility of limited liability. The definition of a trader was extended both by statute and by judicial interpretation but by the mid-nineteenth century it still excluded large numbers of those engaged in business activity including, for example, farmers and builders.

This preferential treatment was probably due to the feeling that traders were the only people liable to become insolvent through no fault of their own. Blackstone,[13] for example said:

> "[traders] are, generally speaking, the only persons liable to acci-
> dental losses, and to an inability of paying their debts, without any
> fault of their own. If persons in other situations of life run in debt
> without the power of payment, they must take the consequences of

---

[9] The direct ancestor of Insolvency Act 1986, s.423 considered in Chap. 30.3 below. The 1570 legislation remained in force until it was replaced by Law of Property Act 1925, s.172.

[10] The 1705 Act also permitted a bankrupt to keep some of his assets for the first time, probably also to encourage co-operation. At the same time as this amelioration of the consequences for the compliant bankrupt, the penalties on those guilty of fraud became harsher with the introduction of the death penalty for the fraudulent debtor who became bankrupt.

[11] In 1849, for example, three categories of bankrupt were identified: the virtuous, the unfortunate and the spendthrift. It was not until 1976 that discharge became almost automatic.

[12] And whose capital was therefore particularly susceptible to being removed by an absconding debtor.

[13] W. Blackstone, *Commentaries on the laws of England*, Vol. 3.

their own indiscretion.... the law holds it to be an unjustifiable practice, for any person but a trader to encumber himself with debts of any considerable value".

Not even all traders fell within the scope of the bankruptcy law since there was a minimum level of debt required before a trader could be made bankrupt. Furthermore, until 1824, it was not possible for a trader to seek discharge by putting himself into bankruptcy.[14]

The history of the law relating to non-trading insolvents is largely the history of imprisonment for debt. Imprisonment could either precede judgment (imprisonment on *mesne* process, designed to prevent flight prior to the hearing) or follow judgment as a coercive means of obtaining payment. The ability of a creditor to imprison his debtor remained part of the law for centuries. Arrest on *mesne* process was not completely abolished until 1838 and imprisonment on judgment for debt, although it became subject to increasing restriction, remained part of the law until 1869.[15]

From the sixteenth century onwards there were those who recognised the futility of imprisoning insolvent debtors in an attempt to extract payment from them. The Privy Council[16] in the sixteenth and early seventeenth centuries and, subsequently, Parliament[17] found ad hoc means of relieving insolvent debtors from imprisonment. The 1759 Act (commonly called the Lord's Act) was the first one to apply prospectively to those not yet imprisoned; it also attempted to deal with problem of those who would rather stay in prison[18] by forcing them to declare their assets. These statutes all allowed the creditor to insist on continued imprisonment on payment of a weekly sum towards the upkeep of the prisoner.

Public opinion became increasingly disturbed by the imprisonment of debtors; both by the harsh treatment[19] and by the inefficiency of the system, since imprisonment put it beyond the debtor's ability to earn and the system was a drain on public expense despite the supposed duty of the creditor to contribute to the cost of the debtor's imprisonment. In 1813 a Court for the Relief of Insolvent Debtors was established to provide a permanent way of addressing the problem. This introduced

---

[14] This reflected the earlier view that bankruptcy was a crime and that men should not be allowed to accuse themselves of criminal behaviour.

[15] See Rubin and Sugarman, *Law, Economy and Society*, Chap. 5 for an account of the continued use of imprisonment for debt after 1869.

[16] By arranging compositions with creditors of a debtor.

[17] By Acts of Parliament releasing imprisoned insolvent debtors.

[18] There were those who were not insolvent and who preferred to use their assets in ensuring themselves a comfortable life in prison rather than in paying their creditors. Those who had no assets were not able to pursue either course.

[19] Graphically described in various Victorian novels, particularly by Charles Dickens.

insolvency as a concept separate from bankruptcy and available to non-traders who, provided their debts were below a certain level, could petition the court for "protection from process". The court could make an interim order protecting the insolvent from legal process and from imprisonment at the suit of a creditor; a final order could be made where, on investigation, the court was satisfied that the insolvency had not arisen from fraud, breach of trust or from becoming indebted without reasonable assurance of being able to repay. This order would probably involve the vesting of the debtor's property in a trustee as well as provision for payment of the remaining debts from after-acquired income or earnings. The problem with this approach[20] was that requiring debtors to meet debts from subsequent income deprived them of any incentive to earn and could not be seen as rehabilitative.

In 1861 the bankruptcy laws were extended to cover non-traders and the Court for the Relief of Insolvent Debtors and the insolvency laws were abolished. These two parallel systems were about to be replaced by a different pair since, with the introduction of the limited liability company, many traders would in future incorporate their businesses. Whereas bankruptcy law was previously the system which dealt with insolvent businesses, that would become the concern of corporate insolvency law and bankruptcy law would deal largely with the non-trading insolvents previously excluded from its provisions.

One of the major issues of dispute during the nineteenth century was the question of who should control the insolvency process.

Parliament's first attempt at a thorough investigation of insolvency was a Select Committee set up in 1817–18. At this time, creditors had virtually full control over the administration of bankrupt estates since the commissioners in bankruptcy (who sat in conditions of extreme chaos) would appoint one or more creditors as assignees of the assets, theoretically under their supervision. Abuses of the system by both creditors and debtors were frequent.

In 1831, Brougham's Bankruptcy Act introduced the concept of official assignees; these were officers attached to the London Bankruptcy Court who would administer the estates. Both the new court and the system of official assignees gave rise to widespread dissatisfaction. The Court was abolished in 1847, the jurisdiction being transferred to the Chancery Court, and in 1869 control of the assets was transferred from the official assignees to the creditors at the insistence of the commercial community, who thought this would be a cheaper system. The principle of decision making by a majority of the creditors had been introduced in 1844 and it soon became apparent that it was too easy for

[20] As a Royal Commission in 1840 pointed out.

a minority of creditors and their advisors to manipulate the proceedings in their own interests through the use of proxies. The creditor-managed system was a particular failure in the case of small bankruptcies where the prospect of realisation was insufficient to engage the interest of the creditors. There was also disquiet at the absence of inquiry into the affairs of debtor who arranged a liquidation of their assets with the consent of their creditors; they obtained a full discharge without any judicial inquiry into their finances.

The basis of the modern system was introduced by Joseph Chamberlain, the President of the Board of Trade, in the Bankruptcy Act 1883. He declared that the law had both to provide for the administration of the estates of those who were bankrupt and to act as a disincentive to behaviour leading to insolvency. There was a requirement for thorough and independent investigation into the causes of insolvency in the public interest rather than leaving matters in the hands of the creditors. Official Receivers, acting under the direction of the Board of Trade, were introduced. The system was intended to be self-financing through fees on bankruptcy petitions, a percentage payable on the assets collected and the interest on amounts collected in the course of the bankruptcy, which were to be paid into the Bank of England.

The provisions of the Bankruptcy Act 1883 lasted, in effect, for over a century until the passage of the Insolvency Act 1986. The Bankruptcy Act 1914 was mainly a measure of consolidation and tidying up. In 1908 the Muir Mackenzie Committee had reported general satisfaction with bankruptcy law and procedure, a view repeated by the Blagden Committee in 1955.

3. History of corporate insolvency

Bankruptcy law had developed well in advance of the introduction of the limited liability company. The Companies Acts contained their own provisions for the winding up of insolvent companies and, whilst the rules borrowed to an extent from the bankruptcy legislation, the two systems developed in parallel.

The Companies Act 1862 laid down the foundation on which subsequent legislation in relation to company winding up has been based. This provided for the possibilities of voluntary liquidation, winding up by court, and winding up under the supervision of the court. The court with jurisdiction was the Chancery Court. The Companies (Winding Up) Act 1890 extended the 1883 bankruptcy innovation of the official receiver's investigatory role to companies. Together with the Directors Liability Act 1890, this was a package of legislation aimed at fraudulent and dishonest company promoters and directors. Complaints about malpractice by promoters and directors of companies remained (and remain) a constant theme of discussion of insolvency law. There were amendments to various aspects of corporate insolvency law in the Companies Acts of 1908, 1929 (which introduced the concept of the creditors voluntary liquidation) and 1947/1948.

Two separate branches of insolvency law had emerged; company liquidation and individual bankruptcy were generally dealt with by different courts and under different sets of procedural rules. The rules of bankruptcy law and corporate insolvency law were similar but there were various differences of substance.

4. Background to the Insolvency Act 1986[21]

In 1973, on the United Kingdom's accession to the European Community, it became necessary to consider the E.C. Draft Bankruptcy Convention; in the course of its report, an advisory committee set up under the chairmanship of Kenneth Cork pointed to the need for revision of a number of areas of national insolvency law. The Justice Report on Bankruptcy in 1975 noted a number of problems highlighted by the recession of early 1970s which lead to small measures of reform in the Insolvency Act 1976; public examination was dispensed with in some cases and discharge made easier.

A further committee under the chairmanship of Sir Kenneth Cork was appointed in 1977 to review the law and practice relating to insolvency, to examine the possibility of harmonising and integrating the existing procedures, to suggest less formal procedures as alternatives to bankruptcy and liquidation and to make recommendations. The full lengthy report was published in 1982. The Cork Committee identified a need for extensive change[22] in order to restore respect for the law of insolvency and to ensure that the solutions provided to situations of insolvency were as fair and equitable as could reasonably be achieved. In particular, they saw a need to simplify and modernise the existing law which they described as "cumbersome, complex, archaic and over-technical" with a view to harmonising and integrating where possible the law and practice relating to companies and to individuals. They saw a need for the law to encourage wherever possible the continuation of businesses as a going concern with consequent preservation of jobs for at least

---

[21] See *Fletcher* [1989] J.B.L. 385.
[22] For a summary of their recommendations, see Chap. 52 of the Cork Report. It should be noted that far from all their recommendations have been implemented.

some of the employees. In the case of an individual debtor, they considered it important to increase the possibility of claims being met out of future wages and income. They were concerned to improve the standard of administration of insolvent estates, to prevent abuse and to encourage the ordinary unsecured creditor to take a more active interest in the proceedings. They were concerned to increase the amount available for the ordinary creditors and to allay the prevalent dissatisfaction with the current distribution of the assets. They recommended relaxing the excessive severity of the law towards the individual insolvent, particularly where incompetent rather than dishonest, but increasing the severity of the law towards the director of the failed company who had acted irresponsibly. They observed that it was unfortunate that their terms of reference did not include a review of the general law of credit and security and remedies for debt enforcement.

After an initially slow response, the government, prompted by public dissatisfaction with insolvency law as seen to be operating during the recession of the early 1980s, brought forward legislation which incorporated some, but by no means all, of the suggestions of the Cork Report. The first attempt at legislation was the Insolvency Act 1985 but this was immediately superseded by the Insolvency Act 1986 so that the 1985 Act never came into force.

5. Summary of current insolvency regimes

a) Bankruptcy

A bankruptcy order may be made in respect of an insolvent individual and will lead to the vesting of most of the bankrupt's assets in a trustee in bankruptcy for distribution amongst his creditors. During the period for which he is an undischarged bankrupt, the individual will be subject to certain legal disabilities and the background to the bankruptcy will be investigated.

b) Individual voluntary arrangement

An individual may be able to avoid bankruptcy by entering into an individual voluntary arrangement under which he may be released from some of his debts or given longer to pay or a combination of both. If the requisite majority of creditors agree, a minority of creditors can be bound by the agreement against their will. Another way of avoiding bankruptcy is the obtaining of a county court administration order.

c) Liquidation

An insolvent company may decide to put itself into voluntary liquidation or may be ordered by the court to go into compulsory winding up.[23] A liquidator will be appointed with the responsibility to realise the company's assets and distribute them between the creditors. At the end of the liquidation process the company is dissolved and ceases to exist. The conduct of those responsible for running the company's affairs in the period leading to the insolvency will be investigated.

d) Company voluntary arrangements and administration orders

A company may be able to avoid a liquidation by entering into a company voluntary arrangement or by obtaining a company administration order giving it a moratorium against creditors whilst it attempts to put its finances in order.

6. Court jurisdiction in insolvency matters

a) Individual insolvency

Jurisdiction in individual insolvency is exercised throughout England and Wales by the High Court, where it will be dealt with by a registrar in bankruptcy, and those of the county courts which exercise an insolvency jurisdiction.[24] The county court has the powers of the High Court in this respect. Jurisdiction is allocated to a particular court on the basis of the debtor's geographical connection with it and the High Court exercises insolvency jurisdiction in relation to the London Insolvency District, those cases in which the debtor does not appear to have a connection with any other court and in certain cases brought by the government.[25]

b) Corporate insolvency

County courts with insolvency jurisdiction may wind up companies with paid-up share capital which does not exceed £120,000 whose registered office is in their insolvency district.[26] The High Court has

---

[23] The terms "liquidation" and "winding up" are synonymous and are used interchangeably in this text.

[24] Insolvency Act 1986, s.373.

[25] Insolvency Rules 1986, r. 6.9, 6.40.

[26] Insolvency Act 1986, s.117(2).

jurisdiction to wind up any company registered in England and Wales.[27] Companies whose registered offices are in London will have to be wound up by the High Court since there is no county court jurisdiction in the London insolvency district. Courts with jurisdiction to wind up companies also have jurisdiction to make company administration orders. Questions may be referred by the county court to the High Court on a case stated basis.[28]

c) Appeals

Every court having jurisdiction in individual insolvency matters may review, rescind or vary any order which it has made.[29] Appeal lies from decisions by the county court or from a registrar in bankruptcy of the High Court to a single judge of the High Court.[30] The procedure normally relating to appeals to the Court of Appeal will apply to such an appeal.[31] Leave may be given, either by the judge or by the Court of Appeal, to appeal to the Court of Appeal. An appeal may be taken to the House of Lords where a point of law of general public interest arises.

---

[27] Insolvency Act 1986, s.117(1).
[28] *ibid.*, s.119.
[29] Insolvency Act 1986 in bankruptcy, s.375(1), Insolvency Rules 1986, r. 7.47 in liquidation.
[30] *ibid.*, s.375(2), Insolvency Rules 1986, r. 7.47(2) in winding up.
[31] Insolvency Rules 1986, r. 7.49.

CHAPTER 6

RECEIVERSHIP[1]

1. Introduction

If insolvency law is taken to be concerned with the collective process of realising and distributing assets amongst the creditors of an insolvent, then receivership strictly has no place in a study of it. This is because the essence of a receivership is that it is a mechanism by which one secured creditor enforces his security against a debtor; historically, no collective considerations arose. It is theoretically possible for a company which has been in receivership to return to financial health and avoid liquidation. More frequently, the receiver will achieve the sale of those parts of the business which are financially healthy and leave behind him a corporate shell which will have to be liquidated.[2]

Receiverships are so bound up with the development and operation of collective insolvency regimes and with the development of the rules of property law which tend to be relevant in an insolvency, that it is very difficult to study insolvency law without at least a basic grasp of the nature of receivership. In addition, administrative receivers are now subject to certain collective responsibilities imposed by the Insolvency Act 1986.

2. The development of receivership

Receivership as a method of enforcing a security originated with court appointments, at the request of a mortgagee, of a receiver to collect the income from mortgaged property and apply it towards payment of the mortgage interest. Over the years, the practice developed of the mortgage deed incorporating a power for the mortgagee to appoint the receiver directly, as agent of the mortgagor. Sections 101 and 109 of the Law of Property Act 1925 now provide a statutory power to appoint a receiver of the income of mortgaged property.

---

[1] See generally Lightman and Moss, *The Law of Receivers of Companies* (2nd ed.).
[2] For an exception, see *Gomba Holdings U.K. Ltd v. Minories Finance Ltd* [1989] 1 All E.R. 261.

During the nineteenth century, with the development of the possibility of taking security over the entire undertaking of a company, lenders began to require the right to appoint a receiver who would manage the business as well as collect the income owing and who would have the power to sell the business, or parts of it, and use the proceeds to pay off the debt. Such a receiver and manager would have the fate of the business and its employees in his hands. The Cork Committee received a considerable amount of evidence about receiverships, much of it hostile, but concluded that a lot of the adverse criticism was really criticism of the all-embracing nature of the floating charge. The Committee considered that there was much to be said for the ability of a receiver and manager to restore an ailing business to profitability or to dispose of it as a going concern. There was, however, recognition of the numerous complaints from ordinary unsecured creditors highly critical of the apparent lack of concern for their interests once a receiver had been appointed and critical of the lack of information available to them about the progress of the receivership. It was also noted that there was criticism of the practice of appointing receivers who were closely connected with the company and not necessarily competent.

As a result of the recommendations of the Cork Committee, the legislation introduced the concept of the administrative receiver, who must be a qualified insolvency practitioner,[3] subject to duties designed to keep the ordinary unsecured creditor informed. The intention is that the ordinary creditors can take steps to have a liquidator appointed if they feel it appropriate.

The Insolvency Act 1986 provides that a liquidator may ask the court to fix the remuneration of any receiver.[4] Where a receiver has been appointed under a charge which as created was floating, the receiver will have to pay those who would be preferential creditors out of the assets subject to the charge.

3. Administrative receivership

a) Definition

Section 29(2) of the Insolvency Act defines an administrative receiver as:

> "(a) a receiver or manager of the whole (or substantially the whole) of a company's property appointed by or on behalf of the holders of any debenture secured by a charge which as created was

---

[3] See Chap. 20 below.
[4] Insolvency Act 1986, s.36.

a floating charge, or by such a charge and one or more other securities; or

(b) a person who would be such a receiver or manager but for the appointment of some other person as the receiver of part of the company's property."

b) Distinction between administrative and ordinary receiver

In many ways the position of an administrative receiver does not differ from that of Law of Property Act receivers or receivers of part only of the property. For example, any receiver appointed under a charge which was floating when created will have first to pay those who would be preferential creditors in a liquidation out of the assets subject to the charge[5] and a liquidator may apply to the court to fix the remuneration of a receiver of any type.[6] In summary, the differences are:

i) a debenture holder with the power to appoint an administrative receiver has the power to veto a company administration order. This has given rise to the so-called "lightweight floating charge" which is not required for the additional assets it secures but in order to protect the lender's rights from being damaged by an administration.[7] An administrative receiver must vacate office if an administration order is made whereas an ordinary receiver may remain in office.[8]

ii) an administrative receiver must be a qualified insolvency practitioner. This requirement does not apply to other types of receiver in respect of whom the only limitation is that they may not be bodies corporate[9] or undischarged bankrupts.[10]

iii) an administrative receiver has obligations to investigate the background to the receivership,[11] report to the creditors, usually within three months of his appointment,[12] and to report to the Insolvency Service if he considers that the conduct of a

---

[5] Insolvency Act 1986, s.40.
[6] *ibid.*, s.36.
[7] This is discussed further in Chap. 10 in the context of the application for an administration order.
[8] The moratorium brought into effect by the order will, however, prevent further enforcement of the security without leave.
[9] Insolvency Act 1986, s.30.
[10] *ibid.*, s.31.
[11] *ibid.*, ss.46, 47.
[12] *ibid.*, s.48.

director requires a disqualification order.[13] Other receivers have no investigatory function and their duty to provide information is restricted to ensuring that all the letters and other documentation of the company state that a receiver has been appointed[14] and accounts of the receiver's receipts and payments must be delivered to the registrar of companies.[15]

iv) an administrative receiver has an extensive range of powers conferred by statute, including the power to apply for an order to dispose of property charged to another creditor[16] whereas other receivers have the powers conferred by the debenture under which they were appointed.

v) an administrative receiver's liability on adopted contracts of employment is restricted to qualifying liabilities.[17]

vi) an administrative receiver can only be removed by court order if he refuses to resign.

4. Appointment and powers of an administrative receiver

In order for the appointment of an administrative receiver to be valid, the following conditions need to be fulfilled: there should be no administration order in force, the security under which the appointment is made must be valid, the obligations secured by the debenture must arise from a valid contract, the power to appoint the receiver must have become exercisable under the terms of the debenture, the appointment must have been made in the manner authorised by the debenture and the person appointed must be qualified to act.

The appointment of the receiver crystallises floating charges which have not already crystallised. It also suspends the directors' powers as regards both assets comprised in the security and the conduct of the business in so far as it falls within the sphere of the receiver; given the width of the receiver's powers this effectively deprives the directors of a role.[18] The appointment will terminate any contracts of employment which are incompatible with the administrative receiver's powers but

---

[13] Company Directors Disqualification Act 1986, s.7(3)(d).

[14] Insolvency Act 1986, s.39.

[15] *ibid.*, s.38.

[16] *ibid.*, s.43.

[17] The liability of other receivers is governed by s.37 of the Insolvency Act 1986 which was not amended by the Insolvency Act 1994 when it amended s.44 of the Insolvency Act 1986.

[18] See *Newhart Developments Ltd v. Co-operative Commercial Bank* [1978] Q.B. 814 and *Gomba Holdings U.K. Ltd v. Homan* [1986] 3 All E.R. 94 for a discussion of their residual powers.

does not affect other contracts of employment.[19] Other contracts are not affected by the appointment since the receiver will be appointed as agent for the company.[20] This agency lasts unless and until the company goes into liquidation.

The source of the receiver's powers is the debenture under which he is appointed but the Insolvency Act 1986 provides[21] that the powers conferred by the debenture are deemed to include those listed in Schedule 1 to the Act in so far as they are not inconsistent with the provisions of the debenture. Schedule 1 contains 23 powers covering virtually every aspect of the management of the business and of the assets comprised in the security. The powers which are exercisable in relation to the assets covered by the security will survive a liquidation of the company but the personal powers given to the receiver to manage the business cease if the company goes into liquidation.

The court has the power[22] to allow the receiver to dispose of property which is subject to a prior or equal ranking security as if it were not subject to the security. This power may be exercised where the court considers that this would be likely to promote a more advantageous realisation of the company's assets than would otherwise be effected. The net proceeds of the sale plus the amount by which those proceeds fall short of the value determined by the court as the net amount which would be realised by a sale on the open market is to be applied in meeting the liabilities secured by the displaced security. This means that any deficiency caused by the manner of disposal comes out of the assets available to the debenture holder and is payable to the secured creditor in priority to other claims.

As an office-holder under the Insolvency Act 1986, an administrative receiver is given power to take possession of documents and to insist on co-operation from officers and employees of the company.[23]

5. Duties of an administrative receiver

a) Duty to the debenture holder

The receiver's chief duty is to his debenture holder to take care to realise the charged assets for their benefit. There is only a very limited duty of

---

[19] *Griffiths v. Secretary of State for Social Services* [1974] Q.B. 468.
[20] Insolvency Act 1986, s.44, which merely gives statutory effect to what would anyway be the position under most debentures. In the case of a Law of Property Act receiver the agency derives from Law of Property Act 1925, s.109(2).
[21] Insolvency Act 1986, s.44.
[22] *ibid.*, s.43.
[23] *ibid.*, ss.234, 235, 236 which are considered in more detail in Part IV.

good faith in equity to the company but no general duty of care in tort. In *Downsview Nominees Ltd v. First City Corp.*[24] it was said that:

> "A mortgagee owes a general duty to subsequent encumbrancers and to the mortgagor to use his powers for the sole purpose of securing repayments of the moneys owing under his mortgage and a duty to act in good faith. He also owes the specific duties which equity has imposed upon him in the exercise of his powers to go into possession and his powers of sale . . . . The decisions of the receiver and manager whether to continue the business or to close down the business and sell the assets chosen by him cannot be impeached if those decisions are taken in good faith while protecting the interests of the debenture holder in recovering the moneys due under the debenture, even though the decisions . . . may be disadvantageous for the company."

The Privy Council adopted a more restrictive view of the duties of the receiver in *Downsview* than had been apparent in some earlier cases in which it appeared that a receiver might be liable in negligence to the company, its guarantors and subsequent encumbrancers.[25] In New Zealand, Canada and Australia, statutory duties have been placed on receivers to act in reasonable manner.

b) Duty to the public at large

There are various duties owed to the public at large: notification of appointment,[26] a duty to investigate the affairs of the company and submit a report to the Registrar of Companies and the creditors[27] and a duty to report anyone whom he thinks should be disqualified from acting as a director.[28]

c) Duty to the preferential creditors

There is also a duty to those who would be preferential creditors on a liquidation to pay them ahead of the chargeholder. Section 40 of the Insolvency Act 1986 is as follows:

[24] [1993] A.C. 295. See *Berg*, [1993] J.B.L. 213. For earlier decisions taking the same restrictive view of the equitable source of the obligations, see *Parker-Tweedale v. Dunbar Bank plc* [1991] Ch. 12 and *China and South Sea Bank Ltd v. Tan Soon Gin* [1990] 1 A.C. 536.

[25] See *Cuckmere Brick Co Ltd v. Mutual Finance Ltd* [1971] Ch. 949, *Standard Chartered Bank Ltd v. Walker* [1982] 1 W.L.R. 1410, *American Express International Banking Corp. v. Hurley* [1985] 3 All E.R. 564.

[26] Insolvency Act 1986, s.46.

[27] *ibid.*, ss.47, 48.

[28] Company Directors Disqualification Act 1986, s.7(3)(d).

"(1) The following applies, in the case of a company, where a receiver is appointed on behalf of the holders of any debentures of the company secured by a charge which, as created, was a floating charge.

(2) If the company is not at the time in course of being wound up, its preferential debts[29] . . . shall be paid out of the assets coming to the hands of the receiver in priority to any claims for principal or interest in respect of the debentures.

(3) Payments made under this section shall be recouped, as far as may be, out of the assets of the company available for payment of general creditors."

There has been some debate recently as to the situation where an administrative receiver is appointed under a debenture to which there was a prior ranking floating charge. In *Griffiths v. Yorkshire Bank plc*[30] Morritt J. held that the wording of section 40 of the Insolvency Act 1986 led to the conclusion that the preferential creditors only ranked in priority over a charge which was created as a floating charge and in respect of which a receiver had been appointed. The same point arose subsequently in *Re H&K Medway Limited*[31] and Neuberger J. reached a different conclusion. The company had granted a floating charge to Ford Credit Europe plc over certain vehicles and their proceeds of sale. Subsequently, it granted a charge in favour of National Westminster Bank plc and then another to 3i plc. The 3i charge subjected the company's vehicle stock to a floating charge. It was agreed between the three creditors that the Ford charge would have priority over the 3i charge in respect of the vehicles. Shortly before January 4, 1995 the company ceased trading, which crystallised the floating charges. On January 4, 1995 3i appointed administrative receivers under its charge. The court had to decide whether or not the preferential creditors had priority over Ford. The preferential creditors argued that the expression "the debentures" at the end of section 40(2) of the Insolvency Act 1986 was a reference back to "any debentures of the company secured by a charge which, as created, was a floating charge" in section 40(1) of the Insolvency Act 1986. Ford argued that "the debentures" in section 40(2) was limited to those debentures under which "a receiver [had been] appointed" so that Ford would have priority over the creditors. Neuberger J. preferred the argument of the preferential creditors and held that they had priority to all the holders of floating charges over a company's assets and not just that under which the receivers were

---

[29] See Chap. 35 below.
[30] [1994] 1 W.L.R. 1427.
[31] [1997] 2 All E.R. 321.

appointed. He was influenced in part by the fact that the consequence of adopting the other interpretation would be that well advised chargees would always be able to avoid section 40 of the Insolvency Act 1986 by requiring the borrower to execute a second floating charge in favour of a nominee with a view to any receiver then being appointed under the second charge.

d) Duty to ordinary creditors

There is no direct duty owed to the ordinary creditors other than to keep them informed; there is provision for the establishment of a creditors' committee to undertake a monitoring function.[32]

6. Liability of an administrative receiver

The administrative receiver will be the agent of the company unless and until it goes into liquidation and, as such, will be able to bind the company to contracts. The receiver is not obliged to fulfil or to permit the company to fulfil existing contracts and will incur no personal liability by repudiating a contract in the name of the company even where this exposes the company to liability.[33]

Section 44 of the Insolvency Act 1986[34] provides that the administrative receiver will be personally liable on any contract entered into by him in the carrying out of his functions unless the contract otherwise provides and, to the extent of any qualifying liability, on any contract of employment adopted by him in the carrying out of these functions. He will not be taken to have adopted a contract by reason of anything done in the first 14 days of his appointment.

---

[32] Insolvency Act 1986, s.49.

[33] *Airlines Airspares Ltd v. Handley Page Ltd* [1970] Ch. 193.

[34] As amended by the Insolvency Act 1994. These amendments followed the furore caused by the Court of Appeal decision in *Powdrill v. Watson* [1994] 2 All E.R. 513, which is discussed in Chap. 12 below.

PART II

AVOIDING BANKRUPTCY OR LIQUIDATION

CHAPTER 7

INTRODUCTION TO PART II

Part II is concerned with the circumstances in which a bankruptcy or liquidation can be avoided despite the fact that the debtor is in fact insolvent. It should be noted that the mere fact of insolvency does not trigger any legal consequences: it is only with the commencement of a liquidation or bankruptcy that the status of the insolvent and the rights of the insolvent's creditors undergo a change. Amongst the list of aims set out in the Cork Report,[1] the Committee included the need to treat imminent insolvencies at an early stage and to provide means for the preservation of viable commercial enterprises which are capable of making a useful contribution to the economic life of the country. This recognition of the desirability of preserving businesses as going concerns where possible has acquired the label of "the rescue culture".[2]

Chapter 8 considers the possibility of dealing with debt problems by obtaining the agreement of all those affected to a rescheduling of the obligations. Many debt problems are resolved by such informal means; where this can be achieved it will be to the benefit of all concerned since the more formal the process the greater the proportion of available assets which will be swallowed up by costs. The difficulty with all informal means is that any one dissentient creditor is likely to be able to destroy the effect of the agreement reached by the rest.

Where unanimous agreement cannot be obtained, it will be necessary to consider using one of the procedures under which the will of the minority may be suborned by that of majority. It will be seen that the will of secured creditors cannot generally be overridden. Chapter 9 explains the procedures currently available to individuals: the county court administration order and the individual voluntary arrangement. Chapter 10 explains the procedures available to companies: a scheme of arrangement under section 425 of the Companies Act 1985, the company voluntary arrangement and the administration order. It also considers the general perception in the United Kingdom that the corporate

---

[1] See Chap. 1.
[2] See Belcher A., "The Economic Implications of Attempting to Rescue Companies" in Rajak (ed.), *Insolvency Law Theory and Practice* for a discussion of what constitutes a "rescue" and the circumstances in which a rescue can be held to have succeeded.

rescue procedures stand in need of reform and looks briefly, by way of comparison, at some of the models operating in other jurisdictions. Chapter 11 explains the rules relevant to a partnership business.

Chapter 12 considers the position of the employee in relation to the attempted rescue of a business. Many of the relevant rules are to be found in the employment protection legislation rather than the insolvency legislation but the rules are clearly relevant in trying to understand the current balance between the interests of the employees and those of the creditors in the context of the "rescue culture".

CHAPTER 8

INFORMAL AGREEMENT

1. Introduction

This Chapter starts by considering the processes which may lead to an informal resolution of debt problems at opposite ends of the debt spectrum. Whether the debtor is an individual with a low income, in debt to his landlord and electricity supplier, or a multi-national enterprise owing millions of pounds to dozens of banks, the basic need is the identical one of agreeing a rescheduling of their obligations in order to remove the threats posed by their indebtedness.

Individuals are likely to need to seek assistance in achieving an informal resolution of their debt problems; if they cannot afford to pay for the advice of professionals, they may be able to seek the assistance of debt-counsellors or other advice agencies. Commercial borrowers with bank loans will find that the bank or banks will become involved in trying to find a solution; even where the bank is adequately secured, it may feel that a successful rescue will keep it a customer and source of future income. Banks are also conscious of the risk of being seen as destroyers of businesses. Bank-led rescues are often referred to as "company workouts" and may involve the introduction of an expert "company doctor" as a replacement for, or addition to, the management of the company. Large companies with finance provided by a number of banks may find themselves the subject of the London Approach, a set of guidelines developed by the Bank of England for co-ordinating multi-bank rescues.

Any agreement to reschedule debts arrived at by the parties will only be binding on them if the principles of contract law so provide. This Chapter considers some of the relevant points of contract law and the rules which apply where a deed is used.

2. Assistance for consumer debtors

The Cork Committee referred both to the recommendation of the Payne Committee[1] that a debt counselling service be established and to the

[1] Cmnd 3909, 1969.

Money Advice Centres set up by the National Association of Citizens Advice Bureaux. The Cork Report observed[2] that "we believe that the development of either of these services would reduce the time spent by county court staff in advising debtors and would assist in sorting out debtors' muddles at an earlier stage".

Various forms of money advice services exist[3] in addition to those provided at the market rate by professionals such as solicitors and accountants; one-to-one debt counselling, telephone helplines and the provision of self-help packs are the main forms.

Debt counselling tends to involve those with multiple debts whose arrears have reached a serious state and who are facing court proceedings, repossession of their homes, disconnection of fuel or water supply or business failure. The objective of this form of money advice is to help debtors maximise their income and minimise their expenses and to assist in negotiating with creditors. This will usually be time-consuming and very demanding of money advice resources. This form of counselling is particularly successful in averting imminently threatened crises such as homelessness[4] and in increasing income by identifying benefits to which the debtor is entitled. Although most debtors seem to feel relief at finding help, not all of them retain an adequate commitment to the repayment schedule. It is not clear that debt counselling achieves its re-educative aims since many of those who have sought debt counselling have come to rely on the counsellor to help with future difficulties.

Telephone helplines and the provision of self-help packs are less resource demanding methods and seemed to appeal to those at a less serious level of indebtedness and who are, therefore, more likely to make a full financial recovery as a result of the assistance. Both these methods usually involve giving the debtor advice designed to enable them to take control of their budgets and give them confidence in dealing with creditors. A survey of National Debtline[5] users showed that three-quarters had eventually been able to make affordable arrangements to repay what they owed.

---

[2] At para. 349.

[3] This account draws heavily on Kempson, *Money Advice and Debt Counselling* published in 1995 for the Policy Studies Institute. See also Berthoud and Kempson, *Credit and Debt: The PSI Report*, Ford, *Consuming Credit* and *d'Ingeo* (1994) N.L.J. 1275.

[4] Representation at a housing repossession hearing greatly reduces the likelihood of a possession order being granted.

[5] The largest and best-funded helpline originally founded in 1987 as Housing Debtline, to prevent homelessness caused by mortgage and rent arrears, based at the Birmingham Settlement but covering the whole of England and Wales.

Money advice of all types appears to have some success in leading to the calculation of more realistic repayment schedules for arrears than would otherwise be the case. Repayment of rent arrears clearly improved with the intervention of a money adviser but the evidence was less compelling in relation to arrears owed to retailers, banks and the utilities.

The evidence suggests that comprehensive provision of money advice would require a ten-fold increase in the number of advisors requiring an additional annual expenditure of more than £60 million. There have been attempts to persuade the credit industry to assist with funding on the grounds that creditors have some responsibility to assist the casualties of the system. The Money Advice Trust has been set up to co-ordinate private sector contribution.

Demand for money advice outstrips supply but should probably be even greater. It is quite clear that money advice does assist debtors[6] but the Policy Studies Institute survey in 1989 identified a reluctance to seek assistance with debt problems. Nearly 60 per cent of those surveyed who had been identified as having had a problem debt in the preceding year had not discussed it with anyone, even family or friends. Only a third had taken formal advice from a money adviser, solicitor, bank manager or accountant. Those who sought advice came disproportionately from amongst owner/occupiers rather than tenants, particularly council tenants. A feeling that financial difficulty was a personal matter to be sorted out in private was the most frequent reason given for failure to seek advice.

3. Bank rescue

a) The Banking Codes

In July 1997 banks and building societies brought into effect a voluntary code[7] to be followed in their relations with personal customers. This provides that they will consider cases of financial difficulty sympathetically and positively and will try to help overcome the difficulties. It suggests obtaining help from debt counselling organisations and undertakes to liaise with such organisations where customers so request. At the same time, they also bought into effect a statement of principles[8]

---

[6] It is less clear that creditors derive a quantifiable benefit.
[7] British Banking Association, *The Banking Code*.
[8] British Bankers Association: *Banks and Businesses Working Together*.

outlining how banks will work with small and medium-sized businesses. The principles reiterate support for the rescue culture.

b) Company "workouts"

Company workouts are reorganisations which result from the contractual agreement of the company's creditors rather than as an arrangement under the Insolvency Act or the Companies Act. Justice observed
in its 1994 report[9] that there were signs that in the more economically
significant cases, rescue operations are increasingly being conducted by
the banks and the commercial community outside the confines of the
insolvency system.

The business's bank may well take the initiative in identifying that
there is a problem and arranging for a business review or viability study.
It may prove possible to avoid receivership or a formal insolvency
regime by considering a sale of the business as a going concern, a
refinancing or a gradual run-down. A main advantage to be derived from
this approach is that it avoids giving harmful publicity to the difficulties
being faced by the business.

c) The London Approach[10]

This is a set of guidelines developed by the Bank of England and the
major banks designed to assist with the informal rescue of companies
where a number of lenders are involved. The Bank of England is
available to provide mediation assistance in resolving disputes amongst
the lenders involved.[11] There are no formal sanctions for breach of the
guidelines other than the disapproval of the Bank of England.

The basic premise is that no one lender will seek to do better out of
the situation than any other lender. It involves the lenders agreeing to
freeze[12] their proportion of the company's indebtedness and any security at its existing level and to provide short term finance whilst a plan
is considered. One bank is appointed as "lead banker" to investigate the
situation, produce a report as a matter of urgency and co-ordinate rescue
plans with the assistance of a steering committee. An inter-creditor debt
rescheduling agreement will then be drawn up.

The plan may sometimes involve the lenders entering into an "equity-
debt" swap under which they exchange some of the unpaid debt for
shares, usually special preference shares giving the lenders priority as to

---

[9] Justice, *Insolvency Law: An Agenda for Reform.*
[10] (1995) 11 I.L.&P. 82
[11] The Bank of England has been involved in more than 160 cases since 1989.
[12] Often referred to as implementing "a standstill".

dividends and repayment and sometimes containing an option to convert to ordinary shares.

The London Approach was first devised during the 1970s at a time when the banks were predominant amongst the providers of finance. The increasing numbers[13] and diverse nature[14] of those with a financial stake in companies has made it more difficult for the banks to remain in control of a rescue operation. Commentators point to the increasing problems, and expense, in operating it given the increased involvement of foreign banks, amongst whom the Bank of England has less influence. The development of a secondary market in debt has both increased the number of creditors in any particular case and made it difficult to know who they are; additionally, there is the problem that where debt is viewed as a commodity there is less incentive to secure the long term existence of the borrower. The problem with any system which does not allow for the overriding of a minority creditor is that such a creditor is then in a strong position to bargain for the other creditors to buy out his blocking interest at an enhanced price.

4. Contractual arrangements

A debtor has always been able to make arrangements with his creditors for the settlement of his debts entirely independently of any court proceedings. It is possible to arrange with an individual creditor that the creditor will accept less or will accept what is owing late. Contract law students all encounter the problems the courts have had in finding sufficient consideration to support a promise by the creditor to accept less than the amount owing in full settlement; the rule in *Pinnels's Case*[15] provides that a promise to accept part of what is owing in settlement of the full sum is not enforceable although consideration can be found if the debtor agrees to pay in a different form, at a different place or at an earlier time than that originally agreed. This principle was recently upheld by the Court of Appeal in *re Selectmove Ltd*[16] despite arguments that changing views of consideration should lead the courts to accept that the creditor does derive a benefit from such an arrangement in that he does receive some payment whereas in absence of the

---

[13] The rescue of Heron International, for example, involved 82 banks.
[14] Amongst those who may be interested parties are bondholders, insurance companies and other institutional shareholders and purchasers of debt from the original holders of it.
[15] (1602) 5 Co. Rep. 117a. Upheld by the House of Lords in *Foakes v. Beer* (1884) 9 App. Cas. 605.
[16] [1995] 2 All E.R. 531.

arrangement he might receive nothing.[17] Selectmove Ltd was fighting a
petition by the Inland Revenue to have it put into compulsory liquidation; it claimed that it had entered into an agreement with the Revenue
to pay off the debt in instalments.[18] The Court of Appeal held that no
such agreement had been reached but that even if there had been, it
would not have been contractually binding.[19]

This problem of a lack of apparent consideration ought logically to
arise in relation to an arrangement (usually called a composition)
between the debtor and all his creditors under which each agrees to
accept a stated percentage of his debt in full satisfaction of what is
owing. The creditors have clearly provided consideration and will be
bound *inter se* but it is not obvious what consideration has been
provided by the debtor. The courts have, however, been prepared to
uphold such arrangements, probably for pragmatic reasons of commercial convenience but purportedly on the basis that it would be a fraud
upon all the parties concerned for one creditor to deny the existence of
the agreement.[20] There will be no problem with consideration where a
deed is used to record the agreement.

5. Deeds of Arrangement

Deeds of Arrangement[21] between insolvent debtors and their creditors
became a source of disquiet during the nineteenth century since they
were often the occasion of fraud against the majority of creditors. These
arrangements usually contemplated that the debtor give up virtually the
whole of his assets to a trustee for the benefit of creditors in return for
a release from their claims. Unscrupulous persons frequently induced
insolvent debtors to execute deeds of arrangement in their favour and
then failed to make proper distribution to the creditors out of the
property. The Deeds of Arrangement Act 1887 was intended to ensure

[17] An argument which Lord Blackburn had produced in *Foakes v. Beer* when he had
pointed out that "all men of business, whether merchants or tradesmen, do every day
recognise and act on the ground that prompt payment of a part of their demand may be
more beneficial to them than it would be to insist on their rights and enforce payment
of the whole".

[18] The Inland Revenue does frequently make such agreements. An article in *The Observer*
on December 15, 1996 on the charity Taxaid which provides advice about tax debts
compared the number of people against whom the Revenue took action in the year to
April 1996 (2,217 made bankrupt, 400 judgment executions) with the number of tax
debts queries dealt with by the CAB in the same period (87,000).

[19] The Court also held that promissory estoppel would not be relevant since the company
had not behaved in such a way as to merit the assistance of equity.

[20] *Wood v. Robarts* (1818) 1 Stakr. 417, *Cook v. Lister* (1863) 13 C.B.N.S. 543, *Couldery
v. Bartrum* (1881) 19 Ch. D. 394, *Hirachand Punamchand v. Temple* [1911] 2 K.B.
330.

[21] The definition of which includes certain instruments not under seal.

adequate publicity for these arrangements and better protection for creditors. The Deeds of Arrangement Act 1914 introduced an element of court and Board of Trade control; if the deed was not registered within seven days of execution it was automatically void. Deeds of Arrangement became very popular for a while after 1914 but by the time of the Cork Report their use had dramatically declined. One problem was the ability of any dissenting creditor to destroy the protection achieved by the agreement with the other creditors. Another problem was that entry into a Deed of Arrangement was an act of bankruptcy available as the basis of a petition for bankruptcy for the following three months; a successful petition for bankruptcy would lead to the setting aside of the deed so the trustee under the deed would not be able to collect or distribute the estate safely within the three-month period.

6. Difficulties in arriving at informal agreement

The main problem encountered by debtors attempting to negotiate a settlement with their creditors arises when they owe multiple debts and are unable to persuade all the creditors to agree to their proposals. Any one dissenting creditor may decide to continue to enforce the debt and may be able to apply for a bankruptcy or winding up order. There is no deterrent to creditors in seeking to pursue their debts aggressively; the preference rules[22] are such that unless the debtor was motivated by a desire to prefer that creditor over the other creditors, the payment will be safe in the event of an ensuing liquidation or bankruptcy.

[22] See Chap. 30.

CHAPTER 9

RESCUE REGIMES AVAILABLE TO INDIVIDUALS

1. Introduction

The two regimes currently available are the county court administration (available where there is a judgment outstanding against a debtor owing less than £5,000 in total), which is the direct descendant of the nineteenth century Court for the Relief of Insolvent Debtors, and the individual voluntary arrangement, introduced by the Insolvency Act 1986 following recommendations by the Cork Committee. The individual voluntary arrangement is only appropriate where the debtor has assets whose realisation will be of interest to the creditors. There is still a gap in the system in that there is no procedure suitable for the insolvent without assets who owes more than £5,000 or against whom there is no judgment.

2. County court administration

a) Current position[1]

Section 112 of the County Courts Act 1984 provides that where a debtor is unable to pay forthwith the amount of a judgment obtained against him and alleges that his whole indebtedness[2] is less than the county court limit of £5,000, the county court has a discretion on his application to make an order providing for the administration of his estate. Any county court has jurisdiction, not just those with insolvency jurisdiction. The request for an administration order must state[3] whether the debtor proposes to pay creditors in full or how much he proposes to pay and the amount of the monthly instalments. It must be accompanied by a list of his creditors. Creditors will be given notice of the hearing and will be

---

[1] County Courts Act 1984, Pt. VI and CCR 1981, Ord. 39.
[2] "Indebtedness" is not defined.
[3] Forms N92 and N93.

able to object to the inclusion of any debt in the list of debts or to the proposals.

An administration order may provide for the payment of the debts by instalments either in full or to such extent as appears practicable to the court under the circumstances and subject to any conditions as to future earnings or income which the court thinks just. The court may vary or subject the order to periodical review. Once an order has been made, creditors will be unable to pursue—

> "any remedy against the person or property of the debtor in respect of any debt: (a) of which the debtor notified the appropriate court before the administration order was made; or (b) which has been scheduled to the order, except with leave of the appropriate court and on such terms as that court may impose."[4]

This has raised an issue[5] in relation to mortgage lenders whose borrowers are in arrears. In most cases they will be able to show that mortgage repayment default has led to the entire outstanding loan becoming repayable at once so that the total indebtedness is too great for an administration order to be possible. Where this argument does not work, it would appear that they might be caught by the freeze since there is no saving of the rights of secured creditors.

Whilst an administration order is in force those creditors whose existence has been notified to the court by the debtor will not be able to present a bankruptcy petition against the debtor without leave of the court[6]; the exception to this is that a creditor owed more than £1,500 may do so within 28 days of being notified of the order. Additionally, execution may be levied if the assets exceed £50 and the creditor requests it.[7] Section 116 of the County Courts Act 1984 preserves the right to distrain for rent for six months up to the date of the order (but not for any rent after the date of levy of distress).

The court takes a fee of not more than ten per cent of the total amount of the debts in relation to the implementation of an administration order.[8] The debtor will be required to make a single regular payment to the court of an agreed amount. Regular payments are then made to creditors by the court according to the terms of the order. The money paid in is applied first in payment of the fees. There is no concept of preferential creditors.

---

[4] County Courts Act 1984, s.114.
[5] see *Harper* 13 I.L.&P. 43.
[6] County Courts Act 1984, s.112(4).
[7] *ibid.*, s.115(1) as amended by Insolvency Act 1985, s.220(3)(4).
[8] *ibid.*, s.117(1).

The order will be discharged automatically when the scheduled creditors have been paid as provided for in the order and costs met.[9] The order may be revoked if the debtor fails without reasonable cause to comply with it.[10] The court may suspend the order or vary it if the debtor is unable to comply for a good reason.

Where a debtor has sought to take advantage of the administration order and has failed to comply with it, the insolvency legislation allows the imposition of some of the disabilities of the undischarged bankrupt on the debtor.[11] The debtor may be prevented from obtaining credit or carrying on business without, in either case, disclosing that an order has been made and may be prevented from acting as a director or being involved directly or indirectly in the promotion, formation or management of a company.[12] These restrictions may last for up to two years.

b) History[13] and suggestions for reform

The administration order procedure was introduced by the 1883 Bankruptcy Act which gave the county courts the power to administer the estates of judgment debtors whose whole indebtedness was less than £50. This vested a loose discretion in the judge to arrange for the relief of the small debtor by reasonable composition; the court was enjoined to take into consideration the circumstances in which the indebtedness had been incurred and whether there had been any fraud, idleness, improvidence, gambling or intemperance. An inquiry in 1887 found that the system was not working well since the cases were too small to support the expense of the machinery.

The procedure was re-enacted in the 1914 Act and transferred into the legislation governing the county courts in the County Courts Act 1934. At that time it was subject to a £50 ceiling which was only raised in 1965 to £300 and then in 1977 to £2,000. As long ago as the Muir Mackenzie Committee in 1908 it was recommended that a debtor should be entitled to apply for an order even where there was no outstanding judgment against him but this has yet to be implemented.

Amendments contained in the Courts and Legal Services Act 1990[14] which have not yet been brought into force would improve the position in some respects. The range of people entitled to apply for such an order would be extended to include debtors against whom there was no

---

[9] County Courts Act 1984, s.117(2).
[10] CCR, Ord. 39.
[11] Insolvency Act 1986, s.429.
[12] Company Directors Disqualification Act 1986, s.12.
[13] See *Cork* paras 68–73.
[14] s.13 amending s.112 of the County Courts Act 1984.

outstanding judgment and the creditor under a judgment. The court would also be able make an order of its own volition or on the application of a creditor. The upper limit on indebtedness would also go. An order would not last longer than three years; the proposed time limit is intended to help persuade creditors that an administration order is not necessarily a worse option than a bankruptcy.

A further unimplemented section of the Courts and Legal Services Act 1990[15] would allow a county court to make a restriction order where it could otherwise make an administration order. A restriction order would provide for a stay of enforcement in that no creditor specified in the order would have any remedy against the debtor or his property in respect of debts specified except with the leave of the court.

The amendments to the County Courts Act 1984 were originally delayed in order to allow for provision to be made for the expected increase in the number of applications for administration orders. The problem of the lack of definition of the debts which are covered by an administration order has given rise to a need for further consideration; the amendment of the administration order is now up for review in the context of the wider question of review of the entire civil justice system.

3. Individual voluntary arrangements

a) Introduction

The introduction of the individual voluntary arrangement ("IVA") followed the recommendation of the Cork Committee that it should be possible to make an effective collective agreement with creditors even where a minority of creditors dissent from the arrangement. It also recognises the need for the protection of the debtor from his creditors whilst the possibility of an arrangement is canvassed; this protection is provided by an interim order.[16]

An IVA may be proposed in an attempt to avoid bankruptcy and also where a bankruptcy order has been made. In the latter case, approval of such an arrangement may lead to the setting aside of the bankruptcy.

A company voluntary arrangement ("CVA") procedure was introduced at the same time as that for the IVA. Many of the provisions are identical and the caselaw is interchangeable to that extent.

---

[15] s.13(5) inserting s.112A into the County Courts Act 1984.
[16] Under Insolvency Act 1986, s.252.

b) Application for an interim order

An application for an interim order may be made[17] where a debtor intends to make a proposal to his creditors for a composition in satisfaction of his debts or a scheme of arrangement of his affairs. The court will not make an interim order if the debtor has applied for such an order during the previous 12 months. In *Hook v. Jewson Ltd*[18] it was held that the court would not allow applications for interim orders to become a means of postponing the making of bankruptcy orders in circumstances where there was no apparent likelihood of benefit to the creditors from the proposal. An application may be made by any debtor who would be able to petition for his own bankruptcy[19] and, where a bankruptcy order has been made, by the bankrupt, the official receiver or trustee in bankruptcy. An interim order will also be made where the court has appointed an insolvency practitioner to report on the possibility of a voluntary arrangement under section 273 of the Insolvency Act 1986.[20]

The application for an interim order allows the court to stay any legal process against the person or property of the debtor.[21]

A successful application for an interim order requires that the proposal for the voluntary arrangement provide for a qualified insolvency practitioner ("the nominee") who has indicated, after seeing a copy of the proposal, that he is willing to supervise the implementation of the arrangement. The court may make an interim order if it thinks that it would be appropriate to do so for the purpose of facilitating the consideration and implementation of the proposal.

The proposal will explain why the debtor thinks a voluntary arrangement is desirable and give reasons why his creditors may be expected to concur with the arrangement. The proposal must[22] give details of the debtor's assets, any assets which are to be excluded from the proposal and any assets which are to be contributed from elsewhere as well as detailing the liabilities of the debtor and how it is proposed to deal with them.

---

[17] Under Insolvency Act 1986, s.253.
[18] [1997] 1 B.C.L.C. 664.
[19] See Chap. 15.1.
[20] See Chap. 15. Justice noted that appointments under s.273 of the Insolvency Act 1986 appeared to have been infrequent probably because of the restrictive circumstances in which they can be made. It was suggested that the monetary limits be broadened and that the powers be extended to creditors' petitions.
[21] Insolvency Act 1986, s.254.
[22] Insolvency Rules 1986, r.5.3 details the required contents.

c) The effect of an interim order

The making of the interim order effects a temporary moratorium in that no bankruptcy petition may be presented or proceeded with and "no other proceedings and no execution or other legal process may be commenced or continued against the debtor or his property except with the leave of the court".[23] The interim order will initially last for 14 days unless the court orders its subsequent extension.[24]

The courts have held that this moratorium only restrains processes of a judicial or adjudicative nature. An interim order will not affect the right to levy distress, to re-enter peaceably, to exercise rights of set off, to disconnect utility supplies, to repossess where no court order is needed or to serve notices. This moratorium is less extensive than the moratorium which applies once a company has gone into administration[25] since the interim order does not prevent the enforcement of security interests or distress. This discrepancy seems illogical and, given that one of the aims of the Insolvency Act 1986 was to harmonise the position as between individuals and companies, undesirable. The anomalous position was noted by the judges in the cases of *Re A Debtor (No. 13A–10–1995)*[26] and *McMullen & Sons v. Cerrone*,[27] both of which concerned the enforcement of remedies by a landlord against an insolvent tenant. The question of a landlord's rights against an insolvent tenant has raised a number of difficult issues in the context of the attempted rescue of the tenant.[28]

Rattee J. had occasion, in *Re A Debtor (No. 13A–10–1995)*[29] to consider whether a landlord should have sought leave before peaceably re-entering premises after the tenant had been granted an interim order. He concluded that, although forfeiture proceedings would require leave, re-entry was a form of extra-judicial self-help and did not require leave: in order to require leave, re-entry would have to fall within the definition "legal process", which the judge held referred to the taking of judicial

---

[23] Insolvency Act 1986, s.252.
[24] Insolvency Act 1986, s.255(6).
[25] See Chap. 10.4.
[26] [1995] 1 W.L.R. 1127.
[27] [1994] B.C.C. 25.
[28] See Milman and Davey [1996] J.B.L. 541 and Anderson 12 I.L.&P. 114 (1996) for articles gathering together the various strands of law relevant to the effect of individual and corporate rescue regimes on the landlord and tenant relationship. Both articles highlight the lack of any considered approach in the legislation to the whole issue of the rights of a landlord in the rescue context.
[29] See above.

or quasi-judicial proceedings.[30] In *McMullen & Sons v. Cerrone* it was held that a landlord owed rent by his tenant, a jeweller, could levy distress against jewellery on the premises despite the grant of an interim order to the tenant.

d) Nominee's report

The next step is for the nominee to report to the court as to whether a meeting of the creditors should be summoned to consider the proposal.[31] The nominee must exercise an independent and objective professional judgment.[32] This report is to be made before the end of the period of the interim order but the court may extend this period to give the nominee more time. If the court agrees that the meeting should be called, the interim order will be extended for that purpose. The court may override the nominee's judgment that a meeting should be called or may alter the suggested time, date or venue.

The court may refuse to continue the interim order if it is satisfied that it is unlikely that the debtor would get a majority at the meeting.[33]

Where there are no bankruptcy proceedings in existence or pending and the nominee files his report with the initial application for an interim order, these first two stages can be combined in what is referred to as a "concertina order". This is not possible where notice of the hearing has to be given[34] to a creditor known to have presented a bankruptcy petition or, where the debtor is an undischarged bankrupt, to whichever of the official receiver, trustee in bankruptcy and bankrupt is not making the proposal.

e) Creditors' meeting

The nominee then has to summon a meeting of all creditors whose debts are or would be bankruptcy debts[35] and that meeting will decide whether or not to approve the proposal. Notice of at least 14 days must

---

[30] Following Millett J. in *Re Olympia and York Canary Wharf Ltd* [1993] B.C.L.C. 453 rather than Harman J. in *Exchange Travel Agency Ltd v. Triton Property Trust plc* (1991) B.C.C. 341. Both cases are discussed in Chap. 10 below.

[31] Insolvency Act 1986, s.256.

[32] (*Re a debtor (No. 222 of 1990)* [1992] B.C.L.C. 137). There were judicial comments about the "deplorably low quality" of the nominee's comments on the proposal, in particular the failure to apply a critical eye to the debtor's statement of assets and liabilities and the lack of attempt to assess whether or not the proposal was in accordance with the Insolvency Rules.

[33] *Re Cove (a debtor)* [1990] 1 All E.R. 949.

[34] Under Insolvency Rules 1986, r.5.5(4).

[35] Insolvency Act 1986, s.257.

be given.[36] The date of the meeting must not be more than 28 days after the nominee's report was filed in court.

The meeting will be chaired by the nominee or his substitute. Approval of an arrangement requires a majority in excess of three-quarters in value of those present in person or by proxy and voting; the resolution will not be valid if opposed by more than half in value of those creditors who are not associates of the debtor.[37] Voting entitlement depends on the amount of unsecured debt owing to the particular creditor; the chairman of the meeting has power to admit or reject a creditor's claim for the purpose of his entitlement to vote.[38] Meetings tend not to be well attended and the arrangement may be accepted by the votes of only a few creditors.[39]

The meeting can be adjourned to attempt to arrive at an agreement from time to time for 14 days from when the meeting was first held. After that time, the proposal will be deemed to have been rejected if agreement is not obtained.[40]

The proposal may be approved with modifications provided that the debtor has consented to the modifications.[41] The meeting may not approve any proposal affecting the rights of secured or preferential creditors[42] without the concurrence of such creditors.[43] There has been some debate as to which creditors count as secured creditors in this context.

f) Who is a secured creditor for these purposes?

Several cases[44] have considered the question of whether the right of re-entry makes a landlord a secured creditor who cannot be deprived of that right without his consent. In *March Estates v. Gunmark Ltd*[45] Lightman J. held that a lessor is a secured creditor in that a voluntary arrangement cannot, without the consent of the landlord, affect the right

---

[36] See Insolvency Rules 1986, r.5.13(2) and (3).

[37] *ibid.*, r.5.18.

[38] *ibid.*, 1986, r.5.17(4).

[39] See Pond [1995] J.B.L. 118 at 121 where he describes an extreme case in which an IVA was accepted on the single vote of a trade creditor representing just over one per cent of the unsecured debts outstanding. Banks, owed in excess of £60,000, were not represented at the meeting.

[40] Insolvency Rules 1986, r.5.19.

[41] Insolvency Act 1986, s.258(2),(3).

[42] See below, Chap. 35.

[43] s.258(4), (5).

[44] The cases relate to both IVAs and CVAs since ss 4(3) and 258(4) of the Insolvency Act 1986 contain identical provisions in this respect with regard to both types of arrangement. The issue of whether a right of re-entry is a security interest has also arisen in the context of an administration order: see chap. 10 below. See n. 28 above.

[45] [1996] 32 E.G. 75.

to forfeit the lease if the full rent is not paid. The judge went on to reject
the earlier view of Hoffmann J. in *Re Naeem*[46] that, although the
landlord retained the right of forfeiture, it was unlikely that any condition of full repayment would be imposed as a condition of relief from
forfeiture given that the arrangement provided for a reduction in the
landlord's right to arrears.

Conceptually, this seems a dubious outcome since a right of re-entry
is not an interest in property conferred by the tenant on the landlord but
a right retained by the landlord when granting the lease; therefore,
although serving a security function, it lacks the essential characteristic
of a security interest. It is to be noted[47] that the courts first decided that
a right of re-entry was a security interest for the purposes of insolvency
legislation in the context of administration; this was a finding that gave
the court power to restrain its use during the administration. In the
context of voluntary arrangement, this characterisation of the right of
re-entry protects the landlord rather than the debtor. This outcome may
be correct[48] given that in an administration the restriction will be merely
a temporary stay of the right whereas a voluntary arrangement will alter
rights permanently.

Peck v. Craighead[49] decided that an execution creditor who had
seized goods was a secured creditor for these purposes. The sheriff had
taken walking possession[50] of many of the chattels used by the debtors
in their hotel business. The creditor was entitled to the proceeds of sale
of the chattels to the extent of his debt and the sheriff's charges: the
voluntary arrangement could not take this right away without his
consent.

g) Effect of approval

Where the meeting approves the proposal, the arrangement will take
effect as if made by the debtor at the meeting. All those who, whether
or not present at the meeting, had been correctly given notice of the
meeting and were entitled to vote at it will be bound as if they were
parties to the arrangement.[51]

---

[46] [1990] 1 W.L.R. 48, an IVA case. This approach had been approved by Knox J. in
Doorbar v. Alltime Securities Ltd [1995] B.C.C. 728.
[47] See Anderson 12 I.L.&P. 114.
[48] Those who consider that a landlord's property based rights should be favoured over the
rights of other suppliers to the debtor would agree with this.
[49] [1995] B.C.C. 525.
[50] That is, had seized the goods but left them in possession of the debtor, thereby obtaining
property rights in them.
[51] Insolvency Act, s.260.

A considerable body of case law is growing up[52] in relation to the question of who can be bound into these arrangements against their will. Most of the cases are concerned with arguments by people with claims against the debtor that they do not fall within the precise description of those bound either because they did not have notice of the meeting or because they were not entitled to vote at it.

One group of cases has considered the issue of when a person had notice of the meeting. In *Re a debtor (No. 64 of 1992)*[53] it was held that notice meant actual notice so that where the notice is sent to the wrong address the creditor will not be bound by the outcome of the meeting, at least where it had no actual notice from any other source. In *Beverley Group v. McClue*[54] the notice was sent correctly but not received until after the meeting but the creditor had learned of the meeting from other sources. Knox J. held that creditor was entitled to vote at the meeting provided that he was aware of it and would be bound by the outcome of the meeting regardless of whether or not he voted. In *Re Bielecki*,[55] in which the notice was sent out late, the court held that if a creditor did not have notice in accordance with the Rules he would not be bound despite that fact that he knew of the meeting in time to attend and vote if he had chosen to do so. It would seem that, where the creditor did actually know of the meeting from other sources, the outcome may depend on whether the notice was sent correctly.

There have also been cases concerned with the question of who was entitled to vote at the meeting; those seeking to argue that they are not bound by the IVA will be arguing that they were not entitled to vote. Rule 5.17 of the Insolvency Rules 1986 provides that every creditor given notice of the meeting is entitled to vote at it.[56] Section 382(3) of the Insolvency Act 1986 provides that, in relation to the insolvency of individuals, references to debt or liability are to be taken as including those which are present, future, certain, contingent, fixed, liquidated or capable of being ascertained by fixed rules or as a matter of opinion. It is quite clear, therefore, that those whose debts are not yet owing[57] are capable of being included in an individual voluntary arrangement.[58] The Rules further provide that "a creditor shall not vote in respect of a debt

---

[52] The provisions governing this issue are identical in a number of respects in relation to both IVAs and CVAs.

[53] [1994] 2 All E.R. 177.

[54] [1995] B.C.C. 751.

[55] October 19, 1995, unreported. See 12 I.L.&P. 97.

[56] In *re a debtor* [1997] 1 W.L.R. 1319, Rimer J. held that r.5.17 was not exhaustive as to who is entitled to vote. A creditor who is not given notice but learns of the meeting from another source is entitled to vote.

[57] Such as landlords in respect of future rent.

[58] This is not so clear in the case of a CVA. See Chap. 10.3.

for an unliquidated amount, or any debt whose value is not ascertained, except where the chairman agrees to put upon the debt an estimated minimum value for the purpose of entitlement to vote".[59]

In *Re Cranley Mansions*[60] it was argued that a creditor who had not agreed the quantification of his debt would not be bound by the arrangement. Ferris J. ruled that the word "agrees" required some element of bilateral concurrence between the chairman and the creditor in question. This appeared to have the unfortunate consequence of allowing a creditor, whose debt was disputed as to amount to frustrate the attempt at concluding an arrangement by refusing to agree the amount put on the debt and, thereby, not having the right to vote and, consequently, not being bound in to the arrangement. In *Doorbar v. Alltime Securities*[61] Knox J. held that what was required was the chairman's agreement to put a minimum value on the claim and not an agreement upon or in relation to the amount of that minimum value itself. In that case the creditor in question was a landlord with a claim to future rent under a lease. The chairman of the meeting was willing to put a substantial value on the claim but not the total rent due until the lease expired as he felt account had to be taken of the landlord's duty to mitigate. He reduced the value of the claim to below an amount which enabled the landlord to block the arrangement. Knox J. held that the landlord was entitled to vote and therefore was bound by the arrangement and this was upheld by the Court of Appeal. *Doorbar* was followed, in the corporate context, in *Re Cancol*.[62]

If the chairman is in doubt whether a claim should be admitted or rejected, he shall mark it as objected to and allow the creditor to vote, subject to his vote being subsequently declared invalid if the objection to the claim is sustained.[63] This was relied on in *Day v. Richardson & Evans*[64] in which the chairman of a meeting admitted a contested claim for voting but marked it as being objected to. If the claim had not been admitted, the arrangement would have been approved. The court subsequently ruled that the claimant had no proper claim and should not have voted. The arrangement was deemed to have been approved at the meeting. In *Re a Company (No. 004539 of 1993)*[65] the court provided some guidance as to the basis on which courts should apply the rules. The onus is on the creditor mounting the appeal. The court must

---

[59] The same provision is relevant to IVAs, CVAs and creditors' meetings in administrations, liquidations, receiverships and bankruptcy.
[60] [1994] 1 W.L.R. 1610.
[61] [1996] 2 All E.R. 948.
[62] [1996] 1 All E.R. 37. See Chap. 10.3.
[63] Insolvency Rules 1986, r.5.17(6).
[64] May 2, 1995, unreported.
[65] [1995] B.C.C. 116.

examine the evidence placed before it and decide whether, on balance, the claim was established and if so in what amount. The court is entitled to consider any evidence, not just that available to the chairman. On the facts of this case, it was established that the disputed claim had in fact been compromised and therefore should not have been admitted for voting.

The question has arisen of the possible effect of a voluntary arrangement on third parties. This issue, again, has arisen in the leasehold context in which a landlord often has rights against third parties, particularly guarantors, in respect of the tenant's defaults.[66] The tenant debtor will be concerned to prevent claims both by the landlord and by any third party who has had to meet a claim by the landlord arising out of the tenant's default and is seeking to enforce an indemnity against the tenant. Questions have also arisen as to the right of the third parties to prevent the landlord from claiming against them.

Where the arrangement does not expressly deal with the situation between creditor and third parties, it will absolve the debtor without affecting the liability of any other party such as a guarantor or assignor of a lease. For example, in *R A Securities Ltd v. Mercantile Credit Co. Ltd*[67] a landlord who was bound by a voluntary arrangement with an assignee of the lease was able to claim from the original tenant. In *Burford Midland Properties Ltd v. Marley Extrusions*[68] creditors were forbidden by the arrangement from claiming against third parties if this might lead to indemnity claims against the debtor, an assignee of a lease. The court held that the original tenant could only take direct advantage of this if the arrangement amounted to a variation of the lease; if the lease had not been varied, the action against the original tenant could only be prevented by the debtor seeking an injunction against the landlord to enforce the agreement. In *Mytre Investments Ltd v. Reynolds*[69] and *March Estates plc v. Gunmark Ltd*[70] it was held that a voluntary agreement could only bind third parties (and thus prevent indemnity claims against the debtor) if it made it clear that it was to affect their rights and they had been given notice of the meeting. Third parties should be entitled to vote as contingent creditors. In *March Estates* it was made clear that the landlord would only be prevented from suing the original tenant or guarantor if this was made clear in an arrangement to which both were bound.

---

[66] See n. 26 above.
[67] [1995] 3 All E.R. 581. See also *Johnson v. Davies* [1997] 1 All E.R. 921, upheld by the Court of Appeal on March 18, 1998, unreported.
[68] [1994] B.C.C. 604.
[69] [1995] 3 All E.R. 588.
[70] [1996] 32 E.G. 75.

Where the arrangement is approved any pending bankruptcy petition will be dismissed unless the court orders otherwise.[71] If the debtor is an undischarged bankrupt, the court may annul the bankruptcy order or give such directions about the conduct of the bankruptcy and administration of the bankrupt's estate as it thinks fit.[72] It will delay making any order for 28 days from receiving the report of the meeting to give time for a challenge to the arrangement to be made under section 262. The interim order remains in effect for 28 days after the report to the court but will then cease to have effect unless the court extends it in connection with a section 262 application.[73]

The arrangement has to be notified to the Insolvency Service[74] which maintains a register open to public inspection[75] but this is the only publicity given to it.

h) Challenge to the decision of the meeting

The decision of the meeting may be challenged under section 262 on the grounds that it unfairly prejudiced the interests of a creditor or that there has been some material irregularity in relation to the meeting. Those with standing to present such a challenge are the debtor, any person entitled to vote at the meeting, the nominee, the trustee in bankruptcy and the official receiver. An application must be made within 28 days[76] of the report of the meeting to the court. The court has power to revoke or suspend any approval or give directions for calling a further meeting and may continue or renew the interim order for this purpose.

Hoffmann J. has said[77] that "unfair prejudice" means unfairness brought about by the terms of the voluntary arrangement itself with respect to the relationships between the creditors themselves. Material irregularities include approving an arrangement wrongly affecting a secured creditor.[78] In *Re a debtor (No. 87 of 1993) (No. 2)*[79] the court held that material irregularities could extend to matters other than the conduct or convening of the meeting. In that case, the debtor's failure to disclose all his assets and liabilities in his statement of affairs was held to amount to a material irregularity. This would also be grounds for

---

[71] Insolvency Act 1986, s.260(5).
[72] *ibid.*, s.261.
[73] *ibid.*, s.260(4).
[74] Insolvency Rules 1986, r.5.24.
[75] *ibid.*, r.5.23.
[76] The court has jurisdiction to extend this period: *Tager v. Westpac Banking Corporation* [1997] 1 B.C.L.C. 313.
[77] *Re a debtor* [1992] 1 W.L.R. 226.
[78] *Peck v. Craighead* [1995] B.C.C. 525.
[79] *The Times*, August 7, 1995.

presenting a bankruptcy petition in respect of the debtor but the court held that it was not illogical to have two remedies in respect of the failure since there might be cases in which a creditor felt that bankruptcy of the debtor would not improve his position.

i) Implementation of the arrangement

The nominee becomes the supervisor of the arrangement with the responsibility of overseeing its implementation: he may apply to the court for directions if necessary.[80] Assets included in the proposal and any income promised by the debtor will be transferred to the supervisor. Anyone dissatisfied by the conduct of the supervisor may apply to the court.[81] The supervisor has to report to the creditors, the court and the Insolvency Service every 12 months on the progress of the arrangement and within 28 days of its completion.[82]

j) Default in connection with an IVA

The supervisor of the arrangement or any person bound by it is entitled to present a petition for the bankruptcy of the debtor[83] on the grounds[84] that the debtor has failed to comply with his obligations under the arrangement or that false or misleading information was given by the debtor to the creditors when they were considering the proposal or that the debtor has failed to comply with the reasonable requirements of the supervisor.

A number of cases have considered the effect of a subsequent bankruptcy order on a voluntary arrangement. In *Re McKeen*[85] the landlord of a tenant who had entered into an IVA with his creditors petitioned for the bankruptcy of the tenant. The tenant thought the landlord was bound by the IVA and did not defend the petition whereupon the court made a bankruptcy order. The debtor applied to annul the bankruptcy order. By the time the High Court considered the matter, the landlord had been paid in full. The creditors bound by the IVA were not paid in full. The court can annul the order[86] if satisfied that the bankruptcy debts and

---

[80] Insolvency Act 1986, s.263(4).
[81] *ibid.*, s.263(3).
[82] Insolvency Rules 1986, r. 5.26, 5.29.
[83] Insolvency Act 1986, s.264(1)(c).
[84] *ibid.*, s.276.
[85] [1995] B.C.C. 412.
[86] Insolvency Act 1986, s.282.

expenses of the bankruptcy have all been paid or secured for, to the satisfaction of the court. Section 382 partially defines bankruptcy debts as "any debt or liability to which [the debtor] is subject at the commencement of the bankruptcy . . . any debt or liability to which [the debtor] becomes subject after commencement . . . by reason of any obligation incurred before the commencement". The High Court held that the pre-existing debts were satisfied by the approval of the arrangement. The bankruptcy order did not automatically terminate the voluntary arrangement and although the assets comprised in the voluntary arrangement were vested in the trustee in bankruptcy, the trustee was bound by the rights of the creditors under the agreement. According to this case a creditor bound by a voluntary arrangement "in satisfaction of the debtor's debts" will not have a bankruptcy debt entitling him to petition for bankruptcy.

Re Bradley-Hole[87] also concerned a bankruptcy on the petition of a creditor not bound by the IVA. The court came to a different conclusion about the assets and held that the assets held by the supervisor of the arrangement were held by him on trust for the creditors who were parties to the arrangement. The bankrupt therefore retained no beneficial interest in the property and none of the assets vested in the trustee.

In *Re Essengein Hussein, Davis v. Martin-Sklan*,[88] the debtor failed to comply with his obligations under a voluntary arrangement which had been approved by his creditors and the supervisor petitioned for his bankruptcy. Blackburne J. held that a bankruptcy order made on the petition of the supervisor of an arrangement pursuant to section 264(1) of the Insolvency Act 1986 would automatically bring the voluntary arrangement to an end.

It can be seen from these cases that there may not be any advantage for a creditor in arguing that he is not bound by the IVA since the IVA is likely to have removed all the assets of the debtor from the reach of a trustee in bankruptcy.

k) Evaluation of the IVA

A fairly substantial percentage of all formal individual insolvencies are now dealt with by an IVA. Recent statistics for individual insolvency provided by the Insolvency Service are:

---

[87] [1995] B.C.C. 418.
[88] [1995] B.C.C. 1122.

	1994	1995	1996
Bankruptcy orders	25,634	21,933	21,803
Deeds of Arrangements	2	2	2
IVAs	5,103	4,384	4,466

The IVA has a number of advantages over bankruptcy: it avoids the stigma of bankruptcy, it involves less publicity and the debtor does not incur the disabilities of a bankrupt.[89] Friends and relatives may be prepared, in order to obtain these advantages for the debtor, to contribute money to an IVA which would not be available in a bankruptcy. Another attraction to creditors is that an IVA does not carry the Insolvency Service fee[90] and more assets therefore remain available for the creditors. Creditors will prefer a bankruptcy where there appears to be the possibility of the trustee in bankruptcy re-opening previous transactions and swelling the assets.[91] There may be problems in future in persuading creditors to agree to an IVA where the debtor has a personal pension which may become available to a trustee in bankruptcy.[92]

The Loughborough University Banking Centre carried out a study in 1989 of 100 IVA proposals followed by a 1992 follow-up survey of 78 of the proposals which had been accepted.[93] About 33 per cent of accepted arrangements subsequently met trouble, of which over two-thirds eventually failed. Some recurrent factors in the failure were identified; these included circumstances beyond the debtor's control such as redundancy and divorce but were often attributable to non-co-operation by the debtor in providing appropriate information in the preparation of the IVA or lack of will to continue to meet the agreed payments. IVAs which provided for payment of income by the debtor over an extended period were the most likely to fail. The survey found that the costs associated with the IVAs were demonstrably lower than would have been the case in a bankruptcy. Dividends for unsecured creditors were higher than would have been the case in bankruptcy. Arrangements which only involved the transfer of assets produced a

---

[89] Such as inability to be a director of a company and restrictions on obtaining credit. See Chap. 15.4.
[90] See Chap. 20.
[91] see Chap. 30.
[92] see Chap. 33.
[93] Pond, *An alternative to bankruptcy—an empirical study of Individual Voluntary Arrangements*, Pond *Do Individual Voluntary Arrangements really work?* Pond [1995] J.B.L. 118, Evans & Pond 11 I.L.&P. 95 [1995].

higher dividend than would have been the case in a bankruptcy because of the lower costs involved. Arrangements which involved subsequent payments from the income of the debtor produced a much higher level of dividend than a bankruptcy where they succeeded but such arrangements were much more likely to fail than asset only arrangements.

4. Evaluation of the regimes available to individuals

It is clear that there is a gap in the legislative provision for insolvency in that there is no provision short of bankruptcy for those who have insufficient assets to interest their creditors in some sort of arrangement and for whom a county court administration order is not a possibility.

The committee set up by the Council of Justice in 1993 to report on the workings of the present insolvency system[94] reported that the IVA was not helping the small consumer debtor who commonly has no assets or income from which it is possible to make a contribution towards past debts. It observed that the advantages of the IVA "seem to be particularly apparent to the more sophisticated type of debtor: such as professionals in private practice with the prospect of some continuing income or directors faced with large guarantees on behalf of an insolvent company". The Report said that the lack of appropriate alternative procedures compels far too many individual debtors to resort to bankruptcy. Justice noted that the level of the deposit and fees had not in practice served as a barrier to the presentation of debtors' petitions and that some charities had been putting aside funds to help with this funding. They felt that the burden of handling the affairs of small insolvent debtors fell to a disproportionate extent and inappropriately upon the Bankruptcy Court.

It seems likely that there are still a large number of consumer debtors who cannot come to any form of agreement, formal or informal, with their creditors and for one reason or another[95] do not seek to take advantage of the bankruptcy laws; it has been argued that for many the alternative is a lifelong burden of unpayable debt.[96]

It should be pointed out that the Cork Committee itself said[97] "We do not regard our proposals as a panacea for solving the problems of all insolvent individual debtors". They envisaged the procedure as being applicable to three main categories of debtor: directors and others who have personally guaranteed the debts of insolvent companies, often with a small number of other creditors and substantial assets; members of

---

[94] Justice, *Insolvency Law: An Agenda for Reform.*
[95] Where cost is not a deterrent, stigma or lack of knowledge may be.
[96] Ford and Wilson, Rajak (ed.), *Insolvency Law Theory and Practice* Chap. 6.
[97] para. 365.

professions not permitted to take advantage of limited liability; and traders who for one reason or another have not formed companies but whose gross business assets might well be sizable. The Cork Committee expected other debtors to use the Debts Arrangement Order which they proposed[98] but which was not implemented. This would have allowed the court to provide for the orderly repayment of the debtor's obligations over a period of time with the possibility of payments of less than 100 pence in the pound and, after a relatively short period of time, the discharge of the debts. The court would have been able to consider applications from debtors without realisable assets or surplus income.

Justice said that the amendments contained in the Courts and Legal Services Act 1990, if brought into force, would go some way to meeting the need for reform but that there was an urgent social need for a complete reassessment of the procedures for dealing with the affairs of insolvent consumer debtors.

The underlying problem is the resource implications given that where the insolvent is assetless the costs of whatever procedure is used to deal with the situation cannot come from the debtor. Greater provision of free money advice services and the extension of the use of the county court administration procedure both require external financing either from the government or from the credit industry itself.

---

[98] In Chap. 6 of the Cork Report.

CHAPTER 10

CORPORATE RESCUE REGIMES[1]

1. Introduction

The Cork Committee said[2]: "we believe that a concern for the livelihood and well-being of those dependent upon an enterprise which may well be the lifeblood of a whole town or even a region, is a legitimate factor to which a modern law of insolvency must have regard. The chain reaction consequent upon any given failure can potentially be so disastrous to creditors, employees and the community that it must not be overlooked". The Committee recognised that what is now administrative receivership was capable of ensuring the survival of viable parts of the company by selling them to new owners. The only other available formal rescue mechanism at that time was a scheme of arrangement under what is now section 425 of the Companies Act 1985. The recommendations in the Cork Report led to the introduction of the company voluntary arrangement and the administration order.

It may be possible to ensure, through informal means, the survival of a company which is unable to pay its debts where all the creditors are in agreement or where there is some pre-existing contractual agreement governing the situation under which a dissenting party can be bound. In other situations it will only be possible to achieve a resolution of the repayment problems on a basis which is acceptable to the majority, but not the totality of the creditors, if there is a procedure which enables the majority to bind the minority. Both section 425 of the Companies Act 1985 and the company voluntary arrangement procedure contained in Part I of the Insolvency Act 1986 make this possible. The dissenting minority can, however, still endanger the achievement of an agreement during the negotiations by taking action against the company either to have it wound up or to enforce rights against the company which will leave it incapable of surviving. The only way of dealing with this

---

[1] Texts specifically on this area include David Brown, *Corporate Rescue*; Fletcher, Higham and Trower, *The Law and Practice of Corporate Administrations*; Grier and Floyd, *Corporate Recovery: Administrations and Voluntary Arrangements*. For a cross-disciplinary approach, see A. Belcher, *Corporate Rescue*.
[2] At para. 204.

problem is the imposition of a freeze on creditors' rights and the only regime which currently makes this possible is the company administration order.

This Chapter explains the three regimes currently available in the United Kingdom. It then goes on to examine the problems associated with them, the proposals for reform and some of the procedures available elsewhere.

2. Schemes of arrangement[3]

A scheme of arrangement under section 425 of the Companies Act 1985 enables a company, whether or not it is insolvent, to enter into a compromise or arrangement with any class of its creditors or members and may be used to restructure the capital of companies in financial difficulties. It may be used as an alternative to liquidation (possibly coupled with an administration order[4]) or within a liquidation as a means of reaching a compromise with creditors. Approval of the scheme requires, first, the consent of each of the various classes of members and creditors affected and, secondly, the sanction of the court. Consent of a class requires a majority of three-quarters in value of those present and voting either in person or by proxy. Once approved the scheme is binding on all the relevant classes of creditors and members and on the company.[5]

The section 425 procedure is initiated by an application to the court for an order summoning a meeting of the relevant class of creditors (which may include contingent creditors[6]) or members affected by the scheme. The application may be made by the company or any creditor, member, liquidator or administrator of it. The application should be supported by an affidavit which explains the need for the proposed scheme and sufficient information to enable the court to determine whether the meetings ought to be summoned. It is for the applicant to identify the composition of the class meetings to be summoned. A class will consist of those persons whose rights are not so dissimilar as to make it impossible for them to consult together with a view to their

---

[3] See *Insolvency Law: Theory and Practice* (ed. Rajak), Chap. 20.
[4] See, for example, *Re Polly Peck International plc* [1996] B.C.C. 486.
[5] This contrasts with the company voluntary arrangement provisions under which only those creditors who had notice of the meeting and were entitled to vote will be bound.
[6] *Re Midland Coal* [1895] 1 Ch. 267, a case on the 1870 provision which was the precursor of Companies Act 1985, s.425. It only applied to insolvent companies and logic required that claims be valued as if being proved in a liquidation.

common interest.[7] Where a class has no interest in the arrangement because of the insolvency of the company, it is unnecessary to summon a meeting of that class.[8]

In order for the court to sanction the scheme,[9] it has, first, to be satisfied that there is strict compliance with the statute, including the obligations to disclose the terms of the arrangement[10] and to convene separate meetings of the different categories of creditors, and that the scheme is a compromise or arrangement within the section. The court also has to be satisfied that the class was fairly represented at the class meeting and that the majority were exercising their power bona fide. Finally, the court must be satisfied that the terms of the arrangement are such that an intelligent and honest member of the class acting in respect of his own interest might normally approve of the arrangement.[11] Once the court has approved the scheme, it may use the wide powers given to it by section 427 of the Companies Act 1985 to assist in the implementation of the scheme; these powers include the ability to transfer property and dissolve a company without winding it up.

The Cork Committee identified[12] a number of problems with this procedure. The absence of a moratorium causes difficulty, particularly given the delay and complexity involved in applying to court and summoning the various meetings. A minimum period of eight weeks will be necessary to get the scheme in place. It can be difficult to identify the relevant classes correctly and there is always the risk that if the classes have been incorrectly defined the scheme will not be sanctioned.

3. Company voluntary arrangements

a) Introduction

The Cork Committee felt that something less complex and speedier than the section 425 arrangement was needed. They also felt that court involvement could be replaced to an extent by that of an insolvency

---

[7] *Sovereign Life Assurance Co. v. Dodd* [1892] 2 Q.B. 573 and *Re Hellenic and General Trust Ltd* [1976] 1 W.L.R. 123 are amongst the substantial body of case law on this point.

[8] *Re Tea Corp.* [1904] 1 Ch. 12, *Re BCH plc (No. 3)* [1992] 1 W.L.R. 672, *Re MCC plc (No. 2)* [1994] 1 B.C.L.C. 1 (contractually subordinated creditors excluded).

[9] See *Re Anglo-Continental Supply Co. Ltd* [1922] 2 Ch. 723 at 736 for a statement of these requirements.

[10] Contained in Companies Act 1985, s.426.

[11] *Re Dorman Long & Co.* [1934] Ch. 635.

[12] At paras. 404–418.

practitioner given the new controls as to who would be eligible to act as such.[13]

The company voluntary arrangement ("CVA") is broadly similar to the IVA considered in the previous Chapter. The main distinction is that there is no moratorium associated with the CVA. Additionally, since the interests of members as well as creditors may be affected, there will need to be two meetings summoned to consider a CVA proposal.

b) Proposal for a CVA

Section 1 of the Insolvency Act 1986 provides that the directors of a company, other than one in liquidation or administration, may propose[14] a voluntary arrangement to the company and its creditors. This must be either a composition in satisfaction of its debts or a scheme of arrangement of its affairs. The proposal must explain why the directors think an arrangement is desirable and why the creditors may be expected to concur in it. It must include a statement of the company's assets, any other assets to be made available, the liabilities and how it is proposed to deal with them. There is no requirement that the company be insolvent or unable to pay its debts. A liquidator or administrator may also propose a voluntary arrangement. The proposal must provide for a qualified insolvency practitioner ("the nominee") to act as supervisor of the arrangement.

The proposal and a statement of the company's affairs[15] must be submitted to the intended nominee, unless he is already liquidator or administrator of the company. The nominee then has 28 days[16] in which to submit a report to the court stating whether he thinks meetings of the company and of its creditors should be summoned to consider the proposal and, if he does, details of the proposed meetings. The meetings must be held not less than 14 and not more than 28 days after the nominee files his report with the court. If the nominee fails to submit the report, the court may, on the application of the person intending to make the proposal, order his replacement by another qualified insolvency practitioner.[17] A nominee who has reported that the proposal should be considered should, unless the court directs otherwise, summon the meetings for the time, date and place proposed in the report.

---

[13] See Chap. 20.
[14] Insolvency Rules 1986, r.1.3 sets out the items which must be included in a proposal.
[15] Whose contents are prescribed by Insolvency Rules 1986, r.1.5. The nominee may request further information.
[16] Insolvency Act 1986, s.2. The court may extend the 28 day period.
[17] Insolvency Act 1986, s.2(4).

A nominee who is already liquidator or administrator does not have to submit a report to the court and may summon the meetings to consider the proposal as he thinks fit, giving at least 14 days notice.[18]

c) Consideration of proposal

Those summoned to the meetings must be sent a copy of the proposal, a summary of the statement of affairs and the nominee's comments on the proposal.[19] Notice of the creditors' meeting must be sent to all creditors of the company of whose claims and addresses the nominee is aware.[20]

The meetings will decide whether to approve the proposed arrangement with or without modification.[21] The meetings may not approve any proposal or modification which affects the rights of a secured creditor to enforce his security[22] or affects the priority of payment of preferential debts unless the creditor affected consents.[23]

The voting rights and the requisite majorities applicable to the meetings are set out in the Insolvency Rules 1986.[24] Members vote in accordance with the rights attaching to their shares and a resolution at a members meeting requires a majority of more than one half of those present in person or by proxy and voting on the resolution.[25]

Every creditor who was given notice of the meeting is entitled to vote at it and votes are calculated according to the amount of the creditor's debt at the date of the meeting or, where relevant, at the start of the liquidation or administration; creditors may not vote in respect of secured claims. The same provisions apply as on an IVA in respect of disputed debts.[26] The requisite majority at the creditors' meeting in respect of a resolution to approve the proposal or any modification of it is a majority in excess of three-quarters in value of the creditors present in person or by proxy and voting on the resolution. Other resolutions at the creditors meeting require a majority in excess of one-half. Any resolution of the creditors will be invalid if those voting against it include more than half in value of the creditors entitled to vote who are not connected with the company.

---

[18] Insolvency Rules 1986, r. 1.11.
[19] *ibid.*, r. 1.9.
[20] *ibid.*
[21] Insolvency Act 1986, s.4.
[22] See Chap. 9.3(f) for discussion of what amounts to a security in the context of a voluntary arrangement.
[23] Insolvency Act 1986, s.4(3)(4).
[24] rr. 1.17 to 1.20.
[25] See Insolvency Rules 1986, rr. 1.17 to 1.20 for voting rights and majorities.
[26] See Chap. 9.3(g) above.

d) Effect of approval

Once approved, the arrangement takes effect as if made by the company at the creditors' meeting and binds every person who had notice of and was entitled to vote at that meeting as if he were a party to the voluntary arrangement.

There has been the same debate as in relation to IVAs about the extent to which those with future and contingent debts can be bound by a voluntary arrangement[27] with the same outcome. In *Re Cancol Ltd*[28] a landlord claimed that he was not a "creditor" of the tenant within the provisions of the Act in relation to future rent under the 20-year lease, was not therefore entitled to vote and was not bound by the company voluntary arrangement. The landlord argued that whereas there was an identical extended definition of creditor for the purposes of liquidation[29] and IVA,[30] there was no such definition for a CVA in the case of a company not in liquidation. Knox J. found that the landlord was a creditor and was bound; consistency dictated that for a company voluntary arrangement creditors should include those with debts payable in the future on a contingency, as that was the position for IVAs and for bankruptcy and winding up procedures. Furthermore, to exclude future rent would also exclude overdrafts and other debts payable on demand if a demand had not been made; such creditors could then avoid being bound by a CVA by not making a demand.[31]

Where the company is in administration or liquidation, the court may stay the winding up or discharge the administration or give directions with respect to their conduct which will facilitate the implementation of the voluntary arrangement. No such order will be made until 28 days after the chairman of the meeting has reported the approval to the court.[32] This is to give time for a challenge to the arrangement to be made under section 6 of the Insolvency Act 1986.

---

[27] See Chap. 9.3(g).

[28] [1996] 1 All E.R. 37.

[29] Insolvency Rules 1986, r. 13.12.

[30] Insolvency Act 1986, s.382(3).

[31] Hermer, 17 Co. Law. 84, points out that s.425 arrangements apply to contingent creditors on the basis of authority at a time when only insolvent companies could use the procedure and that it would be possible to argue a precedent-based distinction between CVAs in liquidation and those not. It would also be possible to differentiate on policy grounds between CVA in liquidation and not in liquidation since if the extended definition were not applicable in a liquidation the creditor would be left without redress. There is, however, no justification for distinguishing between a CVA and an IVA.

[32] The chairman must report the result of the meetings to the court within four days: Insolvency Act 1986, s.4(6) and Insolvency Rules 1986, r. 1.24.

e) Challenge to CVA

A challenge may be made to a CVA[33] within 28 days of the result of the meetings being reported to the court. The challenge may be made by anyone entitled to vote at either meeting, the nominee or a liquidator or administrator of the company. The grounds for challenge are the same as those available in respect of an IVA[34] and have been discussed in the previous Chapter.[35]

f) Implementation of arrangement

Once the arrangement has been approved the nominee becomes the supervisor responsible for overseeing the implementation of the arrangement. The court has a general supervisory function[36] in that the supervisor may apply for directions and anyone dissatisfied by the conduct of the supervisor may seek the assistance of the court.

The supervisor of a CVA has *locus standi* to petition for the winding up or administration of a company.[37]

4. Administration orders

a) Introduction

Essentially, the idea behind the administration order is to give a company facing insolvency a breathing space from the pressures of creditors to see if a means can be found of effecting a rescue. An administration may also allow a more effective realisation of the assets than would be available in a liquidation because of the difficulty a liquidator has in permitting a company to continue trading.

The Cork Committee said that receiverships pursuant to floating charges had proved an important way of preserving businesses and jobs and of raising more from the sale of the assets than resulted from a piecemeal liquidation. The Committee recommended that a new form of proceeding should be made available for those circumstances in which receivers were not or could not be appointed. A receiver cannot be appointed to run the business unless the company has given a floating

---

[33] Under Insolvency Act 1986, s.6.
[34] *ibid.*, s.262.
[35] See Chap. 9.3(h).
[36] See Insolvency Act 1986, s.7.
[37] *ibid.*, s.7(4). For the effect of a subsequent liquidation, see *Re Halson Packaging Limited* [1997] B.C.C. 993 (voluntary liquidation) and *Re Arthur Rathbone Kitchens Limited* [1997] 2 B.C.L.C. 280 (voluntary liquidation followed by compulsory liquidation).

charge over the entire undertaking. Even where there is a floating charge over the entire undertaking, the debenture holder may be unwilling to appoint a receiver of the business; the lender may, for example, be adequately secured by fixed charges over the fixed assets. Where a receiver could not be appointed, the only possibilities were an informal arrangement or a formal scheme of arrangement under the Companies Act which was expensive and time-consuming. The Cork Committee recommended a moratorium in the case of both administration and administrative receiverships.

The Government[38] accepted these proposals with the exception of the suggestion that the moratorium should be extended to receivership: "The Government believes that only a court-appointed official, the administrator, whose duty will be to act in the interests of all creditors and shareholders, should enjoy such temporary protection".

An administration order is an order directing that, during the period for which the order is in force, the affairs, business and property of the company shall be managed by an administrator appointed for the purpose by the court.[39] During the administration, the company is protected from its creditors. The administrator takes control of the company's property and manages its affairs. The administrator draws up proposals to achieve the purposes for which the administration order has been made and should apply to the court for the administration order to be discharged when it appears that the purpose of the administration has either been achieved or has become incapable of achievement or where the creditors of the company require an application to be made.

b) Grounds for seeking an administration order

Three conditions must be satisfied[40] before the court can make an administration order:

  i) the court must be satisfied that the company is or is likely to become unable to pay its debts. The company will be deemed unable to pay its debts in the circumstances specified in section 123 of the Insolvency Act 1986[41] in connection with a petition for compulsory liquidation. These are non-compliance with a statutory demand, unsatisfied judgment execution, inability to pay its debts as they fall due or having

---

[38] *A Revised Framework for Insolvency Law* Cmnd. 9175.
[39] Insolvency Act 1986, s.8(2).
[40] *ibid.*, s.8.
[41] Discussed in Chap. 17.2, below.

assets whose value is less than the amount of the company's liabilities, taking into account its contingent and prospective liabilities. This latter balance sheet test is more likely to be used in this context than in the context of a petition for a compulsory winding up since the petition for an administration is likely to be made by those with access to evidence of balance sheet insolvency.

ii) the court must consider that the making of an order would be likely to achieve one or more of the purposes specified in section 8(3) of the Insolvency Act 1986. The first of the purposes for whose achievement an administration order may be made is the survival of the company and the whole or any part of its undertaking as a going concern. It is to be noted that this purpose envisages the survival of the company as a legal person; the sale of the business to another entity would not come within this purpose.[42] The second possible purpose is the approval of a company voluntary arrangement; seeking an administration order is currently the only method of obtaining a moratorium against creditors whilst the arrangement is set up. The third purpose is the sanctioning under section 425 of the Companies Act 1985 of a compromise or arrangement. The final possible purpose is the achievement of a more advantageous realisation of the company's assets than would be effected on a winding up; this is the most often used goal.[43] The order has to specify for which purpose or purposes it is being made.

One of the first issues facing the courts in implementing these provisions was the meaning to be given to the requirement that an administration order "would be likely to" achieve one of the statutory goals. In *Re Consumer and Industrial Press*,[44] an early decision on the section, Peter Gibson J. took the view that the court had to be satisfied that it was more probable than not that the order would achieve its purpose. Hoffmann J. refused to follow this restrictive view in *Re Harris Simmons Ltd*[45] and said, referring to the explanation in the Cork Report of when it was envisaged that an

---

[42] *Re Rowbotham Baxter* [1990] B.C.L.C. 397.
[43] This purpose does not encompass a more advantageous method of *distribution* of the assets: *Re Powerstore (Trading) Ltd* [1998] 1 All E.R. 121.
[44] [1988] B.C.L.C. 177.
[45] [1989] 1 W.L.R. 368.

administration order would be made, that the question was whether there was a "real prospect" that one of the purposes would be achieved. This view was followed by Vinelott J. in *Re Primlaks*[46] and is now generally accepted.[47] In *Re SCL Services*[48] Peter Gibson J., in using the "reasonable prospect" test, held that only purposes which passed the test could be included in the order. Professor Milman suggests[49] that "the real significance of the 'reasonable prospect' test lies in its symbolic offering of support by the courts for the administration order process".

iii) the company must not be in liquidation and nor must an administrative receiver have been appointed. Even where the company is in administrative receivership, the court may make an administration order if it is also satisfied that the debenture holder who appointed the receiver has consented to the making of the order or, that if an administration order were to be made, the security by virtue of which the receiver was appointed would be avoided as a transaction at an undervalue,[50] a preference[51] or under section 245 of the Insolvency Act 1986.[52] Notice of a petition for an administration order must be given[53] to any person who has appointed or is or may be entitled to appoint an administrative receiver. This gives such a debenture holder the opportunity to appoint a receiver before the hearing of the petition for the administration order. A debenture holder with a floating charge over the whole undertaking of the company is, therefore, in a position to veto the making of an administration order. In *Re Croftbell*[54] Vinelott J. held that a floating charge given by the company to a borrower purely for the purpose of conferring this veto rather than in order to provide any additional real security was effective to achieve its purpose; such a charge has become known as a "lightweight floating charge".

---

[46] [1989] B.C.L.C. 734.
[47] *Re Land and Property Trust Co.* [1991] B.C.C. 446 is an example of a case in which it was held there was no reasonable prospect of success. Costs were awarded against the directors personally.
[48] [1990] B.C.L.C. 98.
[49] See (ed. Rajak), *Insolvency Law Theory and Practice*, p. 373.
[50] Insolvency Act 1986, s.238. See Chap. 30.3.
[51] *ibid.*, s.239. See Chap. 30.4.
[52] See Chap. 29.3.
[53] Under Insolvency Act 1986, s.9(2).
[54] [1990] B.C.C. 781, Oditah [1991] J.B.L. 49.

Where these three requirements are met the court has a discretion as to whether or not to make an order.[55] In *Re Arrows (No. 3)*[56] the court refused to make an administration order on the ground that a compulsory liquidation was appropriate; the administration had been opposed by a majority in value of the creditors and there were serious matters requiring thorough investigation.[57] Less weight will be given to the interests of the secured creditors than to those of the unsecured creditors since the former have less to lose from the administration.[58] In *Re West Park Golf and Country Club*[59] the court held that it was an abuse of process to present a petition, as a means of applying commercial pressure, in circumstances where there were no reasonable grounds for believing that the petition would be granted.

c) Procedure for seeking an administration order[60]

A petition for an administration order may be presented by the company, the directors,[61] a creditor or creditors (including contingent and prospective creditors). An affidavit must be filed in support of the petition—giving grounds for the deponent's belief that the company is or is likely to become unable to pay its debts and stating which of the statutory goals is expected to be achieved by the making of an administration order. The affidavit must give details of the company's financial position, of any secured creditors and of any winding up petition presented against the company. The affidavit should also contain details of other matters which would assist the court in deciding whether to make an administration order. There must also be a statement as to whether an independent report on the company's affairs has been produced and, if not, an explanation of why not. Rule 2.2 of the Insolvency Rules provides for the preparation, and exhibition to the affidavit, of a report by an independent person (who may be the proposed administrator) to the effect that the appointment of an administrator for the company is expedient. In the early days of the administration procedure, the practice developed of submitting highly

---

[55] *Re Manlon Trading Ltd* (1988) 4 B.C.C. 455, *Re Imperial Motors* 1990 B.C.L.C. 29.

[56] [1992] B.C.C. 131.

[57] cf. *Structures & Computers Ltd v. Ansys Inc.*, *The Times*, October 3, 1997 in which Neuberger J. granted an administration order despite the opposition of the majority of the unsecured creditors.

[58] *Re Consumer & Industrial Press* [1988] B.C.L.C. 177, *Re Imperial Motors* [1990] B.C.L.C. 29.

[59] [1997] 1 B.C.L.C. 20.

[60] Insolvency Act 1986, s.9 and Insolvency Rules 1986, rr. 2.1–2.10.

[61] As a board or by one of them with the consent of the board but not by an individual dissenting director: *Re Equiticorp International plc* [1989] B.C.L.C. 597.

detailed and expensive reports under rule 2.2. The court issued a practice direction in an attempt to restrict this.[62] The proposed administrator's consent to accept appointment must also be exhibited to the affidavit.

The petition must be served[63] on, *inter alia,* any person who has appointed or is or may be entitled to appoint an administrative receiver. This must be done at least five clear days before the day fixed for the hearing. The courts have held that, under the wide powers conferred by section 9(4) and (5) of the Insolvency Act 1986, they may shorten the time for service of the petition. In *Re Chancery plc*[64] there was a gap of only a few hours between presentation of the petition and the granting of the order. In *Re Cavco Floors*[65] and *Re Shearing and Loader Ltd,*[66] orders were granted without the petition even having been presented. In *Re Rowbotham Baxter,*[67] however, Harman J. said the practice of granting an order before the petition had been presented should cease since the court should not make an order without hearing any arguments in opposition.

Notice of the petition must be given to any sheriff or other officer known to the petitioner to be charged with an execution or other legal process against the company and against any person who to the knowledge of the petitioner has distrained against the company or its property. There is no general advertisement of a petition for an administration order. The petition cannot be withdrawn except with the leave of the court; this enables the court to deal with vexatious or frivolous petitions.

At the hearing, the court may hear the petitioner, the company, any person who has appointed or is entitled to appoint an administrative receiver, any administrative receiver, anyone who has petitioned for the liquidation of the company, the proposed administrator and, if they give leave, any other person who appears to have an interest justifying his appearance.

Where an administration order is made, the costs of obtaining it form part of the expenses of the administration. Notice of an administration has to be advertised in the *Gazette* and in such newspaper as the administrator thinks appropriate for ensuring that the order comes to the

---

[62] Practice Note [1994] 1 All E.R. 324.
[63] Insolvency Rules 1986, r. 2.6.
[64] [1991] B.C.C. 171.
[65] [1990] B.C.C. 589.
[66] [1991] B.C.C. 232.
[67] [1990] B.C.L.C. 397.

notice of the company's creditors. Notice also has to be given forthwith to the registrar of companies.

d) Consequences of presenting a petition for administration

The presentation of a petition for administration brings about immediate protection for the company.[68] Once a petition has been presented, then, until the administration order is made or the petition dismissed, the company may not go or be put into liquidation. No steps may be taken to enforce any security over the company's property or to repossess goods in the company's possession under hire-purchase agreements[69], no distress may be levied nor any proceedings or execution or other legal process be commenced or continued except, in any case, with the leave of the court. This moratorium does not interfere with the presentation of a petition for winding up[70] nor with the appointment of an administrative receiver or the exercise by such receiver of his functions. Where there is an administrative receiver in office when the petition is presented, the moratorium will not commence unless and until the appointor of the receiver consents.

The court may if necessary restrict the powers of the directors and of the company in general meeting pending the hearing of the petition. The court may be required to exercise these powers if there is a risk of the company's assets disappearing before the hearing can take place. *Re Gallidoro Trawlers*[71] was an *ex parte* application made by the company's bank which was proposing to file a petition for an administration order. It had a charge on the company's ships but feared that it would be rendered valueless by a sale by the company of its fishing licences. Harman J. declined to appoint an interim manager but decided that the company should not dispose of any of its assets except in the ordinary course of business or with the consent of the proposed administrator or of the court; he also abridged the time for service of the petition to not less than two clear days.

There is no power to appoint a provisional administrator but a Practice Note[72] suggests the possibility of the immediate appointment of an administrator required to report back within a short time.

---

[68] Under Insolvency Act 1986, s.10.

[69] Which, by Insolvency Act, s.10(4), includes conditional sale agreements, chattel leasing agreements and retention of title agreements.

[70] But the court may restrict advertisement of the petition: *Re a company (No. 001992 of 1988)* [1989] B.C.L.C. 9, *Re a company (No. 001448 of 1989)* [1989] B.C.L.C. 715.

[71] [1991] B.C.C. 691.

[72] [1994] 1 All E.R. 324.

e) Consequences of making the administration order

Directors do not automatically vacate office on the making of an administration but the administrator does have an unfettered power to remove the directors from office.[73] The directors may not exercise their powers so as to interfere with the administrator in the discharge of his duties. The directors will be under an obligation to co-operate with the administrator.[74]

Once an administration order has been made, an extensive moratorium comes into effect. The court in *Barclays Mercantile Business Finance v. SIBEC*[75] made the point that the rights of creditors are not substantively affected: the moratorium prevents enforcement and is designed to enable the administrator to control the assets free from interference by creditors.[76] As will be seen, this is a more extensive moratorium than is available to an individual debtor.[77]

f) The moratorium[78]

Once an administration order has been made, any petition for winding up is dismissed and any administrative receiver will vacate office. During the period for which the administration order is in force no resolution may be passed or order made for the winding up of the company and no administrative receiver may be appointed. Section 11 of the Insolvency Act 1986 goes on to provide:

> "(c) no other steps may be taken to enforce any security over the company's property, or to repossess goods in the company's possession under any hire-purchase agreement[79], except with the consent of the administrator or the leave of the court and subject (where the court gives leave) to such terms as the court may impose;
>
> and

---

[73] Insolvency Act 1986, s.14.
[74] *ibid.*, ss235, 236. Failure to co-operate might also be grounds for a disqualification order on the grounds of unfitness: see Company Directors Disqualification Act 1986, s.6 and Sched. 1.
[75] [1992] 1 W.L.R. 1253.
[76] See Prentice, Oditah and Segal of Ziegel (ed.), *Current International and Comparative Developments in Corporate Insolvency Law*, Chap. 5.
[77] See Chap. 9.3(c) above and Kruse 12 I.L.&P. 46.
[78] Insolvency Act 1986, s.11. See Goode, *Principles of Corporate Insolvency Law* (2nd ed.) pp. 295 *et seq.*
[79] As defined in Insolvency Act 1986, s.10(4), see n. 69, above.

(d) no other proceedings and no execution or other legal process may be commenced or continued, and no distress may be levied against the company or its property except with the consent of the administrator or the leave of the court and subject (where the court gives leave) to such terms aforesaid."

Section 11(c) and (d) have given rise to litigation to determine the precise scope of the moratorium and the circumstances in which a court would (and, therefore, an administrator should) give leave for an exception to be made. Most of the phrases of both subsections have been subject to judicial scrutiny and it is notable that the courts have frequently referred to the legislative policy behind the legislation.

In *Re Bristol Airport*[80] the Court of Appeal had to consider the meaning of "other steps", "security" and "the company's property". The issue here was whether an airport authority could exercise its statutory right of detention[81] against aircraft leased to a company in administration. The Court held that the taking of a step involved preventing the administrator from doing something with respect to the assets covered by the security which he would otherwise be entitled to do[82] and included the retaking of property. The Court went on to hold that "the company's property" included property held by the company under a lease; it looked to section 436 of the Insolvency Act 1986 and was also influenced by the fact that equipment leasing is commonplace as a method of corporate finance. The Court also held that "security" included a statutory lien.

The meaning of "enforcement of security" has exercised the courts on a number of occasions. It has been held that, in relation to a possessory security, passivity does not constitute enforcement; something more, such as failure to deliver up the property after a request by the administrator, would be required for there to be enforcement.[83] It has been necessary to decide whether a right of re-entry falls within the moratorium. In *Exchange Travel Agency v. Triton Property Trust plc*[84] Harman J. held that the exercise of a right of re-entry would fall within both section 11(3)(c) and (d) as the enforcement of security and the commencement of legal process. He referred to the fact that re-entry would be barred in a liquidation and that it would therefore be astonishing if it were not barred in an administration. *Scottish Exhibition Centre*

---

[80] [1990] Ch. 744.

[81] Under Civil Aviation Act 1982, s.88.

[82] On this basis, s.11 would not stop the service of a demand in respect of an on-demand loan or of a notice rescinding a contract.

[83] *Re Sabre International Products Ltd* [1991] B.C.L.C. 470 which concerned the right of carriers to detain goods.

[84] [1991] B.C.C. 341.

v. Mirestop Ltd[85] proceeded on the basis that leave was needed to re-enter; the court granted leave, noting the length of time which the administrators had been in occupation. In *Re Olympia & York Canary Wharf Ltd*[86] it was held that leave was not required for the service of a notice on a company purporting to terminate a contract on the basis that time was of the essence. In the course of his judgment, Millett J. accepted that exercising peaceable re-entry was enforcement of a security but was not "legal process". A similar finding was made at the full trial of *Scottish Exhibition Centre v. Mirestop Ltd.*[87] In the recent case of *Razzaq v. Pala*,[88] which concerned the application of section 285 of the Insolvency Act 1986, Lightman J., relying on the Court of Appeal authority of *Ezekiel v. Orakpo*[89] which was not referred to in the cases on administrations and individual voluntary arrangements, held that a right of re-entry was not a security interest.[90]

In *Re Atlantic Computers*,[91] the Court of Appeal had to decide, first, whether administrators could continue to receive rents on computers which had been sub-let to customers without handing over the rents to the lessors of the computers and, secondly, whether the owners could repossess the computers from the customers. In answer to the first point, the Court held that it was not improper for the administrators to continue to use the computers.[92] The Court of Appeal held that goods sub-let by a company were still "in the company's possession" as between the company and the lessor and, therefore, leave was required before the lessors could repossess them; the Court went on to give leave for reasons explained below.

Goods will still be held "under a hire-purchase agreement" where the agreement provides for its determination on the presentation of an administration petition.[93]

"Other proceedings" means legal proceedings or quasi-legal proceedings such as arbitration[94] so that an application for an out-of-time

---

[85] [1993] B.C.L.C. 1459.
[86] [1993] B.C.L.C. 453. Later proceedings at (1993) B.C.C. 159.
[87] (1994) B.C.C. 845.
[88] [1997] E.G.C.S. 75 and Chap. 25.2
[89] [1977] 1 Q.B. 260. The Court of Appeal held that a right of forfeiture is not a security since in exercising it the lessor recovers his own property.
[90] See discussion of the right of re-entry in relation to the interim order in an IVA (Chap. 9.3) and the freeze on individual enforcement of unsecured rights in a liquidation (Chap. 25.2).
[91] [1990] B.C.C. 859.
[92] And there was no room for the application of the expenses principle from liquidation (as to which, see Chap. 35, below).
[93] *Re David Meek Plant Hire Ltd* [1994] 1 B.C.L.C. 680.
[94] *Re Bristol Airport* [1990] Ch. 744 holding that the exercise of statutory lien or rights under contract was not proceedings.

registration under section 404 of the Companies Act 1985 was not prevented by the moratorium[95] and nor was an application for the removal of the company's civil aviation licence.[96] Industrial tribunal applications are caught by the moratorium.[97] Although Harman J. in *Exchange Travel Agency v. Triton Property Trust plc*[98] held that "other legal process" included exercise of a right of re-entry, Millett J. refused to follow this *Re Olympia & York Canary Wharf Ltd*[99] and the general view is that "other legal process" only refers to the process requiring the assistance of the court.[1]

In *Re Atlantic Computer Systems plc*[2] the Court of Appeal laid down some general guidelines to assist administrators in deciding whether or not to give consent. They hoped, by so doing, to reduce the number of applications being made to court for consent. The guidelines in summary were:

    i) the onus was on the party seeking leave to make out a case;

    ii) if granting leave would be unlikely to impede the achievement of the purpose of the administration, leave should normally be given;

    iii) in other cases, the court must carry out a balancing exercise, weighing the legitimate interests of the secured creditor against those of the company's other creditors;

    iv) an administration for the benefit of unsecured creditors should not be conducted at the expense of those who have proprietary rights;

    v) it will normally be a sufficient ground for the granting of leave that a refusal would cause significant loss to the applicant but, if substantially greater loss would be caused to others by the grant of leave, that may outweigh the loss caused to the applicant by a refusal;

    vi) in assessing what loss would accrue, the court will consider the financial position of the company; if relevant, its ability to pay rental arrears and continuing rentals; the administrator's proposals; the period for which the administration order has already been in force and is expected to remain in force; the

---

[95] *Re Barrow Borough Transport Ltd* [1990] Ch. 227.

[96] *Air Ecosse Ltd v. CAA* (1987) 3 B.C.C 492.

[97] *Powdrill v. Watson* [1995] 2 All E.R. 65, *Carr v. British International Helicopters* [1993] B.C.C. 855. Leave to bring the action will usually be given but further leave would be needed to enforce any order made by the Tribunal.

[98] [1991] B.C.C. 341.

[99] [1993] B.C.C. 154.

[1] This is the view taken by the cases on the effect of the interim order in an IVA; see Chap. 9.3(c).

[2] [1990] B.C.C. 859.

effect on the administration if leave is given; the effect on the applicant if leave is refused; the end result sought to be achieved by the administration; the prospects of that result being achieved; the history of the administration so far; and the probability of the suggested consequences.

The conduct of the creditor is also relevant. It can be seen from *Re Bristol Airport*[3] that leave will not normally be granted where the creditor has been benefiting from administration. It is more likely that a creditor will get leave if he has made it clear from the start that he is opposed to the administration and wishes to enforce his security.

The company in administration in *Re Atlantic Computers*[4] was in the business of leasing computers, a substantial number of which it held under hire purchase agreements. Two suppliers sought leave to repossess the stock and the Court of Appeal held that leave should be granted despite the fact that this would make it more difficult for the administrators. A failure to grant leave would cause significant loss to the lessors since the computers were a wasting asset. The court said that the starting point in the balancing act was the protection of the security holder and that it would not be fair to leave the secured creditors in the weak bargaining position of not being able to rely on proprietary rights as a bargaining counter. Administration should not be used for redistributional purposes and should not be conducted for the benefit of unsecured creditors at the expense of those with proprietary claims.

g) Overreaching power to deal with charged property

An administrator is empowered[5] to dispose of assets which are subject to a security interest or which are in the possession of the company under a hire-purchase agreement[6] without the consent of the security holder or owner. In the case of a fixed charge, court approval is necessary unless the security holder agrees.[7] The court will give the necessary authority where it is satisfied that the disposal of the assets would be likely to promote one or more of the purposes specified in the administration order.[8] It will be a condition of the court order that the net proceeds of the disposal will be applied towards discharging the

---

[3] [1990] Ch. 744.
[4] [1990] B.C.C. 859.
[5] Under Insolvency Act 1986, s.15.
[6] Which is defined by Insolvency Act 1986, s.15(9) as including conditional sale agreements, chattel leasing agreements and retention of title agreements.
[7] *Re ARV Aviation Ltd* [1989] B.C.L.C. 664.
[8] Insolvency Act 1986, s.15(2).

sums secured by the security or payable under the hire-purchase agreement. If disposal generates less than the open market price which would be obtained by a willing vendor, the shortfall has to be made good by the administrator.

No consent is needed to deal with property subject to a charge which, as created, was a floating charge.[9] The rights of the floating chargee are transferred to the proceeds obtained by the administrator from the disposal.

g) Powers and responsibilities of the administrator

The administrator, who must be a qualified insolvency practitioner, is appointed by the administration order.[10] If a vacancy subsequently occurs by death, resignation or otherwise, the court may fill the vacancy by an order which may be sought either by any continuing administrator or, if there is no administrator, by a creditors' committee or, if there is no committee, by the company, the directors or any creditor of the company. The administrator may resign on grounds of ill health or because he intends to cease acting as an insolvency practitioner or because of a conflict of interest or change in personal circumstances which precludes or makes impracticable his continuation as administrator or on other grounds with the leave of the court,[11] which also has the power to remove an administrator at any time.

An administrator is empowered by section 14 of the Insolvency Act 1986 to do all such things as may be necessary for the management of the affairs, business and property of the company. In particular, the administrator has the powers specified in Schedule 1 to the Act and also has[12] the power to remove any director of the company and to appoint any person to be a director of it, whether to fill a vacancy or otherwise, and to call meetings of the members or creditors of the company. The company and its officers lose the right to exercise any power which might interfere with the exercise of the administrator's powers.[13] The administrator is deemed to act as the company's agent in the exercise of these powers[14] so that the company will be responsible for his acts and omissions and, in particular, for contracts made or broken by the administrator.

---

[9] Insolvency Act 1986, s.15(1) and (3).
[10] *ibid.*, s.13.
[11] The provisions, explained below, which apply to the release of the administrator and to his remuneration and expenses at the end of the administration also apply where one administrator is replaced by another.
[12] By Insolvency Act 1986, s.14(2).
[13] *ibid.*, s.14(4).
[14] *ibid.*, s.14(5).

On appointment, the administrator takes into his custody or under his control all the property to which the company is or appears to be entitled.[15] The administrator must within 28 days of the making of the order notify all the creditors of the company so far as he is able.[16] A statement of the affairs of the company must be sought by the administrator from those who are or have been officers of the company, those who have taken part in the company's formation at any time in the year before the order, employees and those who have been employed by the company in the past year and whom the administrator thinks capable of giving the information required and those who are or have been within that year officers of or in the employment of a company which is, or within that year was, an officer of the company.[17] The administrator may release any of these people from the obligation to deliver a statement; those who are not released will have 21 days in which to deliver the statement unless given longer by the administrator.

An administrator also has the power to seek orders setting aside floating charges,[18] transactions at an undervalue,[19] preferences[20] and extortionate credit bargains.[21]

h) The administrator's proposals

The administrator has three months[22] (or such longer period as the court may allow) to send to the registrar of companies and creditors a statement of his proposals for achieving the purposes of the order. He must also lay a copy of the statement before a meeting of the company's creditors summoned for the purpose on not less than 14 days' notice. The members of the company must also be given notification of the proposals.

The meeting of the creditors[23] will decide whether or not to approve the administrator's proposals. Creditors have votes according to such of the debt owing to them at the time of the making of the administration order as remains outstanding at the time of the meeting. A creditor whose debt is secured will not be entitled to vote. Approval requires a majority in value of those present and voting, in person or by proxy. Any resolution will be invalid if those voting against it include more

---

[15] *ibid.*, s.17(1).
[16] Insolvency Act 1986, s.21.
[17] *ibid.*, s.22.
[18] *ibid.*, s.245, see Chap. 29.
[19] *ibid.*, s.238, see Chap. 30.
[20] *ibid.*, s.239, see Chap. 30.
[21] *ibid.*, s.244, see Chap. 30.
[22] *ibid.*, s.23.
[23] *ibid.*, s.24.

than half in value of the creditors, who are not connected with the company, to whom notice of the meeting was sent. The meeting may approve the proposals with modifications where the administrator has consented to each modification. The administrator must report the result of the meeting to the court and to the registrar of companies. Where the meeting has declined to approve the proposals, the court may discharge the administration order or adjourn the hearing or make any other order that it thinks fit. Any substantial revisions to proposals which have been approved must themselves be approved in the same way.[24]

Once the proposals have been approved the administrator is under a duty[25] to manage the affairs, business and property of the company in accordance with the proposals.

i) Protection of interests of creditors and members

The administrator must summon a meeting of the creditors at any stage if requested to do so by one-tenth in value of the creditors or if directed to do so by the court.[26]

A creditors' meeting which approves the administrator's proposals may, if it thinks fit, establish a committee of creditors which may require the administrator to explain the progress of the administration to it.[27] The committee will consist of between three and five creditors of the company elected at the meeting. Members of the committee will have one vote each and a resolution requires a simple majority of those voting. The administrator must call a meeting of the committee within three months of its establishment and thereafter when so requested by the committee or a member of it. The committee will be involved in deciding the level of remuneration of the administrator; if there is no committee, this will be decided by a meeting of the creditors as a whole.

Section 27 of the Insolvency Act 1986 gives creditors and members of the company the right during the administration to petition the court for an order on the ground that the company's affairs, business and property are being or have been managed by the administrator in a manner which is unfairly prejudicial to the interests of the creditors or members generally or of some part of its creditors or member (including at least himself) or that an actual or proposed act or omission of the administrator is or would be so prejudicial. The court may make such

---

[24] Insolvency Act 1986, s.25.
[25] *ibid.*, s.17(2)(b).
[26] *ibid.*, s.17(3).
[27] *ibid.*, s.26.

order as it thinks fit if the petitioner is successful in establishing his case.[28] *Re Charnley Davies Ltd*[29] concerned an application under section 27 brought by creditors who complained that the administrator had negligently failed to get the best price available for the assets. Millett J. found that the evidence did not support the claim of negligence and went on to say that, in any event, a sale at a negligent undervalue would not, *per se*, fall within the section. He said that "an allegation that the acts complained of are unlawful or infringe the petitioners' legal rights is not a necessary averment in a section 27 petition. In my judgment, it is not a sufficient averment either". He went on to say that a complaint that the administrator was showing insufficient regard for the interests of the creditors would be appropriate under section 27 but that if the whole gist of the complaint lay in the unlawfulness of the conduct, it could be adequately redressed by the remedy provided by the law for that wrong. In the case of professional negligence by the administrator, the appropriate remedy would be to have the administration order discharged and the company put into liquidation so that the liquidator could pursue the former administrator under section 212 of the Insolvency Act 1986.[30]

j) The end of the administration

The administrator may apply at any time to the court for the administration order to be discharged[31] and must do so if it appears to him that the administration has either achieved its purpose or is incapable of achieving its purpose. He must also seek a discharge of the order if he is required to do so by a meeting of the company's creditors summoned for the purpose in accordance with the Insolvency Rules. The court may make such order as it thinks fit in response to such an application.

The administrator will be released from liability in relation to the administration and his conduct as administrator at such time as the court determines[32]; release of the administrator will not prevent the exercise of the court's powers under section 212 of the Insolvency Act 1986.[33] The remuneration and proper expenses of the administrator will be charged on and paid out of any property of the company which is in his custody or control when he ceases to be administrator in priority to any security which, as created, was a floating charge.[34] Sums payable under

[28] *ibid.*, s.27(4) makes some specific suggestions of possible remedies.
[29] [1990] B.C.C. 605.
[30] As to which, see Chap. 31.3.
[31] Insolvency Act 1986, s.18.
[32] *ibid.*, s.20.
[33] See Chap. 31.3.
[34] Insolvency Act 1986, s.19(4).

contracts entered into or, to the extent that the sums payable are qualifying liabilities, adopted by the administrator[35] in the course of the administration will be paid in priority to the administrator's expenses and remuneration.[36] This super-priority given to contractual obligations incurred by the administrator in relation to contracts which he has adopted has chiefly been an issue in relation to liability on contracts of employment and is explained, in Chapter 12, in the context of the consideration of the position of the employee in the rescue culture.

k) Comparison of administration and administrative receivership

Debenture holders with the power to appoint an administrative receiver may find themselves in the position of having to decide whether to make such an appointment or whether a proposed administration should be allowed to go ahead.[37] The chief differences between the two regimes are that the administrator is an officer of the court who should consider the interests of all concerned in a balanced fashion whereas the receiver is appointed by and chiefly owes his duties to the debenture holder. The administrator is under no threat of personal liability unlike the receiver. The administration brings about a moratorium which the receivership does not although the existence of the receivership will usually render creditor action pointless. An administrator has the power to avoid previous transactions at an undervalue and preferences which are not available in a receivership.

5. Comparative evaluation of the U.K. regimes

a) Introduction[38]

The conditions for a successful rescue include the need for the company to seek help sufficiently early; this can be encouraged either by providing heavy sanctions against directors who fail to seek such help or by making the rescue regime sufficiently attractive to them. Directors are

---

[35] Or his predecessor.

[36] Insolvency Act 1986, s.19(5).

[37] For a full discussion see Anderson, 12 I.L.&P. 9, 54.

[38] See, generally, Goode, *Principles of Corporate Insolvency* (2nd ed.) pp. 335 *et seq.*; Segal of Ziegel (ed.), *Current Developments in International and Comparative Corporate Insolvency*, Chap. 1; Phillips (1996) Insol. Law 14.

likely to view rescue regimes which involve divesting them of their powers and subjecting them to investigation as options of last resort. Another necessary condition of financial recovery is the ability to find funding during the reorganisation; this will require that new lenders can be provided either with a right to priority of repayment or adequate security, which will be easier if the giving of blanket security rights over all assets including after-acquired property is either impermissible or not commercial practice. Success is also likely to require a stay on creditors' rights during the negotiation period and for the ability to prevent dissenting creditors from upsetting an agreement which meets general approval or from exercising influence disproportionate to their true entitlement by threatening to block plans. The ability to persuade, or insist on, suppliers maintaining their relationship with the company is also a factor of a successful rescue. Finally, success depends on having a procedure which does not swallow up a large proportion of the assets in expenses. A large number of rescues take place outside the formal insolvency system[39] and it is desirable that this should remain the case. Formal rescue regimes are only necessary for those cases in which informal recovery is not possible and it may be that there is a relatively small number of cases in which an informal rescue is not possible but a formal one would be, particularly if rescue is defined as the survival of the original entity.

The Department of Trade and Industry published a consultative document in 1993[40] which highlighted the fact that the use of the company rescue provisions brought into effect by the Insolvency Act 1986 has been low compared with the overall number of insolvencies; the document observed that between 1990 and 1993 there had been 88,000 corporate insolvencies in England of which 21,500 were receiverships but only 296 were company voluntary arrangements and 447 were administration orders. More recent figures show that in 1996 there were 13,461 liquidations, 2,701 receiverships, 210 appointments of administrators and 459 CVAs. It is apparent that neither the company voluntary arrangement nor the administration order is being much used although there have been some high profile administrations including those of Maxwell Communications, Polly Peck International, Olympia

---

[39] The first survey by the Society of Practitioners of Insolvency of members' activities outside formal insolvency appointments, carried out in 1996, showed that 57% of bank-instructed cases (the overwhelming majority of cases in the survey) and 42% of director-instructed cases led to a recovery without a formal insolvency procedure.

[40] DTI, *Company Voluntary Arrangements and Administration Orders: A Consultative Document*.

and York and Barings.[41] This contrasts with the success of the individual voluntary arrangement.[42]

The main problem with the company voluntary arrangement is perceived as being the lack of moratorium. It was envisaged that where a moratorium was necessary the company would apply for an administration order but this has proved to be an unattractive option. The main deterrent to the use of the administration order, apart from the existence of the veto which can be exercised by those with security over the whole undertaking, seems to be the expense of the exercise which can be attributed partly to the need for the insolvency practitioner to replace the existing management. This replacement of the existing management is also seen as a disincentive to the directors to seek an administration until it is likely to be too late to effect a successful rescue. Receivership was seen by the Cork Committee as a rescue regime but it is subject to the criticism that, where the debenture holder is adequately secured, there is a lack of incentive to maximise returns. Furthermore, a receivership requires there to be a cash sale despite the fact that the company might be more valuable if not sold for cash but left in the hands of some of the existing claimants which is possible in workouts, administrations and CVAs.

A comparison of the rescue provisions which exist in other jurisdictions demonstrates considerable variety in the possible procedures available. The brief descriptions which follow of some of the other models serve to illustrate the diversity. Some of the proposals for reform of the U.K. system, considered later in the Chapter, would adopt features which form part of some of these models. All the systems provide for some kind of freeze of creditors' rights but the types of creditor and the extents to which they are affected vary widely. The extent to which there is judicial involvement in the process also varies. Most of the procedures replace the existing management but some, most notably the United States, have debtor in possession[43] regimes. The different views on the question of the debtor in possession probably reflect to some extent cultural differences of attitude to entrepreneurial risk-taking. The historical legacy in the United Kingdom is an attitude that allowing a business to get into a state of insolvency is culpable whereas in the United States there has been greater acceptance of the view that a

---

[41] See Hogan 12 I.L.& P. 90 for an account of the administration of Barings and two other merchant banks: banks were initially excluded from the administration process but the Banks (Administration Proceedings) Order 1989 made under the Insolvency Act 1986, s.422 extended administrations to banks.

[42] See Chap. 9.3(k).

[43] The term used where the pre-insolvency management remains in office.

growing economy requires risk-taking which will inevitably lead to instances of insolvency.

b) United States[44]

Chapter 11 of the Bankruptcy Code 1978 provides a mechanism for reaching agreement among the relevant parties for the reorganisation of a company which may or may not be insolvent.[45] An automatic stay comes into effect once a petition has been filed in the U.S. Bankruptcy Court commencing a case under the Code. The secured creditor will be able to lift the stay against them unless the court finds that they are "adequately protected"; this will be the case if it is clear that the creditor has adequate security which will keep its value or where the debtor agrees to make periodic payments to offset any decline in value. Post-petition financing is often enabled by the provision of super-priority for such financing. The management of the debtor company remains in office but will have to provide the court with constant information and cannot take actions outside the normal course of its business without court consent which creditors will have the opportunity to oppose. As debtor in possession, the management will negotiate with creditors, working through the creditors' committee if one has been appointed, for approval to a plan of reorganisation. Every class of creditor must approve the plan unless the court can override the objection of an opposing class; this is referred to as the "cramdown" of creditors. Secured creditors may be forced to agree if they receive at least the value of their security. Unsecured creditors cannot be overridden unless claimants below them in priority receive nothing.

c) Canada[46]

The Canadian Bankruptcy and Insolvency Act of 1992 introduced new commercial reorganisation provisions which bring secured creditors within the scope of a stay. Secured creditors have to give notice of any intention to enforce security so that the company can seek commercial reorganisation and obtain a stay preventing enforcement. The commercial reorganisation process is initiated by the filing of a notice of intention to make a proposal which brings about an automatic stay of

---

[44] See Westbrook, of Rajak (ed.), *Insolvency Law Theory and Practice*, Chap. 11 and Ziegel (ed.), *Current Developments in International and Comparative Corporate Insolvency.*

[45] One prevalent criticism of the procedure is its use for non-insolvency purposes such as forcing the compromise of litigation or avoiding onerous employment contracts.

[46] See Ogilvie [1994] J.B.L. 304.

proceedings against both secured and unsecured creditors for an initial period of 30 days, renewable for up to six months. The Act includes a provision preventing the termination of contracts as against company during restructuring period as well as the automatic stay. The court does not have to become involved until creditors have approved the proposal by the requisite majority. There are sharp differences between this procedure and the United States Chapter 11 procedure. This process does not provide for a debtor in possession; a trustee takes over management and there is no possibility of overriding the rights of a particular class of claimant in the restructuring.

These new provisions do not repeal the extensively used[47] Companies' Creditors Arrangement Act 1985 which provides for a debtor in possession arrangement leading to a restructuring which can affect secured and unsecured creditors. This Act gives the court very wide discretion to impose a stay which the courts have interpreted as being intended to restrain conduct which would impair the ability of debtor company to stay in business during the negotiation period, maintain the status quo as amongst the creditors and restrain conduct which would seriously impair the debtor's ability to concentrate its efforts on negotiating compromise or arrangement. Each class of creditors must approve the plan by a three-quarters majority. Courts have prohibited suppliers and other parties contracting with the debtor from termination of contracts without court approval; suppliers have normally been required to continue to supply throughout the reorganisation on normal market terms without enjoying super-priority.

d) Australia[48]

The Australian Corporate Law Reform Act 1992 introduced a new voluntary administration regime which may be invoked by any company which is insolvent or likely to become so and does not involve an application to court. The object is to maximise the possibility of saving the company or its business or to provide a better rate of return to creditors than under a liquidation. The appointment of the administrator brings about a stay of enforcement against the company and its property. Fully secured creditors will be caught by the stay unless they elect within 14 days to enforce their security. The administrator controls the

---

[47] Including the Olympia and York reconstruction which involved both a U.K. administration and Canadian CCCA proceedings.

[48] See Harmer, in Ziegel (ed.), *Current Developments in International and Comparative Corporate Insolvency Law*, Chap. 4.

affairs of the debtor and has to decide whether to recommend a deed of company arrangement, the termination of the administration or liquidation. The creditors decide which of the options is to be accepted. The court has a general, supervisory role.

New Zealand, which has had a draconian statutory manager regime which suspends all claims and the exercise of all enforcement rights against the company, is likely to adopt the Australian model in the interests of harmonisation.

e) France[49]

France introduced a "redressement judicaire"[50] procedure in 1986 with an emphasis on saving businesses and employment[51]; following criticism, particularly by creditors who felt their rights were being eroded, reform of the system took place in 1994 and the court no longer has to consider rescue where all business activity has ceased or where rescue is manifestly impossible. Where a debtor goes into *redressement judicaire*, there will be a period of observation lasting at least six months during which the business of the debtor is scrutinised and a stay will affect all creditors. A court appointed administrator and a representative of the creditors will manage the business under the supervision of the court. The administrator has the power to demand that third parties perform their contractual obligations, irrespective of breaches by the debtor, provided the administrator pays the required consideration; contracts in France may not validly contain provisions for termination on the grounds of the insolvency of the other party. The administrator will make a report to the court at the end of the observation period. The court will decide either to permit the debtor to reorganise its business or sell it to a third party or wind up the business. The court will only agree to reorganisation or sale if there is a serious chance that the business will survive. The court will consider the interests of all parties before making a decision and if the proposed reorganisation includes redundancies it must hear representatives of the workers. Creditors must agree to any reduction of their claims before the plan will take effect.

---

[49] See Omar 12 I.L.&P. 39, 81.
[50] See de Dree, of Rajak (ed.), *Insolvency Law Theory and Practice*, Chap. 18.
[51] The objectives of the procedure are stated to be the reorganisation of the debtor, the continuation of the activity of the debtor and of the employment of its workforce and the repayment of debts to the creditors; at one time there was an argument that this was an ordered hierarchy of objectives but the view now prevails that the objectives are of equal importance.

f) Germany[52]

Germany enacted a new insolvency law in 1994, after long discussions about reform which began in 1978, which will come into effect at the beginning of 1999 and will replace bankruptcy law which dates back to 1877. The new law is based on the principle that the role of insolvency law is to organise collective action in such a way that the value of the debtor's assets will be maximised so that all benefit. The proceedings will be unified, in that the same procedure may result in liquidation or in reorganisation, and creditor—driven in that it is for the creditors to decide which outcome best suits them. Creditors will decide whether or not the debtor will remain in possession. Action by secured and unsecured creditors will be stayed. Interference with pre-bankruptcy entitlements particularly security interests is to be kept to a minimum and there will be no preferential creditors in bankruptcy. Secured creditors will be entitled to regular interest payments despite the stay as a disincentive to junior creditors to delay proceedings. The plan may be confirmed by the court only when each dissenting claimant receives the full cash equivalent of its claim as that claim would be realised in a liquidation. In addition the class or debtor must be treated fairly and adequately as against all other classes.

g) Republic of Ireland[53]

The system in the Republic of Ireland is of particular interest given the common ancestry with U.K. insolvency law. The Irish Companies (Amendment) Act 1990 as amended introduced the Examinership procedure into Irish law.[54] This involves the appointment of an examiner by the court and the placing of the company concerned under the protection of the court for a three or four month period. The grounds on which the court may appoint an examiner are more flexible than those for a U.K. administration: an examiner may be appointed in circumstances where the company is likely to be unable to pay its debts and no order has been made or resolution subsists for its winding up. The Irish Supreme Court has said[55] that the purpose of an examinership is to examine the

---

[52] Burger and Schelberg 11 I.L.& P. 8.

[53] McCormack, of Rajak (ed.), *Insolvency Law Theory and Practice*, Chap. 17.

[54] The immediate impetus for the legislation was collapse of the Goodman Group following the embargo on trade with Iraq. Iraq was a major destination of Irish meat exports and the Goodman group controlled about 40 per cent of the Irish meat trade. It appeared that Goodman companies owed their bankers £460 million and might be insolvent to the extent of at least £70 million and probably much more. All its borrowing was unsecured so there was no possibility of a receiver being appointed.

[55] In *Re Atlantic Magnetics Ltd* (1993) 2 I.R. 561.

situation, affairs and prospects of the company and that the court only has to be satisfied that the company has some prospect of survival. The court may not consider appointing an examiner if a receiver has been appointed to the company for a continuous period of at least three days prior to the presentation of the petition (originally 14 days but reduced to three). Company management and creditors have to make up their minds immediately on the appointment of a receiver whether they wish to apply for an examiner. Those in a position to appoint a receiver but who have not done so do not have the power to veto the examinership. The appointment of an examiner does not automatically bring the powers of the directors to an end although the examiner may seek an order from the court restricting the powers of the directors.

The court protection brings about a moratorium during which neither secured nor unsecured creditors may pursue their claims against the company. The examiner has a wide statutory power[56] to halt, prevent or rectify the effects of any act, omission, course of conduct, decision or contract by or on behalf of the company, its officers, employees, members or creditors or any other person in relation to the income, assets or liabilities of the company which, in his opinion, is or is likely to be to the detriment of the company, or any interested party. This allows the examiner to ignore the negative pledge in a bank debenture and raise new finance on the security of book debts.[57] The examiner must report to the court within 21 days unless the court extends the time period. If the examiner feels that the company is capable of survival, he has to put a plan to meetings of members and creditors and report back to the court within the three month court protection period, which may be extended by the court by a further month. If the court approves, the plan will become binding on all concerned and the Examinership comes to an end.

Where the examiner certifies that expenses during the court protection period have been incurred to avoid prejudicing the chances of the survival of the company as a going concern, the expenses will be paid in full in any subsequent receivership or liquidation. The remuneration, costs and expenses of the examiner are to be paid out of the revenue of the company or the proceeds of realisations of the assets ahead of secured and unsecured creditors. The examiner is required to use the staff of the company so far as possible rather than his own staff in an effort to keep down costs. The examiner may bring proceedings in respect of reckless or fraudulent trading (difficult given the short period

---

[56] Companies (Amendment) Act 1990, s.7(5).
[57] *Re Holidair Limited* (1994) 1 I.L.R.M. 481. The court also held that the moratorium prevented the banks from withdrawing consent to the use of book debts in the ordinary course of trade and designating an account into which they were to be paid.

of examinership) and there is an equivalent provision to section 15 of the Insolvency Act 1986.

The plan needs the approval of a class of members or creditors with impaired rights. Any creditor or member whose rights are to be impaired by the proposals is entitled to be heard by the court when it considers whether to approve the plan. The court has a wide discretion in relation to the proposed plan but the scheme must be fair and equitable towards any class of members or creditors whose interests are impaired and no interested party must be unfairly prejudiced.

h) Suggestions for reform in the United Kingdom

There has been considerable discussion in the United Kingdom as to the necessity for the expensive option of replacing the incumbent management with an insolvency practitioner before a company is able to get the benefit of a moratorium.[58]

In 1993, the Insolvency Service published a consultative document[59] containing the recommendations of a working party set up to consider the apparent under-use of the company voluntary arrangement provisions. The working party included representatives from the legal and insolvency professions, the academic world, banks, the CBI, the Bank of England, the Treasury and the Insolvency Service. It concluded that the company voluntary arrangement procedure should be reformed so that it could be initiated speedily by the mere filing of a notice of a prospective arrangement, together with the consent to act of the proposed nominee, and would provide a 28 day period in which the company would be protected against all claims and enforcement procedures, including the appointment of an administrative receiver. It also recommended that those proposing to appoint an administrative receiver should have to give notice of this intention so that the company could consider applying for CVA protection. Other more radical ideas for consideration included the possibility of the company being able to use assets subject to a fixed charge on book debts, a proposal that debts incurred during the moratorium should be given super-priority and the idea that the court might be able to override the appointment of an administrative receiver with an administration order where the value of the chargee's security was sufficient to ensure that the loan would be repaid in full. There was even a tentative suggestion that receivership itself should be abolished.

---

[58] See Segal in Ziegel (ed.), *Current Developments in International and Comparative Corporate Insolvency*, Chap. 1, at p. 10.
[59] DTI, "Company Voluntary Arrangements and Administration Orders: A Consultative Document".

In the meantime, debate was generated by a more radical proposal that a scheme of debt-equity swap should be introduced.[60] Professors Aghion, Hart and Moore put forward a proposal for reform, "The Economics of Bankruptcy Reform", which was briefly summarised in Appendix E of the October 1993 Consultative Document. The Treasury subsequently commissioned them to carry out a more detailed study and they subsequently issued a revised proposal for debt-equity swaps which they described[61] as using the best parts of receivership and administration while dealing with certain fundamental difficulties from which the procedures suffer. Their basic premise is that none of the existing procedures guarantees that those who determine the outcome of an insolvency have an incentive to maximise the returns to claimants. Receivership leaves the decision with the bank which will only be concerned to recover the debt owing to itself whilst decision-making in administrations and CVAs may rest with ordinary creditors whose chances of recovery are so slight that they are biased in favour of high risk strategies and lengthy processes. The debt-equity swap would apply in administrations but only in receiverships if it were triggered by either the floating charge holder or a junior creditor.

Their proposal is that all debt, other than that secured by fixed charges, should be converted to equity or options to buy equity. The floating charge should be given to the floating charge holder or the most senior class of creditors if there is no floating charge. The other claimants (junior creditors and former shareholders) are given options to buy the shares with exercise prices reflecting the amount of debt senior to their claims. All options would expire on a set date. The insolvency practitioner would meanwhile be running the business so as to maximise the value of the equity and so would be accountable for fraud or negligence to those who hold the shares at the end of the exercise. The plan for the future of the company is presented to the shareholders after the expiry of the option procedure so that the decisions are taken by the new shareholders. There has been considerable hostility to these ideas, particularly from practising lawyers and accountants, mainly because of the feeling that there is substantial scope for abuse of unsecured creditors.[62]

Justice appended a response to the DTI's 1993 consultative document to its 1994 publication "Insolvency Law. An Agenda For Reform". It

---

[60] See Aigon, Hart and Moore, 11 I.L.&P. 67, Campbell 12 I.L.&P. 14.
[61] 11 I.L.&.P 67.
[62] See Campbell 12 I.L.&P. 14. The Joint Insolvency Law Sub-Committee of the Law Society said that it was dubious about use of debt/equity swaps since it considered that the combination of circumstances in which such a swap is feasible and desirable does not often arise.

favoured gradual change to the existing system rather than radical solutions. It felt that unless there was cogent evidence of necessity, the pattern of lending secured by debentures containing floating charges should not be upset. It suggested that in small cases judges could dispense with a rule 2.2 report and adjourn the administration petition pending the passing of a CVA. It pointed out that the legislation already contained the power to do this and that it would provide a considerable saving in costs coupled with protection against creditors. Justice recognised that there were two problems which could only be dealt with by legislation; the problem of funding and priority of new debts incurred during trading while the petition is adjourned. It suggested that the directors could be allowed to use assets subject to a floating charge and, in absence of floating charge, uncharged assets. Legislation could give new creditors priority unless they had notice that the debt was not incurred for the benefit of creditors. It also suggested that contractual provisions which allowed termination on the sole grounds of entry into administration should be made void. It suggested that consideration should be given to extending the prohibition on utilities demanding payment of arrears as a condition of future supply to other suppliers.[63] Justice was hostile to the notion of obtaining a moratorium simply by filing without any court supervision or effective insolvency practitioner control since they felt the system would be open to abuse. They also felt that the 28-day proposal was pointless since this would be too short to achieve anything useful but would be a longer than desirable period of uncertainty.

The general response to the Insolvency Service's consultative document was hostile and led not to proposals for legislation but to a further Insolvency Service Consultative Document[64] in 1995. This abandoned the more radical proposals and suggested the introduction of a requirement of an independent assessment by the nominee as to whether the proposed CVA was a viable proposition and whether a moratorium would be appropriate in the circumstances. It has been suggested that this would be likely to re-introduce the cost problem which exists in relation to the administration order.

The DTI then put forward a more limited set of proposals for legislation than that envisaged by the Insolvency Service.[65] This envisaged an additional form of voluntary arrangement which would be available

---

[63] See Insolvency Act 1986, s.233.

[64] *Revised Proposals for a New Company Voluntary Arrangement Procedure*, April 1995.

[65] Press Notice P/95/839, November 1995. The proposals have yet to find Parliamentary time although the Policy Unit of the Insolvency Service say that it is still intended that legislation will be brought forward to implement them.

only to small companies[66] which were not in administration or liquidation. This would involve a moratorium binding on all creditors including secured creditors provided that a nominee certified to the court that there was a reasonable prospect of the CVA being successful. The nominee would supervise management during the moratorium and should bring it to an end if he became of the opinion that the CVA would not succeed. The company would not be able to dispose of assets subject to any kind of charge without the consent of the chargee. The creditors would not be able to agree to a package which affected the rights of a secured creditor without the agreement of that creditor.

---

[66] As defined in Companies Act 1985, s.247.

CHAPTER 11

PARTNERSHIP RESCUE

1. Introduction

The possibility of partnership rescue was introduced into insolvency law by the Insolvent Partnerships Order 1994[1] ("IPO"). A partnership voluntary arrangement ("PVA") and partnership administration procedure were introduced which are similar to the corporate procedures contained in the Insolvency Act 1986.

The IPO provides appropriate interpretations for the partnership context of the corporate terminology used in the Insolvency Act 1986. References to companies are to be construed as references to insolvent partnerships and all references to the registrar of companies are to be ignored. An "officer of the company" will be a member of a partnership or a person who has management or control of the partnership business. Article 3(4) provides that "other expressions appropriate to companies shall be construed, in relation to an insolvent partnership, as references to the corresponding person, officers, documents or organs (as the case may be) appropriate to a partnership".

In most cases any solvent partners will be expected by the creditors to make contributions to the rescue package. Where the partners, as well as the partnership business, are insolvent, a successful rescue will require individual voluntary arrangements to be interlinked with the partnership rescue package.

2. Partnership voluntary arrangements

Article 4 provides that the provisions of Part I of the Insolvency Act 1986 (the company voluntary arrangement provisions) shall apply in relation to an insolvent partnership as modified in Schedule 1 to the IPO. Article 5 provides that where winding up and bankruptcy orders are made against an insolvent partnership and an insolvent member of that partnership in his capacity as such, Part I of the Insolvency Act 1986 applies to corporate members and Part VIII (individual voluntary

[1] S.I. 1994 No. 2421.

arrangements) to individual members of that partnership, with the modification that references to the creditors of the company or of the debtor include references to the creditors of the partnership.

This procedure follows the structure of the company voluntary arrangement.[2] As with a CVA, there is no interim order and so there is no protection for the partnership whilst the proposal is being considered. Partners are given the roles played by both directors and shareholders in a CVA so that, in addition to making the proposal for the arrangement they also have to hold a members' meeting to consider the proposal.

Individual partners may also seek to enter into interlocking IVAs in order to lock in their own personal creditors as well as the creditors of the firm.

3. Partnership administration orders

Article 6 provides that the provisions of Part II (company administration orders) of the Insolvency Act 1986 shall apply in relation to an insolvent partnership as modified in Schedule 2 to the Order. Article 6 extends the application in connection with an administration order of certain other parts of the Insolvency Act 1986, including section 212 (which provides a remedy for misfeasance or breach of duty against insolvency practitioners and members of the partnership) and the provisions of the Act relating to preferences and transactions at an undervalue, to insolvent partnerships.

A partnership administration order may be made for one or more of the following three purposes provided that the partnership is unable to pay its debts[3]:

a) the survival of the whole or any part of the undertaking of the partnership as a going concern;
b) the approval of a partnership voluntary arrangement;
c) a more advantageous realisation of the partnership property than would be effected on a winding up.

A petition may be presented by any or all of the members of the partnership in their capacity as such and a creditor or creditors (including contingent and prospective creditors). An agricultural chargeholder,[4] who may be granted a floating charge over partnership assets, is given the same veto as those entitled to appoint administrative receivers are given in relation to company administrations. There is no other floating

---

[2] See Chap. 10.3.
[3] Not also "likely to become unable" as with a company.
[4] Under the Agricultural Credits Act 1928.

charge possible over partnership assets. Since lenders to partnerships (with the exception of agricultural lenders) will not be in a position to appoint an administrative receiver, it is possible that they may choose to make more use of the administration procedures for partnerships than has been the case in relation to companies.

The order brings a moratorium on creditors' actions against the partnership but not against the partners individually; for this they would have to propose IVAs and apply for interim orders. An agricultural receiver, in common with any other receiver,[5] will only have to leave office if requested to do so by the administrator. The power of the administrator to deal with charged property under section 15 of the Insolvency Act 1986 permits the administrator to dispose of property which is subject to a charge which, as created, was floating as if it were not subject to a charge unless an agricultural receiver has been appointed under it. The administrator will need a court order to dispose of property subject to any other form of security.

Section 14 of the Insolvency Act 1986 is amended in relation to insolvent partnerships[6] to provide that the administrator may prevent any person from taking part in the management of the partnership business and to appoint any person to be a manager of that business. Section 14(6) as modified provides that an officer of the partnership shall not, unless he otherwise consents, be personally liable for the debts and obligations of the partnership incurred during the period of the administration order.

---

[5] But unlike an administrative receiver in respect of a company in administration.
[6] By para. 8 of Sched. 2 to the IPO.

CHAPTER 12

THE PLACE OF THE EMPLOYEE IN THE RESCUE CULTURE

1. Introduction[1]

A major difficulty faced by the law is the balancing of the legitimate interests of those involved in an insolvent business. It has to be decided how the inevitable losses should be shared between the providers of capital, trade creditors, workforce and customers and, in particular, what emphasis should be placed on the preservation of jobs. The question of priority of claims against a business which is being liquidated is considered in Chapter 35. Where the insolvency practitioner is attempting to rescue a business, two specific questions may arise; first, the extent to which continuing to employ the workforce during an insolvency gives rise to liability and, secondly, the extent to which the rights of the workforce reduce the value to a purchaser of the business as a going concern. The first question is dealt with by the insolvency legislation but the provisions relating to the second, although clearly affecting distributional rights within an insolvency, are to be found within the ambit of employment law.

2. Liability for continuing to employ the workforce

a) Introduction

This issue is relevant both to the question of whether an administrative receiver will decide to shut down the business subject to the charge or attempt to keep trading and sell it as a going concern and to the question of whether an administration is a viable proposition. It is obvious that keeping the business going and retaining the workforce will involve meeting the ongoing entitlements of the employees to salary. The controversial question has been that of the extent to which their continued employment bestows on the employees priority over other creditors and gives them claims against the insolvency practitioner with

---

[1] See Upex, *The Law of Termination of Employment* (5th ed.), particularly Chap. 13.

regard to payments due to them on termination which would have been ordinary unsecured claims in a liquidation. It has been argued that any such favourable treatment, whilst apparently beneficial to the employees, would in fact result in the closure of businesses and the loss of jobs which might otherwise have been rescued.

b) Consequence of immediate dismissal by insolvency practitioner

When an insolvency practitioner taking control of an insolvent business immediately dismisses the employees, they are likely to have a number of claims against the employer. There will be contractual claims for wrongful dismissal because they have not been given the notice of dismissal to which their contract entitles them[2] and claims under the employment protection legislation. The employment protection legislation will enable those with sufficient accrued service to claim redundancy payments and, possibly, unfair dismissal compensation although where the entire workforce is dismissed the latter claim is unlikely to be successful. Partial dismissal of the workforce might entitle those dismissed to claim that they had been unfairly selected for dismissal. Where a sufficient number of employees are made redundant at the same time, there will be an obligation on the employer to consult and failure to comply with this obligation may lead to the making of a protective award.[3]

These claims will all be unsecured ordinary claims against the employer[4] although some of the payments will be guaranteed by the National Insurance Fund[5] which will be subrogated to the claims against the employer.

c) Effect on employees of administration

The appointment of an administrator has no effect upon the contracts of the employees since section 14(5) of the Insolvency Act 1986 deems him to act as the agent of the company. The administrator has the power to dismiss employees but the moratorium will prevent any proceedings

---

[2] There may also be contractual claims for arrears of pay and accrued holiday pay.
[3] See below.
[4] See Chap. 35.
[5] See Chap. 34.

being taken against the company without the consent of the administrator or the court during the administration.[6] Section 19 of the Insolvency Act 1986[7] provides that sums payable under new contracts entered into by an administrator and certain obligations to those whose contracts of employment have been adopted[8] by the administrator are to be paid out of the company's assets in priority to the administrator's own fees and expenses. The obligations arising under adopted contracts which acquire priority are wages, salaries and pension contributions arising during the administration. The administrator will not be taken to have adopted a contract of employment by reason of anything done or not done in the first 14 days after his appointment. Administrators will, therefore, be unwilling to retain the services of employees unless confident that there will be sufficient assets remaining to meet the costs of the administration after paying the employees.

d) Effect on employees of administrative receivership

It was decided by the case of *Griffiths v. Secretary of State for Social Services*[9] that the appointment of a receiver as agent of the company by debenture holders did not automatically terminate the contracts of employment. The court held that contracts would only be terminated by a concurrent sale of the business[10] or if the receiver entered into new contracts or if the contract was inconsistent with the existence of a receiver. In some circumstances the role of a managing director might be inconsistent with that of a receiver; this was an argument raised in the *Griffiths* case although on the facts this particular managing director had not been dismissed. If a company in receivership goes into liquidation, the receiver's agency comes to an end[11] and a compulsory liquidation is said to bring the contracts of employment to an end.[12] It seems therefore that if an administrative receiver continues to trade after the company goes into liquidation, he must be trading and employing those working in the undertaking as principal.

---

[6] As seen above in Chap. 10.4, leave would usually be given to obtain, but not to enforce, a decision.

[7] As amended by the Insolvency Act 1994.

[8] This concept is discussed below in the context of dismissal by the insolvency practitioner.

[9] [1974] 1 Q.B. 468.

[10] This has since been altered by the Transfer of Undertakings Regulations explained below.

[11] Insolvency Act 1986, s.44 which enacts the common law rule in *Gaskell v. Gosling* [1897] A.C. 575.

[12] See Chap. 17.4.

Section 44 of the Insolvency Act 1986[13] provides that administrative receivers will be personally liable for any new contracts which they make and will be liable for wages, salaries and pension contributions arising during the receivership of those whose contracts of employment they have adopted.[14] This is an amendment to the common law position under which the receiver, as agent of the company, would incur no personal liability. Since 1947 receivers have been statutorily personally liable on new contracts of any type entered into by them unless such liability is specifically excluded by the contract. The Insolvency Act 1986 imposed liability on them in relation to adopted contracts of employment which has since been restricted by the Insolvency Act 1994 to the obligations arising during the currency of the employment. The receiver will not be taken to have adopted the contract of any employee dismissed within 14 days of the start of the receivership. An administrative receiver will be entitled to an indemnity out of the company's assets in respect of this personal liability but if the assets prove insufficient the loss will fall on the receiver. Receivers will, therefore, only retain the services of employees where they are confident that funds will be available to meet these obligations without putting themselves or their debenture holders at risk.

e) Dismissal during an administration or administrative receivership

An employee dismissed in the course of an administrative receivership or administration is likely to be redundant, will have a wrongful dismissal claim if dismissed without the correct notice and may have an unfair dismissal claim. The employee may be able to claim some of these payments from the National Insurance Fund[15] which will be subrogated to the employee's rights. If liability for these termination payments were to be treated in the same way as liability for obligations arising during the currency of the employment, the insolvency practitioner would have to weigh up in the first 14 days whether the risk to the rescue operation and to himself of a potential large bill on later dismissal required the immediate dismissal of any employees whom the business might subsequently seek to dismiss. Sections 19 and 44 of the Insolvency Act 1986 as amended now make it quite clear that claims for termination payments are claims against the company and do not affect the insolvency practitioner. The history of this area of insolvency law

---

[13] As amended by the Insolvency Act 1994.
[14] This concept is discussed below in the context of dismissal by the insolvency practitioner.
[15] See Chap. 34.

has been described as an example of "the British system of law making at its worst".[16]

Until 1986 the position was that an administrative receiver could only have any liability on a contract of employment if he had entered into the contract. For example, in *Re Mack Trucks*[17] the receiver expressly terminated the old contracts because he erroneously thought this was the effect of the company going into receivership and entered into new contracts of employment on the same terms in November 1964. The company ceased trading in July 1965 and it was held that the receiver could be sued for the wrongful dismissals since he was personally liable on the new contracts. That the receiver had no liability on continuing contracts was demonstrated by *Nicoll v. Cutts*[18] in which the plaintiff managing director, who had been on sick leave since the start of the receivership, was dismissed by the receivers some weeks after the start of the receivership; the Court of Appeal held that he had no claim against the receivers since they had not entered into a contract with him. This case prompted an amendment to the insolvency legislation then going through Parliament which imposed liability on receivers in respect of contracts "adopted" by them. The same terminology was used in relation to the new provisions on administration in which priority over the administrator's costs was given to claims arising under "adopted" employment contracts.

No definition was provided by the legislation of the circumstances in which a contract would be adopted. Receivers and administrators took to sending letters to the workforce informing them that they would continue to be employed but that their contracts were not being adopted. The efficacy of this practice was upheld by Harman J. in the unreported case of *Re Specialised Mouldings*,[19] a judgment on which insolvency practitioners placed great reliance.[20] In *Powdrill v. Watson*,[21] however, it was held at first instance, by the Court of Appeal and by the House of Lords that letters of this type do not work and that the contract of any employee whose services are retained after the 14 day grace period will be taken to be impliedly adopted. This case concerned claims brought by employees dismissed by a company in administration in respect of salary, including pension contribution, in lieu of the notice to which they were entitled under their contracts and arrears of holiday pay. They also

---

[16] Pollard (1995) 24 I.L.J. 141 at 151.
[17] [1967] 1 All E.R. 977.
[18] [1985] B.C.L.C. 322.
[19] February 3, 1987 (Ch.D).
[20] Unwisely as it transpired and as several commentators had warned might prove to be the case. See, for example, Goode *Principles of Corporate Insolvency Law* (1st ed.) pp. 101 *et seq.*
[21] [1994] 2 All E.R. 513, CA; [1995] 2 All E.R. 65, HL.

brought unfair dismissal claims but Evans-Lombe J. held that the right not to be unfairly dismissed arose under the employment protection legislation and not under the contract of employment so that unfair dismissal rights did not fall into the category of liabilities given priority by section 19 of the Insolvency Act 1986 and there was no appeal from this decision. The House of Lords heard the case jointly with two cases on the same point in relation to administrative receivership: *Re Leyland DAF Ltd* and *Re Ferranti International plc*.[22] Lord Browne-Wilkinson, delivering the judgment of the House of Lords, expressed his sympathy for the position of receivers and administrators and recognised the difficulty of having to decide within 14 days whether to close down the business, dismiss the employees and sell on a break up basis or to continue the business, keep on the employees and try to sell it as a going concern. His Lordship adopted a basis of statutory interpretation which was as generous as possible to the insolvency practitioners in that he held that if the words of the legislation had a meaning which was consistent with the presumed intention not to frustrate the rescue culture and produce unworkable results, that construction should be adopted. Otherwise, the literal meaning of the provisions could only be rejected if they produced an absurd result. He then proceeded to reject the first instance decision of Lightman J. in *Re Leyland DAF*[23] that section 44 of the Insolvency Act 1986 imposed liability on a receiver for all sums claimed under an adopted contract on the basis that it was most improbable that Parliament had intended such a discrepancy between those dismissed in the first 14 days and those kept on and that such a construction would make the position of the receiver almost impossible; to interpret the section in this way would be absurd. The interpretation of section 44 must be that it was subject to the same limitation as applied to an administrator's liability under section 19 of the Insolvency Act 1986 and that liability would only relate to debts in respect of the period of office of the receiver. He felt constrained to decide that adoption connoted some conduct by the insolvency practitioner which amounted to an election to treat the continued contract of employment with the company as giving rise to a separate liability in the administration or receivership and that it was not possible to adopt part only of a contract. The outcome was that, in addition to the liability to pay the employees during the currency of their employment during the insolvency, there would also be an obligation to pay wages during the contractual notice period including pension contributions, or damages in

[22] See Fletcher [1995] J.B.L. 596.
[23] [1994] 4 All E.R. 300.

lieu thereof, and holiday pay referable to the employment since the appointment of the office-holder.

Within less than two months[24] of the Court of Appeal decision in *Powdrill v. Watson*,[25] the Insolvency Act 1994 had been enacted to amend the offending provisions of the Insolvency Act 1986 and restrict the potential liability of administrative receivers[26] and administrators to claims arising from the currency of the employment, which the insolvency practitioners had always been quite happy to meet. The government refused, however, to make the legislation retrospective[27] further back than the date when the proposed amendment to the law had been announced to Parliament; it only applies, therefore, to contracts adopted on or after March 15, 1994. There have been reports of at least some large claims having been brought in respect of the period between 1986 and 1994 although the limitation rules will have prevented those affected in the early days from bringing actions and the principle of mitigation of loss will have cut down other potential claims. Those who will have benefited from the *Powdrill v. Watson* decision are employees whose contractual entitlement to notice monies exceeded the amount of notice money guaranteed by the National Insurance Fund[28] either because they were contractually entitled to a longer period of notice than that provided by the employment protection legislation or because their weekly salary exceeded the National Insurance Fund ceiling. This has been argued to be particularly unfair since these employees are the most likely to have been responsible for any mismanagement leading to the collapse of the business.

f) Consultation about collective redundancies

Section 188 of the Trade Union and Labour Relations (Consolidation) Act 1992,[29] re-enacting section 99 of the Employment Protection Act

---

[24] Lord Browne-Wilkinson described this as "almost unprecedented speed". Several businesses which went into receivership immediately after the judgment were shut down which might previously have been allowed to continue trading; this highlighted the need for immediate action to keep "the rescue culture" afloat.

[25] [1994] 2 All E.R. 513.

[26] But not of Law of Property Act receivers who are subject, under Insolvency Act 1986, s.37, to liability identical to that under the unamended version of s.44.

[27] The lobbying power of the banks and the insolvency practitioners with respect to a situation which they were powerless to do anything about was insufficient to overcome the usual antipathy to retrospective legislation as being contrary to the rules of natural justice.

[28] See Chap. 34.

[29] As amended by the Collective Redundancies and TUPE Amendment Regulations 1995, S.I. 1995 No. 2587 which were necessary to deal with the failure of the original U.K. provisions to comply with the Directive in relation to employees without a recognised union.

1975 which was passed to implement Directive 75/29 on Collective Redundancies, gives employees the right to have their representatives consulted about proposed collective redundancies. An employer proposing to dismiss as redundant 20 or more employees at one establishment within a period of 90 days or less is obliged to consult the appropriate representatives of the employees. Where the proposal is to dismiss at least 100 employees the consultation shall begin at least 90 days before the first dismissal; in other circumstances the consultation period is at least 30 days. Appropriate representatives are either employee representatives elected by them or representatives of an independent trade union recognised by the employer.

In the event of a failure to consult, a "protective award" may be sought[30] from an industrial tribunal by the representatives who have not been consulted or, where there are no representatives, by the employees themselves. A protective award is an order that the employees be paid remuneration beginning with the date on which the first dismissal takes place for such period as the tribunal determines to be just and equitable in all the circumstances having regard to the seriousness of the default but not exceeding the length of the appropriate consultation period.[31] If the employer fails to pay the protected award, individual employees are then able to enforce it.[32]

There is a defence[33] which provides that if there are "special circumstances which render it not reasonably practicable" for the employer to comply with the provisions "the employer shall take all such steps towards compliance with that requirement as are reasonably practicable in those circumstances" which may mean no steps at all. The Collective Redundancies Directive contains no "special circumstances" defence but it does not apply to "workers affected by the termination of an establishment's activities where that is the result of judicial decision". This fails to take account of the fundamentally different nature of U.K. insolvency procedures which do not necessarily involve the court. According to the Court of Appeal in *Clarks of Hove Ltd v. Bakers Union*[34] the correct approach to the defence provided by the U.K. legislation is to ask, first, were there special circumstances; secondly, if so, did they render compliance not reasonably practicable and, thirdly, had the employer taken such steps as were reasonably practicable. The

---

[30] Under Trade Union and Labour Relations (Consolidation) Act 1992, s.189.

[31] *ibid.*, s.190, contains further details of the calculation of the award which is subject to a statutory maximum weekly amount of, from April 1, 1998, £220.

[32] *ibid.*, s.192. Protective awards will be preferential debts and guaranteed by the National Insurance Fund.

[33] *ibid.*, s.188(7).

[34] [1978] I.C.R. 366.

Court then went on to hold that, whilst a sudden disaster leading to the closure of the business might be special circumstances, there was nothing special about a gradual run-down of the company. This was followed in *GMB v. Messrs Rankin & Harrison*[35] and in *Re Hartlebury Printers Ltd.*[36] The latter case was one in which the directors, and subsequently administrators, had failed to consult the trade unions over dismissals which were held to have occurred when the administration was superseded by a liquidation. It was held, however, that the administrators, and directors before them, did not actually "propose" to make redundancies although they were aware of the financial difficulties and realised that redundancies might become necessary; the redundancies occurred because of the decision of the court. Morrit J. rejected the argument that administrators were not subject to the consultation provisions.

There are similar rights provided to employees on the transfer of a business.[37] The transferring employer must give information to representatives of all those affected by the transfer and consult in relation to all those employees in respect of whom he envisages that measures will be taken. Failure to comply may lead to a complaint[38] by the representatives or, if there are none, by the employees to the industrial tribunal which may award appropriate compensation not exceeding four weeks' pay.

3. Employees' rights on the sale of the business

a) The pre–1981 position

Prior to 1981 a receiver was able to sell the business as a going concern divested of any accrued liability to its employees. The employees would be made redundant by the insolvency practitioner prior to the transfer of the business and the transferee would offer employment to such of the workforce as were wanted under new contracts. The employees would be paid redundancy payments whether or not they were going to be

---

[35] [1992] I.R.L.R. 514 (Scottish EAT case on receivership).
[36] [1992] I.C.R. 559. The case was actually an application under Insolvency Act 1986, s.130(2) (see Chap 25.2 below) for leave to commence proceedings and was heard in the Chancery division.
[37] Transfer of Undertakings (Protection of Employment) Regulations 1981, Reg. 10, as amended by the 1995 Amendment Regulations, see n. 28 above.
[38] Under Reg. 11.

re-engaged and those who were re-employed would begin their employment with the transferee without any accrued rights.

b) The Transfer of Undertakings Regulations[39]

Since the Transfer of Undertakings (Protection of Employment) Regulations 1981 ("TUPE") were enacted to implement Directive 77/187 on Business Transfers (the Acquired Rights Directive), and particularly since the House of Lords interpretation of them in *Litster v. Forth Dry Dock*,[40] it has been difficult to sell a business without its employees.

Regulation 5 provides for an automatic transfer of the contracts of employment and acquired rights of those employed in the business "immediately before the transfer". The transferee employer is treated as having been responsible for anything done by the transferor in relation to the contract and takes over the terms of the contract under which the employee has been employed except for rights in relation to pensions.[41] The employee's accrued continuous service is transferred. Continuous service is relevant both for determining entitlement to bring claims under the employment protection legislation and to the calculation of amounts to be paid where the claim is successful. It was held in *Angus Jowett Ltd v. NUTGW*[42] that a transferor's liability for a protective award under section 188 of the Trade Union and Labour Relations (Consolidation) Act 1992 in respect of failure to consult on collective redundancies would not pass to the transferee since it was not a right arising under a contract.[43]

The term "immediately before" is not defined in TUPE and there was considerable controversy as to whether the practice of dismissing employees before completion of the sale prevented their being employed in the business "immediately before" so that they did not transfer with it. In *Secretary of State v. Spence*[44] the Court of Appeal held that Regulation 5 only applied to employees employed by the transferor at the moment of the transfer so that dismissal only hours previously would be fatal to their continuity; even those re-engaged by

---

[39] See Pollard (1996) 25 I.L.J. 191.
[40] [1989] 2 W.L.R. 634.
[41] TUPE, Reg. 7. This is in accordance with the Directive: *Adams v. Lancashire C.C.* [1997] I.R.L.R. 436.
[42] [1985] I.C.R. 646.
[43] The decision is longstanding but appears questionable, see Upex, above, para. 2.58. The question has been raised as to whether a protective award made on the complaint of an individual employee, which has been possible since the Amendment Regulations of 1995, would be treated differently.
[44] [1987] Q.B. 179.

the transferee would be entitled to redundancy payments and their new employer would inherit no obligations in relation to them.

Spence provided certainty at the expense of rendering TUPE more or less a dead letter. This potentially major gap in the protection intended to be provided by TUPE was rectified by the House of Lords in *Litster v. Forth Dry Dock*.[45] Their Lordships, following *Pickstone v. Freemans*,[46] gave a purposive interpretation of TUPE and said that Article 4 of the Directive required that Regulation 5(3) be read as if there were inserted after the words "immediately before the transfer" the words "or would have been so employed if he had not been unfairly dismissed in the circumstances described in Regulation 8(1)". Regulation 8(1) provides that dismissals in connection with the transfer of the business will be automatically unfair.[47]

There has been a considerable amount of case law on the issue of the circumstances in which the dismissals will be in connection with the transfer; the position is still not clear in some respects. There are conflicting cases on whether a dismissal can be in connection with a transfer when there is no definitely identified transferee.[48] It has also been held that an indication by a potential transferee that he would want to retain specified employees does not amount to a request to dismiss the others.[49]

Employees who have been employed in an insolvent business immediately before its transfer will, therefore, be able to bring their claims against the solvent transferee instead of against the insolvent transferor and can be sure that the claims will be met in full. The transferee will insist on an adjustment to the price to take account of this potential liability and the insolvency practitioner will recover less for distribution amongst the other creditors. Where the value of the business falls below the amount the insolvency practitioner could obtain by selling the assets on a break-up basis, the business will be closed in order to maximise realisations. There is, therefore, a risk that more jobs will be lost than if

[45] [1989] 2 W.L.R. 634.

[46] [1989] A.C. 66.

[47] Reg. 8(2) provides that if some economic, technical or organisational reason can be shown for them they are potentially fair. The Court of Appeal in *Warner v. Adnet Ltd*, *The Times*, March 12, 1998, held that an employee made redundant before the sale as a going concern of a business in receivership had not been unfairly dismissed since the reason for his dismissal was an economic one and the dismissal was reasonable and fair in the circumstances.

[48] See, *e.g.*, *Harrison Bowden v. Bowden* [1994] I.C.R. 186, *Ibex Trading v. Walton* [1994] I.R.L.R. 564, *Michael Peters Ltd v. Farnfield* [1995] I.R.L.R. 190.

[49] *Longden & Paisley v. Ferrari Ltd and Kennedy International* [1994] I.R.L.R. 157.

the Regulations did not apply.[50] On this basis it has been argued that the Regulations should not apply to transfers of insolvent businesses.[51]

c) Applicability of the Acquired Rights Directive to insolvency

There is no specific mention in the Directive of insolvency. In the English language version, Article 1(1) provides that the Directive applies to the transfer of an undertaking "as a result of a legal transfer or merger". The other language versions of the Directive, however, with the possible exception of the Danish version, were drafted more restrictively to refer to contractual transfers. In the *Abels*[52] case the European Court of Justice considered the argument that transfers by insolvent transferors are not, at least in some Member States, considered to be genuinely consensual and therefore fall outside the Directive.

The Court, having held that it was not possible to determine the question as a matter of interpretation and that it was necessary to consider the purpose of the Directive, held that the Directive was intended to safeguard workers' rights when an undertaking was transferred. The argument that insolvency was an exception to the directive was prima facie tenable as "insolvency law is characterised by special procedures intended to weigh up the various interests involved, in particular those of the various classes of creditors; consequently, in all Member States there are specific rules which may derogate, at least partially, from other provisions of a general nature including provisions of social law". Whether this was intended in the case of this Directive depended upon whether the protection of employees would be furthered by not applying the Directive to insolvent transferors. There was a serious possibility that workers would be more at risk if the Directive applied to transfers of insolvent businesses because purchasers would be unwilling to take on obligations and would refuse to buy the business. Insolvency law provisions and proceedings differed between the various Member States and the Court said that it was impossible to conclude that Member States were obliged to extend the Directive to transfers taking place in the context of insolvency proceedings where insolvency was proved and there was judicial control of the insolvency proceedings which should involve a liquidation of the transferor. This would seem to

---

[50] There is some evidence that this happened in Germany. See Schumacher (1994) 23 I.L.J. 101.
[51] See Collins (1989) 18 I.L.J. 144, Floyd [1989] I.L.&P. 177, Davies (1989) 9 Yearbook of European Law 21.
[52] *Abels v. The Administrative Board of the Bedrijfsvereniging voor de Metaalindustrie en de Electrotechnische Industrie* [1987] 2 C.M.L.R. 406.

exclude receiverships and voluntary liquidations from the scope of any possible exemption unless it could be argued that the strict licensing of insolvency practitioners in the United Kingdom provided sufficient control. In the *d'Urso*[53] case, the European Court of Justice came to the same conclusion as in *Abels* but laid more stress on the insolvency being a liquidation than on its being subject to court control.[54] An exemption on this basis would not apply to administrations since these do not necessarily envisage a liquidation.

The Directive permits Member States to confer more favourable rights on employees than are required and this appears to be what TUPE does, presumably because at the time TUPE was drafted it was assumed that the Directive applied to transfers by insolvent businesses. Application of TUPE to insolvencies is clearly envisaged by Regulation 4 which deems the transfer of a business hived-down by a receiver, administrator or voluntary liquidator not to take place until either the hive-down company ceases to be wholly owned by its insolvent parent or its business is sold, whichever happens first, and provides that employees still employed by the parent to work in the business "immediately before" that time will be deemed to transfer to the hived-down business and its new owner.[55] In *Belhaven v. Berekis*[56] it was held by the Scottish Employment Appeal Tribunal that TUPE applied to the transfer of a business by a trustee in bankruptcy.

Discussions about proposed amendments to the Directive have been in progress for several years; the Commission proposed the most recent version in February 1997.[57] This would allow Member States to dis-apply most of the Directive in cases where the undertaking "is the subject of bankruptcy proceedings or any other analogous proceedings instituted with a view to the liquidation of the assets of a natural or legal person and under the supervision of a competent public authority". Member States would also be allowed to provide that in the context of other insolvency proceedings, such as administration, the transferor's debts to the employees would not transfer provided that the proceedings

---

[53] [1992] I.R.L.R. 136.

[54] Current proposals by the European Commission for a new version of the Acquired Rights Directive reflect this view.

[55] Reg. 4 may, in fact, be unnecessary since Reg. 5 is expressed to transfer contracts which "would otherwise have been terminated by the transfer" and in *Pambakian v. Brentford Nylons* [1978] I.C.R. 665 the Employment Appeal Tribunal held that the parent company had retained the business activity of providing employees to the hive-down company and that the execution of the hive-down agreement did not, therefore, automatically terminate the contracts.

[56] March 17, 1993, EAT, unreported.

[57] [1997] O.J. C124/48.

were "conducted under the supervision of a competent public authority, which may be an insolvency practitioner authorised by a competent public authority" and gave rise to guaranteed payment in accordance with Directive 80/987.

PART III

BANKRUPTCY AND LIQUIDATION PROCEDURES

CHAPTER 13

INTRODUCTION TO PART III

Part III deals with the formal regimes applicable to an insolvent debtor incapable of rescue. It explains the procedures by which such regimes are initiated, the conduct of the regimes and the consequences for the insolvent of being subject to such regimes.[1] The mere fact of being in a state of insolvency does not have any legal consequences until either the debtor or a creditor relies on that state to invoke one of the formal regimes provided by the insolvency legislation.

Since the routes into compulsory liquidation and bankruptcy frequently commence with the service of a statutory demand by a creditor, Chapter 14 starts this Part by looking at the rules relating to such demands.

The regime relevant to an insolvent individual is bankruptcy, which is considered in Chapter 15. Individual insolvency law has to make provision not just for the distribution of the assets of the insolvent to the creditors but also for the continued existence and eventual discharge from bankruptcy of the insolvent.

Insolvent companies may be wound up (or put into liquidation, the terms are synonymous) either voluntarily on the resolution of the members, as explained in Chapter 16, or compulsorily by order of the court, as explained in Chapter 17. Liquidation will result in the termination of the existence of the company. The majority of liquidations are voluntary; in many cases this will suit all the interested parties since a winding up ordered by the court will swallow up more of the available assets, the liquidator will have less freedom of action and there will be a greater degree of investigation into the background to the insolvency than is the case in a voluntary liquidation. The rules governing all types of liquidation, even of solvent companies, are to be found in the Insolvency Act 1986 which removes a number of the previous procedural distinctions between the processes of bankruptcy and liquidation. Individual and corporate insolvency law are, however, still distinct and are dealt with in separate parts of the Act although this is an improve-

---

[1] The consequences for the creditors are considered in Pt V.

ment on the previous position under which the corporate provisions were contained in the Companies Acts and the individual provisions in the Bankruptcy Act.

The rules relating to insolvent partnerships are currently to be found in the Insolvent Partnerships Order 1994 and are explained in Chapter 18. Partnership insolvency law has been largely assimilated to corporate insolvency law but has the additional complication that the partners are likely to have individual liabilities in addition to their liability for the partnership debts.

CHAPTER 14

THE STATUTORY DEMAND

1. Introduction

The statutory demand procedure was first introduced as a method for creditors to establish evidence of their corporate debtors' inability to pay. The Insolvency Act 1986 implemented the recommendation of the Cork Committee that the statutory demand procedure be extended to individuals to replace the ancient and complex procedure under which the creditor of an individual could present a petition to the court within three months of the debtor having committed an "act of bankruptcy".[1] "Acts of bankruptcy" comprised a list of events thought to be indications of the debtor's inability to meet his liabilities which had been added to in a piecemeal fashion over the years and still included such arcane provisions as "with intent to defeat or delay his creditors he does any of the following things, namely, departs out of England, or being out of England remains out of England, or departs from his dwellinghouse, or otherwise absents himself, or begins to keep house".[2] The most commonly relied on act of bankruptcy was the debtor's failure to comply with a "bankruptcy notice" requiring him to pay a judgment debt due to a creditor.

The provisions relating to companies and individuals are still not identical. In particular, a statutory demand served on a company can only relate to a debt which is currently payable whereas a statutory demand served on an individual may relate either to a debt which is currently payable or to one which is not yet due. Unless the petitioner can show unsatisfied judgment process, a statutory demand will have to be served before a creditor can petition to have a debtor declared bankrupt. In the case of a debtor company, however, the statutory demand is only one method open to the creditor who has complete

---

[1] The complexities were compounded by the relation back of the bankruptcy to the earliest act of bankruptcy proved to have been committed within the three months preceding the presentation of the bankruptcy petition.

[2] This was s.1(d) of the repealed Bankruptcy Act 1914.

freedom as to how he seeks to persuade the court that the debtor is unable to pay its debts.[3]

One issue with which the courts have had to grapple is the extent to which a creditor should be permitted to use a statutory demand to apply pressure on a probably solvent debtor to pay.

2. Service of a statutory demand[4]

A statutory demand is a document requiring the debtor to pay the debt or to secure or compound it to the creditor's satisfaction if the debt is payable immediately. In the case of an individual debtor not under an immediate obligation to pay, the demand will require the debtor to establish to the satisfaction of the creditor that there is a reasonable prospect that the debtor will be able to pay when the debt does fall due.

There are various prescribed forms of statutory demand; the precise form depends on whether the debtor is an individual or a company, on whether or not the debt is a judgment debt and whether it is payable immediately or at some time in the future. A statutory demand must explain that the potential consequence of the demand, if not complied with, is that proceedings for winding up or bankruptcy, whichever is appropriate, may be instituted. The demand must give details of the time within which it must be complied with and how the debtor can enter into negotiations with a view to securing or compounding for the debt to the creditor's satisfaction.

A creditor must, where practicable, effect personal service of the statutory demand on an individual debtor.[5] If personal service is not possible, it may be effected by other means such as first class post or insertion through a letter box. Where the post is used, service is taken to have been effected on the seventh day after posting. Advertisement may be used by way of substituted service where the demand is in respect of a judgment debt, the debtor is keeping out of the way with a view to avoiding service and there is no real prospect of the debt being recovered by execution or other process.[6]

---

[3] see Chap. 17.2(c).
[4] In the case of a company, see Insolvency Act 1986, s.123(1)(a) and rr. 4.4–4.6 of the Insolvency Rules 1986. For bankruptcy, see Insolvency Act 1986, s.268 and rr. 6.1–6.5 of the Insolvency Rules 1986.
[5] Insolvency Rules 1986, r. 6.3.
[6] Practice Note [1987] 1 W.L.R. 82 and 85.

A demand served on a company must be shown to have been delivered at the company's registered office.[7]

3. Challenge to a statutory demand

a) Introduction

The statutory demand is intended as a method of establishing the insolvency of the debtor. It should not, therefore, be used as a method of obtaining payment of a debt in circumstances where the debtor has a reason other than insolvency for failing to pay. The courts have shown concern for the problems faced by creditors in extracting payment from recalcitrant debtors and a mere desire to delay payment has not been treated as such a reason. At the same time, the courts are alive to the potential for abuse by creditors of the system.[8] It is difficult, however, to prevent abuse of the system where a debtor responds to an improper statutory demand without involving the courts. Justice observed[9] that there was disturbing evidence that statutory demands were being used as a means of intimidating debtors who might have a genuine defence to the claim into paying the amount claimed in the belief that the demand emanated from the court and without realising that it could be challenged. They suggested that it might be desirable for there to be a more stringent test to be satisfied before a statutory demand could be issued in respect of debts other than judgment debts.

The procedural aspects of challenging a statutory demand differ between individual and corporate debtors. The previous bankruptcy law provisions under which a bankruptcy notice could be challenged are reflected to an extent in the Insolvency Rules although the courts have refused to take the previous over-technical approach to the content of a statutory demand where it is clear that the debtor has not been prejudiced by defects in the drafting.

b) Individual debtor

The Insolvency Rules 1986[10] set out the circumstances under which an application may be made to set aside a statutory demand served on an individual debtor. The application has to be made within 18 days and

---

[7] *Re a Company* [1985] B.C.L.C. 37.
[8] This is a problem which also arises in the context of petitions for compulsory liquidation presented on the basis of evidence other than a statutory demand; see Chap. 17.2(c).
[9] *Insolvency Law: An Agenda for reform*, paras 4.14 *et seq.*
[10] Insolvency Rules 1986, rr. 6.4–6.5.

stops the time for compliance with the demand from running unless and until the application is dismissed. If the court is satisfied that the application is without merit, then it may be dismissed without a hearing or notice to the creditor. There are four grounds for setting a demand aside; these are, first, that the debtor appears to have a counterclaim, set-off or cross demand at least equal to the amount specified in the demand[11]; secondly, that the debt is disputed on grounds which appear to the court to be substantial; thirdly, that the creditor appears to be secured for at least the amount of the debt; and, finally, that the court is satisfied on other grounds that the demand ought to be set aside.

The Court of Appeal had occasion to consider the provisions dealing with the setting aside of statutory demands in *Re a debtor (No. 1 of Lancaster 1987).*[12] The debtor challenged the demand on the grounds that the wrong form had been used and, at a later stage in proceedings, that the amount of the debt was incorrectly stated. Warner J., whose decision to dismiss the application was upheld by the Court of Appeal, said that it was not appropriate to follow the old law applicable to bankruptcy notices which placed supreme importance on strict adherence to technicalities. Defects in the statutory demand should only cause it to be set aside where they had positively misled the debtor not, as under the old law, where they might reasonably have misled him. Nicholls L.J. pointed out that the purpose of the statutory demand was to activate a presumption of inability to pay and that the residual discretion to set the demand aside should only be used where circumstances would make it unjust for the demand to give rise to that presumption. He then observed that "there may be cases where the terms of the statutory demand are so confusing or misleading that, having regard to all the circumstances, justice requires that the demand should not be allowed to stand. There will be other cases where, despite such defects in the contents of the statutory demand, those defects have not prejudiced and will not prejudice the debtor in any way and to set aside the demand in such a case would serve no useful purpose".[13] This case fell into the latter category since although the amount of the debt was incorrectly stated, the debtor had clearly not been confused by it since he did not raise the issue until a late stage in the proceedings and had originally relied on the technical defect that the wrong form had

---

[11] *AIB Finance v. Debtors* [1997] 4 All E.R. 677 (and Court of Appeal decision reported in *The Times*, March 11, 1998) illustrates the need for the counterclaim to be at least equal to the debt specified in the statutory demand.

[12] [1989] 1 W.L.R. 271 (first instance decision of Warner J. reported at [1988] 1 W.L.R. 419.

[13] The test was applied in *Re a debtor (No. 51 of 1991)* [1992] 1 W.L.R. 1294 and in the cases mentioned in the next footnote.

been used. Nicholls L.J. did warn creditors and their advisors not to take the decision as an invitation to draft demands in a slipshod manner.

Re a debtor (No. 1 of Lancaster of 1987) is also authority for the proposition that it will not necessarily be fatal to the statutory demand that the extent of the indebtedness has been overstated. Where part of the amount claimed is disputed, the debtor will have to pay the undisputed element before applying to the court to have the demand set aside aside in respect of the disputed balance.[14]

Where a statutory demand is based on a judgment debt, the court should not go behind the judgment on an application to set aside the statutory demand nor inquire into the validity of the debt nor, as a general rule, adjourn the application to await the result of an application to set aside the judgment.[15]

If the application to set the demand aside succeeds, the court may make a penalty order for cost against the creditor and the creditor's advisors. The Court of Appeal in *Platts v. Western Trust & Savings Ltd*[16] held that the court hearing the application has a wide discretion as to how to deal with the matter.

The court may review, rescind or vary[17] an order made on an application to set aside a statutory demand. In *Re a Debtor (No. 32 of 1991)*[18] Millett J. held that this was a jurisdiction which should be rarely exercised since it allowed what amounted to a renewed application to set aside a demand after the period limited for making such an application. The question for the court is whether the order ought to remain in force in the light of changed circumstances or fresh evidence, whether or not such evidence might have been available at the time of the hearing.

The decision of the court may also be the subject of an appeal.[19] A decision to set aside a statutory demand on the basis that the applicant's case appears to have merits which ought to be further investigated is not a hearing "on the merits" so as to block the introduction of new evidence at the appeal stage.[20] The decision as to whether or not to allow new evidence in such a case will be a matter of discretion for the appeal court.

---

[14] *Re a debtor (No. 490 of 1991), ex p. the debtor v. Printline (Offset) Ltd* [1992] 1 W.L.R. 507, *Re a debtor (No. 657 of 1991)* [1993] B.C.L.C. 181.

[15] Practice Direction [1987] 1 W.L.R. 119, *Re a debtor (No. 657 of 1991)* [1993] B.C.L.C. 181.

[16] (1993) 22 L.S. Gaz. 38.

[17] Under Insolvency Act 1986, s.375(1).

[18] [1993] 1 W.L.R. 314.

[19] Insolvency Act 1986, s.375(2). See Chap. 5.6 above.

[20] *AIB Finance v. Debtors* [1997] 4 All E.R. 677. New evidence may always be admitted in special circumstances, see *Ladd v. Marshall* [1954] 1 W.L.R. 1489.

c) Corporate debtor

There is no specific provision in the Insolvency Rules permitting a company to challenge a statutory demand but where a company disputes a statutory demand which has been served on it and the creditor refuses to withdraw it, the company may apply for an injunction to restrain the issue of a winding up petition. This procedure was used, for example, in *Cannon Screen Entertainment Ltd v. Handmade Films (Distribution) Ltd*[21] in which the creditor had served a statutory demand in respect of a debt which transpired to be disputed. Warner J. said that there was nothing improper in a creditor who has no notice of a substantial defence to his claim taking a short cut and serving a statutory demand rather than pursuing the normal course of issuing a writ against the debtor but that the creditor took such a course of action at his own risk as to costs if it should turn out that there was a defence to the claim.

In *Cornhill Insurance plc v. Improvement Services Ltd*[22] the plaintiff insurance company sought an injunction to restrain the defendants from presenting a petition for winding up on the basis of a statutory demand which had been served on them. Cornhill claimed that such a petition would constitute an abuse of the process of the court since it was clear that they were solvent. Harman J. refused the injunction on the basis that persistent non-payment of a debt suggested insolvency[23] and that Cornhill had its own remedy in that it could make payment.

Hoffmann J. made it clear in *Re a Company No. 0012209 of 1991*[24] that a statutory demand should not be used as a method of debt collection against a solvent company where the debt is disputed in good faith. An injunction restraining the issue of a winding up petition in such circumstances was granted and the petitioner was ordered to pay the applicant's costs on an indemnity basis to make it clear that abuse of the petition procedure in this way was a high risk strategy. The judge said:

> "It does seem to me that a tendency has developed, possibly since the decision in *Cornhill Insurance plc v. Improvement Services Ltd,*[25] to present petitions against solvent companies as a way of putting pressure upon them to make payments of money which is bona fide disputed rather than to invoke the procedures which the rules provide for summary judgment. I do not for a moment wish

[21] [1989] 5 B.C.C. 207.
[22] [1986] B.C.L.C. 26.
[23] Relying on observations of Ungoed-Thomas J. in *Mann v. Goldstein* [1968] 2 All E.R. 769 at 773.
[24] [1992] 2 All E.R. 797.
[25] [1986] 1 W.L.R. 114.

to detract from anything which was said in the *Cornhill Insurance* case . . . It was, however, a somewhat unusual case in which it was quite clear that the company in question had no grounds at all for its refusal. . . . if, as in this case, it appears that the defence has a prospect of success and the company is solvent, then I think that the court should give the company the benefit of the doubt and not do anything which would encourage the use of the Companies Court as an alternative to the RSC, Ord. 14 procedure."

CHAPTER 15

BANKRUPTCY

1. Introduction

This chapter explains how a debtor may be declared bankrupt, the consequences of the bankruptcy order for the bankrupt and the duration of the bankruptcy. It also explains the role of the official receiver[1], the appointment of the trustee in bankruptcy and the duties, powers and potential liability of the trustee. The law relating to the investigation of the background to the bankruptcy is considered in Part IV and the rules governing the collection, realisation and distribution of the assets are considered in Part V.

2. Initiating bankruptcy

(a) Who may be made bankrupt?

Section 265 of the Insolvency Act 1986 provides that a bankruptcy petition can only be presented by a creditor or the debtor where the debtor is either domiciled in England or Wales, personally present in England or Wales on the day on which the petition is presented or, during the previous three years, has either been resident or carried on business in England and Wales.

(b) Who may petition for a bankruptcy order?[2]

The bankruptcy procedure may be initiated either by an unpaid creditor[3] or creditors together or by a debtor who considers that bankruptcy is the only way out of financial difficulty. Where an individual voluntary arrangement is in existence, the supervisor and those bound by the arrangement also have *locus standi* to petition. The overwhelming majority of petitions are presented by creditors but the percentage of

---

[1] See also Chap. 20.3.
[2] Insolvency Act 1986, s.264.
[3] *ibid.*, s.383(1) defines a creditor as a person to whom a bankruptcy debt (defined in Insolvency Act 1986, s.382) is owed.

petitions which result in bankruptcy orders is much larger in the case of petitions presented by debtors than those presented by creditors[4] since bankruptcy petitions presented by creditors often result in payment of the debt and withdrawal of the petition. The Justice report[5] said that bankruptcy orders were being sought by far too many debtors because of the absence of a suitable alternative.

(c) The debtor's petition

The sole ground for a debtor's petition is that the debtor is unable to pay his debts.[6] The petition has to be accompanied by a statement of the debtor's affairs containing prescribed particulars[7] including details of the debtor's creditors and liabilities and assets. The debtor will also have to meet the court fee (currently £25) and pay an amount (currently £250) on account of the official receiver's costs.

Inability to pay debts means inability to meet payments currently due; this was demonstrated by *Re a debtor (No. 17 of 1966)*,[8] an example of an attempted abuse of the insolvency legislation by a debtor. The debtor had been ordered to pay £2,400 damages as a result of an incident in which he had shot the judgment creditor in the eye. The damages were to be paid by weekly instalments of just over £1. The debtor presented a petition for his own bankruptcy, accompanied by a statement of affairs showing that he owed £2,400 in damages, £34 for clothes and £8 in respect of a moped. His assets were shown as £10 cash and the moped valued at £10. He was adjudicated bankrupt. His victim successfully applied for annulment of the order. The court held that only the instalments of the damages currently payable should be taken into account in deciding whether the debtor was able to pay his debts and that the debtor could pay those.

A debtor's petition may lead to the court ordering an investigation into the possibility of setting up an individual voluntary arrangement rather than the making of a bankruptcy order.[9] This is possible where the unsecured liabilities which would be bankruptcy debts are less than the small bankruptcies level (currently £20,000), the value of the debtor's estate in a bankruptcy would be at least £2,000 and the debtor has not been adjudged bankrupt or entered into a composition with his creditors

---

[4] See the statistics contained in Chapters 6 and 7 of Rajak (ed.) *Insolvency Law: Theory and Practice.*
[5] *Insolvency Law: An Agenda for Reform.*
[6] Insolvency Act 1986, s.272.
[7] See Insolvency Rules 1986, 6.41, 6.68.
[8] [1967] 1 All E.R. 668.
[9] Insolvency Act 1986, s.273.

or scheme of affairs in the previous five years. If the court considers it appropriate to investigate the possibility of the debtor entering into an individual voluntary arrangement, it will appoint an insolvency practitioner to investigate and to make a report to the court. The report may lead to the making of an interim order[10] and the calling of a meeting of creditors to consider the proposal. The approval of the proposal by the creditors will cause the deemed dismissal of the bankruptcy petition, unless the court orders otherwise.[11]

In any case in which a bankruptcy order is made and the liabilities are below the small bankruptcies level and the bankrupt has neither been adjudged bankrupt within the previous five years nor made a composition with his creditors nor entered into a scheme of arrangement, the court has the power to issue a certificate for the summary administration of the bankrupt's estate.[12] This will have the consequence that the bankruptcy remains under the control of the official receiver rather than a private sector insolvency practitioner, will probably end in two rather than three years and will involve less investigation than would otherwise be the case. A certificate for summary administration may be revoked by the court at any time if it appears that, on grounds existing at the time the certificate was issued, it should not have been issued.

(d) Petition in connection with default under an IVA

Section 264 of the Insolvency Act 1986 gives the supervisor of an individual voluntary arrangement[13] or any person bound by it *locus standi* to petition to have the debtor made bankrupt. The grounds for such a petition[14] are that the debtor has failed to comply with his obligations under the arrangement or has given false or misleading information in the process of having the IVA approved or has failed to comply with the reasonable requirements of the supervisor in connection with the arrangement.

(e) Creditor's petition

A petition may be presented by a single creditor or by several creditors jointly on the basis of a liquidated and unsecured debt or debts which at least equal the bankruptcy level, which is currently £750, and which the debtor appears either unable to pay or, where the debt is not currently

---

[10] See Chap. 9.3.
[11] Insolvency Act 1986, s.260(5).
[12] *ibid.*, s.275.
[13] See Chap. 9.3.
[14] Insolvency Act 1986, s.276.

payable, to have no reasonable prospect of being able to pay.[15] In determining whether there is a reasonable prospect of the debtor being able to pay when the debt falls due, it is to be assumed that the prospect given by the facts and other matters known to the creditor at the time he entered into the transaction resulting in the debt was a reasonable prospect.[16] A creditor may petition in respect of a secured debt[17] if willing to give up the security or in respect of that part of the debt which will not be covered by the security.[18] Where a secured creditor gives up a security, the security passes to the trustee in bankruptcy for realisation for the benefit of all the creditors; the security is not destroyed and, therefore, any subordinate security over the property is not accelerated.[19]

Section 268 of the Insolvency Act 1986 provides that inability to pay a debt is to be established only by reference either to the unsatisfied execution of a judgment debt in favour of a petitioning creditor[20] or to non-compliance with a statutory demand[21] and[22] by no other means. No petition may be presented if there is an application outstanding to have the statutory demand set aside.[23] In *Re a debtor (No. 340 of 1992)*,[24] the petition was presented on the basis of unsatisfied execution of judgment in that the sheriff was unable to obtain access to the debtor's premises. Millett L.J. held that the wording of section 268 of the Insolvency Act 1986 contemplated that an execution would actually have taken place and that it was not possible to present a petition on the basis of inability to obtain access to effect execution. The petition had, therefore, to be dismissed. The petitioner in that case would have been able to proceed by way of the statutory demand route although that would have caused a delay of three weeks.[25]

---

[15] Insolvency Act 1986, s.267.

[16] *ibid.*, s.271(4).

[17] *ibid.*, s.383 provides that a debt is secured to the extent that the person to whom the debt is owed holds any security for the debt (whether a mortgage, charge, lien or other security) over any property of the person by whom the debt is owed.

[18] *ibid.*, s.269.

[19] *Cracknell v. Jackson* (1877) 6 Ch.D. 735.

[20] See Chap. 4.4.

[21] See Chap. 14, above.

[22] Unlike the grounds for compulsory liquidation of a company where inability to pay debts may be established by reference to any evidence.

[23] Insolvency Act 1986, s.267(2)(d). An informal letter asking that the statutory demand be set aside which did not comply with the appropriate formalities prescribed by the Insolvency Rules did not prevent presentation of a petition: *Ariyo v. Sovereign Leasing plc*, *The Times*, August 4, 1997.

[24] [1996] 2 All E.R. 211, CA.

[25] It is apparent that the petitioner wanted to obtain a bankruptcy order before the passing of two years since the debtor had transferred property to his wife. See Chap. 30 for the relevance of this.

There is provision[26] for presentation of a petition after the service of a statutory demand before the three-week period for compliance has expired if there is a serious possibility that the debtor's property or its value will be significantly diminished during that period.[27] The bankruptcy order may not be made until at least three weeks have elapsed since the service of any statutory demand but, once a petition has been presented, the court may appoint an interim receiver to take immediate possession of the debtor's property.[28] The person applying for the appointment of an interim receiver will have to deposit or secure for such sum as the court directs to cover the expenses of the interim receivership; if a bankruptcy order is subsequently made, the sum will, provided there are sufficient funds, be repaid out of the bankrupt's estate.

In most cases, the court will not hear the bankruptcy petition until at least 14 days after it has been served on the debtor.[29] The debtor must give at least seven days notice of an intention to oppose the petition at the hearing. In addition to the petitioning creditor and the debtor, the supervisor of any voluntary arrangement in force for the debtor and any creditor who has given the requisite notice[30] may be heard by the court.

A bankruptcy petition is viewed as a class action brought on behalf of all the creditors with the consequences that once a petition has been presented it may only be withdrawn with the leave of the court at the hearing of the petition.[31] Other creditors may be substituted[32] for the original petitioning creditor and the court will take into account the interests of all the creditors in deciding whether or not to make the order. The court has a general power to dismiss a bankruptcy petition or stay proceedings, on such terms as it thinks fit, where it thinks it appropriate to do so.[33] In *Re Williams*[34] it was held that the court should not grant repeated adjournments of bankruptcy proceedings on the basis that the debtor had indicated that he would eventually (but not within a reasonable time) be able to repay what was owing by instalments.

---

[26] Insolvency Act 1986, s.270.
[27] See *Re a debtor (No. 22 of 1993)* [1994] 2 All E.R. 105.
[28] Insolvency Act 1986, s.286. This will either be the official receiver or may be an insolvency practitioner previously appointed under Insolvency Act 1986, s.273 to consider the possibility of an IVA.
[29] Insolvency Rules 1986, r. 6.18.
[30] *ibid.*, r. 6.23.
[31] *ibid.*, r. 6.32.
[32] *ibid.*, r. 6.30.
[33] Insolvency Act 1986, s.266.
[34] *The Times*, July 16, 1997.

The debt must be outstanding at the time of the petition[35] but a debtor cannot ensure the avoidance of bankruptcy simply by paying the amount owed to the petitioning creditor since the court may substitute[36] another creditor for the petitioning creditor. Substitution requires that the petitioning creditor is unable or does not wish to pursue the petition and that the substituted creditor would have been able to present a bankruptcy petition on the date when the petition was presented because he could show either an unsatisfied execution or an unsatisfied statutory demand at that time. Where a payment is made to the first petitioner and a bankruptcy order is made after the substitution of another petitioner, the payment will be a void disposition within section 284 of the Insolvency Act 1986.[37]

It is possible for a creditor who could not have presented a bankruptcy petition at the same time as the petitioner to apply for a "change of carriage" order enabling him to take control of the proceedings without being substituted as the petitioner[38]; the court may make such an order if satisfied that the petitioning creditor does not propose to pursue proceedings diligently or at all. It was held in *Re Purvis*[39] that where the debt in respect of which the petition was presented has been paid, a change of carriage order is not possible since section 271 of the Insolvency Act 1986 provides that the court cannot make a bankruptcy order where, if the petition was based on a debt currently payable, the debt has been paid, secured or compounded for. Chadwick J. held that section 271 overrides the provisions of rule 6.31 of the Insolvency Rules 1986 despite the fact that the rule appears to give the court power to make a change of carriage order unless the payment has been made by someone other than the debtor or with the approval of the court.[40]

Re Purvis[41] demonstrates the operation of a bankruptcy petition as a class action. A bankruptcy petition was presented by the debtor's bank but, before the hearing of the petition, the bank and the debtor achieved a compromise of the debt, which was to be paid by instalments from some personal injury damages which the debtor expected to receive, and the bank sought to withdraw the petition. Customs and Excise gave

---

[35] *Re Patel* [1986] 1 W.L.R. 221.
[36] Insolvency Rules 1986, r. 6.30.
[37] See Chap. 30.2.
[38] Insolvency Rules 1986, r. 6.31.
[39] [1997] 3 All E.R. 663.
[40] Such approval validating the payment for the purposes of Insolvency Act 1986, s.284 (see Chap. 30.2). The purpose behind rule 6.31 seems to be an attempt to prevent a creditor from using the presentation of a bankruptcy petition as a means of exerting pressure on the debtor to pay him at the expense of other creditors in that if the bankruptcy order were to be made at the behest of another creditor the payment would be invalidated by Insolvency Act 1986, s.284.
[41] [1997] 3 All E.R. 663.

notice of their intention to appear on the hearing of the petition and
applied at the hearing for a change of carriage order; they were not in
a position to seek to be substituted as the petitioner. Chadwick J. held
that section 271 of the Insolvency Act 1986 prevented him from making
a bankruptcy order but did not require him to dismiss the petition and
that it would be appropriate to adjourn the petition to see if the payments
due under the compromise agreement were in fact made. The judge
ordered carriage of the petition to be given to Customs and Excise both
to give them dominion in relation to the petition debt[42] and to reflect the
court's view that the original petitioning creditor was using the bankruptcy procedure improperly and for his own ends to the detriment of
the creditors generally.

The court may refuse to make a bankruptcy order if it is satisfied that
the debtor is able to pay all his debts (taking into account contingent and
prospective liabilities) or is satisfied that the petitioner has unreasonably
refused an offer by the debtor to secure or compound for a debt in
respect of which the petition is presented.[43] *Re a debtor (No. 32 of
1993)*[44] shows that it will be rare for the petitioner's refusal of the
debtor's offer to be unreasonable. The Court of Appeal held that before
it could be said that the refusal was unreasonable the court had to be
satisfied that no reasonable hypothetical creditor in the position of the
petitioning creditor and in the light of the actual history as disclosed to
the court would have refused the offer and that the refusal was therefore
beyond the range of possible reasonable actions in the circumstances.
The Court of Appeal held that a reasonable creditor might well wish for
the full investigation that a bankruptcy would occasion even if there was
little to be gained financially by the creditor.[45]

In *Eberhardt & Co. Ltd v. Mair*[46] it was held that, since the bankruptcy court has a duty to ensure that it does not make an order in
circumstances which would cause injustice, it was not bound by any
previous decision arising in connection with any judgment on the debt
or an application to set aside a statutory demand; it could reconsider
afresh the question of whether the debt was due.

---

[42] Chadwick J. obviously thought that Insolvency Act 1986, s.271 would not prevent a
bankruptcy order being made if the debtor did not perform his obligations under the
compromise agreement. It is not clear, however, that non-performance would revive the
original debt.

[43] Insolvency Act 1986, s.271.

[44] [1995] 1 All E.R. 628.

[45] In *ex p. Travel and General Insurance* [1990] 3 All E.R. 984 it was held that a refusal
to vote in favour of a proposal for an IVA is not within Insolvency Act 1986, s.271 since
a proposal of an IVA is not to be regarded as an offer to each creditor individually.

[46] [1995] 3 All E.R. 963.

f) Notification of bankruptcy petition

The court will forthwith send notice to the Chief Land Registrar of the filing of a petition for bankruptcy. This will be registered in the register of pending actions.[47]

g) Notification of bankruptcy order

The making of the bankruptcy order will be advertised by the official receiver in a local newspaper and in the London Gazette.[48] The Insolvency Service's Bankruptcy Public Search Room in Birmingham contains public records of all bankruptcies taken from the official notification to the Gazette.

h) Appeal against bankruptcy order

The court which made the bankruptcy order may be asked to review or rescind the order.[49] An application must be based on a change in circumstances since the order was made or on the discovery of further evidence which it would not be possible to adduce on appeal. In *Fitch v. Official Receiver*[50] the Court of Appeal held that a change of mind by the petitioning creditor would amount to changed circumstances and, since the change of mind had happened since the making of the bankruptcy order, it could not be raised on appeal. It is also possible to appeal in the normal way against the decision of the court to make or refuse a bankruptcy petition.[51]

3. Conduct of the bankruptcy

a) Official receiver's role

The official receiver[52] performs a caretaking role in relation to the bankrupt's estate under section 287 of the Insolvency Act 1986 until a trustee in bankruptcy is appointed. This is restricted to protecting the property but he is entitled to sell or otherwise dispose of any perishable goods comprised in the estate and any other goods so comprised the value of which is otherwise likely to diminish. The official receiver must

---

[47] Insolvency Rules 1986, rr. 6.13, 6.43.
[48] *ibid.*, rr. 6.34, 6.46.
[49] Insolvency Act 1986, s.375(1).
[50] [1996] 1 W.L.R. 242.
[51] See Chap. 5.6 above.
[52] See Chap. 20.3.

not incur expense at this stage without the sanction of the court. Provided the official receiver has reasonable grounds for believing that he is entitled to do so, he is protected from liability in respect of any loss or damage resulting from seizure or disposal of assets which are subsequently determined not to form part of the bankrupt's estate.

Whether the official receiver becomes trustee in bankruptcy or is replaced by a private sector insolvency practitioner, he retains investigatory obligations in relation to the bankruptcy which are explained in Part IV below.[53]

If, at any stage in the bankruptcy, a vacancy arises in the office of trustee in bankruptcy, the official receiver will be the trustee until the vacancy is filled.[54]

b) The function of the trustee in bankruptcy

Section 305 of the Insolvency Act 1986 provides that the function of the trustee is to get in, realise and distribute the bankrupt's estate in accordance with the provisions of the Act.[55] This considered in detail in Part V below.

c) Appointment of trustee in bankruptcy[56]

Where a certificate of summary administration has been issued, the official receiver will usually become trustee in bankruptcy as from the time of issue of the certificate.[57]

Where the bankruptcy order has followed an insolvency practitioner's report that an IVA is not feasible, the court may if it thinks fit appoint that insolvency practitioner as trustee in bankruptcy.[58] If there is an IVA already in existence, the court may appoint the supervisor as trustee in bankruptcy.[59] In either of these cases, the trustee must give notice of his appointment, stating whether he proposes to call a meeting of the creditors for the purpose of establishing a creditors' committee and, if he does not, stating the power of the creditors to require him to call one.

---

[53] See Chap. 21.
[54] Insolvency Act 1986, s.300.
[55] If not also the official receiver, he will have a duty to co-operate with the official receiver in the investigatory aspects of the bankruptcy; see Chap. 21.
[56] See Chap. 20.4 for qualification to act as a trustee in bankruptcy.
[57] Insolvency Act 1986, s.297. The court does have the power to make a substitute appointment.
[58] *ibid.*, s.297(4).
[59] *ibid.*, s.297(5). This would not be possible where there was a potential conflict of interest between the IVA creditors and the bankruptcy creditors.

In all other cases, section 293 of the Insolvency Act 1986 provides that the official receiver must decide in the first 12 weeks of the bankruptcy whether to summon a general meeting of the bankrupt's creditors for the purpose of appointing a trustee of the bankrupt's estate. He will be assisted in coming to this decision by the statement of the bankrupt's affairs and the other information to which he is entitled in relation to the bankrupt's affairs.[60] If he decides within the 12-week period not to summon such a meeting, he must give notice[61] of this decision to the court and to every known creditor of the bankrupt and, as from the giving to the court of the notice, the official receiver becomes the trustee in bankruptcy.[62]

The official receiver may be compelled, under section 294 of the Insolvency Act 1986, to summon a meeting of the creditors to appoint a private sector insolvency practitioner as trustee; this will require the concurrence with the request for the meeting of not less than one-quarter in value of the bankrupt's creditors, including the creditor making the request. If a meeting is called and fails to appoint a trustee, the official receiver has to decide whether to refer the need for an appointment to the Secretary of State for Trade and Industry who may decide to make an appointment.[63] If the official receiver decides to make no reference or if no appointment is made, the official receiver will give notice of this to the court and will become trustee at that time. Where the official receiver has become trustee, he may at any time ask the Secretary of State to appoint an insolvency practitioner instead.[64]

d) Appointment of a creditors' committee

Provision is made[65] for the appointment of a committee of creditors to oversee the conduct of the bankruptcy. Where the official receiver is trustee the committee cannot operate but its functions will be vested in the Secretary of State.[66]

e) Powers of the trustee in bankruptcy[67]

The trustee in bankruptcy has the powers conferred on him by section 314 of the Insolvency Act 1986 which are particularised in Schedule 5

---

[60] See Chap. 21.2.
[61] Insolvency Act 1986, s.293(2).
[62] *ibid.*, s.293(3).
[63] *ibid.*, s.295.
[64] *ibid.*, s.296.
[65] *ibid.*, s.301. See s.5 of Chap. 20.5 which deals with the control of the insolvency system.
[66] *ibid.*, s.302.
[67] The power to disclaim onerous property is considered in Chap. 26.3.

of the Act. Part I of the Schedule lists the powers which may be exercised with the permission of the creditors' committee or the court, Part 2 lists the powers for the exercise of which the trustee does not need such permission and Part 3 lists the powers which may be exercised ancillary to any of the powers in Parts 1 or 2. The Part 2 general powers include the power to sell property comprised in the bankrupt's estate, to give receipts for money which discharge the payer from responsibility and to pursue debts comprised in the estate. The Part 1 powers requiring sanction include the power to continue the bankrupt's business for its beneficial winding up, the power to litigate as plaintiff or defendant in relation to the bankrupt estate, the power to raise money by granting security over the property in the bankrupt's estate, the power to accept postponed payment for property in the estate, the power to exercise rights, options or powers comprised in the estate and the power to enter settlements of claims. The trustee is also given the power,[68] with the sanction of the creditors or the court, to appoint the bankrupt to assist in the managing of the estate or the carrying on of a business for the benefit of the creditors.

f) Ceasing to be trustee in bankruptcy[69]

The trustee will vacate office if the bankruptcy order is annulled or when the administration of the estate is complete and a final meeting of the creditors has been held.[70] A trustee in bankruptcy must vacate office if he ceases to be qualified to act as such and may also resign on grounds of ill health or where there is some conflict of interest or change of personal circumstances which precludes or makes impracticable the further discharge by him of the duties of a trustee.[71] A trustee appointed by the Secretary of State may also be removed by the Secretary of State.[72] In other circumstances, a trustee in bankruptcy may be removed from office only by an order of the court[73] or by a general meeting of the bankrupt's creditors summoned for that purpose in accordance with the rules.[74]

A trustee on ceasing to hold office will be given his release from all liability in respects of acts and omissions of his in the administration of the estate and otherwise in relation to his conduct as a trustee at the time

---

[68] Insolvency Act 1986, s.314(2).
[69] See generally Insolvency Act 1986, s.298.
[70] *ibid.*, s.331.
[71] *ibid.*, s.298(7). Insolvency Rules 1986, rr. 6.126–6.128.
[72] *ibid.*, s.298(5); Insolvency Rules 1986, r. 6.133.
[73] Insolvency Rules 1986, r. 6.132.
[74] Insolvency Act 1986, s.298, Insolvency Rules rr. 6.129–6.131.

prescribed by section 299 of the Insolvency Act 1986. Nothing will prevent the court from imposing liability under section 304[75] of the Insolvency Act 1986 on a trustee who has been guilty of the misapplication of property or of misfeasance or breach of fiduciary or other duty in the carrying out of his functions. The trustee is given protection[76] from claims of those whose property he has wrongfully seized or disposed of provided that he reasonably believed at the time that he was entitled so to act unless any damage was caused by his negligence.

4. Consequences of being an undischarged bankrupt

a) Loss of property

As explained in Part V below,[77] the bankrupt will be under an obligation to hand over most of his property to his trustee in bankruptcy for distribution to his creditors.

b) Freedom from harassment by creditors

The creditors of the bankrupt lose the right to take individual action against the bankrupt and his assets as explained below.[78]

c) Investigation and possible criminal liability

The bankrupt will be under an obligation to co-operate with the official receiver's investigation into the background to the bankruptcy.[79] There are a number of criminal offences which can only be committed by undischarged bankrupts. These are explained below[80] and it will be seen that some of the offences arise from the pre-bankruptcy actions of the bankrupt whereas others are committed during the currency of the bankruptcy.

d) Personal disabilities

An undischarged bankrupt is subject to a number of personal disabilities. Under section 11 of the Company Directors Disqualification Act 1986 it is an offence for an undischarged bankrupt to act as a director of,

---

[75] See Chap. 20.5(e).
[76] By Insolvency Act 1986, s.304(3).
[77] See Chap. 27, in particular.
[78] See Chap. 25.
[79] See Chap. 21.
[80] In Chap. 22.

or directly or indirectly to take part in or be concerned in the promotion, formation or management of, a company without the leave of the court by which the bankruptcy order was made. The official receiver must be given notice of any intention to apply for such leave and will oppose it where he considers that it is contrary to the public interest.

A bankrupt is also barred from a number of public offices; in particular, section 427 of the Insolvency Act 1986 prevents an undischarged bankrupt from taking part in parliamentary proceedings or from being elected as Member of Parliament. An undischarged bankrupt cannot be a member of a local authority[81] or a justice of the peace.[82] A number of other occupations are barred to undischarged bankrupts; for example, it is not possible for an undischarged bankrupt to practice as a solicitor.[83]

The undischarged bankrupt will find it difficult to obtain credit.[84] Under section 360 of the Insolvency Act 1986 a bankrupt will be guilty of an offence if he obtains credit of £250 or more without informing the creditor of his status as an undischarged bankrupt. Obtaining credit includes taking possession of goods under a hire-purchase or conditional sale agreement and being paid in advance for the supply of goods or services. It will also be an offence for a bankrupt to engage directly or indirectly in a business under a name other than that in which he was adjudged bankrupt without disclosing to all those with whom he enters into any business transaction the name in which he was made bankrupt.

Section 371 of the Insolvency Act 1986 allows the court to order the re-direction of a bankrupt's mail to the official receiver or the trustee in bankruptcy.

5. Ceasing to be bankrupt

a) Discharge from bankruptcy

Section 278 of the Insolvency Act 1986 provides that the bankruptcy of an individual commences with the day on which the bankruptcy order is made and continues until the individual is discharged. It used to be the case that a bankrupt had to apply for his discharge and large numbers of bankrupts never did so.[85] Automatic discharge from bankruptcy was

---

[81] Local Government Act 1972, s.80.
[82] Justices of the Peace Act 1979, s.63A.
[83] Solicitors Act 1974.
[84] Even after discharge his creditworthiness will not recover easily.
[85] Particularly since public examination of the bankrupt was at that time a necessary prerequisite to obtaining discharge.

first introduced in 1976. Under the current provisions, the bankruptcy will usually expire automatically either at the end of two years, in the case of a summary administration, or at the end of three years in other cases. The period of a bankruptcy which will end automatically may be extended[86] if the court is satisfied on the application of the official receiver that the bankrupt has failed or is failing to meet his obligations under the Insolvency Act 1986. In such a case, the court may order that the period of two or three years shall cease to run for such period, or until the fulfilment of such conditions, as may be specified in the order.

Where the individual has previously been an undischarged bankrupt within the 15 years before the bankruptcy order, a court order will be required to bring the bankruptcy to an end.[87] An application for such an order may not be made until five years after the commencement of the bankruptcy and the court may refuse to grant it or may grant it with or without conditions. At the hearing of such an application, the official receiver, trustee in bankruptcy and creditors may appear, make representations and put to the bankrupt such questions as the court allows. The official receiver will make a report to the court which has usually carried great weight with the court in making its decision. Conditions imposed by the court may relate to the time at which the discharge is to take effect or to what is to happen to after-acquired property of the discharged bankrupt.

The Cork Committee said[88] that the written evidence presented to it was fairly evenly balanced between those, mainly practitioners, who supported the new automatic procedure and those who did not. The latter were mainly creditors and some individuals who had themselves been bankrupt. The Committee suggested that in more serious cases, there should be an automatic review of whether discharge should be granted rather than an automatic discharge.

Discharge has no effect on the distribution of the assets which vested in the trustee in bankruptcy during the bankruptcy nor on the right of any creditor to prove in the bankruptcy.[89] The discharged bankrupt is, however, released from most bankruptcy debts. The exceptions are fines and debts which were incurred in respect of, or forbearance in respect of which was secured by means of any fraud or fraudulent breach of trust to which the bankrupt was a party. The bankrupt will not be discharged

---

[86] Under Insolvency Act 1986, s.279(3).
[87] Insolvency Act 1986, ss279(1), 280; Insolvency Rules rr. 6.217, 6.218.
[88] para. 607.
[89] Insolvency Act 1986, s.281. The discharged bankrupt remains under an obligation to co-operate with the trustee in the performance of his duties: Insolvency Act 1986, ss333, 366.

from bankruptcy debts consisting of liability for damages for personal injury or arising under an order made in family or domestic proceedings[90] unless and to the extent ordered by the court.[91] Discharge does not affect the right of any secured creditor of the bankrupt to enforce his security for the payment of a debt from which the bankrupt is released. Discharge only releases the bankrupt; it does not affect the liability of any guarantor or anyone else with liability for the released debts.

(b) Annulment of bankruptcy order

The court may annul a bankruptcy order under section 282 of the Insolvency Act 1986 if it appears that, on any grounds existing at the time the order was made, the order ought not to have been made. The order may also be annulled if the bankruptcy debts and the expenses of the bankruptcy have all been either paid or secured for to the satisfaction of the court since the making of the order. A bankruptcy may be annulled even if the bankrupt has been discharged from the bankruptcy. The other circumstance in which a bankruptcy order may be annulled[92] is where a bankrupt has entered into an individual voluntary arrangement.

Transactions carried out by or under the authority of the official receiver, the trustee in bankruptcy or the court before the annulment under either section will be valid but any of the bankrupt's estate vested in the trustee at the time of the annulment shall revert to the bankrupt unless the court orders that it shall vest in another person.[93] Any time when a person was a bankrupt by virtue of an order that was subsequently annulled will be disregarded in establishing entitlement to be discharged from a subsequent bankruptcy. Annulment has the effect that the bankruptcy order is regarded as never having been made.[94]

---

[90] Or maintenance proceedings under the Child Support Act 1991.

[91] Insolvency Act 1986, s.281(6) provides that discharge does not release the bankrupt from such other bankruptcy debts, not being debts provable in his bankruptcy, as are prescribed.

[92] *ibid.*, s.261.

[93] This enables the court to order the vesting of property in the supervisor of an IVA.

[94] Insolvency Act 1986, s.282(4) preserves the validity of any acts done by the official receiver or the trustee before the annulment.

Chapter 16

VOLUNTARY LIQUIDATION

1. Introduction

A voluntary winding up is set in motion by a resolution of the members of the company. It may be either a members' voluntary liquidation or a creditors' voluntary liquidation; in the case of an insolvent company, it will have to be a creditors' voluntary liquidation. The distinction is that in a creditors' voluntary liquidation the creditors have ultimate control over the conduct of the liquidation.

2. Commencement of the winding up

a) Resolution of the members

A company may be wound up voluntarily in the three circumstances outlined in section 84 of the Insolvency Act 1986. The relevant provision in the context of insolvency is section 84(1)(c) of the Insolvency Act 1986 which provides that a company may be wound up voluntarily if the company resolves by extraordinary resolution of its members to the effect that it cannot by reason of its liabilities continue its business and that it is advisable to wind up. A company may be wound up voluntarily in any circumstances by special resolution of its members under section 84(1)(b) of the Insolvency Act 1986. The distinction between an extraordinary and a special resolution is that the former only requires 14 days' notice of the meeting at which the resolution is to be passed whereas a special resolution requires 21 days' notice. Both types of resolution require a three-quarters' majority of those members voting.[1]

A voluntary winding up is deemed to commence at the time of the passing of the resolution by the company. The company must then within 14 days give notice of the resolution by advertisement in the

---

[1] Companies Act 1985, s.378.

Gazette.[2] The Registrar of Companies must be notified within 15 days after the passing of the resolution.[3]

b) Inability to swear statutory declaration of solvency

Where the directors cannot swear a statutory declaration of solvency under section 89 of the Insolvency Act 1986 within the five weeks before the winding up resolution, a voluntary liquidation will have to be a creditors' voluntary liquidation. The directors will only be able to swear such a declaration if they think that the company will be able to pay its debts in full, together with interest, within 12 months from the commencement of the winding up[4]; it is a criminal offence to make such a declaration without reasonable grounds for believing it.

c) Creditors' meeting

Where the winding up is to be a creditors' voluntary winding up, a meeting of the creditors must be called under section 98 of the Insolvency Act 1986 to be held not later than 14 days after the day of the company meeting. Creditors must be given at least seven days' notice of the meeting and the notice must give the name and address of the insolvency practitioner to whom they can apply free of charge for such information about the company's affairs as they may reasonably require. Alternatively, creditors may be given details of a place in the relevant locality, where on the two business days before the meeting, a list of the names and addresses of the company's creditors will be available for inspection. The directors must prepare a statement of the affairs of the company to be laid before the meeting and one of their number must preside at the meeting.[5]

d) Consequences of going into voluntary liquidation

The company ceases from the commencement of the winding up to carry on its business except so far as may be required for its beneficial winding up.[6] The directors lose most of their powers with the appointment of a liquidator.[7] The corporate state and powers of the company

[2] Insolvency Act 1986, s.85(1).
[3] Companies Act 1985, s.380(1) and (4).
[4] See *Re Corbenstoke Ltd (No. 2)* (1989) 5 B.C.C. 767.
[5] Insolvency Act 1986, s.99.
[6] *ibid.*, s.87(1).
[7] *ibid.*, ss.114, 103.

continue until the company is dissolved.[8] Any transfer of shares made without the sanction of the liquidator or alteration in the status of the company's members after the commencement of the liquidation is void.[9] All business documentation must contain a statement that the company is being wound up.[10]

e) Conversion from members' to creditors' voluntary liquidation

If a winding up commences as a members' voluntary winding up but the liquidator forms the view that payment of all debts will not be possible, a meeting of creditors must be summoned[11] for a date within a month of the liquidator coming to that conclusion. The liquidation will be converted to a creditors' voluntary winding up as from the day of the creditors' meeting, which will be treated as a meeting called under section 98 of the Insolvency Act 1986.

3. Control of the winding up

a) Appointment of liquidator[12]

In most cases, the creditors will choose the liquidator. Both the creditors and the members at their respective meetings may nominate a person to be liquidator. The liquidator will be the person nominated by the creditors or, where no person has been so nominated, the person nominated by the members. If the two meetings nominate different liquidators, any director, member or creditor of the company may within seven days of the creditors' nomination apply to the court for a decision as to who should be liquidator. The court may order that either nominee be the sole liquidator or that both be joint liquidators or that some other person be liquidator.

A liquidator nominated by the company meeting will be unable,[13] without the sanction of the court, to exercise any powers during the period before the holding of the creditors' meeting; the exception to this is that the liquidator will be able to take custody of the company's property, to dispose of perishable goods and other goods the value of which is likely to diminish if they are not immediately disposed of and

[8] Insolvency Act 1986, s.87(2).
[9] *ibid.*, s.88.
[10] *ibid.*, s.188.
[11] *ibid.*, s.95.
[12] *ibid.*, s.100.
[13] *ibid.*, s.166.

to do all such other things as may be necessary for the protection of the corporate assets. These restrictions are intended to prevent the dissipation of corporate assets by a liquidator friendly to those in control of the company; this practice is referred to as Centrebinding since it was held in the case of *Re Centrebind*[14] that, under the then law, the acts of a liquidator subsequently displaced by the creditors were valid.

If a vacancy occurs in the office of a liquidator, other than a liquidator appointed by, or by the direction of the court, the creditors may fill the vacancy.[15] If for any reason, there is no liquidator acting, the court may appoint a liquidator.[16] The liquidator must publish notice of his appointment in the Gazette within 14 days of the appointment and also notify the registrar of companies.[17]

b) Ceasing to be liquidator[18]

The court may, on cause shown, remove a liquidator and appoint another.[19] A liquidator may also be removed from office by a general meeting of the company's creditors summoned for that purpose in accordance with the rules[20]; if the liquidator was appointed by the court such a meeting will only be summoned if requested by at least half in value of the creditors, otherwise the meeting must be called if requested by at least 25 per cent in value of the creditors. The liquidator must vacate office if he ceases to be qualified to act as an insolvency practitioner and may resign because of ill health or where some conflict of interest or other circumstance makes it impracticable for him to continue to act; resignation requires the calling of a creditors' meeting and notice to the registrar of companies.[21] The liquidator will also vacate office after the liquidation is complete.

A liquidator who has ceased to hold office will be given his release from potential liability in connection with the liquidation at the time prescribed in section 173 of the Insolvency Act 1986. Nothing will prevent the exercise of the court's powers under section 212 of the Insolvency Act 1986 in relation to a liquidator guilty of breach of fiduciary or other duty or of misapplying company property.

---

[14] [1966] 3 All E.R. 889.
[15] Insolvency Act 1986, s.104.
[16] *ibid.*, s.108.
[17] *ibid.*, s.109.
[18] See, generally, Insolvency Act 1986, s.171 and Insolvency Rules 1986, rr.4.108—4.123.
[19] Insolvency Act 1986, s.108(2). See Chap. 20.5(e).
[20] *ibid.*, s.171(2)(b).
[21] The courts have shown themselves willing to order the removal of an insolvency practitioner where this avoids the need for calling a large number of creditors' meetings: *Bullard v. Taplin* [1996] B.C.C. 973, *Re Sankley Furniture* [1995] 2 B.C.L.C. 594

c) Liquidation committee[22]

The creditors may elect a liquidation committee of not more than five persons to exercise the functions conferred on it by the insolvency legislation. If such a committee is appointed, the company may appoint up to five members to sit on the committee. The creditors may resolve to object to some or all of the members appointed by the company in which case those members may not act unless the court directs that they may. On an application to the court, the court may appoint substitutes to act as members of the committee.

d) Cessation of directors' powers

Once the company is in liquidation, the powers of the directors are limited to calling the creditors' meeting, drawing up the statement of affairs and protecting the assets of the company unless the court allows them to do something else.[23] On the appointment of a liquidator, all the powers of the directors cease, except so far as the liquidation committee (or, if there is no such committee, the creditors) sanction their continuance.[24]

e) Function and powers of the liquidator

The liquidator will proceed to wind up the company's affairs in accordance with the provisions of the Insolvency Act.[25]

Section 165 of the Insolvency Act 1986 sets out the powers of a liquidator in a voluntary liquidation, partly by reference to Schedule 4 to the Act. The liquidator may call meetings of the company. He is to pay the company's debts and adjust the rights of the contributories amongst themselves.[26] He may exercise the powers specified in Part II of Schedule 4 without any further permission[27]; these allow him to institute and defend legal proceedings and to carry on the business of the company so far as necessary for its beneficial winding up. Part III of

---

[22] Insolvency Act 1986, ss.101, 102.
[23] *ibid.*, s.114.
[24] *ibid.*, s.103.
[25] *ibid.*, s.107. See Part V below.
[26] As to contributories, see Chap. 31.2.
[27] A liquidator in a compulsory liquidation will need permission to exercise these powers.

Schedule 4 contains a list of powers which any liquidator has; these include the power to sell the company's property, the power to appoint agents to do any business the liquidator is unable to do himself and a general power to do all such other things as may be necessary for winding up the company and distributing its assets. Part I of Schedule 4 lists the powers which the liquidator can only exercise with the consent of the court, the liquidation committee or, where there is no committee, a meeting of the creditors; these are the power to pay any class of creditors in full and the power to enter compromises with those claiming against the company or against whom the company has a claim. Where the whole or part of the company's business or property is proposed to be transferred to another company, section 110 of the Insolvency Act 1986 gives the liquidator the power to accept shares or other interests in the transferee company instead of cash for distribution amongst the members of the transferor company provided, in the case of a creditors' voluntary liquidation, that the court or the liquidation committee consents.[28]

The liquidator, any contributory or any creditor may apply to the court to determine questions arising in the course of the liquidation or to exercise any of the powers which the court would have if the company were being wound up by the court.[29] Where the liquidation takes longer than one year, the liquidator has to call meetings of the members and of the creditors at the end of the first year from the commencement of the liquidation, and of each succeeding year, or at the first convenient date within three months from the end of the year or such longer period as the Secretary of State may allow.[30] At these meetings, the liquidator presents an account of his acts and dealings and of the conduct of the winding up during the preceding year.

4. Stay of liquidation

Once a resolution for voluntary liquidation has been passed, it is not possible to rescind it. An application may be made to the court under section 112 of the Insolvency Act 1986[31] to exercise the power which it has to stay a compulsory liquidation.[32]

---

[28] Which is not likely unless all the creditors have been paid in full.
[29] Insolvency Act 1986, s.112.
[30] *ibid.*, s.105.
[31] Which allows the court to exercise in a voluntary liquidation any power which it could exercise in a compulsory liquidation.
[32] Under Insolvency Act 1986, s.147.

5. End of the winding up

As soon as the company's affairs are fully wound up, the liquidator will make up an account of the winding up, showing how it has been conducted and the disposition of the company's property, and will lay this account before meetings of the company and of the creditors.[33] The liquidator will then send to the registrar of companies a copy of the account and a return of the holdings of the meetings. The company will be deemed to be dissolved under section 210 of the Insolvency Act 1986 three months after registration of this return unless the court makes an order deferring dissolution.

[33] Insolvency Act 1986, s.106.

CHAPTER 17

COMPULSORY LIQUIDATION[1]

1. Introduction

This Chapter considers the circumstances in which the court will order that an insolvent company be wound up, the consequences of the winding up order and the rules governing the conduct of the liquidation.

2. Obtaining a winding up order

a) Introduction

Obtaining a winding up order involves the presentation of a petition by one of the categories of eligible petitioner asking that the court make a winding up order and appoint a liquidator. The High Court has jurisdiction[2] to wind up any company registered in England and Wales. If the company in question has a paid up share capital which does not exceed £120,000, the county court has concurrent jurisdiction.

b) Eligibility to petition[3]

Those eligible to petition for a winding up order are:

> (i) the company, which may by special resolution resolve to seek a winding up order, although it would more normally resolve to go into voluntary liquidation;

---

[1] See, generally, Pennington *Corporate Insolvency Law* (2nd ed.) Chap. 2.

[2] See Insolvency Act 1986, s.117 as to jurisdiction. Insolvency Act 1986, s.118 deals with the situation where proceedings have been started in the wrong court. Insolvency Act 1986, s.119 provides for the county court to refer questions by case stated to the High Court.

[3] See generally Insolvency Act 1986, s.124. There are additional rules allowing regulators to petition for the winding up of insurance companies, banks, investment businesses and charities.

(ii) the directors all acting together[4];

(iii) any creditor or creditors, including those with contingent or prospective claims.[5] Creditors may petition in respect of both legally and equitably assigned debts.[6] A person claiming to be a creditor on the basis of a debt which is bona fide disputed by the company is not a creditor and the company will be able to have the petition struck out.[7] In practice, the vast majority of petitions are presented by creditors.

(iv) any contributory.[8] A shareholder must have held his shares for at least six of the 18 months before the presentation of the petition unless either the company is a public or unlimited company and the number of members has fallen below two[9] or the shares devolved on him through the death of a former holder. A contributory will only be permitted to bring a petition if he can show some financial interest in a liquidation[10]; this means that either he must have some outstanding liability on his shares[11] or that the company must be solvent or that investigation resultant on a liquidation may swell the funds and make a surplus possible.

(v) the official receiver where the company is already in voluntary liquidation. The court will not make a winding up order on the petition unless it is satisfied that the voluntary winding up cannot be continued with due regard to the interests of the creditors or contributories.[12]

(vi) administrators and administrative receivers have the power both to present and defend winding up petitions.[13]

---

[4] *Re Instrumentation Electrical Services Ltd* [1988] B.C.L.C. 550. The normal powers delegated to the directors of managing the business on a majority basis do not give them authority to present a petition for winding up: *Re Emmadart* [1979] Ch. 540.

[5] In practice, they will have to be owed at least £750 before the court will agree to grant the order.

[6] Insolvency Act 1986, s.123 (1)(a). *Re Steel Wing Co.* [1921] 1 Ch. 349; held that although equitable assignees of part of a debt could petition for winding up, they did not have standing to serve a statutory demand and would have to find another method of establishing inability to pay.

[7] *Re a company (No. 0012209 of 1991)* [1992] B.C.L.C. 865.

[8] This broadly means the past and present members of the company. See Insolvency Act 1986, ss74,79.

[9] In which case, after six months the member becomes personally liable for the company's debts: Companies Act 1985, s.24 as amended by the Companies (Single Member Private Companies) Regulations 1992.

[10] *Re Rica Gold Washing Co.* (1879) 11 Ch.D. 36.

[11] Either because the shares were issued partly paid or the company is unlimited or limited by guarantee.

[12] See below.

[13] Insolvency Act 1986, Sched. 1, para. 21.

(vii) The Secretary of State may petition on the just and equitable ground if it appears, as a result of various forms of statutory investigation,[14] expedient in the public interest that the company should be wound up.

c) Grounds for petition

There are seven permissible grounds on which a petition may be based; the only one relevant to insolvency law[15] is section 122(f) of the Insolvency Act 1986, that "the company is unable to pay its debts".

Section 123 of the Insolvency Act 1986 defines the situations in which a company in England or Wales will be deemed unable to pay its debts. The first is where the company has been served with a statutory demand[16] by a creditor to whom the company is indebted in a sum exceeding £750 and the company has for three weeks thereafter neglected to pay the sum or to secure or compound for it to the reasonable satisfaction of the creditor. It would appear not to be possible for creditors with debts smaller than £750 to band together to serve a statutory demand. In *Re London and Paris Banking Corporation*[17] it was held that neglecting to pay means omitting to pay without reasonable excuse so that refusal to pay where the existence of the debt is disputed on substantial grounds does not give rise to a ground for a winding up order. In *Re Tweeds Garages*[18] it was held that if there is no dispute as to the fact of the indebtedness but there is a dispute as to the amount, then, provided the undisputed balance exceeds £750, a statutory demand can be served for that amount. Where there is a genuine dispute as to the company's liability to pay the creditor, the court will usually dismiss the petition and the creditor will have to sue the company for the debt to establish his right to base a petition on it.[19]

Section 123(1)(e) provides that a company will be deemed unable to pay its debts if it is proved to the satisfaction of the court that the company is unable to pay its debts as they fall due. This provides an

---

[14] See Insolvency Act 1986, s.124A.
[15] Although, somewhat oddly, all the provisions relating to the winding up of solvent companies are also contained in the Insolvency Act 1986.
[16] See Chap. 14.
[17] (1874) L.R. 19 Eq. 444.
[18] [1962] Ch. 406.
[19] *Re Boston Timber Fabrications Ltd* [1984] B.C.L.C. 328. In the recently reported 1981 case of *Re Claybridge Shipping Co. SA* [1997] 1 B.C.L.C. 572, the Court of Appeal held that this was only a rule of practice and that it was possible for the court to determine the issue in the course of the winding up proceedings where appropriate and possible without undue inconvenience. This was something the court might do where the likely result of striking out the petition would be to deprive the petitioner of a remedy altogether.

alternative, not available in bankruptcy, to the statutory demand route and creditors who are satisfied that they have the evidence to establish the company's insolvency may dispense with the three week period required by the statutory demand; in *Taylors Industrial Flooring v. M & H Plant Hire (Manchester) Ltd*[20] the Court of Appeal made it clear that there is no obligation to proceed via the statutory demand route and held that, if a debt is due from a company and is not disputed, failure to pay is evidence of an inability on the part of the company to pay its debts. Dillon L.J. observed that "The practice for a long time has been that the vast majority of creditors who seek to petition for the winding up of companies do not serve statutory demands".

Both sections 123(1)(a) and (e) of the Insolvency Act 1986 refer to non-payment of debts. This is a cash-flow test of insolvency since the concept of a debt is narrower than that of a liability: a debt is a liquidated demand presently due and a person is not to be treated as unable to pay his debts because at some future time he will have to pay a debt which he would be unable to meet if it were presently payable.[21] Since 1907 the court has also been able to look to the balance sheet test which is currently contained in section 123(2) of the Insolvency Act 1986. This provides that a company is also deemed unable to pay its debts if it is proved to the satisfaction of the court that the value of the company's assets is less than the amount of its liabilities, taking into account its contingent and prospective liabilities. In *Winter v. IRC*,[22] Lord Reid defined a contingent liability as one which, by reason of something done by the person bound, will necessarily arise or come into being if one or more of certain events occur or do not occur. He said that the term could not be extended to include everything that a prudent businessman would think it proper to provide against. In *Re Byblos Bank*[23] the court held that in comparing the company's assets with its future liabilities, it was not appropriate to take into account assets which it hoped to acquire.[24]

The company's inability to pay its debts may also be established by showing that execution or other process issued on a judgment, decree or order of any court in favour of a creditor of the company has been returned unsatisfied in whole or in part.

---

[20] [1990] B.C.L.C. 216.
[21] *Re European Life Assurance Society* (1869) L.R. 9 Eq. 122.
[22] [1961] 3 All E.R. 855.
[23] [1987] B.C.L.C. 232.
[24] Although this might be relevant in deciding whether or not to exercise the discretion to make the winding up order.

d) Advertisement of the petition[25]

A creditor's petition must be advertised once in the *Gazette*, at least seven business days before the day appointed for the hearing and not less than seven days after service of the petition on the company, unless the court otherwise directs.[26] The court may direct that the advertisement may be placed in a specified newspaper, instead of the London *Gazette*, if it is not reasonably practicable to place it there. The advertisement serves the purpose of informing creditors and other interested parties and of notifying the public generally. If the petition is not duly advertised, the court may dismiss it.[27] The court may also dismiss a petition which has been advertised too early; the seven-day gap between service of the petition on the company and its advertisement is intended to give the company a chance to apply to the court for the petition to be struck out before the damage of an advertisement is done.[28] In *Re Roselmar Properties Ltd*[29] the court declined to strike out a petition which had been advertised too early on the grounds that the company was already in voluntary liquidation and, therefore, the advertisement could have done no harm. There has been some disagreement as to whether notifying third parties individually before the end of the seven-day gap justifies the court in dismissing the petition.[30]

e) Application to strike out petition

It may be possible for the company to apply for the petition to be struck out before the date on which it is due to be heard on the ground that the company has a defence to the petitioner's claim. The court may order the petitioner to refrain from advertising the petition before the striking out motion has been heard. The court will treat as an abuse of the process of the court a petition which is presented upon the basis of a

---

[25] For details of the procedure involved in presentation and service of the petition see Insolvency Rules 1986, rr. 4.7–4.19.

[26] Insolvency Rules 1986, r.4. 11.

[27] Practice Direction [1996] 1 W.L.R. 1255 stresses that this is a mandatory provision designed to ensure that a compulsory liquidation is a class remedy made available to all creditors not just a way of applying pressure on a debtor company to pay. The court will only rarely dispense with the need for an advertisement. See *Applied Data Base ltd v. Secretary of State for Trade and Industry* [1995] 1 B.C.L.C. 272.

[28] *Re Signland Ltd* [1982] All E.R. 609.

[29] (1986) 2 B.C.C. 157.

[30] See *Re a Company (No. 001127 of 1992)* [1992] B.C.C. 477, *Re Bill Hennessey Associates* [1992] B.C.C. 386, *SN Group plc v. Barclays Bank plc* [1993] BCC 506. In *Re Doreen Boards Ltd* [1996] 1 B.C.L.C. a contributory's petition was struck out as an abuse of process on the basis of publicity which she had given to the petition before the time provided by the Rules which had caused the bank to freeze the company's account.

debt which is bona fide disputed on substantial grounds.[31] Hoffmann J. explained in *Re R.A. Foulds Ltd*[32] that this was because the presentation of a winding up petition puts very great pressure on the company and it is not right for that pressure to be used in order to induce the company to abandon a fairly arguable defence to the claim. He went on to express his doubts about the effect of the court being required to strike out such a petition without regard to the question of whether the company was in fact solvent and held that, since the creditor had clearly had *locus standi* at the time of presentation (in that the debtor had subsequently paid the undisputed part of the debt), he could exercise his discretion more widely in deciding whether the petition should be allowed to go on to advertisement and hearing. The evidence suggested that there might be other creditors who would seek to support the petition.

It has been held, however, that a petition will not be stayed or dismissed merely because the company clearly could pay the petitioner's debt where the company has persistently failed to do so: *Cornhill Insurance plc v. Improvement Services Ltd.*[33] As seen above,[34] however, in *Re a Company (No. 0012209 of 1991)*[35] the court warned that creditors should not be tempted to use insolvency procedures to pressurise debtors where there is a bona fide dispute about the existence of the debt.

It is not appropriate to stay a petition for more than a short time since any eventual winding up will be deemed to have commenced at the time of presentation of the petition, the company would have to trade with the petition hanging over it and the other creditors would be prevented from presenting their own petitions.[36] Where there is some matter which needs to be resolved before the right to pursue the petition can be established, the appropriate course will normally be to dismiss the petition.

f) Withdrawal of petition

The court can allow the petitioner to withdraw the petition up to five days before the hearing date if it has not been advertised and no notices in support or opposing the petition have been received and the company

---

[31] *Mann v. Goldstein* [1968] 1 W.L.R. 1091. See Chap. 14.3 in relation to statutory demands. In *Re Euro Hotel (Belgravia) Limited* [1975] 3 All E.R. 1075, Megarry J. held that where an undisputed debt was overtopped by a disputed cross-claim, the court would have a discretion as to whether or not to strike it out.

[32] (1986) 2 B.C.C. 99, 269 at 99,273.

[33] [1986] 1 W.L.R. 114.

[34] See Chap. 14.3(c).

[35] [1992] 2 All E.R. 797. See also *Re a company* (1983) 1 B.C.L.C. 98, 939.

[36] *Re Boston Timber Fabrications Ltd* [1984] B.C.L.C. 328.

consents (on such terms as to costs as the parties may agree).[37] The court may substitute as petitioner any creditor or contributory who in its opinion would have a right to present a petition and who is desirous of prosecuting it.[38]

g) Consequences of presentation of petition

Once a petition has been presented, an application may be made to the court by the company or by any creditor or contributory to restrain any action or proceeding pending against the company.[39] The court may appoint a provisional liquidator; the official receiver or any other fit person may be appointed.[40] The court will establish the functions and powers of the provisional liquidator; in practice, these will be confined to taking possession of the company's assets and preserving and protecting them.

If a winding up order is made, the liquidation will be deemed to have commenced at the time of presentation of the petition.[41] Any attachment, sequestration, distress or execution put in force against the company after commencement of the winding up will be void.[42] Any disposition of the company's property or transfer of shares or alteration in status of the members after the commencement of the winding up will be void unless the court orders otherwise[43]; it is, therefore, difficult for a company against whom a petition has been served and advertised to continue trading normally.

h) Court's powers on hearing the petition

Those who wish to appear on the hearing of the petition will only be able to do so with the leave of the court unless they have given notice of intention to appear either in support of the petition or in opposition to it in accordance with the Insolvency Rules.[44]

The court may make a winding up order, dismiss the petition, adjourn the hearing or make an interim order or another order that it thinks fit but the court may not refuse to make a winding up order only on the ground that there are no assets available for distribution[45]: this ensures

[37] Insolvency Rules 1986, r. 4.15.
[38] ibid., r. 4.19.
[39] Insolvency Act 1986, s.126. See Chap. 25.2.
[40] ibid., s.135.
[41] ibid., s.129.
[42] See Chap. 25.2.
[43] Insolvency Act 1986, s.127. See Chap. 30.2.
[44] r. 4.16
[45] Insolvency Act 1986, s.125.

that those in control of companies cannot avoid the investigation pursuant on a winding up order by disposing of all the company's assets. In *Bell Group Finance (Pty) Ltd v. Bell Group (U.K.) Holdings Ltd*[46] Chadwick J. held that bringing about investigation of an insolvent company's affairs where there was a prospect of benefit to creditors justified making an order notwithstanding the lack of immediate prospect of assets for distribution.

A petition for winding up invokes a class right and the court will take into account the wishes of other creditors and contributories and may in its discretion decline to make a winding up order even where the petitioner makes out a valid ground.[47] The wishes of the shareholders and of creditors who rank after the petitioning creditor will carry less weight than those of creditors of equal status. The court may refuse to make a winding up order where it finds that the petitioner is motivated by some reason other than recovery of the amount owing to him.

i) Rescission[48] or stay of the order

Any court which has the jurisdiction to wind up a company also has the power to review, rescind or vary any order made in the exercise of that jurisdiction.[49] Any application for the rescission of a winding up order must be made within seven days from the date of the order although the court has the power to extend the time limit in appropriate circumstances.[50] It has been held that only a party able to appear on the petition to wind up the company has *locus standi* to apply to rescind the winding up order.[51] The validity of a winding-up order cannot be impeached in the context of an application made under it.[52]

The court may at any time, on the application of the liquidator or the official receiver or any creditor or contributory, make an order that the winding up be stayed either altogether or for a limited time, on such terms and conditions as the court thinks fit. The court may permit the directors to resume the management of the company. Liquidations have

---

[46] [1996] 1 B.C.L.C. 304.
[47] See, *e.g.*, *Re Pleatfine Ltd* [1983] B.C.L.C. 102, *Re Esal Commodities* [1985] B.C.L.C. 450, *Re Crigglestone Coal Co. Ltd* [1906] 2 Ch. 327, *Re Lines Bros Ltd* [1983] Ch. 1.
[48] *Re Dollar Land (Feltham) Ltd* [1995] 2 B.C.L.C. 370.
[49] Insolvency Rules 1986, r. 7.47.
[50] *Re Virgo Systems* (1989) 5 B.C.C. 833.
[51] *Re Mid East Trading* [1997] 3 All E.R. 481. Chadwick L.J. observed that it was unnecessary for the Court of Appeal to consider whether or not this was correct: [1998] 1 All E.R. 577 at 582.
[52] *Re Mid East Trading* [1998] 1 All E.R. 577, CA.

been stayed where the company has paid or settled all the claims of the creditors and provided for the liquidator's remuneration and expenses.[53]

3. Petition against company in voluntary liquidation

The voluntary winding up of a company does not bar the right of any creditor or contributory to have it wound up by the court.[54] The court should not make an order unless it is satisfied that the voluntary winding up cannot be continued with due regard to the interests of the creditors and contributories.[55] Creditors are only likely to seek conversion of the liquidation into a more expensive compulsory one where they are dissatisfied with the progress of the voluntary liquidation or feel that additional investigation is necessary. This should happen less often since the introduction of stricter rules as to who can be a liquidator.

The general rule is that the court will follow the wishes of the majority in value of the creditors. In *J. D. Swain*[56] Harman J. said that where a liquidation in progress was supported by the majority of creditors, it was necessary for a petitioner to show some reason why the majority of the class should not prevail over the minority. The cases show that the court will give greater weight to the wishes of independent creditors than to creditors who also happen to be connected with the company.

Re Hewitt Brannan[57] is an example of a case in which a petition was presented by the official receiver. The company had been in voluntary liquidation for six years during which time a substantial sum had been collected by receivers appointed on behalf of certain secured creditors. Once the secured creditors had been paid off, the receiver handed a substantial balance over to the liquidator who paid himself generously out of it. The liquidation continued to proceed slowly and eventually the official receiver petitioned for a compulsory winding up. The petition was opposed actively by 10 per cent of the creditors and not actively supported by any of them. The liquidator had just offered a dividend of 38.6p in the pound which they preferred to the delay and extra cost of a compulsory liquidation. Harman J. granted the compulsory winding up order, saying that the liquidator had shown a deplorable attitude and needed investigation; winding up by the court was in the public interest

[53] *Re South Barrule Slate Quarry Co* (1869) L.R. 8 Eq. 688, *Re Lowston Ltd* [1991] B.C.L.C. 570, *Re Calgary and Edmonton Land Co. Ltd* [1975] 1 All E.R. 1046.
[54] Insolvency Act 1986, s.116.
[55] *ibid.*, s.124(5).
[56] [1965] 1 W.L.R. 909.
[57] [1990] B.C.C. 354.

and the conduct of the creditors in failing to keep the liquidator up to the mark counted against them.

A similar finding was made in *Re Pinstripe Farming Co Ltd*,[58] in which it was held that the liquidator in the voluntary winding up may appear but should confine himself to pointing out relevant facts and should not adopt a partisan view in favour of or against the petition.

4. Consequences of a winding up order

The liquidation will be deemed to have commenced at the time of presentation of the petition unless the company was already in voluntary liquidation in which case the commencement of the liquidation will be the date of the resolution for voluntary liquidation.[59] The registrar of companies[60] and the official receiver[61] must be notified forthwith.

No action or proceeding can be started or proceeded with against the company without the consent of the court.[62]

A compulsory winding up order is always said to bring contracts of employment and agency[63] to an end automatically. *Chapman's Case*[64] is always taken as authority for the proposition in relation to employees although the issue in that case was when the notice of termination (whose existence was assumed in that case) was given and not whether a winding up necessarily involves termination of employment. *Re English Joint Stock Bank, ex p. Harding*[65] did not assume that a court order for winding up terminates contracts but in *Macdowell's Case*[66] Chitty J. held that a winding up order operated as a dismissal, apparently on the basis that *Chapman's Case* had been universally accepted as based on this proposition. The Privy Council in *Commercial Finance Co. Ltd v. Ramsingh-Mahabar*[67] has recently accepted the view, although it is not apparent that any obligation universal to every employer is necessarily rendered incapable of performance as a result of a winding up order if the company continues to trade and retain employees through the agency of the liquidator.

The powers of directors cease forthwith on the appointment of a liquidator.[68]

---

[58] [1996] 2 B.C.L.C. 295.
[59] Insolvency Act 1986, s.129.
[60] *ibid.*, s.130(1).
[61] Insolvency Act 1986, r. 4.20.
[62] Insolvency Act 1986, s.130(2).
[63] *Gosling v. Gaskell* [1897] A.C. 575.
[64] (1866) L.R. 1 E.Q. 346.
[65] Law Rep. 3 Eq. 341.
[66] (1886) 32 Ch. D 366.
[67] [1994] 1 W.L.R. 1297.
[68] *Fowler v. Broad's Patent Night Light Co.* [1893] 1 Ch. 724.

5. Control of the liquidation

a) The role of the official receiver

Section 136 of the Insolvency Act 1986 provides that the official receiver will be the liquidator of the company unless and until replaced by another liquidator and will be the liquidator during any vacancy. The official receiver also has the investigatory duties explained below.[69]

b) Appointment of a liquidator

The official receiver must decide within 12 weeks of the winding up order being made whether or not to summon meetings of the company's creditors and of the company's contributories for the purpose of choosing a person to be liquidator in his place.[70] If he decides not to call such meetings he must give notice of that decision to the court and to the creditors and contributories. Any notice to the creditors must explain that one-quarter in value of the creditors may require the official receiver to summon a meeting. Section 139 of the Insolvency Act 1986 provides that the liquidator will be the person nominated by the meeting of the creditors or, where no person has been so nominated, the person nominated by the contributories. In the case of different persons being nominated, any contributory or creditor may, within seven days after the date on which the nomination was made by the creditors, apply to the court for an order either appointing the person nominated as liquidator by the contributories to be liquidator instead of, or jointly with, the person nominated by the creditors or appointing some other person to be liquidator instead of the person nominated by the creditors.

If the winding up order is made immediately upon the discharge of an administration order or at a time when there is a supervisor of a voluntary arrangement approved in relation to the company, the court may appoint as liquidator the person who was the administrator or is the supervisor instead of the official receiver.

The official receiver may at any time, including where meetings have been held which have not resulted in the appointment of an liquidator, ask the Secretary of State to appoint a liquidator in his place.[71]

---

[69] See Chap. 21.
[70] Insolvency Act 1986, s.136(5).
[71] *ibid.*, s.137.

c) Liquidation committee

Meetings of creditors and contributories may establish a liquidation committee[72] where the liquidator is not the official receiver.[73] A liquidator who is not the official receiver must call such meetings if requested to do so by one-tenth in value of the company's creditors. Where only one of the meetings decides to establish a committee, a committee will be established unless the court orders otherwise.

d) Function and powers of the liquidator

Section 143 of the Insolvency Act 1986 provides that the functions of the liquidator of a company which is being wound up by the court are to secure that the assets of the company are got in, realised and distributed to the company's creditors and, if there is a surplus, to the persons entitled to it.[74] Where the liquidator is not the official receiver, the liquidator also has a duty to co-operate with the official receiver in the performance of his functions.

The liquidator may, with the sanction of the court or the liquidation committee, exercise any of the powers specified in Parts I and II of Schedule 4 to the Act and, without needing any sanction, exercise any of the general powers specified in Part III of that Schedule.[75] The liquidator has an obligation to notify any liquidation committee where he disposes of property of the company to a person connected with the company or employs a solicitor. The liquidator has the power to summon general meetings of creditors and contributories and may apply to the court for directions in relation to any matter arising in the winding up.

e) Ceasing to be liquidator[76]

The liquidator may be removed from office only by order of the court or by a meeting of the creditors summoned for that purpose. A liquidator appointed by the Secretary of State may be removed by the Secretary of State. A liquidator may resign in the prescribed circumstances by giving notice to the court[77]; he must resign where he ceases to be qualified to

---

[72] Insolvency Act 1986, s.141.
[73] Where the official receiver is the liquidator, the functions of the committee are vested in the Secretary of State.
[74] See Pt V, below.
[75] Insolvency Act 1986, s.167. See Chap. 16.3(e) for discussion of content of Sched. 4.
[76] Insolvency Act 1986, ss172, 174.
[77] Insolvency Rules 1986, rr. 4.108–4.112.

act. A liquidator also vacates office on the giving of notice to the court and to the registrar of companies that the final meeting has been held.

The liquidator will be released from potential liability in connection with the liquidation at the time specified by section 174 of the Insolvency Act 1986. Nothing will release a liquidator from potential liability under section 212 of the Insolvency Act 1986 for misuse of company property or breach of duty.

6. End of the liquidation

Section 202 of the Insolvency Act 1986 allows the official receiver to apply to the registrar of companies for the early dissolution of the company where he is liquidator and it appears to him that the realisable assets of the company are insufficient to cover the expenses of the winding up and that the affairs of the company do not require any further investigation. At least 28 days' notice of intention to make this application must be given to the creditors, the contributories and any administrative receiver, all of whom have the right to apply to the Secretary of State for directions enabling the winding up to proceed.[78]

In other cases, where it appears to the liquidator, not being the official receiver, that the winding up of the company is for practical purposes complete, he shall summon a final general meeting of the creditors which will receive the report of the winding up and determine whether the liquidator should have his release.[79] The company will be dissolved three months after notice of the holding of the final meeting is given to the registrar of companies.[80] Where the official receiver has been the liquidator, the company will be dissolved three months after the registrar receives notice from him that the winding up is complete.[81]

---

[78] Insolvency Act 1986, s.203. There is a right to appeal to the court from the decision of the Secretary of State.
[79] *ibid.*, s.146.
[80] *ibid.*, s.205.
[81] *ibid.*, s.205.

CHAPTER 18

WINDING UP INSOLVENT PARTNERSHIPS

1. Introduction

Since 1986 it has been possible for the court to make an order putting an insolvent partnership into liquidation under Part V of the Insolvency Act 1986 as if it were an unregistered company.[1] The relevant provisions are currently contained in the Insolvent Partnerships Order 1994[2] which "translates" the corporate terminology used in the Insolvency Act 1986 into the appropriate references for the partnership context.[3] Where a firm is wound up as an unregistered company each present and former partner liable to contribute is classified as a contributory as is anyone who has been held out as a partner. Each contributory will be liable to contribute up to the extent of their assets.

If the partners can between them meet the claims of the creditors, any insufficiency in partnership assets will fall on the partners and will be borne between them in accordance with the terms of the partnership. It will frequently happen that when the partnership business becomes insolvent, at least some of the individual members of the partnership will be unable to bear their share of the loss and will themselves become insolvent; a partner may be an individual or a company so the relevant regime may be either bankruptcy or liquidation. The question then arises as to how the estate of an insolvent partner should be distributed as between his private creditors and the creditors of the firm or his solvent partners, who will have had to pay more than their share of the business losses to make up for his shortfall.

The Insolvent Partnerships Order 1994 makes provision for the presentation by creditors of a petition against the partnership alone[4] and also for the simultaneous presentation of petitions against the partnership and one or more of the partners in their capacity as such.[5] It is also

---

[1] Insolvency Act 1986, ss221, 420.
[2] S.I. 1994 No. 2421 made under Insolvency Act 1986, s.420.
[3] See Insolvent Partnership Order 1994, Arts. 2, 3 and Chap. 11.1 above.
[4] Insolvent Partnerships Order 1994, art. 7.
[5] *ibid.*, art. 8.

possible[6] for all the members to present a joint petition for the bankruptcy of each of them in his capacity as a member of the partnership and the winding up of the partnership business without the partnership being wound up as an unregistered company. Article 19 of the Order permits proceedings to be commenced against an individual partner for a partnership debt without petitioning against the partnership or against any other partner. The court is, however, given a general power by article 14[7] of the Insolvent Partnerships Order 1994 to make orders as to the future conduct of the insolvency proceedings where a petition for winding up or bankruptcy has been presented against any person and the court's attention is drawn to the fact that the person is a member of an insolvent partnership. Any such order may apply the provisions of the Insolvent Partnerships Order 1994 to the future conduct of the insolvency proceedings and may include provisions as to the administration of the joint estate of the partnership and how it and the separate estate of any member are to be administered. It is likely that in any situation where an insolvent partnership is being wound up and bankruptcy or compulsory liquidation orders are made against individual partners that the provisions of article 8 of the Insolvent Partnerships Order 1994 will be applied in order to achieve a fair distribution of the assets amongst the various creditors.

The law on insolvent partnerships is enacted in a somewhat complex way by modifying the relevant provisions of the Insolvency Act 1986. The position is somewhat better than under the previous regulations in that the Insolvent Partnerships Order 1994 does set out the modified provisions in its Schedules. A considerable amount of cross-referencing still has to take place. In this account of the various regimes provided under the Insolvent Partnerships Order, the introduction to each regime explains[8] which provisions of the Insolvency Act 1986 apply, which have been modified and in which Schedule the modified provisions are to be found. It should be noted that section 229 of the Insolvency Act 1986 provides that the provisions of Part V of the Act with respect to insolvent partnerships are in addition to and not in restriction of any provisions in Part IV with respect to winding up of companies by the court. It also provides that the court or liquidator may exercise any powers or do any act in the case of insolvent partnerships which might be exercised or done by it or him in winding up a company registered under the Companies Acts.

---

[6] Under Insolvent Partnerships Order 1994, art. 11.
[7] Which amends Insolvency Act 1986, ss168, 303.
[8] As does the Insolvent Partnerships Order itself.

2. Winding up of insolvent partnership on petition of creditor

a) Introduction

Article 7 of the Insolvent Partnerships Order 1994 provides for the presentation of a petition for winding up an insolvent partnership in circumstances where no petition is presented by the petitioner against any member or former member of the partnership in his capacity as such. The provisions of Part V of the Insolvency Act 1986 will apply to the winding up as modified by the Insolvent Partnerships Order 1994 so that the modified provisions are as set out in Schedule 3 of the Order; the provisions modified by Schedule 3 are sections 117, 131, 133, 220 to 223, 234 and Schedule 4 of the Insolvency Act 1986. Sections 73(1), 74(2)(a) to (d) and (3), 75 to 78, 83, 122, 123, 202, 203, 205 and 250 of the Insolvency Act 1986 will not apply.

b) Jurisdiction

The courts will have jurisdiction if the partnership has a principal place of business in England and Wales or if the debt on which the petition is based arises from business carried on by the insolvent partnership within the three years before presentation of the petition at a place of business within England and Wales, even if that is not the principal place of the partnership's business.[9]

c) Eligibility to petition

Creditors, the Secretary of State and certain insolvency practitioners may present a petition against the partnership under article 7.[10] The insolvency practitioners with *locus standi* are the liquidator or administrator of a corporate member or of a former corporate member, the administrator of the partnership, the trustee of an individual member or former member's estate or the supervisor of voluntary arrangement approved in relation to a corporate or individual member or the partnership.

---

[9] Insolvency Act 1986, s.221 as modified by the Insolvent Partnerships Order 1994, Sched. 3. There are specific provisions relating to partnerships with principal places of business in either Scotland or Northern Ireland.
[10] Insolvency Act 1986, s.221(A) (as modified).

d) Grounds for petition

The grounds for winding up a partnership as an unregistered company are the following[11]:

   (i) the partnership is dissolved or has ceased to carry on business or is carrying on business only for the purpose of winding up its affairs;

  (ii) the partnership is unable to pay its debts;

 (iii) the court is of the opinion that it is just and equitable that the partnership should be wound up.

e) Inability to pay debts

Inability to pay debts will be shown by any of the following[12]:

   (i) failure of the partnership to comply with a statutory demand[13] in respect of a sum exceeding £750;

  (ii) the bringing of an action or other proceeding against one or more partners personally in respect of a partnership debt of which notice has been given to the partnership and in respect of which the partnership has taken no action for three weeks to pay, secure or compound for the claim or procured a stay of the action or indemnified the defendant against liability from the action;

 (iii) execution or other process issued on a judgment against the partnership is returned unsatisfied;

 (iv) it is proved to the satisfaction of the court that the value of the partnership's assets is less than the amount of its liabilities taking into account its contingent and prospective liabilities.

If a petitioning insolvency practitioner can satisfy the court that a bankruptcy or winding up order has been made against the member whose trustee or liquidator he is on the grounds of that member's inability to pay a joint debt, the order shall be rebuttable proof that the partnership is unable to pay its debts.

---

[11] Insolvency Act 1986, s.221(7), Insolvent Partnerships Order 1994, Sched. 3.

[12] ss222, 223 (both as modified by the Insolvent Partnerships Order 1994, Sched. 3) and Insolvency Act 1986, s.224.

[13] Insolvency Act 1986, s.222(2), Insolvent Partnerships Order 1994, Sched. 3 sets out the requirements for service of the demand.

f) Conduct of the insolvency

The winding up of the partnership will be conducted as if it were a compulsory winding up of a company.[14]

Where the petition has been presented by an insolvency practitioner who is already trustee or liquidator of a member, the court may appoint that practitioner as provisional liquidator of the partnership under section 135 of the Insolvency Act 1986.[15] Such an insolvency practitioner may also be appointed as liquidator by the court on the making of a winding up order, in which case the official receiver will not become a liquidator.[16]

3. Winding up of partnership on member's petition

a) Introduction

Article 9 of the Insolvent Partnerships Order 1994 is the appropriate article where a member petitions for the winding up of an insolvent partnership whilst not petitioning for the insolvency of any member of the partnership. Part V of the Insolvency Act 1994 will govern the winding up with the modifications to sections 117, 131, 133, 234 and Schedule 4 of the Insolvency Act 1986 set out in Part II of Schedule 3 of the Insolvent Partnerships Order 1994 and with the modifications to sections 117 and 221 of the Insolvency Act 1986 set out in Schedule 5 of the Insolvent Partnerships Order 1994. Sections 73(1), 74(2)(a) to (d) and (3), 75 to 78, 83, 122, 123, 124(2) and (3), 202, 203, 205 and 250 Insolvency Act 1986 will not apply.

b) Jurisdiction

The court has jurisdiction where the partnership has, or has had within the previous three years, a principal place of business in England or Wales.

c) *Locus standi* and grounds for petition

Any member of a partnership which consists of not less than eight members may petition under article 9.[17] The grounds for petitioning are[18] that:

---

[14] See Chaps 17 and 21.
[15] Insolvency Act 1986, s.221(A)(4) as modified.
[16] *ibid.*, s.221(A)(5) as modified.
[17] *ibid.*, s.221A(1), Insolvent Partnerships Order 1994, Sched. 5.
[18] Insolvent Partnerships Order 1994, s.221(7), Sched. 5.

(i) the partnership is dissolved, or has ceased to carry on business, or is carrying on business only for the purpose of winding up its affairs; or

(ii) the partnership is unable to pay its debts[19]; or

(iii) the court is of the opinion that it is just and equitable that the partnership should be wound up.

Any member of any sized partnership may petition[20] with the leave of the court if the court is satisfied that the member has served a demand on the partnership in respect of a joint debt exceeding £750 due from the partnership, but paid by the member other than out of partnership property, which the partnership has for three weeks failed to pay and the member has obtained a judgment, decree or order of the court for reimbursement which all reasonable steps have failed to enforce.

d) Conduct of the liquidation

The winding up of the partnership will be conducted in the same way as a winding up under article 7 of the Insolvent Partnerships Order 1994.

4. Winding up of partnership and concurrent insolvency of partners on petition of creditor

a) Introduction

Article 8 of the Insolvent Partnerships Order 1994 provides for the presentation by a creditor of petitions both for the winding up of an insolvent partnership and at the same time for the bankruptcy or liquidation of one or more members or former members of the partnership in their capacity as such. Article 7, explained above, will be the relevant article if petitions are presented against the partners in their individual capacities.

Under article 8, the provisions of Part V of the Insolvency Act 1986, apart from sections 223 and 224, will apply (as modified by Schedule 4 of the Insolvent Partnerships Order 1994[21]) to the winding up of the partnership. Corporate partners against whom a petition has been concurrently presented may be wound up under Parts IV, VI, VII and XII to XIX of the Insolvency Act 1986 as modified by Schedule 4 of the

[19] As established under Insolvency Act 1986, ss222 to 224, as modified.

[20] Insolvency Act 1986, s.221A, Insolvent Partnerships Order 1994, Sched. 5.

[21] Para. 1 of Insolvent Partnerships Order 1994, Sched. 4 lists more than 50 provisions of the Insolvency Act 1986 which it modifies.

Insolvent Partnerships Order 1994. Individual members against whom concurrent petitions have been presented will be subject to the bankruptcy provisions of Part IX (other than sections 269, 270, 287 and 297) and Parts X to XIX, as modified by Schedule 4 of the Insolvent Partnerships Order 1994. A member of a partnership against whom an insolvency order is made under article 8 will not be treated as a contributory[22] under the Insolvency Act 1986 unless the contrary intention appears.

Jurisdiction in respect of article 8 of the Insolvent Partnerships Order 1994 is the same as under article 7, explained above.

b) Eligibility and grounds to petition

Creditors to whom the partnership and its members are indebted in respect of a liquidated sum payable immediately may petition on the grounds that the partnership is unable to pay its debts. An insolvent partnership will be deemed unable to pay its debts where a statutory demand in respect of a debt in excess of £750 has been served on the partnership and on any one or more members or former members liable to pay the sum due and the partnership and its members have for three weeks neglected to pay the sum or to secure or compound for it to the creditor's satisfaction.[23] This is the only basis on which the petitioner can establish inability to pay debts. Sections 122, 123, 267 and 268 of the Insolvency Act 1986 are amended[24] so that the only basis for the concurrent petitions against the members of the partnership is inability to pay partnership debts exceeding £750, such inability to be established by the statutory demand route.

The petition to wind up the partnership will be heard first and the court will not make orders in respect of the members until either an order has been made to wind up the partnership or the petition to do so has been dismissed.[25] The court has the power to make any order that it thinks fit on the hearing of the petition against the partnership and the order may contain directions as to the future conduct of any insolvency proceedings in existence against any insolvent member in respect of whom an insolvency order has already been made.[26] When a winding up order has been made against the partnership, the court may make orders against the members in respect of whom concurrent petitions have been presented. If no such orders are made within 28 days of the order against

[22] Insolvency Act 1986, s.221(7), Insolvent Partnerships Order 1994, Sched. 4.
[23] Insolvency Act 1986, s.222, Insolvent Partnerships Order 1994, Sched. 4.
[24] By Insolvent Partnerships Order 1994, Sched. 4, Pt. II.
[25] *ibid.*, Sched. 4, s.124(6) and 125A.
[26] *ibid.* 1994, s.125(2), Sched. 4.

the partnership, the winding up of the partnership will be treated as taking place under article 7. If the petition against the partnership has been dismissed, proceedings under any order made against a member will take place without the modifications made by the Insolvent Partnerships Order 1994.

c) Conduct of concurrent insolvencies of partnership and members

The winding up of the partnership and of any corporate partner will be conducted as if it were a compulsory liquidation of a company[27] and the bankruptcy of any individual member will be conducted in accordance with the usual rules,[28] in both cases as modified by Schedule 4 of the Insolvent Partnerships Order 1994.

The official receiver will become the responsible insolvency practitioner in respect of both the partnership and any member in respect of whom an order has been made unless and until he is replaced by an insolvency practitioner either chosen by a combined meeting of the creditors of the partnership and the creditors of an insolvent member or appointed by the Secretary of State in like manner to a compulsory liquidation of a company.[29] The official receiver will have to call a meeting to appoint a private sector insolvency practitioner if he is required to do so by one quarter in value of the partnership creditors or by one quarter in value of the creditors of an insolvent partner.[30] Any combined meeting of creditors will be conducted as if it were a meeting of a single set of creditors.[31] The meeting may also appoint a committee which will act as liquidation committee of the partnership and for any insolvent corporate partner and as creditors' committee for any insolvent individual partner.[32]

The responsible insolvency practitioner can become trustee of any member who is subsequently made bankrupt in respect of a partnership debt.

If the responsible insolvency practitioner feels there is likely to be a conflict of interest between the various estates, he may call separate meetings of creditors to ascertain their wishes. He may also be requested to summon a meeting at any time by one tenth in value of the creditors

---

[27] See Chap. 17 above.
[28] See Chap. 15.
[29] Insolvent Partnerships Order 1994, Sched. 4, ss136, 136A, 137, 137A.
[30] *ibid.*
[31] *ibid.*, s.139, Sched. 4.
[32] *ibid.*, ss141, 141A, Sched. 4.

or contributories. He may apply to the court for directions.[33] The court may decide to appoint additional insolvency practitioners either to act jointly with or to replace the existing practitioner.

d) Collection and distribution of the assets

The Insolvent Partnerships Order 1994 makes some amendments, in the case of an article 8 insolvency, to the provisions of the Insolvency Act which deal with the collection and distribution of the assets.[34] The insolvency practitioner will keep distinct accounts of the joint estate of the partnership and of the separate estate of each member of that partnership against whom an insolvency order has been made.

The definition of exempt property in the bankruptcy of an individual partner is amended[35] so that any assets which are partnership property fall into the estate.

Provision is made for the payment of the expenses in relation to the various estates.[36] Joint expenses will first be applied against joint assets. Expenses of the individual estates will first be applied against the separate assets. If there is a shortfall in the joint estate, the unpaid balance will be apportioned equally between the separate estates of the insolvent partners and rank *pari passu* with those expenses. If there is a shortfall in any of the separate estates, the unpaid balance will form part of the expenses to be paid out of the joint estate. Any balance remaining will be apportioned equally between the other estates and will continue to be apportioned equally until the balance has been paid. If the creditors' committee agree or if the court gives leave, the responsible insolvency practitioner may pay any expenses incurred for any separate estate as part of the expenses to be paid out of the joint estate, or pay out of any separate estate any part of the expenses incurred for the joint estate which affects that separate estate.

An insolvency practitioner appointed under article 8 of the Insolvent Partnerships Order 1994 will deal first with the expenses of the various estates and then with the claims of the joint estate creditors. Any shortfall will then be proved for in the individual insolvencies. The Cork Committee recognised[37] that it was correct in principle that the separate creditors should have no resort to the joint estate until the joint estate creditors were paid in full since a partner would not be entitled to receive any share of the firm's assets until the firm's debts were paid and

---

[33] *Ibid.*, s.230A, Sched. 4.
[34] See generally Pt V below.
[35] Insolvent Partnerships Order 1994, s.283, Sched 4.
[36] *ibid.*, s.175, Sched. 4.
[37] para. 1689.

there was no reason why his private creditors should be in a better position. A distribution from the individual estate will be paid up to the joint estate and then distributed to the joint estate creditors. The aggregate amount of the shortfall is claimable against each individual estate but the rule against double proof means that the liquidator cannot recover more than once on behalf of the joint estate.

The priority of debts in both joint and separate estates is that expenses will be paid first, then preferential debts followed by ordinary debts and then interest on joint debts (other than postponed debts), followed by postponed debts and then, finally, interest on postponed debts. Where there is a shortfall in the joint estate, the debts will be a claim on the estate of each insolvent partner against whom an order has been made under article 8. The claims will rank equally with debts of the same category in the separate insolvencies. This abrogates the previous rule that where there was any joint estate the joint estate creditors were postponed to the separate estate.

Schedule 4, s.175C(2) contains the common law rule[38] that a partner cannot prove against either the joint estate or the separate estate of his bankrupt co-partner in competition with the firm's creditors who are in fact his own creditors; he will have to wait until the partnership liabilities have all been discharged. If all the joint creditors have been paid and the separate estate of the co-partner is clearly insolvent, the rule does not apply. There are exceptions in the case of fraud and where debts have arisen in the ordinary course of a separate business. A partner who has incurred personal liability in reliance on an indemnity from his partners will find that his claim is subordinated to the claims of joint estate creditors until they have been paid out in full.

e) End of the insolvencies

When it appears to the insolvency practitioner, not being the official receiver, that the winding up of the partnership or any corporate member or the administration of the estate of any individual member is for practical purposes complete, he must summon a final general meeting of the relevant creditors, which may be a combined meeting, to receive his report and to determine whether the practitioner should have his release from potential liability.[39]

---

[38] *ex p. Collinge* (1863) 4 De. G. & J. 533.
[39] Insolvent Partnerships Order 1994, ss146, 331, Sched. 4.

5. Winding up of partnership and insolvency of all members on member's petition

a) Introduction

Article 10 is the relevant article where a member of a partnership presents a petition against the partnership and against all its members in their capacity as such. Many of the provisions are the same as apply under article 8 where a petition has been presented by a creditor against the partnership and some of the partners but the provisions as to eligibility to petition and grounds for petition are different.

The partnership may be wound up as an unregistered company under Part V of the Insolvency Act 1986. Sections 220, 225 and 227 to 229 of the Insolvency Act 1986 will apply modified as set out in Part II of Schedule 4 of the Insolvent Partnerships Order 1994. Sections 117, 124, 125, 221, 264, 265, 271 and 272 of the Insolvency Act 1986 will apply modified as set out in Schedule 6 of the Insolvent Partnerships Order 1994. Sections 73(1), 74(2)(a) to (d) and (3), 75 to 78, 83, 124(2) and (3), 154, 202, 203, 205, 222, 223, 224 and 250 of the Insolvency Act 1986 will not apply.

The winding up of any corporate members of the partnership will be governed by Parts IV, VI, VII and Parts XII to XIX of the Insolvency Act 1986. The bankruptcy of individual members will be governed by Part IX (other than sections 273, 274, 287 and 297) and Parts X to XIX. Those of these provisions which are modified by the Insolvent Partnerships Order 1994 are set out in Schedule 4 of the Order, with the exception of the provisions on summary administration which will apply as set out in Schedule 7 to the Order. Unless the contrary intention appears, members against whom an order has been made will not be treated as contributories for the purposes of the Insolvency Act 1986.[40]

Jurisdiction is the same as under article 9 of the Insolvent Partnerships Act, explained above.

b) *Locus standi* and grounds for petition[41]

A member can present a petition if the partnership is unable to pay its debts and if petitions are presented at the same time by that partner for insolvency orders against every partner of the partnership (including himself) and each partner is willing for an insolvency order to be made

---

[40] Insolvent Partnerships Order 1994, s.221(7), Sched. 6.
[41] *ibid.*, s.124 IA, Sched. 6.

against him and the petition against him contains a statement to this effect. The court may allow the petitioner to leave out some partners where it considers it impracticable to present petitions against them. The court will have the same powers on hearing the petitions as under article 8 of the Insolvent Partnerships Order 1994, explained above.

c) Conduct of the insolvencies

The conduct of the insolvencies and the rules as to priority of expenses and debts will apply as under article 8 of the Insolvent Partnerships Order 1994, explained above. The court may issue a certificate for summary administration if the total of the partnership debts and the separate debts of the member is less than £20,000 and the member concerned has neither been adjudged bankrupt nor made a composition with his creditors in satisfaction of his debts nor a scheme of arrangement of his affairs within the five years before the presentation of the joint petition.

6. Joint bankruptcy petition by all members

a) Introduction

Under article 11 of the Insolvent Partnerships Order 1994, the court can make orders for the bankruptcy of all the members and the winding up of the business, but not as a registered company, on the joint petition of all the members. Parts IX (other than sections 273, 274 and 287) and X to XIX of the Insolvency Act 1986 will apply in so far as they relate to the insolvency of individuals where a bankruptcy petition is presented by a debtor and modified as set out in Schedule 7 to the Insolvent Partnerships Order 1994. The provisions which Schedule 7 modifies are sections 264 to 266, 272, 275, 283, 284, 290, 292 to 301, 305, 312, 328, 331 and 387. The Company Directors Disqualification Act 1986 will not be applicable in this situation.

For there to be jurisdiction under this article, the partnership must have or have had within the previous three years a principal place of business in England and Wales.

b) Grounds and eligibility to petition[42]

A joint bankruptcy petition may be presented under article 11 of the Insolvent Partnerships Order 1994 by all the partners, in their capacity

---

[42] Insolvent Partnerships Order 1994, ss264, 265, 266 and 272, Sched. 7.

as such, provided that they are all individuals and that none of them is a limited partner. The court may allow the presentation of a petition by only some of the members of the partnership where it is satisfied that it would be impracticable to require presentation by all the members. The only ground for presentation of the petition is that the partnership is unable to pay its debts and the petition shall be accompanied by a statement of affairs of each member and of the partnership. The court may issue a certificate for summary administration if the total of the partnership debts and the separate debts of the member is less than £20,000 and the member concerned has neither been adjudged bankrupt nor made a composition with his creditors in satisfaction of his debts nor a scheme of arrangement of his affairs within the five years before the presentation of the joint petition.

c) Conduct of the bankruptcies

The official receiver will be appointed as trustee of the estates of the members and of the partnership until a replacement trustee is appointed. The provisions which apply to the conduct of a partnership winding up and concurrent insolvencies of members under article 8 of the Insolvent Partnership Order 1994[43] also apply, appropriately modified, in this situation.

7. Personal consequences for individual partners

A partner of an insolvent partnership will be deemed to be an officer or director for the purposes of the Insolvency Act 1986 and the Company Directors' Disqualification Act 1986 and may face liability for criminal offences, civil liability for wrongful and fraudulent trading[44] and disqualification under the Company Directors Disqualification Act.[45]

Schedule 8 of the Insolvent Partnerships Order 1994 contains the modifications of the Companies Directors Disqualification Act 1986. Disqualification orders may be made against those who are or have been officers of partnerships which have become insolvent. Officers of partnerships are those who are members of the partnership and those who

---

[43] Explained in s.3(e)–(g) above.
[44] These provisions will be of no consequence to a partner whose liability is anyway unlimited.
[45] Except under Insolvent Partnerships Order 1994, Art. 11.

have management or control of the partnership business. In many cases the partners will be disqualified because they are undischarged bankrupts but a longer period of disqualification could be imposed under section 6 of the Companies Directors Disqualification Act 1986.

PART IV

MAINTAINING PUBLIC CONFIDENCE

CHAPTER 19

INTRODUCTION TO PART IV

Part IV focuses on what the Cork Committee described as one of the main aims of insolvency law: the maintenance of public confidence in the system as being one under which those to whom credit is extended should not be lightly released from their obligation to pay. The Cork Committee observed[1] that "it is a basic objective of the law to support the maintenance of commercial morality and encourage the fulfilment of financial obligations. Insolvency must not be an easy solution for those who can bear with equanimity the stigma of their own failure or their responsibility for the failure of a company under their management". Later in the Report,[2] the Committee observed that society requires to be satisfied in respect of four distinct matters: first, whether or not fault or blame attaches to the conduct of the insolvent; secondly, if it does, that the insolvent will be suitably punished; thirdly, that the insolvent's opportunity to repeat such conduct in the future should be controlled whilst at the same time allowing re-establishment of legitimate trading activities; finally, whether and to what extent the responsibility for the insolvency is attributable to someone other than the insolvent.

A fundamental requirement of public confidence in the system is the integrity and competence of those charged with the implementation of the insolvency procedures. There has been considerable debate in the course of the history of insolvency law about who should control the process of collection and distribution of the assets in order to prevent abuse by debtors, creditors or by those in control of the assets. Chapter 20 considers the issue of who controls the insolvency system and looks, in particular, at the licensing and control of trustees in bankruptcy, liquidators, administrators and administrative receivers. It also deals with the debate about the cost of the insolvency system.

Insolvency does not necessarily involve criminal liability but it does indicate a state of affairs which requires public explanation and inquiry. The Cork Committee said[3] "If the basic objectives of the law are to be

[1] para. 191.
[2] At para. 1735.
[3] At para. 194.

achieved, it is essential that proper investigation will be made in every case in which it is warranted. Justice and fairness to those whose conduct is liable to be investigated, and the proper constraints on public expenditure alike, require that no investigation will be undertaken unless it is warranted". At one time, all bankrupts had to undergo a public examination before they could obtain their discharge but this is now seen as unnecessarily draconian. Chapter 21 explains the extent to which the insolvency legislation provides for the investigation of those who, or whose companies, become insolvent. An intractable problem in this area is that of how to reserve the more onerous and expensive procedures for those deserving thorough investigation.

Chapter 22 sets out the criminal offences which may be committed in connection with an insolvency. The personal consequences for the individual insolvent of becoming bankrupt have already been explained[4] and the extent to which the bankrupt loses his property is explained in detail later.[5]

An evaluation of whether the consequences of bankruptcy provide a sufficient sanction to maintain public confidence in the system depends in part on the view taken of the extent to which being unable to pay is a culpable state. A tension between the feeling that being unable to pay one's debts is a state of affairs which should be punished and the recognition that the debtor has sometimes merely been unlucky has existed throughout the history of insolvency law. The latter view now prevails together with a recognition that some risk-taking is an inevitable aspect of a growing economy and that failure on occasions is a necessary concomitant. At the same time the system should not favour the debtor to such an extent that there is no incentive for debtors to meet their obligations. The Justice report suggested[6] that the current combination of automatic discharge from bankruptcy and the infrequency with which income payments orders[7] are sought amounts to a relaxed regime which "can only encourage debtors who started out as essentially honest people to repeat the process".

The existence of limited liability increases the potential for abuse of the system. Prevention of abuse of this privilege requires investigation into the conduct of those responsible for the insolvent company and the incorporation into the law of measures designed to deter them from allowing their companies to become insolvent. The provisions of the Company Directors Disqualification Act 1986, considered in Chapter 23, are designed to achieve this end; the measures relating to fraudulent

---

[4] See Chap. 15.4.
[5] See Chap. 27.
[6] *Insolvency Law: An Agenda for Reform* at para. 4.30.
[7] See Chap. 27.5 for income payment orders.

and wrongful trading[8] also impose a sanction on directors who allow a company to continue to incur obligations which it will be unable to meet. The Cork Committee recognised that there was particular concern about the prevalence of what are referred to as "phoenix companies". These arise where those who have been running their business through the medium of a company which has become insolvent buy the assets from the liquidator, often at a bargain price, and transfer them into a new company trading under a name which leads customers to think that they are still dealing with the same entity. The liabilities of the old company are not transferred: the "phoenix company" rises from the ashes of the insolvent company having shed its debts. The new company may well meet the same fate as the old and it has not been uncommon for the process to be repeated by the same people on a number of occasions. Section 216 of the Insolvency Act 1986, which is also explained in Chapter 23, is intended to prevent this happening.

[8] See Chap. 31.

CHAPTER 20

CONTROL OF THE INSOLVENCY SYSTEM

1. Introduction

The Cork Committee observed that "the success of any insolvency system is very largely dependent upon those who administer it"[1] and that "while the method of control over the administration of bankruptcy varies from country to country, in almost all bankruptcy systems creditors were originally given the primary responsibility for administering the process. In country after country, however, this had led to scandal and abuse, and exclusive control has been progressively removed from creditors and varying degrees of official control have been introduced as it has been increasingly accepted that the public interest is involved in the proper administration of the bankruptcy system".[2]

In England and Wales, creditors were given control of the system by the 1869 Bankruptcy Act[3] as a consequence of persuasive argument by the commercial community that, since the estates were being administered primarily for the benefit of the creditors, they were the persons best calculated to look after their own interests. The reality turned out to be very different and the overwhelming indifference of the vast majority of those owed small amounts or who stood to gain nothing from the bankruptcy meant that there was little control exercised. In many cases bankrupts and their advisers found it possible to take control of the administration of the bankruptcy in their own interests to the prejudice of the majority of creditors.

In consequence, official control was re-introduced by the Bankruptcy Act 1883 with the introduction of a public official to be known as the official receiver, under the control of the Board of Trade which had overall responsibility for bankruptcy law. The intention was that the official receiver would carry out an impartial and independent examination into the causes of each bankruptcy and the conduct of each bankrupt. The cost was to be met from a fee levied on each petition, a small

---

[1] para. 732.
[2] para. 702.
[3] See Chap. 5 on the history of insolvency law.

percentage on the assets collected and interest on amounts collected which would be paid into an account at the Bank of England. The official receiver's role was subsequently extended to compulsory liquidations. A Department of Trade and Industry consultation document published in July 1980 suggested that there should no longer be official involvement in personal insolvencies but this suggestion met with a hostile reaction from the insolvency profession and from the Cork Committee and was not pursued.

The Cork Committee was concerned about the lack of control over who could be appointed as liquidator in a voluntary liquidation or as receiver and manager to enforce a floating charge over the undertaking of a company. Whilst the appointment of trustees in bankruptcy and liquidators in compulsory liquidations was subject to control by the courts and the Department of Trade and Industry, anyone could be appointed as a voluntary liquidator or receiver. Evidence was presented to the Cork Committee of abusive practices such as the sale of the assets of the company to those previously connected with it at prices prejudicial to the creditors. It was also felt that directors of companies in voluntary liquidation were not being properly investigated. The Cork Report recommended subjecting all insolvency practitioners to proper regulation in order to maintain standards both of competence and of integrity and these recommendations were given effect in the Insolvency Act 1986. The introduction of regulation of insolvency practitioners was linked to a lessening of court involvement in certain areas of insolvency practice; it has been seen,[4] for example, that there is no need for a court to be actively involved in a company voluntary arrangement.

2. The Insolvency Service

Overall responsibility for the administration of insolvency law in England and Wales lies with the Department of Trade and Industry. This has been delegated to the Insolvency Service, which is an executive agency under the direction of the Inspector General of Insolvency. The Insolvency Service has a controlling and supervisory function with regard to all official receivers and insolvency practitioners. The Disqualification Unit within the Insolvency Service is responsible for pursuing applications to disqualify directors on the grounds of unfitness.[5] The Insolvency Service maintains registers of voluntary arrangements and

[4] In Chap. 10.3.
[5] See Chap. 23 below.

disqualification orders. It produces an annual report giving statistics for the various insolvency regimes.

3. Official Receivers.[6]

The official receiver is not a single person. The functions of the official receiver are carried out by a number of people appointed to the office of official receiver by the Secretary of State for Trade and Industry. Every person holding the office of official receiver is attached either to the High Court or to one or more specific county courts having an insolvency jurisdiction and will exercise the functions of the official receiver in relation to bankruptcies and liquidations falling within the jurisdiction of that court. The official receiver has the status of officer of the court in relation to which he exercises the functions of his office.[7]

As has been seen,[8] the official receiver will serve as trustee in bankruptcy or liquidator in compulsory liquidations where no private sector insolvency practitioner has been appointed; these will be insolvencies where the assets are insufficient to bear the cost of a private sector appointment. The official receiver also has an investigatory function to perform in relation to all bankruptcies and compulsory liquidations. The White Paper of 1984, which preceded the current insolvency legislation, envisaged that the official receivers should be able to concentrate strongly on their investigative duties. As Justice reported[9], the increased caseload of the Insolvency Service has been such that the resources available to undertake these investigatory functions have fallen, comparatively speaking, to a very low level. Consideration was given by the government in the mid–1990s to the privatisation of the role of official receiver and various tenders were considered but it was eventually decided that it would not be cost-effective to proceed.

4. Qualification of insolvency practitioners

a) Requirement of qualification

The Insolvency Act 1986 prohibits unqualified persons from acting as insolvency practitioners[10] and requires that holders of the office of

---

[6] See Pt XIV of the Insolvency Act.
[7] Insolvency Act 1986, s.400(2).
[8] In Chaps 15.3, 17.5.
[9] *Insolvency Law: An Agenda for Reform* (1994) para. 4.28.
[10] Insolvency Act 1986, s.389.

liquidator, administrator and administrative receiver be qualified insolvency practitioners.[11] The Act defines acting as an insolvency practitioner[12] in relation to a company as acting as a liquidator, provisional liquidator, administrator, administrative receiver or supervisor of a voluntary arrangement. In relation to an individual, a person acts as an insolvency practitioner by acting as a trustee in bankruptcy, interim receiver of property, a trustee under a deed of arrangement, administrator of the insolvent estate of a deceased individual or supervisor of an individual voluntary arrangement. Official Receivers do not act as insolvency practitioners for the purposes of requiring qualification. Any other person who acts as an insolvency practitioner at a time when not qualified to do so is liable to imprisonment, a fine or both.[13]

b) General prohibitions

Insolvency practitioners must be individuals; companies cannot be qualified to act as insolvency practitioners.[14] Undischarged bankrupts, persons subject to disqualification orders under the Companies Directors Disqualification Act 1986 and "patients" within the mental health legislation are all disqualified from acting as insolvency practitioners.

c) Authorisation

Qualification to act as an insolvency practitioner requires authorisation to act either by virtue of membership of a recognised professional body which has granted authorisation or by virtue of an authorisation granted in response to a direct application to the Department of Trade.[15] Seven professional bodies have been recognised as able to grant authorisation[16]; a member of any of these bodies may be licensed to act as an insolvency practitioner by complying with their rules. In 1996 there were a total of 1,810 authorised insolvency practitioners, nearly half of whom were authorised by the Institute of Chartered Accountants in England and Wales.

Both the recognised bodies and the Department of Trade must consider whether applicants are fit and proper persons to act as insolvency

---

[11] Insolvency Act 1986, s.230.
[12] *ibid.*, s.388.
[13] *ibid.*, s.389.
[14] *ibid.*, s.390(1).
[15] *ibid.*, s.390.
[16] *ibid.*, s.391, Insolvency Practitioners (Recognised Professional Bodies) Order 1986 (S.I. 1986 No. 1764). The recognised bodies are the Chartered Association of Certified Accountants, the Insolvency Practitioners Association, the Institute of Chartered Accountants in England and Wales (and the equivalent bodies in Ireland and Scotland), the Law Society and the Law Society of Scotland.

practitioners and meet educational, training and experience require-ments. The Insolvency Practitioners Regulations 1990[17] lay down requirements to be applied by the Department of Trade. The recognised bodies are required to have "acceptable" rules and the Regulations clearly provide a guideline as to what is acceptable. A body which departed markedly from the rules prescribed for the Department of Trade would be likely to find its status as a recognised body at risk.

Authorisation to act as an insolvency practitioner will only be given to those who have reached a certain educational standard, which will include examination on insolvency law, and have had a certain amount of practical experience. Matters specified in the Insolvency Practitioners Regulations 1990 as relevant to the question of whether an applicant is a fit and proper person to be an insolvency practitioner include the honesty, integrity and competence of the individual. Where the appli-cant has previously been an insolvency practitioner it will be relevant to consider whether he has been guilty of any contraventions of insolvency law, whether he has adequate systems of control and accounting records and whether he has allowed himself to get into a position of conflict of interest.

The issue of conflict of interest[18] has given rise to particular concern. It is clear that insolvency practitioners should be, and be seen to be, independent and not subject to any conflicts of interest in their admini-stration of the insolvent estate and investigation of the background to the insolvency. The Insolvency Rules contain express provisions enabling insolvency practitioners to resign on the ground of conflict of interest. There is considerable guidance provided by the code of conduct issued for practitioners licensed by the Secretary of State which emphasises the need for practitioners to avoid relationships and commit-ments which might affect, or appear to affect, their objectivity. If there is a conflict of interest the insolvency practitioner should refuse the appointment and if he might appear to have a conflict of interest he should disclose this to interested parties and allow them to decide whether or not he should act. It will usually be possible to accept an appointment following on from monitoring or advisory work carried out for bankers of a company but insolvency practitioners should not accept an appointment where they have previously held office in relation to a company as director, auditor or administrative receiver since they might subsequently find themselves in the position of having to investigate their previous actions. The case of *Re Corbenstoke Ltd (No. 2)*[19] was a

---

[17] S.I. 1990 No. 439.
[18] See generally Anderson, *Current Issues in Insolvency Law* (Clarke ed.), Chap. 1.
[19] (1989) 5 B.C.C. 767.

particularly striking example of a liquidator in a position of conflict of interest since the liquidator had been a director of the company being wound up, was a debtor of the company and was the trustee in bankruptcy of an individual with a claim against the company.[20]

One situation which could cause difficulty is that of the insolvency of a group of companies where it would be impractical in many cases to appoint more than one firm of insolvency practitioners. The Insolvent Partnerships Order 1994 expects that there will be a single practitioner where a partnership is being wound up and there are bankruptcy petitions against insolvent members but that the practitioner can apply for directions if a conflict arises. In *Re Esal (Commodities) Ltd*,[21] where a company in liquidation had members of the liquidator's firm as either liquidator or directors of several of its subsidiaries, Dillon L.J. remarked that the possible conflicts of interest "do not in practice give rise to any serious difficulty because they are well-known to the experienced insolvency practitioners". *Re P Turner (Wilsden) Ltd*[22] is an example of a case where the court decided that conflict of interest meant that separate liquidators were necessary; this case involved two companies in liquidation, only one of which was solvent, owned by the same two shareholders where there was a possibility that the solvent company had prospered by milking the insolvent company of its assets.

Authorisation will only be given for three years at a time and in order to renew the licence the insolvency practitioner will have to show that he has maintained his level of practical involvement by having been appointed as office-holder in at least one case or having acquired at least 500 hours of higher insolvency work experience in the previous three years.

Any person whose authorisation is withdrawn or refused by the Secretary of State may refer his case to the Insolvency Practitioners Tribunal (and, on appeal therefrom, to the High Court) under section 396 of the Insolvency Act 1986. Decisions of the recognised bodies are subject to judicial review by the High Court.

d) Insurance

Before a person is qualified to act as an insolvency practitioner, he must furnish security for the proper performance of his functions by depositing with the recognised body which authorised him, or with the Secretary of State, a bond issued by an insurance company by which it makes

---

[20] The court ordered his removal under Insolvency Act 1986, s.172(2): see Chap. 17(5)(e).
[21] (1988) 4 B.C.C. 475.
[22] [1987] B.C.L.C. 149.

itself jointly and severally liable with him for the proper performance of his duties.[23] The bond must be for a general sum of £250,000 and for additional specific sums in accordance with the prescribed limits applicable to particular cases in which he is to act. The amount of the required cover in relation to any specific appointment is calculated by reference to the value of the assets of the insolvent with a minimum of £5,000 and a maximum of £5,000,000.

5. Control of insolvency practitioners

a) Introduction

The conduct of insolvency practitioners is controlled partly by self-regulation involving monitoring by the authorising bodies[24], partly by the creditors in any particular insolvency and, ultimately, by the court.

b) Monitoring

Insolvency practitioners are required to keep records of prescribed information in respect of each insolvency in relation to which they act and to produce the record on request to the body which authorised them.[25] The Joint Insolvency Monitoring Unit (JIMU) came into being in 1994 to monitor insolvency practitioners as an agent for the larger recognised professional bodies in carrying out their obligations to monitor their appointees and report on the monitoring to the Insolvency Service. JIMU pursues a programme of random monitoring of licence-holders. It reported in 1995 that it found the main areas of breach fell into the areas of bonding, retaining Insolvency Service Act funds, late filing of Directors' disqualification returns, failing to hold annual meetings, sending receipts and payments accounts in late, taking remuneration without authority and keeping inadequate statutory records. The disciplinary response to breach varies with the gravity of such a breach but could lead to the withdrawal of a licence.

---

[23] Insolvency Act 1986, s.390. Insolvency Practitioners' Regulations 1990.
[24] A working party comprising members of the Insolvency Service and of the recognised professional bodies published, under the aegis of the DTI, a Consultative Document on Insolvency Practitioner Regulations in December 1997 which may lead to changes in the system of regulation.
[25] Insolvency Practitioners Regulations 1990, rr. 16, 17, Sched. 3.

c) Withdrawal of licence

Those aggrieved by the actions of an insolvency practitioner may put the renewal of his licence in jeopardy by complaining to the practitioner's professional body or to the Department of Trade. Withdrawal of authorisation during the currency of the licence may be effected by the Secretary of State[26] on the grounds either that the holder is no longer a fit and proper person or that he has failed to comply with the obligations imposed on insolvency practitioners or has furnished false, inaccurate or misleading information in purporting to comply with those obligations.

d) Creditors and creditors' committees

The creditors as a body are given certain powers by the legislation in relation to the conduct of the insolvency. The power of any particular creditor will be in proportion to the amount owed to him since this is how his voting rights at a meeting of the creditors will be calculated. A creditor will need to prove his debt before he is entitled to vote.

The creditors will usually determine the identity of the liquidator in a voluntary liquidation.[27] They may determine the identity of the liquidator in a court liquidation[28] and of the trustee in a bankruptcy[29] although this might require a sufficient percentage of them being willing to override the official receiver's decision not to summon a meeting of creditors to make an appointment. In each case, the creditors also have the power to remove the office-holder.[30] The creditors' meeting may refuse to release the liquidator from liability in which case he will need to apply to the Secretary of State for release from liability in relation to the insolvency. The creditors as a body may bring an administration to an end.[31] Any creditor owed a sufficient amount will be in a position to present a petition for compulsory liquidation in respect of a company in administrative receivership with a view to the liquidator taking steps to address any malpractice by the receiver.

As has been seen,[32] supervising committees may be established in liquidations and bankruptcies unless the official receiver is acting as

---

[26] Under Insolvency Act 1986, s.393(4). The rules of the recognised bodies contain similar provisions.

[27] See Chap. 16(3)(a).

[28] See Chap. 17(5)(b).

[29] See Chap. 15(3)(c).

[30] Insolvency Act 1986, ss298, 171(2)(b), 172(2).

[31] *ibid.*, s.18(2)(b).

[32] In Chaps 15.3 (creditors' committee in bankruptcy), 16.3 (liquidation committee in voluntary liquidation), 17.5 (liquidation committee in compulsory liquidation).

liquidator or trustee and in administrations and administrative receiverships. Any creditor other than a fully secured creditor will be eligible to be elected on to the committees. These are intended to monitor the conduct of insolvency practitioners and, to the extent that a liquidator or trustee in bankruptcy requires permission to exercise some powers, to exercise some control over the conduct of the insolvency.[33] They must be kept informed of the progress of the insolvency and may request information, although the insolvency practitioner may refuse to comply with the request where he considers it frivolous or unreasonable or that the cost of complying would be excessive or would not be covered by the assets. Where there is a committee, it will be responsible for deciding the remuneration of administrators, liquidators and trustees in bankruptcy.[34] Where there is no creditors' committee, its powers and functions will be usually be exercisable by the Secretary of State, acting through the official receiver.[35]

The major problem with creditor control of insolvency is that creditors are often not interested in becoming involved particularly if they are only owed relatively small sums or it is clear that there will be no assets left for the ordinary creditors. It has been argued that committees tend to be dominated by banks whose interests tend to be in a speedy resolution of the insolvency rather than the maximisation of assets for the benefit of all the creditors.

e) Court control over office-holders

The court has the power to remove liquidators,[36] trustees in bankruptcy,[37] administrative receivers,[38] administrators[39] and the supervisors

---

[33] For the powers of the liquidator, see Chaps 17.5(d) and 16.3(e). For the trustee in bankruptcy see Chap 15.3(e).

[34] Insolvency Rules 1986, r. 2.47 (administrator), r. 4.127 (liquidation), r. 6.138 (bankruptcy). If there is no committee, the remuneration is decided by the creditors as a body. If not fixed by the creditors, an administrator's fees will be fixed by the court and those of a liquidator or trustee will be in accordance with the official receiver's scale. A receiver's fees will be fixed by the debenture holder; the liquidator may apply under s.36 of the Insolvency Act 1986 for the court to adjust the remuneration.

[35] Insolvency Act 1986, s.141(5) (compulsory liquidation), Insolvency Act 1986, s.302 (bankruptcy).

[36] Insolvency Act 1986, s.172 in compulsory liquidation. Insolvency Act 1986, s.108 in voluntary liquidations.

[37] *ibid.*, s.298.

[38] *ibid.*, s.45. This is the only method of removing an administrative receiver; this is intended to prevent the placing of undue pressure by the debenture holder on the receiver to follow a particular course of action.

[39] *ibid.*, s.19(1).

of voluntary arrangements.[40] In *Re Keypak Homecare Ltd*,[41] an application to remove a voluntary liquidator, Millett J. held that an order for removal did not require that the liquidator had been guilty of personal misconduct; it was sufficient that he had failed to carry out his duties with sufficient vigour.

Any person who is "aggrieved"[42] by an act or decision of the liquidator or "dissatisfied" by the conduct of the trustee in bankruptcy may apply to the court which may confirm, reverse or modify an act or decision and make such order as it thinks just.[43] The term "aggrieved" previously applied to bankruptcy as well. In *Port v. Auger*[44], Harman J. refused to decide whether "dissatisfied" is wider than "aggrieved" but said "a person can only be dissatisfied if he can show that he has some substantial interest which has been adversely affected by whatever is complained of". The court will not readily interfere in the administration of an insolvency; in *Re a debtor (No. 400 of 1940)*[45] the court said that administration in bankruptcy would be impossible if the trustee must answer at every step for the exercise of his powers and discretions in the management and distribution of the property. The court will intervene only if the insolvency practitioner proposes to act illegally or in breach of his duties[46] or wholly unreasonably, or has already done so. In *Re Hans Place Ltd*[47] the court said that it would not interfere with the exercise of a discretionary power unless the insolvency practitioner has been guilty of fraud or bad faith or his decision was perverse. The Court of Appeal in *Re Edennote Ltd*[48] confirmed that, fraud and bad faith apart, the court will only interfere with the act of a liquidator if he had done something so utterly unreasonable and absurd that no reasonable person would have done it; Nourse L.J. went on to hold that a reason-

---

[40] Insolvency Act 1986, ss7(5), 263(5).

[41] [1987] B.C.L.C. 409.

[42] Nourse L.J. in *Re Edennote Ltd* [1996] 2 B.C.L.C. 389 said it was "neither necessary nor desirable to attempt a classification of those who may be aggrieved" but that it must include the unsecured creditors of an insolvent company.

[43] Insolvency Act 1986, s.168(5), s.112(1) in liquidations, Insolvency Act 1986, s.303(1) in bankruptcy. In a liquidation any creditor or contributory may apply to the court with respect to the exercise or proposed exercise of the liquidator's powers: Insolvency Act 1986, s.167(3).

[44] [1994] 3 All E.R. 200.

[45] [1949] 1 All E.R. 510.

[46] *e.g., Re Armstrong Whitworth Securities Co. Ltd* [1947] Ch. 673, a liquidator had admitted an inflated claim for proof and the court gave directions for the future distribution of the assets so as to correct the error.

[47] [1993] B.C.L.C. 768. Previous influential cases in this area include *Re Peters, ex p. Lloyd* (1882) 47 L.T. 64, *Re a debtor (No. 400 of 1940)* [1949] 1 All E.R. 510, *Leon v. York-o-matic* [1966] 3 All E.R. 272.

[48] [1996] 2 B.C.L.C. 389.

able liquidator was a properly advised liquidator and that since the liquidator in this case had failed to take advice[49] which would have caused him to act differently, his act[50] could be set aside.

It has already been seen[51] that creditors or members of the company who are aggrieved by the actions of an administrator may apply to the court under section 27 of the Insolvency Act 1986. Where an administrator or administrative receiver is in breach of duty, the appropriate course of action will be for the company to be put into liquidation and action taken under section 212 of the Insolvency Act 1986.[52] An action may be brought under section 212 of the Insolvency Act 1986 against a liquidator, administrator or administrative receiver of a company in liquidation for misapplication of property of the company or breach of fiduciary or other duty in relation to the company. The equivalent section in case of a trustee in bankruptcy is section 304 of the Insolvency Act 1986. In either case the application may be made by the official receiver, Secretary of State or creditor. In the case of a bankruptcy, an application may be brought by the bankrupt himself and, in the case of a liquidation, by a contributory. If the insolvency practitioner has been given his release, an application may only be brought with the leave of the court. The court may order the insolvency practitioner to restore or account for the property or to pay a sum by way of compensation.

In addition to the duties laid on the insolvency practitioner by the legislation, the practitioner will also be under common law duties of care and good faith to the company.[53] Liquidators in compulsory[54] windings up, trustees in bankruptcy and administrators are considered to be officers of the court and therefore subject to the rule in *ex p. James, Re Condon*[55] that an officer of the court must act honourably and may not, therefore, always be entitled to insist on his strict legal rights.

f) The need for an ombudsman?

The Justice report viewed the introduction of qualification requirements for insolvency practitioners as the "most spectacular" of the achievements of the 1986 legislation. They observed that, although there had

---

[49] Although rather oddly the Court then decided not to uphold Vinelott J.'s removal of the liquidator on the basis that he had acted honestly and on advice.
[50] Of selling a cause of action (see Chap. 32.3).
[51] In Chap. 10.4.
[52] See Chap. 31.3(a) on Insolvency Act 1986, s.212.
[53] *Pulsford v. Devenish* [1903] 2 Ch. 625, *Re Home and Colonial Insurance Co. Ltd* [1930] 1 Ch. 102, *Re Windsor Steam Coal Co. (1901) Ltd* [1929] 1 Ch. 151, *Re AMF International Ltd (No. 2)* [1996] 2 B.C.L.C. 9.
[54] But not voluntary.
[55] (1874) 9 Ch. App. 609. See Dawson [1996] J.B.L. 437.

been some lapses in the required standards of independence and objectivity, the situation was generally a great improvement on the previous unregulated position. They did however note that it was very difficult to challenge the conduct of an insolvency practitioner. They adverted to the Cork Committee proposal, which had not been accepted, that an Insolvency Ombudsman should be appointed and argued[56] that the need for such an appointment had increased.

6. Cost of the system

a) Insolvency practitioners' charges

Throughout the history of insolvency law there has been concern at the possibility of those involved in administering insolvent estates making an undue profit for themselves at the expense of the creditors. More generally, a recurring theme has been the need to balance the benefits to be derived from the insolvency system with the costs of obtaining them. For instance, the Justice report[57] remarked on the improvements to the system brought about by the licensing of insolvency practitioners but went on to observe that "these improvements have, however, been obtained at a price, in the shape of additional costs and expenses which have by and large fallen upon the insolvent estate to the ultimate financial detriment of the general body of creditors".

The level of insolvency practitioners' charges is the subject of considerable controversy. There has been adverse comment from a number of quarters both on the level of remuneration charged and on the extent of the expenses incurred by office-holders. The House of Commons social security select committee into the Maxwell affair concluded in July 1993 that the accountants and their legal advisers were on the whole too expensive, too slow and too unaccountable. Ferris J. commented unfavourably in July 1997[58] on the fact that all but £40,000 of the £1.67 personal estate of the late Robert Maxwell had been swallowed up in fees; the following day a judge in Luxembourg reduced by a million pounds the fees of nearly £3 million claimed by the liquidators of BCCI. Lightman J., commenting extra-judicially,[59] referred to the

---

[56] *Insolvency Law: An Agenda for Reform*, para. 5.19.
[57] *ibid.*
[58] *MGN plc v. Maxwell, The Times*, July 15, 1997. Ferris J. observed that "I cannot escape saying that I find [the charges] profoundly shocking . . . the receivership will have produced substantial rewards for the receivers and their lawyers and nothing at all for the creditors of the estate".
[59] [1996] J.B.L. 113. For the other side of the debate, see 11 I.L.&P. 161. For a more recent view, see 13 I.L.&P. 141.

perceived[60] unacceptably high level of costs as being a matter of concern and suggested that the main problem was a lack of monitoring in practice, particularly in relation to receiverships.

The fees charged by liquidators, trustees in bankruptcy and administrators are subject to agreement by the creditors, who also have the right to appeal against the level of the remuneration.[61] The fees will be fixed either as a percentage of the value of property dealt with or by reference to the time given by the insolvency practitioner and his staff in attending to the insolvency. The creditors will decide which of these two methods should be used and, if it is the former, the percentage to be applied.[62] The creditors should take into account the degree of complexity of the case, the extent to which the practitioner is subject to any exceptional responsibility, the effectiveness with which the duties appear to have been carried out and the value and the nature of the assets with which the practitioner has had to deal. In guidance to practitioners, the Society of Practitioners of Insolvency has suggested[63] that notification should be sent to creditors of their rights in relation to remuneration in order to avoid subsequent dissatisfaction.

In *MGN plc v. Maxwell*[64] Ferris J. made a number of general observations about the level of costs incurred by office-holders in managing insolvent estates. He said that there was a perception that insolvency practitioners and their lawyers were subject to little or ineffective control. If this were true, it should be addressed and, if it was not, there was a need for a clear exposition of the controls and procedures. The judge pointed out that office-holders were in a fiduciary position and had an obligation to account for the way in which they exercised their powers and dealt with the property under their control. Office-holders should therefore both consider whether they should incur expenditure out of the insolvent estate and be able to produce evidence that such consideration has taken place. This approach was supported by Lightman J., again speaking extra-judicially,[65] who suggested that the onus

---

[60] He observed that he was in no better position than the public to judge whether the costs were in fact excessive or justly earned.

[61] Insolvency Rules 1986, r. 2.47–50 (administrator), r. 4.127–131 (liquidation), r. 6.138–142 (bankruptcy).

[62] The latter is generally preferred by insolvency practitioners. Lightman J. in [1996] J.B.L. 113 remarked on the need to discount unproductive and valueless expenditure of time. See also *Re Tony Rowse NMC Ltd* [1996] 2 B.C.L.C. 225.

[63] Statement of Insolvency Practice 9.

[64] *The Times*, July 15, 1997.

[65] At the Institute of Advanced Legal Studies on December 11, 1997; see 19 Co. Lawyer 72.

should be very much on office-holders to show that they had considered carefully whether to incur costs, particularly in relation to litigation.[66]

b) Insolvency Services Account

The issue of the cost of maintaining the public interest aspect of insolvency law has been a central focus throughout the development of modern insolvency law. The bankruptcy reports of the Board of Trade in the latter half of the last century were noticeably concerned to show that the insolvency department of the Board operated economically in its supervision of bankruptcy law, presumably in response to the earlier arguments of the commercial community that official control introduced unnecessary expense. There is currently a feeling that the cost of the system falls too heavily on those creditors whose debtors have become insolvent rather than being borne by society as a whole. This is because of the requirement for the payment of funds realised in bankruptcies and liquidations to be paid into the Insolvency Services Account maintained by the Department of Trade and Industry at the Bank of England which does not pay a commercial rate of interest. The intention is that the amounts earned on this account should be used to fund the Insolvency Service: this deprives the ordinary creditors of funds which could be earned by placing the money in deposit accounts earning more interest. It is questionable whether the cost of the Service, in which there is general public interest, should be borne by the victims of specific insolvencies. Furthermore, the government has been making more than the amount necessary to fund the Insolvency Service. Justice pointed out that the Insolvency Service Annual Report 1992/93 disclosed that the government derived an income of £50.6 million from running the Insolvency Services Account and gained a surplus of £9 million after setting off the costs of running the Insolvency Service.

[66] See Chap. 32 for more detail on the funding of litigation. Amongst Lightman J.'s suggestions were that office-holders should consider mediation as an alternative to litigation, should attempt to sell any causes of action in the insolvent estate rather than pursue the litigation themselves, should limit the risk of costs by entering into contingency agreements so far as possible, should negotiate market rates of payment for advisers, should ensure thorough advice on the percentage chance of success before going ahead with litigation and should attempt to keep the costs of litigation down by co-operation with the other side.

CHAPTER 21

INVESTIGATION OF THE INSOLVENT

1. Introduction

The Cork Committee saw the investigative processes of insolvency law as the means by which the demands of commercial morality could be met; they said[1]:

> "Creditors and debtors alike must know that in the event of insolvency proceedings taking place there is a risk that an investigation, fully and competently carried out, will take place with a view to uncovering assets concealed from creditors, to ascertaining the validity of creditors' claims and to exposing the circumstances surrounding the debtor's failure. Anything less would, we believe, be unacceptable in a trading community such as our own and would be bound to lead to a lowering of business standards and an erosion of confidence in our insolvency law."

The current structure of investigation in bankruptcy and compulsory liquidation is based on that introduced by the Bankruptcy Act 1883 which was designed to ensure that an impartial and independent examination should be undertaken into the causes of each bankruptcy as well as into the conduct of each bankrupt. Powers to gather information[2] and obligations to take notice of criminal activity are provided in the case of all collective insolvency regimes, with the exception of individual and company voluntary arrangements, but the extent to which there is an obligation on anyone actively to investigate varies.

The aims of the investigatory provisions are to punish wrongdoing and to deter others from engaging in behaviour prejudicial to creditors as well as to assist in the discovery of the assets. The legislation provides the court with powers to assist the insolvency practitioner in discovering the true state of the insolvent's affairs. There is, however, a balance to be struck between the needs of the investigatory processes

---

[1] At para. 238.
[2] Given to liquidators, administrators and administrative receivers who are referred to collectively as "office-holders".

and the need to avoid oppressive and unreasonable behaviour on the part of the investigators; this is an issue which has given rise to a considerable amount of case law in recent years.

2. Extent of the obligation to investigate

a) Bankruptcy

The official receiver has a duty[3] to investigate the conduct and affairs of every bankrupt and, if he thinks fit, to make a report to the court. The exception is where a certificate for the summary administration of the bankrupt's estate is in force, in which case the official receiver will only carry out an investigation if he thinks fit.

b) Corporate insolvency

There are varying degrees of scrutiny into the conduct of those involved in a company which has become insolvent depending upon the insolvency regime to which it has become subject.

On a compulsory winding up, the official receiver has a duty[4] to investigate the causes of failure and the promotion, formation, business, dealings and affairs of the company and to make such report to the court as he thinks fit. Where the liquidator is someone other than the official receiver, the liquidator has an obligation to furnish the official receiver with such information, assistance and documents as the official receiver reasonably requires for the purposes of carrying out his investigatory powers. There is[5] an obligation on the liquidator to notify the official receiver where it appears that a criminal offence has been committed by any past or present officer or member of the company. The court may, on the application of a person interested in the winding up or of its own motion, direct the liquidator to refer the matter to the Director of Public Prosecutions.[6]

In the case of a voluntary liquidation there is no mandatory requirement of investigation. The liquidator will wish to investigate the whereabouts of assets which might be available for the creditors and may ask the court[7] to exercise all or any of the powers which it might exercise in a compulsory winding up, including those which assist with the

---

[3] Insolvency Act 1986, s.289.
[4] *ibid.*, s.132.
[5] *ibid.*, s.218(3).
[6] *ibid.*, s.218(1).
[7] *ibid.*, s.112.

investigatory process. There is[8] an obligation on the liquidator to notify the Director of Public Prosecutions where it appears that a criminal offence has been committed by any past or present officer or member of the company. The court may, on the application of any person interested in the winding up or of its own motion, direct the liquidator to make such a report.[9]

The directors of an insolvent company will, therefore, face a lesser degree of investigation if the company decides to go into voluntary liquidation rather than being put into compulsory liquidation by a creditor. Since the introduction of the requirement that a liquidator in a voluntary liquidation be a qualified insolvency practitioner, it is less likely that a court will feel the necessity to make a winding up order for compulsory liquidation in respect of a company already in voluntary liquidation in order to achieve an adequate investigation.

Creditors of companies in administrative receivership will be able to seek a compulsory winding up order where they feel that further investigation and punishment is required. Creditors of a company in administration will, if sufficient of them agree, be able to seek a discharge of the administration order and a winding up order to enable further investigation and punishment.

Section 7 of the Company Directors Disqualification Act 1986 places an obligation on office-holders in all forms of corporate insolvency to make a report to the Secretary of State where it appears that a disqualification order should be made under section 6 of that Act.[10]

3. Obligation on the insolvent to supply information

a) Bankruptcy

All bankrupts have an obligation to supply the official receiver with information. A person made bankrupt on his own petition will have submitted a statement of affairs[11] with the petition. A person made bankrupt on a creditor's petition is required,[12] unless released from the obligation by the official receiver, to provide a statement of affairs within 21 days of the bankruptcy order unless court or official receiver allows longer. In either case, the statement, verified by affidavit, must give details of the assets and liabilities of the bankrupt. The official

---

[8] Under Insolvency Act 1986, s.218.
[9] *ibid.*, s.218(6).
[10] See Chap. 23.
[11] Insolvency Act 1986, s.272 and Insolvency Rules 1986, rr. 6.41, 6.68. The statement will contain the particulars required by Form 6.28.
[12] Insolvency Act 1986, s.288 and Insolvency Rules 1986, rr. 6.58–6.63.

receiver may employ someone at the expense of the estate to assist in preparing the information.

The bankrupt has a duty[13] to hand over to the official receiver all[14] books, papers and other records of which he has possession or control and which relate to his estate and affairs. The bankrupt also has a duty to give the official receiver such information as is reasonably requested.[15] The official receiver can require that accounts relating to three years prior to the bankruptcy be submitted and the court can order submission of accounts for earlier years.[16] The court may, on the application of the official receiver or the trustee in bankruptcy, order that the bankrupt's mail be re-directed for up to three months.[17]

In addition to the provision of documentary information, the bankrupt may have to answer questions in person. The bankrupt may be required to attend on the official receiver at such times as the official receiver may reasonably require in order to assist with the provision of information.[18]

Section 333 of the Insolvency Act 1986 also provides that the bankrupt shall give to the trustee such information as to his affairs, attend on the trustee at such times, and do all such other things as the trustee may reasonably require. In *Morris v. Murjani*,[19] the Court of Appeal held that the provision gave the court jurisdiction to issue an injunction preventing the bankrupt from leaving the country since any departure might deprive the trustee of information to which he was entitled. The trustee in bankruptcy, where not the official receiver, has an obligation[20] to furnish the official receiver with such information, assistance and documents as the official receiver may reasonably require.

b) Corporate insolvency

Where the court has made a winding up order or appointed a provisional liquidator, the official receiver may require some or all of the persons specified to provide him with a statement in the prescribed form as to the affairs of the company.[21] This must be done within 21 days unless the official receiver extends the time available. Those who may be asked

---

[13] Insolvency Act 1986, s.291.
[14] Including any which would be privileged from disclosure in any proceedings.
[15] Insolvency Act 1986, s.291(4).
[16] Insolvency Rules 1986, rr. 6.64–65, rr. 6.69–71.
[17] Insolvency Act 1986, s.371.
[18] *ibid.*, s.291(4).
[19] (1996) B.C.C. 278.
[20] Insolvency Act 1986, s.305.
[21] *ibid.*, s.131 and Insolvency Rules 1986, rr. 4.32–4.38 deal generally with the statement of affairs. Insolvency Act 1986, s.131(2) sets out the required contents.

to submit the statement are those who are or have been officers of the company (or were officers or employees of a company which was an officer of the insolvent company in the year before liquidation); those who have taken part in the formation of the company during the year before the liquidation; and those who are in the company's employment, or have been within the year before the liquidation, and whom the official receiver thinks can give the information required. If any of these people fail without reasonable excuse to comply with the request they will be liable to a fine and, for continued contravention, a daily default fine.

In the case of a voluntary liquidation, a statement of affairs will have to be presented to the creditors[22] as part of the process of going into liquidation.

Where an administration order has been made, the administrator is under an obligation[23] to require a statement of affairs in the manner which would be required if the company had gone into compulsory liquidation.[24] There is a similar obligation placed on an administrative receiver.[25]

4. Court assistance in investigation

a) Bankruptcy

Section 366 of the Insolvency Act 1986 gives the court various powers with which to support the investigation of the bankrupt. The court may on application by the official receiver or the trustee in bankruptcy summon before it the bankrupt, the bankrupt's spouse and anyone else thought to be in possession of property comprised in the bankrupt's estate or to be indebted to the bankrupt or otherwise able to give information. Anyone who fails to appear without reasonable excuse or who appears likely to abscond to avoid appearing may be arrested in order that they may be brought before the court. These are essentially private proceedings and the court may exclude others from the hearing; those summoned to appear may be examined on oath about the bankrupt and his dealings, affairs and property.[26]

---

[22] Insolvency Act 1986, s.99.
[23] *ibid.*, s.22 and Insolvency Rules 1986, rr. 2.11 to 2.16.
[24] See above.
[25] Insolvency Act 1986, s.47 and Insolvency Rules 1986, rr. 3.3–3.7.
[26] *ibid.*, s.367(4).

Section 366 of the Insolvency Act 1986 also gives the court the power to request those whom it can summon before it[27] to provide evidence on affidavit. They may also be asked to produce any documents in their possession or control which relate to the bankrupt or his dealings, affairs or property and, if they fail to do so, the court may issue a warrant authorising seizure of the documents. Inland Revenue officials may also be requested[28] by the court to produce documents submitted by the bankrupt, assessments made by the Inland Revenue in relation to the bankrupt and any correspondence between the Inland Revenue and the bankrupt.

b) Corporate insolvency[29]

Section 234 of the Insolvency Act 1986 allows the court to require anyone with possession of or control over tangible[30] property, books, papers or records, to which the company appears to be entitled, to hand them over to the office-holder.

Section 235 of the Insolvency Act 1986 imposes an obligation on specified persons to give to the office-holder such information as may reasonably be required and to attend for interview at such times as may reasonably be required. The specified persons are those who are or who have been officers of the company; those who have taken part in the formation of the company at any time within a year before the insolvency; those who are employed by the company, or were employed in the year before the insolvency, and whom the office-holder thinks capable of giving information; those who are, or were within the year before the insolvency, officers or employees of a company which is, or was within that year, an officer of the insolvent company; and, in the case of a company being wound up by the court, anyone who has acted as administrator, administrative receiver or liquidator of the company.

Section 235 of the Insolvency Act 1986 enables information to be obtained on a quick and informal basis which nonetheless overrides any duty of confidentiality. The office-holder will often proceed on the basis that any information obtained will only be used for the purpose of

---

[27] Other than the bankrupt and bankrupt's spouse or former spouse who need not be included in the section since the official receiver already has adequate powers to obtain information and documents from them.

[28] Insolvency Act 1986, s.369.

[29] See Mitchell 13 I.L.&P. 66, 118.

[30] See *Welsh Development Agency v. Export Finance* [1992] B.C.C. 270.

administration of the insolvency.[31] Failure to comply with section 235 without reasonable excuse is a criminal offence leading to a fine and, for continued contravention, to a daily default fine.[32] The office-holder may enforce the obligations contained in section 235 by application to the court.[33] The Court of Appeal has held[34] that such an application would entitle the office-holder to seek interlocutory relief such as an *Anton Pillar* or *Mareva* injunction. Alternatively, failure to comply with obligations under section 235 of the Insolvency Act 1986 may lead to a successful application under section 236 of the Insolvency Act 1986 for a formal examination.

Under section 236 of the Insolvency Act 1986 the court may, on the application of the office-holder[35] summon specified persons before it to be examined on oath or order them to submit an affidavit to the court, in either case as to their dealings with the company. They may also be required to produce any books, papers or other records in their possession or under their control relating to the company and its affairs[36]. Those who are subject to this section[37] are the officers of the company, those known or suspected to have in their possession any property of the company or supposed to be indebted to the company and those whom the court thinks capable of giving information concerning the promotion, formation, business, dealings, affairs or property of the company.[38] The court may order the arrest of those who fail to appear without reasonable excuse or appear likely to abscond. The court may also order the seizure of books, papers, records, money or goods in their possession. An examination under section 236 of the Insolvency Act 1986 takes place before a registrar or judge and both the office-holder and the respondent are entitled to be represented. The procedure can be lengthy and expensive. Examinees are entitled to be given advance notice of the topics of questioning.[39] Evidence obtained under this procedure is not

---

[31] See Mitchell, above.

[32] Insolvency Act 1986, s.235(5).

[33] See Insolvency Rules 1986, r. 7.20; *Re Wallace Smith Trust Company Ltd* [1992] B.C.C. 707.

[34] *Morris v. Murjani* [1996] 1 W.L.R. 848.

[35] Not of a creditor: *Re James McHale Automobiles Ltd* [1997] 1 B.C.L.C. 273.

[36] They may not be asked to produce other documents: *Re Mid East Trading* [1998] 1 All E.R. 577, CA.

[37] A wider category of people than those subject to the obligations contained in section 235.

[38] Including inspectors appointed by the Secretary of State to investigate the company: *Soden v. Burns* [1996] 3 All E.R. 967, in which it was held that section 236 binds the Crown.

[39] *Re Norton Warburg Holdings* (1983) 1 B.C.C. 98, 907.

available to anyone other than the office-holder or other persons who could have applied for an order under section 236.[40]

The House of Lords in *Re British & Commonwealth (Nos 1 and 2)*[41] described the section 236 procedure as "an extraordinary and secret mode of obtaining information necessary for the proper conduct of the winding up" and held that, in deciding whether or not to make an order, the court had to balance the reasonable requirements of the office-holder in the carrying out of his functions with the need to avoid making an order which worked wholly unreasonably, unnecessarily or oppressively on the person concerned. It was not necessarily unreasonable to make the order simply because it was inconvenient to the addressee of the application or caused him a lot of work or might make him vulnerable to future claims or was addressed to a person who was not an officer or an employee or contractor of the company which was in insolvency.[42] Earlier guidance had also been provided by the Court of Appeal in *Cloverbay v. BCCI*[43] in which it was indicated that it would be harder to obtain an order against a third party than against an officer or former officer of the company. The production of documents was more likely to be ordered than oral examination. The question of whether or not the office-holder had reached a firm decision to sue the examinee was merely a factor to be taken into account. Vinelott J. reached a similar conclusion in *Re Arrows Ltd (No. 2)*[44] in which a criminal charge had actually been preferred but where the criminal proceedings lay sufficiently far in the future for a section 236 examination not to be oppressive[45].

Evans-Lombe J. in *Re Mid East Trading*[46] said that an application under section 236 had to pass through two stages. In the first stage, the office-holders had to satisfy the court that they reasonably required the information for the purpose of carrying out their task and must raise a prima facie case that the respondent is able to provide the information.

---

[40] Insolvency Rules 1986, r. 9.5(4) and see section 6 of this Chapter. In *Re Mid East Trading* [1997] 3 All E.R. 481 Evans-Lombe J. observed that the results of the inquiry are confidential to the court and may not be used outside the winding up proceedings without the court's leave.

[41] [1993] A.C. 426.

[42] Lightman J. in *Re Galileo Group Ltd*, [1998] 1 All E.R. 545 refused to make an order for disclosure in circumstances where he held that the liquidator had an insufficient need for the document in question to counterbalance the difficulty and potential oppression which would be involved in complying with the order.

[43] [1991] Ch. 90.

[44] [1992] B.C.L.C. 1176.

[45] See *England v. Purves*, *The Times*, January 29, 1998 for a discussion of the different approach in Australia.

[46] [1997] 3 All E.R. 481, approved on appeal: [1998] 1 All E.R. 577.

Secondly, the court has to balance the requirements of the office-holder against the burden that the inquiry will impose on the respondent.

5. Public examination

a) Bankruptcy

The public examination under section 290 of the Insolvency Act 1986 is a more draconian exercise than a court hearing under section 366. Public examination was first introduced by section 19 of the Bankruptcy Act 1869 which provided "the bankrupt . . . shall produce a statement of his affairs to the first meeting of creditors and shall be publicly examined thereon on a day to be named by the court, and subject to such adjourned public examination as the court may direct". This was re-enacted in the 1883 Act and carried into the 1914 Act with amendments which made it clear that the bankrupt could be examined as to "his conduct, dealings and property". A bankrupt was until 1976 compelled to undergo a public examination into the circumstances surrounding the bankruptcy before he could obtain his discharge; the requirement of public examination was probably one factor leading to a large number of bankrupts never seeking their discharge. The public examination is no longer compulsory and now requires an order of the court. Application for such an examination must come from the official receiver but if half in value of the creditors request it, an application must be made.

Questions may be asked by the official receiver, the trustee in bankruptcy and creditors who have tendered proof of debts. The bankrupt must answer on oath all questions which the court allows to be put and may not refuse to answer questions on the grounds of self-incrimination but if criminal proceedings have been commenced and the court thinks the examination may prejudice a fair trial, the examination may be adjourned. A written record of evidence may be used as evidence against the bankrupt in any proceedings.

The Cork Report considered[47] that a public examination was intended to serve three principal purposes. First, it would form the basis of reports which the official receiver might have to submit to the Department of Trade and Industry concerning the affairs of the bankrupt. Secondly, it would provide an opportunity to obtain material information for the administration of the estate which could not as well be obtained privately. Thirdly, it would give publicity, for the information

---

[47] At para. 655.

of creditors and the community at large, to the salient facts and unusual features connected with the failure.

Failure by the bankrupt without reasonable excuse to comply with any of the obligations outlined above will amount to contempt of court and the bankrupt will be liable to be punished accordingly.

b) Public examination in the case of a liquidation

Where a company is in compulsory liquidation the official receiver may at any time before the dissolution of the company apply to the court under section 133 of the Insolvency Act 1986 for a public examination.[48] There is no longer any need for the official receiver to allege fraud to justify the holding of a public examination.[49] The official receiver must make such a request, unless the court orders otherwise, where one-half in value of the company's creditors or three-quarters in value of the company's contributories so request. Those liable to public examination are those who are or have been officers of the company or have acted as liquidator, administrator, receiver or manager in relation to it or have otherwise been concerned, or taken part, in the promotion, formation or management of the company. They may be questioned on oath by the official receiver, liquidator, creditors and contributories as to the promotion, formation or management of the company or as to the conduct of its business and affairs or their conduct or dealings in relation to the company. The written record of the answers may be used as evidence in any other proceedings. If criminal proceedings have been instituted against the examinee, the court may adjourn the hearing if it thinks that continuance would prejudice a fair criminal trial. The court may order the arrest of anyone who fails to attend a public examination or looks likely to abscond in order to avoid it and may also order the seizure of books, papers, records, money or goods in that person's possession.[50]

6. The right to silence?

One of the basic freedoms secured by English law is that (subject to any statutory provisions to the contrary) no one can be forced to answer

---

[48] Insolvency Rules 1986, rr. 4.211 to 4.217 relate to public examination of company officers and others.
[49] The position in relation to bankruptcies and liquidations is now the same in that public examination is not compulsory for either and can be requested in the same circumstances for both.
[50] Insolvency Act 1986, s.133.

questions or produce documents which may incriminate him in subsequent criminal proceedings. Lord Browne-Wilkinson explained in *Re Arrows (No. 4)*[51] that the principle has evolved from the abhorrence felt for the procedures of the Star Chamber under which the prisoner was forced, by the use of torture, to answer self-incriminating questions on the basis of which he was subsequently convicted. This is a principle observed by all common law countries and is one of the basic rights protected by the European Convention on Human Rights.[52] Balancing this freedom with the need in civil proceedings to discover what has happened to property obtained by fraud has proved problematic. In some areas the problem has been addressed by removing the privilege in civil proceedings but then providing partial protection to the witness against the use in subsequent criminal proceedings of the self-incriminating answers.

There has been considerable debate in recent years as to the extent to which those involved in an insolvency are entitled to refuse to answer questions on the grounds of self-incrimination.[53] The entire purpose of an examination under section 236 or 366 of the Insolvency Act 1986 would be likely to be frustrated if witnesses were able to rely on the privilege against self-incrimination since the examination frequently happens because there is suspicion of fraud. It had been thought that a person examined under these provisions could refuse to answer self-incriminatory questions but in *Re Bishopsgate Investment Management Ltd*[54] the Court of Appeal held that the statutory provisions of the Insolvency Act impliedly overrode the privilege against self-incrimination.[55]

The extent to which information obtained by office-holders should be available to the prosecuting authorities was the issue before the House of Lords in *Re Arrows (No. 4)*[56] in which it had to be decided whether the Serious Fraud Office should have access to transcripts of the examination, under section 236, of a person "N" who had been involved in running a company which had become insolvent. The Serious Fraud Office had acted under powers conferred by section 2(3) of the Criminal

[51] [1995] 2 A.C. 75.
[52] See *Saunders v. United Kingdom* (1997) 23 E.H.R.R. 313 in which the European Court of Justice held that the Convention was breached by the use in a trial for theft and false accounting by the prosecution of statements given by the defendant under legal compulsion to inspectors appointed under the companies legislation.
[53] Fletcher [1992] J.B.L. 442 and [1994] J.B.L. 282, McCormack [1993] J.B.L. 425, Paulden 57 M.L.R. 280.
[54] [1993] Ch. 1.
[55] The same position was reached in relation to inspections under s.432 of the Companies Act 1985 by *Re London United Investments plc* [1992] B.C.C. 202.
[56] [1995] A.C. 75.

Justice Act 1987 in requiring the liquidators to produce the transcripts of the examination with a view to using them as evidence in criminal proceedings against N. The House of Lords was considering an appeal against the Court of Appeal's reversal of Vinelott J.'s decision that the Serious Fraud Office should only be allowed access if they gave undertakings not to use the transcripts in evidence against N save in the circumstances specified in section 2(8) of the Criminal Justice Act 1987. Section 2(8) of the Criminal Justice Act 1987 limits the circumstances in which the Serious Fraud Office may use statements obtained under the powers given to it which impliedly override the privilege against self-incrimination.[57] The protection afforded by section 2(8) does not apply to documents obtained under section 2(3) and there is no other provision in the Criminal Justice Act restricting the use that may be made by the Serious Fraud Office of documents obtained by use of a section 2(3) notice. The effect of this, on the face of it, is that the Serious Fraud Office can use self-incriminating answers given in the course of a section 236 examination which section 2(8) would prevent them from using if the answers had been given to the Serious Fraud Office itself under section 2(2).

Lord Browne-Wilkinson said that a person examined under section 236 can be compelled to give self-incriminatory answers but that a record of his answers is not available to outsiders without an order of the court under rule 9.5(4) of the Insolvency Rules 1986. He then proceeded to consider whether the court should have made such an order in this case.

Counsel for N submitted that the judge had a discretion whether or not to order the handing over of the transcripts on three different grounds: a private law right to confidentiality, public interest immunity (on the basis of the public interest in encouraging the free and speedy flow of essential information to liquidators and of ensuring that information extracted under statutory powers should be used only for the purpose for which the power is provided) and rule 9.5(4) of the Insolvency Rules. The first argument failed on the basis of the wording of the Criminal Justice Act apart from any other consideration. The second argument was also rejected although the *obiter* observation was made that in the case of information obtained under section 235 of the Insolvency Act 1986 there was a much greater public interest in ensuring the free flow of such informally obtained information. Given that liquidators have a wide range of duties to report suspected dishonest conduct, it was not possible for them to give an assurance to a person examined under section 236 that his answers would remain confidential;

[57] *ex p. Smith* [1993] A.C. 1.

there could not therefore be any argument of public interest immunity on the grounds of preserving confidentiality or in giving an assurance to witnesses that their answers would be kept confidential. It was held that the Court of Appeal had been wrong to hold that Rule 9.5(4) gave the court no discretion to withhold the transcripts: "the extraction of private and confidential information under compulsion from a witness otherwise than in the course of *inter partes* litigation is an exorbitant power. It is right that such information should not be generally available but should be used only for the purposes for which the power was conferred". However, it was not for the Companies Court judge to exercise any discretion so as to prevent the prosecuting authorities from using the transcripts.[58] The judge should have left the matter to be decided by the judge at the criminal trial as in the *Barlow Clowes*[59] case. The judge at the criminal trial would know all the facts both as to the means whereby the documents were obtained and their significance or impact in the criminal proceedings and would have a discretion under section 78(1) of the Police and Criminal Evidence Act to refuse to allow the prosecution to rely on the transcripts if admission would "have such an adverse effect on the fairness of the proceedings that the court ought not to admit it". Lord Browne-Wilkinson expressed the view that the failure of the Criminal Justice Act to extend the section 2(8) protection to section 2(2) was an unexplained anomaly which the criminal trial judge would be entitled to take into consideration.

Soden v. Burns[60] was something of a mirror image of *Re Arrows Ltd (No. 4)* in that the office-holders were seeking disclosure of transcripts of evidence given to inspectors appointed under the companies legislation to investigate the affairs of the company. Robert Walker J. held that the transcripts of evidence should be disclosed but only after prior notification to the witnesses and subject to any application by any of them to set aside the order.

---

[58] See *Rank Film Distributors Ltd v. Video Information Centre* [1982] A.C. 380.
[59] [1992] Ch. 208 in which Millett J. ordered the office-holders to apply to the Crown Court to set aside on grounds of public interest immunity a witness order that transcripts of section 235 interviews be produced. The criminal court judge nonetheless ordered the disclosure: *R. v. Clowes* [1992] B.C.L.C. 1158.
[60] [1996] 3 All E.R. 967.

CHAPTER 22

CRIMINAL OFFENCES

1. Introduction

Insolvency is not itself a crime but some conduct which would not normally be criminal will become so in the context of an insolvency. The investigations described in the previous chapter may reveal the commission of such offences; failure to co-operate with the investigation will itself constitute an offence. The existence of the offences will only assist in the maintenance of public confidence if they are perceived as material deterrents to malpractice. The Cork Committee observed[1] that "we cannot stress too strongly our view that bankruptcy offences are serious matters, and need to be prosecuted more frequently, and with greater vigour, than is the case at present".

The offences contained in the Insolvency Act 1986 fall into two broad groups: conduct relating to acts done before the commencement of the insolvency which becomes criminal on the advent of insolvency and conduct relating to acts done after the commencement of the insolvency. It is frequently the case that those who have been involved in criminal activity in relation to an insolvency are charged with offences under the Theft Acts rather than under the insolvency legislation. The relevant offences are likely to be obtaining property by deception,[2] obtaining a pecuniary advantage by deception,[3] false accounting,[4] dishonestly obtaining services by deception[5] and evasion of liability by deception.[6] Penalties under the Theft Acts may be greater than under the insolvency legislation.

In 1996, the official receivers submitted 1,132 reports regarding possible criminal offences and assisted the police or other investigatory authorities in a further 295 criminal investigations. Convictions were obtained in 1996 in 243 cases in which official receivers had submitted

---

[1] At para 1901.
[2] Theft Act 1968, s.15.
[3] *ibid.*, s.16.
[4] *ibid.*, s.17.
[5] *ibid.*, s.1.
[6] *ibid.*, s.2.

reports which resulted in 260 people being convicted of 380 offences. In addition there were 117 cases where the official receiver had assisted the police and others which resulted in 127 persons being convicted. Warning letters were issued to 404 individuals in circumstances where there was evidence of an offence having been committed but where it was considered that proceeding with a prosecution would not be in the public interest.[7]

2. Bankruptcy offences

a) General

Someone who is made bankrupt becomes vulnerable to the criminal offences set out in sections 350 to 362 to the Insolvency Act 1986. The offences are applicable even where the bankruptcy order has been annulled but no proceedings will be instituted after an annulment.[8] Conduct by the bankrupt after he has been discharged will not lead to liability under these provisions.[9] The offences are all subject to the defence of innocent intention[10] which requires the bankrupt to establish that he had no intent to defraud or conceal the state of his affairs. It is not a defence that anything relied on by the prosecution as constituting criminal activity took place abroad.[11] An undischarged bankrupt will also commit a criminal offence[12] by acting in the management of a company.

b) Non-disclosure

A bankrupt will be guilty of an offence under section 353 Insolvency Act 1986 if he does not to the best of his knowledge and belief disclose all the property comprised in his estate[13] to the official receiver or the trustee or does not inform the official receiver or the trustee of any disposal of any property (other than a disposal in the ordinary course of business or by way of payment of the ordinary expenses of the bankrupt

---

[7] Statistics throughout this Chap. are from the Insolvency Service Annual Report for 1996. The 1995 Report contains very similar figures for that year.

[8] Insolvency Act 1986, s.350(2).

[9] *ibid.*, s.350(3).

[10] *ibid.*, s.352.

[11] *ibid.*, s.350(4).

[12] Under Company Directors Disqualification Act 1986, s.11, 48 convictions were obtained under this section in 1996 as a result of official receivers' reports.

[13] As defined in Insolvency Act 1986, s.351(a).

or his family) which would otherwise have fallen into the estate. There were 22 convictions under this section in 1996.[14]

c) Concealment of property

Under section 354 of the Insolvency Act 1986, the bankrupt is guilty of an offence if he does not deliver up any property in his possession which the law requires him to deliver up to the official receiver or trustee. It is also an offence to conceal any debt due to or from him or to conceal property exceeding £500 in value which he is required to deliver up to the official receiver or trustee; conduct in the period of 12 months before the presentation of the petition and between the petition and order can also form the basis of this offence. The bankrupt will also be guilty of an offence if he removes, or removed between petition and order, property exceeding £500 which should have been handed over to the official receiver or trustee. The final offence under this section is that of failing, without reasonable excuse, to account for or explain when so required by the official receiver or the court, the loss of any substantial part of his property in the 12 months before the presentation of the petition or between the petition and the order. There were 35 convictions under section 354 of the Insolvency Act 1986 in 1996.

d) Concealment or falsification of books and papers

Section 355 of the Insolvency Act 1986 provides that a bankrupt will be guilty of an offence if he does not deliver up possession to the official receiver or the trustee all books, papers and other records of which he has possession or control and which relate to his estate or his affairs. It will also be an offence to prevent the production of such documents once a petition for bankruptcy has been presented. It will be an offence where, at any time after the 12 months before the petition, the bankrupt has concealed, disposed of, destroyed, altered, mutilated or falsified such documents (or has permitted such conduct) or has made, caused or permitted the making of any false entries in such documents. There were four convictions under this provision in 1996.

e) False statements

The bankrupt will be guilty of any offence under section 356 of the Insolvency Act 1986 if he makes or has made any material omission in

---

[14] The information on numbers of convictions obtained in 1996 throughout the Chap. relates to convictions obtained as a result of the official receiver's report.

any statement made under the bankruptcy provisions of the Insolvency Act 1986 relating to his affairs. It will also be an offence for a bankrupt to fail to inform the trustee that he thinks a false debt has been proved in the bankruptcy or to attempt to account for any part of his property by fictitious losses or expenses. Section 356 of the Insolvency Act 1986 also provides that it will be an offence to attempt to account for his property by fictitious losses or expenses at a meeting of his creditors from the 12 months before the petition or, at any time, to have been guilty of fraud in an attempt to obtain the consent of creditors to an agreement with reference to his affairs. There were 22 convictions under this provision in 1996.

f) Fraudulent disposal of property

A bankrupt is guilty of an offence under section 357 of the Insolvency Act 1986 if he causes to be made any gift or transfer of, or charge over his property in the five years leading up to the bankruptcy. It is also an offence for the bankrupt to conceal or remove any part of his property after, or within two months before, the date on which a judgment or order for the payment of money has been obtained against him, being a judgment or order not satisfied before the commencement of the bankruptcy. There were 10 convictions under this provision in 1996. In *R. v. Mungro*[15] a custodial sentence was imposed on a bankrupt of previously unblemished character who had failed to declare the receipt of a sum of money. Ognall J. said that the conduct of those who sought to obtain their discharge and at the same time concealed assets attacked the whole basis on which the bankruptcy legislation was founded.

g) Absconding

Absconding or preparing to abscond from England and Wales at any time after the date six months before presentation of the petition for bankruptcy with property to the value of more than £500 which he is required to deliver up is an offence under section 358 of the Insolvency Act 1986. There was one conviction under this section in 1996.

h) Fraudulent dealing with property obtained on credit

Disposing of (including pawning), otherwise than in the ordinary course of business, property which was acquired on credit and has not yet been paid for will be an offence from a year prior to the petition under

---

[15] *The Times*, July 3, 1997.

section 359 of the Insolvency Act 1986 . This offence is also committed by anyone who acquires, otherwise than in the ordinary course of the business of the bankrupt, property from the bankrupt knowing or believing that the bankrupt owed money in respect of the property which he did not intend, or was unlikely to be able, to pay. In determining for this section whether a transaction is in the ordinary course of the business of the bankrupt, it will be relevant to consider the price paid to the bankrupt for the property. There do not appear to have been any convictions for this in 1996.

i) Obtaining credit or engaging in business

The bankrupt is guilty of an offence under section 360 of the Insolvency Act 1986 if either alone or jointly with any other person, he obtains credit of more than £250 without telling the creditor that he is an undischarged bankrupt. Obtaining credit involves the receipt of goods under a hire-purchase or conditional sale agreement and the payment in advance for goods or services to be provided by the bankrupt. It is also an offence under this section for the bankrupt to engage directly or indirectly in a business under a name other than that in which he was adjudged bankrupt without disclosing to everyone which whom he enters into any transaction the name under which he was made bankrupt. There were 59 convictions under this provision in 1996.

j) Failure to keep proper accounts of business

Where the unsecured liabilities of the bankrupt at the commencement of the bankruptcy exceed £20,000, it will be an offence under section 361 of the Insolvency Act 1986 not to have kept proper accounts, as defined in the section, of any business run for any of the two years before the petition unless the omission was honest and excusable in the circumstances. Those who run their businesses through a limited liability company have an obligation to keep proper accounts whether or not they become insolvent; those who do not will only fall under criminal liability for not doing so if they become bankrupt. Failing to keep proper accounting records will, of course, make it far more likely that a business will get into financial difficulties. There were 31 convictions under this provision in 1996.

k) Gambling

Materially contributing to or increasing the extent of the insolvency by gambling or rash and hazardous speculations during the two years prior to the presentation of the petition will be an offence under section 362 of the Insolvency Act 1986. In determining for the purposes of the section whether any speculations were rash or hazardous, the financial position of the bankrupt at the time when he entered them is to be taken into consideration. There were 13 convictions under this provision in 1996.

3. Liquidation offences

a) General

Sections 206 to 211 of the Insolvency Act 1986 set out a series of offences which may be committed by the officers of the company and, in some cases, others; many, but not all, of the offences may be committed by shadow directors. In addition to these offences and the Theft Act offences[16] mentioned above, it should also be noted that, under section 458 of the Companies Act 1985, any person knowingly a party to the carrying on of the business with intent to defraud creditors of the company or creditors of any other person or for any fraudulent purpose will be guilty of a criminal offence.[17] There is also an argument that the wrongful trading[18] and disqualification of directors[19] provisions are quasi-criminal in effect.[20]

b) Fraud in anticipation of winding up

Under section 206 of the Insolvency Act 1986, any past or present officer (including a shadow director) will have committed an offence if, within the 12 months leading up to the winding up or after the commencement of the winding up, he has done any of the following:

  i) concealed any part of the company's property to the value of £500 or more, or concealed any debt due to or from the company;

  ii) fraudulently removed any part of the company's property to the value of £500 or more;

---

[16] 44 convictions were obtained under the Theft Acts in consequence of reports by the official receiver in 1996.

[17] Civil liability for fraudulent trading is considered in Chap. 31.4 below.

[18] See Chap. 31.5 below.

[19] See Chap. 23.2 below.

[20] See, *e.g.*, *Dine* [1994] J.B.L. 325. Breach of a disqualification order is a criminal offence: 5 such convictions were obtained in 1996.

iii) concealed, destroyed, mutilated or falsified any book or paper affecting or relating to the company's property or affairs or been privy to the doing of this by others;

iv) made any false entry in any book or paper affecting or relating to the company's property or affairs or been privy to the doing of this by others;

v) fraudulently parted with, altered or made any omission in any document affecting or relating to the company's property or affairs or been privy to the doing of this by others;

vi) pawned, pledged or disposed of any property of the company which has been obtained on credit and has not been paid for (unless the pawning, pledging or disposal was in the ordinary way of the company's business). Anyone who takes in pawn or pledge, or otherwise receives, property knowing of these circumstances will also commit an offence.

The accused will have a defence in respect of i) or vi) above if he can prove that he had no intent to defraud and under iii) or iv) if he can prove that he had no intent to conceal the state of affairs of the company or to defeat the law. There was one conviction under section 206 in 1996.

c) Transactions in fraud of creditors

An offence under section 207 of the Insolvency Act 1986 will be committed by anyone who was an officer of the company at the time and who either makes or causes to be made any gift or transfer of, or charge on, or causes or connives at the levying of any execution against, the company's property within the five years before the commencement of the winding up. It will also be an offence if such a person conceals or removes any part of the company's property since, or within two months before, the date of any unsatisfied judgment or order for the payment of money obtained against the company. In either event it will be a defence for the accused to establish that he had no intent to defraud the company's creditors. There were three convictions under this provision in 1996.

d) Misconduct in the course of a winding up

Section 208 of the Insolvency Act 1986 provides that any past or present officer, including a shadow director, of a company in liquidation will commit an offence if he:

i) does not give full discovery to the best of his knowledge and belief of the company's property and of its disposal other than in the ordinary way of the company's business unless he can prove he had no intent to defraud;

  ii) does not deliver up company property in his custody and control which he is required to deliver up unless he can prove he had no intent to defraud;

 iii) does not deliver up company books and papers in his custody or control which he is required to deliver up unless he can prove he had no intent to defraud;

 iv) fails to inform the liquidator as soon as practicable of any false debts which he knows or believes to have been proved;

  v) after the start of the liquidation, prevents the production of any book or paper affecting or relating to the company's property or affairs unless he can prove that he had no intent to conceal the state of affairs of the company or to defeat the law;

 vi) attempts to account for any part of the company's property by fictitious losses or expenses within the 12 months preceding the winding up at a meeting of the company's creditors or after the start of the winding up.

There was one conviction under section 208 in 1996.

e) Falsification of company books

When a company is being wound up, any officer or contributory of the company commits an offence under section 209 of the Insolvency Act 1986 by destroying, mutilating, altering or falsifying any, books, papers or securities, or making or being privy to the making of any false or fraudulent entry in any register, book of account or document belonging to the company with intent to defraud or deceive any person.

f) Material omissions from statement of affairs

Past or present officers (including shadow directors) of a company in liquidation commit an offence under section 210 of the Insolvency Act 1986 by making, or having made prior to the commencement of the liquidation, a material omission in any statement relating to the company's affairs. It is a defence to prove there was no intent to defraud.

g) False representations to creditors

Under section 211 of the Insolvency Act 1986, any past or present officer, including a shadow director, of a company in liquidation will commit an offence if he makes, or has made prior to the winding up, any false representation or commits any other fraud for the purpose of obtaining the consent of the company's creditors to an agreement with reference to the company's affairs or to the winding up.

CHAPTER 23

PREVENTING ABUSE OF THE PRIVILEGE OF LIMITED LIABILITY

1. Introduction

There has long been recognition of the potential for abuse of the privilege of limited liability by those running their businesses through the medium of companies.[1] The Cork Committee observed that both the Greene Committee in 1926 and the Jenkins Committee in 1962 had made recommendations in this respect which had not been implemented. The Committee noted[2] considerable dissatisfaction with the perceived leniency of the law with regard to directors of insolvent companies and quoted[3] by way of example the evidence of a divisional consumer protection officer of the South Yorkshire County Council who had said:

> "The doctrine of limited liability may have its good points but it also leads to some indifference and lack of concern when company officials know that if the company goes down, they will not have any financial liability . . . There are many fraudulent practices concerned with the formation and liquidation of companies. Companies are formed, debts run up, the assets milked and the company put into liquidation. Immediately a new company is formed and the process is repeated ad infinitum. Associated with the basic fraud is the practice of new companies buying the remaining stock of the old company at give-away prices, taking on the premises complete with fittings which are unpaid for, again at nominal prices".[4]

This Chapter considers the provisions of the 1986 legislation intended to deal with the concerns expressed by the Cork Committee about "delinquent" directors and "phoenix" companies. The mischief of the "phoenix" company is addressed in the legislation by providing for the

---

[1] Refer back to Chap. 3.4.
[2] In Chap. 45 which is entitled "Delinquent Directors and others".
[3] para. 1741.
[4] See *Re Keypak Homecare* [1987] B.C.L.C. 409 at 411 for a judicial description of this syndrome. The directors involved were subsequently disqualified for three years: see [1990] B.C.L.C. 440.

complete disqualification by court order of some directors from being involved in limited liability companies and by the automatic disqualification of all directors from re-using the name of the insolvent company in a misleading fashion. The introduction of tighter controls on the conduct of voluntary liquidation[5] was prompted partly by a desire to prevent the mischief of the sale at an undervalue of the assets of the original company to those involved in its management.

2. Disqualification of directors[6]

a) Introduction

Statutory disqualification of certain people from being company directors was introduced by the Companies Act 1928, following the recommendations of the 1926 Greene Committee.[7] The provisions were re-enacted in the Companies Act 1948 and prevented undischarged bankrupts from acting as directors unless given leave by the court and made possible the disqualification of those convicted of fraudulent trading from being involved in the management of companies. In 1976 the disqualification provisions were extended to cover cases of misconduct in insolvency, the possible period of disqualification was increased to 15 years and the first proper provision was made for the registration of disqualification orders.

Disqualification on the grounds of unfitness under the 1976 legislation required involvement with two companies which had become insolvent within five years of one another, a provision which was re-enacted in the Companies Act 1985.[8] When the current legislation was under discussion, there was a suggestion that any director of an insolvent company should have to obtain permission from the court to continue to act as a director (thus equating directors of insolvent companies with bankrupts).[9] The Insolvency Bill of 1985 required that, on making a winding up order on grounds of the company's inability to pay its debts, the court should make a provisional order disqualifying all the directors who would then have three months to apply for annulment of the order on grounds that they had "acted in a manner which in the

---

[5] By introducing qualification requirements for liquidators (see Chap. 20.4) and removing the powers of the directors once a company is in voluntary liquidation (see Chap. 16.3).

[6] See generally L. Sealy, *Disqualification and Personal Liability of Directors* (4th ed.), A. Mithani and S. Wheeler, *The Disqualification of Company Directors*.

[7] See Leigh (1986) 7 Co. Lawyer 179 on the history of disqualification.

[8] Companies Act 1985, s.300. Cases on the concept of "unfitness" under this section are still relevant under the current legislation.

[9] para. 46 of the White Paper, *A Revised Framework for Insolvency Law*, Cmnd 9175.

circumstances was in the best interests of the company's creditors". This proposal provoked strong opposition on the grounds that the mandatory disqualification would catch the innocent, would cast an unfair burden on the director and would inhibit non-executive directors from accepting office and contributing their expertise on company boards.[10] The clause was defeated twice in the House of Lords and the requirement for a court order of disqualification was substituted. The provisions are contained in the Company Directors Disqualification Act 1986.

The following quotation from the judgment of Henry L.J. in *Re Grayan Services Ltd*[11] is typical of a number of judicial observations on the mischief at which the legislation is directed.

> "The concept of limited liability and the sophistication of our corporate law offers great privileges and great opportunities for those who wish to trade under that regime. But the corporate environment carries with it the discipline that those who avail themselves of those privileges must accept the standards laid down and abide by the regulatory rules and disciplines in place to protect creditors and shareholders. And, while some significant corporate failures will occur despite the directors exercising best managerial practice, in many, too many, cases there have been serious breaches of those rules and disciplines, in situations where the observance of them would or at least might have prevented or reduced the scale of the failure and consequent loss to creditors and investors . . .
>
> The parliamentary intention to improve managerial safeguards and standards for the long term good of employees, creditors and investors is clear."

Some directors may be regarded as delinquent in that they abuse the privilege of limited liability with dishonest intent. More frequently, the business of the company will fail because of the incompetence of the directors running it; limited liability may protect them from the consequences of their incompetence at the expense of the creditors. It is noteworthy that there are no qualification requirements to become a director so control over dishonest and incompetent directors can only be exercised after the event.[12] A survey by the Institute of Directors in

---

[10] The Singapore government enacted a provision for automatic disqualification on insolvent liquidation in 1984; after three years of criticism it repealed the provision in 1987. See Hicks [1988] J.B.L. 27.

[11] [1995] 3 W.L.R. 1. This was the first appeal to the Court of Appeal against a refusal to disqualify (the first appeal to the High Court from a county court refusal to disqualify was *Re Hitco 2000 Ltd* [1995] B.C.C. 161).

[12] See Finch (1992) 55 M.L.R. 179 at 210, noting that the prospective company director does not have to cross a threshold of minimal competence.

1990 indicated that fewer than 10 per cent of directors had received any training as such and that fewer than a quarter possessed any professional or managerial qualifications.[13] It could be argued that it might be better to impose qualifications on directors, in the same way that auditors and insolvency practitioners have to be qualified, rather than disqualifying them after the event as currently happens.[14]

b) Definition of disqualification order

Section 1 of the Company Directors Disqualification Act 1986 defines a disqualification order as an order that a person shall not, without leave of the court, be a director, liquidator, administrator of a company or a receiver or manager of a company's property or be in any way, either directly or indirectly, concerned or take part in the promotion, formation or management of a company for a specified period. Anyone who acts in contravention of a disqualification order commits a criminal offence[15] and will be personally liable for the debts of the company incurred whilst he was so acting.[16] Anyone involved in the management of a company who acts or is willing to act on the instructions of someone he knows to be disqualified will also become personally liable for the debts of the company incurred at that time.[17] The effect of a disqualification order, therefore, may be to make the disqualified person almost unemployable in the corporate sector.[18]

The Secretary of State maintains a register of disqualification orders which is open to public inspection.[19]

c) Grounds for disqualification[20]

The Companies Directors Disqualification Act 1986 provides for the disqualification from office of directors under nine different sections[21] of the Act.

[13] *ibid.*
[14] See Hicks [1988] J.B.L. 27.
[15] Company Directors Disqualification Act 1986, ss.13, 14.
[16] *ibid.*, s.15.
[17] *ibid.*, s.15.
[18] See Hicks 8 Co. Lawyer 243 at 244 for a discussion of what is "management" and the suggestion that a disqualified person cannot be certain what employment he may take without committing a criminal offence.
[19] Company Directors Disqualification Act 1986, s.18; Companies (Disqualification Orders) Regulations 1986 (S.I. 1986 No. 2067).
[20] See, *inter alia*, Leigh (1986) 7 Co. Lawyer 179, Hicks (1987) 8 Co. Lawyer 243, Drake [1989] J.B.L. 474, Hoey (1997) 18 Co. Lawyer 130.
[21] Including s.11 which automatically disqualifies undischarged bankrupts (see Chap. 15.2) and s.12 which provides for the possibility of an order where there has been a failure to pay under a county court administration order (see Chap. 9.2).

A person[22] convicted of an indictable offence in connection with the promotion, formation, management or liquidation of a company, or with the receivership or management of a company's property may also be disqualified for a maximum period of five years where the order is made by a court of summary jurisdiction and 15 years in other cases.[23] Persistent default in relation to the requirements of company legislation with regard to returns of information to the registrar of companies may result in disqualification for up to five years.[24] A person may be disqualified[25] for up to 15 years where it appears that he has been guilty, whether or not convicted, of knowingly being party to fraudulent trading or, while an officer[26] or liquidator of a company or receiver or manager of its property, of any fraud in relation to the company or breach of duty. An application in respect of any of the foregoing may be made by the Secretary of State or the official receiver, or by the liquidator or any past or present member or creditor of any company in relation to which that person has committed or is alleged to have committed an offence or other default.[27]

If the court orders a person, on the application of the liquidator, to make a contribution to the company's assets under sections 213[28] or 214[29] of the Insolvency Act 1986, it may also disqualify that person for up to 15 years.[30]

The Secretary of State may apply for a disqualification order[31] against any person who is or has been a director or shadow director of a company if, after investigation of a company under one of the relevant statutory provisions, it appears expedient in the public interest; the court may make a disqualification order of up to 15 years on such an application if it is satisfied that the conduct of the director in relation to the company makes him unfit to be concerned in the management of a company.

Section 6 of the Company Directors Disqualification Act 1986 is the central provision in this context. The majority of disqualification orders

---

[22] Whether or not a director.
[23] Company Directors Disqualification Act 1986, s.2; *R. v. Corbin* (1984) 6 Cr.App.R. 17, *R. v. Austen* (1985) 1 B.C.C. 99, 528, *R. v. Goodman* [1992] B.C.C. 625, *R. v. Georgiou* (1988) 4 B.C.C. 322.
[24] Company Directors Disqualification Act 1986, s.3.
[25] *ibid.*, s.4.
[26] Including a shadow director.
[27] Company Directors Disqualification Act 1986, s.16(2).
[28] Fraudulent trading, see Chap. 31.4, below.
[29] Wrongful trading, see Chap. 31.5, below.
[30] Company Directors Disqualification Act 1986, s.10.
[31] *ibid.*, s.8.

are made under section 6[32] which provides that it is the duty of the court to make a disqualification order of between two and 15 years against a person where two conditions are met. The first condition is that the person is or has been a director or shadow director of a company which has at any time during or after his directorship become insolvent. The second condition is that the conduct of the director in connection with that company (either taken alone or taken together with his conduct as a director of any other company or companies) makes him unfit to be concerned with the management of the company. A company becomes insolvent for these purposes if it goes into liquidation at a time when its assets are insufficient for the payment of its debts and other liabilities and the expenses of the winding up[33] or it goes into administration or administrative receivership. The director must be shown to have been unfit in relation to the company which has become insolvent; the evidence of his conduct in connection with the "collateral" companies, which need not have become insolvent, should assist the court in reaching a conclusion of unfitness in connection with the "lead" company but need not be the same or similar as the conduct in relation to that company.[34] Where the court decides that the conduct had fallen below the appropriate standard (which is discussed at greater length below), it must make a disqualification order of at least two years and may not take into account that the director is unlikely to repeat the conduct in the future.[35]

A non-exhaustive list of matters relevant to the determination of unfitness is contained in section 9 and Schedule 1 of the Company Directors Disqualification Act 1986. Matters which the Schedule makes applicable in all cases include:

   (i) any misfeasance or breach of duty by the director in relation to the company;

   (ii) any misapplication or retention by the director of or conduct giving rise to an obligation to account for property of the company;

   (iii) the extent of the director's responsibility for the company entering into any transaction liable to be set aside under Part

---

[32] *e.g.*, *Companies in 1995–96* Table D1 shows 903 orders notified, 718 related to unfitness, one to wrongful trading, 3 to investigations and 181 to the other provisions.

[33] Company Directors Disqualification Act 1986, s.6(2). *Re Gower Enterprises Ltd* [1995] B.C.C. 293.

[34] *Secretary of State for Trade and Industry v. Ivens* [1997] 2 B.C.L.C. 334.

[35] *Re Grayan Ltd* [1995] 3 W.L.R. 1. Evidence of subsequent conduct may be relevant in deciding whether or not to give leave to act as a director under Company Directors Disqualification Act 1986, s.17.

XVI of the Insolvency Act 1986 (transactions defrauding creditors)[36];

(iv) the extent of a director's responsibility for any failure of the company to comply with the accounting and notification requirements of the companies legislation.

Where the company has become insolvent, the court also has to take into account any failure by the director to provide specified information and assistance[37] in the insolvency and the extent of[38] the director's responsibility for any of the following:

  (i) the causes of the company becoming insolvent;

 (ii) the company entering into transactions liable to be set aside under sections 127 or 238 to 240 of the Insolvency Act[39];

(iii) the company's failure to supply goods or services which have been paid for;

(iv) any failure by the directors to comply with the obligation to call a creditors' meeting in a creditors' voluntary winding up.[40]

d) Obtaining a disqualification order on the grounds of unfitness

An application for a disqualification order under section 6 may be made by the Secretary of State or the official receiver where it appears expedient in the public interest.[41] Disqualification is viewed as a public function which should be the concern of a neutral public body rather than being urged on the court by discontented creditors. The cost of the process, however, is to a large extent not a charge on public funds but is funded by the creditors of insolvents since the initial investigatory work is carried out by the office-holders who will be paid from the available assets.

---

[36] See Chap. 30.
[37] The failure of a director in *Secretary of State v. McTighe* [1996] 2 B.C.L.C. 477 to co-operate with the office-holder and the official receiver led to an increase in the length of the disqualification order which would otherwise have been imposed.
[38] In *Secretary of State v. Gash* [1997] 1 B.C.L.C. 341 the court pointed out that the legislation required it to consider not just whether the director was responsible but the extent of the responsibility.
[39] See Chap. 30. See *Re Grayan Ltd* [1995] 3 W.L.R. 1 in which the Court of Appeal overruled Arden J.'s view that the giving of preferences need not be taken into account because the liquidator had pursued other remedies in that respect.
[40] Insolvency Act 1986, s.98, see Chap. 16.2 above.
[41] Company Directors Disqualification Act 1986, s.7.

Office-holders under the Insolvency Act 1986 have a duty[42] to report to the Secretary of State if they form the opinion that someone should be disqualified under section 6 of the Company Directors Disqualification Act 1986. The Secretary of State or official receiver may require an insolvency practitioner to provide additional information about the conduct of any director of the company or to allow inspection of documentation relevant to the conduct of a director.[43]

Proceedings on an application for an order on the grounds of the directors' unfitness are governed by the Insolvent Companies (Disqualification of Directors) Proceedings Rules 1987[44] and Practice Direction [1996] 1 All E.R. 442. The application will be supported by affidavits which must set out the case against the person sought to be disqualified with sufficient clarity and identification of the evidence for the respondent to know where he stands.[45] The Court of Appeal[46] has said that it is on the basis of these allegations that the court must decide whether the conduct has "fallen below the standards of probity and competence appropriate for persons fit to be directors of companies". If the respondent wants evidence taken into account which is not contained in the affidavits, he must file an affidavit in opposition.

A considerable amount of the recent litigation on disqualification of directors has revolved around procedural issues, often arising out of a need to balance the Department of Trade and Industry's struggle to find cost-effective ways of making the system work adequately[47] with the impropriety of the court being used as a rubber-stamp in respect of decisions which the legislation requires to be made judicially.

Where there is no dispute between the two sides as to the facts of the case and the parties have reached broad agreement on the appropriate

---

[42] Company Directors Disqualification Act 1986, s.7(3) and the Insolvent Companies (Reports on Conduct of Directors) Rules 19(9)6 (S.I. 1996 No. 1909). The Rules (which strictly apply to voluntary liquidation but in practice are also followed by the official receiver in compulsory liquidations) require the making of a return in a prescribed form (referred to as a D form). A D3 return will state that the liquidator has not become aware of any information which would require him to make a report under s.7(3). Reports made under s.7(3) are not protected from disclosure to respondent directors: *Secretary of State v. Baker, The Times*, October 23, 1997.

[43] Company Directors Disqualification Act 1986, s.7(4).

[44] (S.I. 1987 No. 2023).

[45] r. 3(3) of the Insolvent Companies (Disqualification of Unfit Directors) Proceedings Rules 1987 (S.I. 1987 No. 2023). *Re Rex Williams Leisure Centre Ltd* [1993] 2 All E.R. 741 at 752. If the affidavit evidence is too vague or imprecise, the allegations (and possibly the entire application) may be struck out: *Re Sutton Glassworks* [1997] 1 B.C.L.C. 26.

[46] In *Re Grayan Services Ltd* [1995] 3 W.L.R. 1.

[47] See Henry D, "'Disqualification of Directors: A View from the Inside", in Rajak (ed.), *Insolvency Law Theory and Practice* for an account of the process from the DTI viewpoint.

length of disqualification order, the summary *Carecraft*[48] procedure may be adopted to avoid a full-scale hearing. This involves placing before the court an agreed statement of facts which include some evidence of unfitness on which the court can act. In *Secretary of State v. Banarse*[49] the judge observed of a somewhat indeterminately worded agreed statement that "A *Carecraft* statement should not mince its words. Either the parties are in agreement as to the facts or they are not." If they were not, a trial will in the long run be the appropriate course of action. The Court of Appeal took the opportunity to make some general observations on the *Carecraft* procedure in *Secretary of State for Trade and Industry v. Rogers*[50] and said that where the parties invite the court to deal with the case on the basis of a statement in which the parties agree certain facts and agree not to pursue other disputed allegations, it is not for the court to insist that other allegations be pursued or that cross-examination take place.[51] If the judge felt strongly that the course being taken by the Secretary of State was ill-advised, it would be possible to adjourn the case for a short time and invite the Secretary of State to reconsider but that was all. Scott V.-C. expressed the view[52] that it would be sensible in such cases if the disqualification could be imposed by a formal undertaking entered into by the director without the necessity for a court order; this would, however require statutory amendment. The current position is that the parties cannot require the judge to find that the agreed conduct warrants a disqualification order although it was almost inconceivable that in a case where the director agreed that his conduct warranted a disqualification order the judge would not so agree. The question of the length of the disqualification order must also remain a question for the judge, although it would be unusual for the judge to disagree with both parties on the issue.

The application for a disqualification order must be brought within two years from the day on which the company became insolvent, a time limit which the Insolvency Service often has difficulty meeting. The courts have had to consider applications for an extension of time on a

---

[48] So-called after the case of *Re Carecraft Construction Ltd* [1994] 1 W.L.R. 172 in which the procedure was first used.

[49] [1997] 1 B.C.L.C. 653.

[50] [1996] 2 B.C.L.C. 513.

[51] In the *Rogers* case, the director was very concerned that there should be no finding of dishonesty against him and the Secretary of State was content not to pursue any such allegation. It was clear that if dishonesty had been alleged, the director would have refused to agree to the use of the *Carecraft* procedure. The Court of Appeal held that it was not, therefore, open to the judge to find that the director had been dishonest.

[52] Previously expressed by him in Practice Direction [1996] 1 All E.R. 445.

number of occasions and have laid down guidelines as to the circumstances in which an extension will be granted[53]; amongst the factors
which the court will consider are the length of the delay, the reasons for
the delay, the strength and gravity of the case and the degree of
prejudice caused by the delay. In *Secretary of State v. Davies*[54] the Court
of Appeal held that the mere fact that there was no good reason for the
delay was not necessarily enough by itself to justify a refusal to proceed
out of time; there, the alleged conduct was particularly serious, there
was an obvious public interest in having the allegations determined and
the delay had occasioned no prejudice to the directors.

There have been several cases[55] in which the courts have considered
the propriety of accepting an undertaking not to act as a director in the
future in return for not proceeding with an application for a disqualification order. In *Secretary of State v. Davies (No. 2)*[56] the respondent was
a wealthy man who said he had no need or desire to be involved in the
management of a company again, offered undertakings which mirrored
the effect of an order under the legislation and argued that the proceedings should be stayed since it would be an abuse of the process of the
court for the Secretary of State to continue the proceedings at substantial
cost to the public purse, as well as being unfairly oppressive to himself.
Alternatively, he sought permission to pursue an application for judicial
review of the decision to continue the proceedings on the grounds that
it was outside the range of reasonable decisions which could be made by
the Secretary of State.[57] Rattee J. held[58] that since the legislation laid
down machinery for protecting the public by disqualification orders
made by the court, it would normally be wrong in principle for the court
to stay proceedings solely because the respondent had offered undertakings since such undertakings would not have all the effects of an
order of the court; in particular, breach of an order would be a criminal
offence whereas breach of the undertakings would be a purely civil
matter, it would not be straightforward to hold personally liable third

---

[53] *Secretary of State for Trade and Industry v. Langridge* [1991] 3 All E.R. 591, *Re Probe
Data* [1992] B.C.L.C. 405, CA , *Re Tasbian Ltd (No. 3)* [1992] B.C.C. 358, *Re Manlon
Trading* [1995] B.C.C. 579, *Secretary of State for Trade and Industry v. McTighe* [1996]
2 B.C.L.C. 284, *Secretary of State v. Davies* [1997] B.C.C. 235.

[54] [1996] 4 All E.R. 289.

[55] *Re Homes Assured Corporation plc* [1996] B.C.C. 297, *Secretary of State v. Cleland*
[1997] B.C.C. 473, *Secretary of State v. Davies (No. 2)* [1997] B.C.C. 488.

[56] [1997] 2 B.C.L.C. 96.

[57] Relying on *Associated Provincial Picture Houses Ltd v. Wednesbury Corp.* [1947] 2 All
E.R. 680, *R. v. Ministry of Defence, ex p. Smith* [1996] 1 All E.R. 257 at 263.

[58] Referring to the observations of Scott V.C. in the *Rogers* case as to the need for a
statutory amendment before an undertaking could have the same effect as an order.
Rattee J's judgment has been approved by the Court of Appeal (*The Times*, December
9, 1997) *sub nom. Re Blackspur Group plc.*

parties[59] acting on the instructions of someone known to have given such undertakings and there would be no entry in the public register of disqualifications. Where there were circumstances which might make a trial of the proceedings unfairly oppressive the matter would be different; an example was *Re Homes Assured Corp plc*[60] in which Robert Walker J. agreed, on the application of the Secretary of State and the respondent, to stay disqualification proceedings on undertakings not in future to act as a director given by the respondent whose poor health made a lengthy trial a hazardous proposition.

e) Who may be disqualified under section 6

Under section 6 of the Company Directors Disqualification Act 1986 only those who have been directors or shadow directors of a company which has become insolvent may be disqualified.[61] A shadow director is a person in accordance with whose directions or instructions the directors of the company are accustomed to act (but so that a person is not deemed a shadow director by reason only that the directors act on advice given by him in a professional capacity).[62] A *de facto* director is someone who holds himself out as a director without having been properly appointed; it has been held that a *de facto* director can be disqualified.[63] In *Re Richborough Furniture Ltd*[64] the court held that in order to be a *de facto* director, the alleged director had either to be the sole acting director or to be acting on an equal footing with the properly appointed directors; in that case, although the defendant had considerable responsibility and was viewed by a number of creditors as a director, he was not a signatory to the company bank account as were the properly appointed directors and should not be treated as a *de facto* director.

A disqualification order may be made against foreigners just as much as against British subjects and it is irrelevant whether or not they were present in the jurisdiction at the time the alleged activities took place.[65]

---

[59] As under Company Directors Disqualification Act 1986, s.15(1)(b).
[60] [1996] B.C.C. 297.
[61] Officers and members of partnerships are treated as directors by the Insolvent Partnerships Order 1994 (see Chap. 18).
[62] Company Directors Disqualification Act 1986, s.22(5).
[63] *Re Lo-Line Electric Motors Ltd* [1988] B.C.L.C. 698, *Re Tasbian* [1992] B.C.C. 358, *Re Moorgate Metals Ltd* [1995] B.C.C. 143, *Re Richborough Furniture Ltd* [1996] 1 B.C.L.C. 507, *Secretary of State v. Laing* [1996] 2 B.C.L.C. 324. See *Re Hydrodan (Corby) Ltd* [1994] 2 B.C.L.C. 180 for Millett J.'s discussion of the distinction between a *de facto* and a shadow director.
[64] [1996] 1 B.C.L.C. 507.
[65] *Re Seagull Manufacturing Co. Ltd (No. 2)* [1994] 2 All E.R. 767.

f) Judicial interpretation of "unfitness"

The courts have had to decide what conduct makes a director "unfit" to be concerned in the management of a company and the cases contain various statements as to the sort of behaviour which justifies disqualification. Fraudulent and dishonest behaviour is obviously likely to lead to a finding of unfitness. Those who have been involved in "phoenix" companies are also clearly at risk of disqualification.[66] *Re Ipcon Fashions Ltd*[67] was an early clear example of such a case. The court found that, although there was no personal dishonesty on the part of the director, there was a cynical exploitation of the privilege of limited liability, including a reckless disregard of all creditors' interests including in particular the Crown, which was the sort of behaviour from which the public clearly needed to be protected. Subsequently, the Court of Appeal in *Re Swift 736 Ltd*,[68] describing "a deplorable pattern of six companies succeeding one another, carrying on the same business of shirt manufacturing from the same premises, as each became insolvent, one after the other", approved the comments of Hoffmann J. at first instance in which he observed that this sort of behaviour was the very thing which the provisions for disqualification of directors were intended to prevent.

Directors will clearly be risking disqualification if they fail to comply with the statutory obligations in relation to maintaining proper books of account and filing information at Companies House.[69] In *Re Swift 736 Ltd*[70] the Court of Appeal said that, in addition to conducting their companies with due regard to the ordinary standards of commercial morality, directors must be "punctilious in observing the safeguards laid down by Parliament for the benefit of others who have dealings with their companies . . . Isolated lapses in filing documents are one thing and may be excusable. Not so persistent lapses which show overall a blatant disregard for this important aspect of accountability. Such lapses are serious and cannot be condoned even though, and it is right to have this firmly in mind, they need not involve any dishonest intent". The failure to comply with filing obligations resulted in the difference

---

[66] See, *e.g.*, *Re Travel Mondial (U.K.) Ltd* [1991] B.C.L.C. 120, *Re Linvale Ltd* [1993] B.C.L.C. 654, *Re Swift 736 Ltd* [1993] B.C.L.C. 1.

[67] (1989) 5 B.C.C. 773.

[68] [1993] B.C.L.C. 896.

[69] *Re Majestic Recording Studies Ltd* [1989] B.C.L.C. 1, *Re City Investment Centres Ltd* [1992] B.C.L.C. 956, *Re New Generation Engineers Ltd* [1993] B.C.L.C. 435, *Re Firedart* [1994] 2 B.C.L.C. 340, *Secretary of State v. Van Hengel* [1995] 1 B.C.L.C. 545 *Re Continental Assurance Co. of London plc* [1977] 1 B.C.L.C. 48.

[70] [1993] B.C.L.C. 896 increasing the period of disqualification ordered by Hoffmann J. whose judgment is reported at [1993] B.C.L.C. 1.

between disqualification in *Secretary of State v. Arif*[71] and non-disqualification in *Secretary of State v. Gash*[72] where the misconduct was otherwise similar. In *Re Hitco 2000 Ltd*[73] the judge held that a failure on the part of a sole director to monitor and control the company's financial position or to ensure that he had the requisite professional guidance amounted to unfitness.

In the early days of the application of this provision,[74] there was considerable debate as to whether disqualification demanded dishonesty or whether incompetence would suffice.[75] Many of the cases drew a clear distinction between commercial immorality and honest commercial misjudgment[76] and blameworthiness was clearly an issue. In *Re Lo-Line Electric Motors Ltd*[77] Browne-Wilkinson V.C. said:

> "Ordinary commercial misjudgment is in itself not sufficient to justify disqualification. In the normal case, the conduct complained of must display a lack of commercial probity, although I have no doubt in an extreme case of gross negligence or total incompetence disqualification could be appropriate".

Peter Gibson J. in *Re Bath Glass Ltd*[78] stated a test requiring a lower degree of blameworthiness:

> "To reach a finding of unfitness the court must be satisfied that the director has been guilty of a serious failure or serious failures, whether deliberately or through incompetence, to perform those duties of directors which are attendant on the privilege of trading through companies with limited liability".

In *Re Sevenoaks Stationers (Retail) Ltd*,[79] which was the first case on the provision to reach them, the Court of Appeal held that whilst such judicial statements might be helpful they should not be treated as judicial paraphrases of the words of the statute and that the question is one of fact in each case. Dillon L.J. said:

> "It is beyond dispute that the purpose of section 6 is to protect the public, and in particular potential creditors of companies, from

---

[71] [1997] 1 B.C.L.C. 34.
[72] [1997] 1 B.C.L.C. 341.
[73] [1995] B.C.C. 161.
[74] And its immediate predecessor, Companies Act 1985, s.300.
[75] Or, to put the issue another way, whether the measure was intended mainly to punish delinquent directors or to protect the public from inadequate (for whatever reason) directors. See Finch (1990) 53 M.L.R. 385.
[76] See, *e.g.*, *Re C U Fittings Ltd* (1989) 5 B.C.C. 210.
[77] [1988] Ch. 477.
[78] (1988) 4 B.C.C. 130.
[79] [1990] B.C.C. 765.

losing money through companies becoming insolvent when the directors of those companies are people unfit to be concerned in the management of a company. The test laid down is . . . whether the person's conduct as a director of the company or companies in question 'make him unfit to be concerned in the management of a company'. These are ordinary words of the English language and they should be simple to apply in most cases. It is important to hold to those words in each case."

In the *Sevenoaks* case, which involved the disqualification of a director, who was a chartered accountant who had been extremely negligent in regard to the running of the business, the unfitness was established by reference to the incompetence of the director; there was no suggestion of dishonesty and, in fact, the director had lost significant quantities of his own money. Recent cases which have stressed the need for adequate levels of competence are *Re Continental Assurance Ltd*,[80] in which a senior employee of a bank who became a non-executive director of a client was disqualified despite his argument that he had no knowledge of the objectionable conduct since "any competent director would have known" and *Secretary of State v. Arif*[81] in which the court observed "It is no answer . . . to say 'I did what I could'. If a director finds that he is unable to do what he knows ought to be done, the only proper course is to resign". In *Secretary of State v. Gash*[82] the court held that although a director whose advice was not being heeded would be prudent, in his own interests, to resign, failure to do so would not necessarily lead to disqualification. In that case, it was clear that some of the directors of the company should be disqualified; the director in question had advised the others that there was a risk of insolvency and had proposed improvements which were ignored and the judge held that the stage had not yet been reached when resignation was the only acceptable course of conduct.

Another issue which originally gave rise to a certain amount of judicial disagreement was the question of whether failure to pay Crown debts was worse than failure to pay other types of creditor and, therefore, more likely to merit disqualification. Hoffmann J. in *Re Dawson Print Group*[83] observed that failure to pay such debts was not to be regarded as a particularly immoral breach of duty: Vinelott J. in *Re Stanford Services Ltd*[84] and Peter Gibson J. in *Re Churchill Hotel*

---

[80] [1997] 1 B.C.L.C. 48.
[81] *ibid.* at 34.
[82] *ibid.* at 341.
[83] (1987) 3 B.C.C. 322.
[84] *ibid.* at 326.

(Plymouth) Ltd[85] thought otherwise. The Court of Appeal, whilst recognising the particular difficulties which the Crown has in pressing for prompt payment, has held[86] that no distinction should be made between failure to pay Crown debts and failure to pay ordinary trade creditors. Directors who have failed to pay any of their creditors unless pressed to do so are likely to be considered unfit particularly if continuing to pay themselves well at the same time.[87]

In *Re Grayan Ltd*[88] the Court of Appeal held that it was not relevant that the director was unlikely to repeat the conduct which had made him "unfit" in relation to the insolvent company. Hoffmann L.J. said that the purpose of making disqualification mandatory was to ensure that everyone whose conduct had fallen below the appropriate standard was disqualified for at least two years: "Parliament has decided that it is occasionally necessary to disqualify a company director to encourage the others". The Court of Appeal also indicated in this case that it would usually be reluctant to overturn the decision of a first instance judge on unfitness particularly where there is dispute on the primary findings of fact on which the trial judge will have had the advantage of seeing and hearing the witnesses. There would, however, be cases such as this where the trial judge reached an incorrect conclusion as to whether the conduct measured up to the standard of probity and competence fixed by the court when it would be appropriate for the appellate court to interfere.

f) The nature of disqualification proceedings

As has been observed,[89] and as can be seen from the views expressed by the Court of Appeal in *Re Grayan Services Ltd* there is a penal element to the disqualification provisions as well as an intention that the public should be protected from future failings. This gives rise to the question of the extent to which defendant directors should be accorded the same protections as are given to those who stand accused in criminal trials.

Browne Wilkinson V.-C. in *Re Lo-Line Electric Motors Ltd*,[90] having said that the primary purpose of the disqualification provisions was "not

---

[85] (1988) 4 B.C.C. 112.
[86] *Re Sevenoaks Stationers Ltd* [1991] B.C.L.C. 325, *Secretary of State v. McTighe* [1996] 2 B.C.L.C. 477.
[87] *Re Synthetic Technology Ltd* [1993] B.C.C. 549, *Secretary of State v. Van Hengel* [1995] 1 B.C.L.C. 545.
[88] [1995] 3 W.L.R. 1. See also *Re Pamstock Ltd* [1994] 1 B.C.L.C. 716.
[89] By Professor Dine, in particular; see, *e.g.*, in Rajak (ed.), *Insolvency Law Theory and Practice*, p. 173, 9 Co. Lawyer 213, [1994] J.B.L. 325. See also Finch (1993) 22 I.L.J. 35.
[90] [1988] B.C.L.C. 698 (on Companies Act 1985, s.300).

to punish the individual but to protect the public against the future conduct of companies by persons whose past records as directors of insolvent companies have shown them to be a danger to creditors and others", went on to hold that, since disqualification involves a substantial interference with the freedom of the individual, the rights of the individual should be fully protected. In that case, natural justice required that the director be given prior notice of a change in the case against him from an allegation of commercial dishonesty to one alleging gross commercial negligence.[91]

There has been considerable discussion of whether the appropriate standard of proof in disqualification cases is the civil one of "balance of probabilities" or whether it should be the more onerous criminal standard of proof beyond reasonable doubt.[92] The expressed view of the court has tended to be that the unfitness must be proved on the balance of probabilities but in reality a much more conclusive weight of evidence seems to be required. In *Re Swift 736 Ltd* [93] Hoffmann J. said that the director should be allowed the benefit of any reasonable doubt, a view also expressed by Lindsay J. in *Re Polly Peck International plc*[94] who said that section 6 was "plainly quasi-penal in effect". In *Re Living Images Ltd* [95] Laddie J. said that criminal burden of proof was not appropriate and that the court should not allow the director the benefit of any reasonable doubt. He did say that, as disqualification proceedings were likely to introduce serious charges of moral condemnation, the courts should be wary of giving credence to allegations affecting a director's moral character without substantial evidence to confirm their validity. The judge also said that the court must be careful not to fall into the trap of being too wise after the event and that the evidence of unfitness must be overwhelming in terms of probability rather than marginally indicative. This seems at least to be approaching the criminal standard of proof.

In *Re Dawes and Henderson (Agencies) Ltd*,[96] the court held that disqualification proceedings are not criminal proceedings and therefore are subject to the usual rule in civil proceedings that evidence of the general reputation of the defendant is not admissible. Blackburne J. adverted to the suggestion that the proceedings were akin to criminal

---

[91] This was cited with approval in *Langridge* [1991] B.C.L.C. 543, *Re Living Images Ltd* [1996] 1 B.C.L.C. 348.
[92] Griffin 18 Co. Lawyer 24.
[93] [1993] B.C.L.C. 1.
[94] [1994] 1 B.C.L.C. 574.
[95] *ibid.* at 348.
[96] [1997] 1 B.C.L.C. 329.

proceedings and said[97] "it is sufficient to say that disqualification proceedings are civil in nature and the fact that allegations of dishonesty are levelled against the respondents does not alter that fact".

In *R. v. Secretary of State, ex p. McCormick*[98], the Court of Appeal held that proceedings for a disqualification order did not involve a criminal charge so as to prevent the use of evidence which the director had been compelled to give to inspectors appointed under section 434 of the Companies Act 1985.

h) Length of disqualification

Although the intention of the legislation is said to be primarily the protection of the public, the length of the disqualification is calculated according to seriousness of the conduct by what seems to be a backward rather than forward looking approach.[99]

The Court of Appeal has held[1] that it has the power to interfere with the length of disqualification ordered by the judge in the usual limited circumstances in which it may intervene with the exercise by a judge of a discretion vested in him. In *Re Sevenoaks Stationers Ltd*[2] the Court of Appeal issued guidance, of a sort, as to the appropriate length of a disqualification order[3]. It was held that periods of 10 years or more should be reserved for particularly serious cases[4] including those where a director already previously had a disqualification order made against him; disqualification for between six and 10 years should apply for "serious cases which do not merit the top bracket"[5]; and the minimum bracket of two to five years should be applied where "though disqualification is mandatory, the case is, relatively, not very serious".

The court has an inherent power to stay or suspend a disqualification order pending an appeal but this will only be exercised in exceptional

---

[97] Referring to a similar statement by the Court of Appeal in *Re Southbourne Sheet Metal* [1993] B.C.L.C. 135.

[98] *The Times*, February 10, 1998.

[99] See Davies, *Gower's Principles of Modern Company Law* (6th ed.), p. 683.

[1] *Secretary of State v. Ettinger* [1993] B.C.L.C.

[2] [1991] Ch. 164.

[3] It has been said that these guidelines bear a resemblance to guidelines on sentencing in criminal cases.

[4] A subsequent Court of Appeal held that one of the directors in *Secretary of State v. McTighe* [1996] 2 B.C.L.C. 477 should be disqualified for 12 years since his conduct was particularly serious, in that he had caused three companies successively to trade at the risk of their creditors, caused the assets of two of them to be removed from creditors and failed to co-operate with liquidator or official receiver. The other director in that case was equally responsible for trading at the risk of creditors in 3 companies and for some misappropriation of property and was disqualified for 6 years.

[5] *ibid.*

circumstances.[6] In most cases an interim order giving leave to act as a director would be more appropriate since the public interest may be protected by obtaining undertakings from the director and by limiting the permission to act to an identified company.

i) Leave to act despite disqualification

If the application for the order was made by the Secretary of State, official receiver or liquidator, they will appear on an application for leave to act despite a disqualification order and call the attention of the court to any matters which appear to be relevant.[7] Hoffmann L.J. in *Re Grayan Services Ltd*[8] said that the question of whether the director was likely to repeat the offending conduct would be highly material to whether he is granted leave or not. If the conditions attached by the court to leave are not complied with, the director is in breach of the disqualification order and so exposed to personal liability.[9] The court will usually want to have financial and management information in relation to the company in question before deciding whether or not to give leave.

Examples of cases in which a disqualified director has been given leave to manage a specified company include *Re Majestic Recording Studios*,[10] *Re Goodwin Warren Control Systems*[11] and *Secretary of State v. Arif*.[12] In *Re Majestic Recording Studios* the director was regarded as the "moving spirit" behind the company and was consequently given leave to act as a director during his five-year disqualification period. This was because the business would otherwise cease and 55 employees would lose their jobs. The court imposed safeguards in the form of an independent chartered accountant approved by the court acting as a co-director and an assurance that the previous year's accounts were properly audited. In *Re Goodwin Warren Control Systems*, non-executive directors of a company, Systems, which had gone into voluntary liquidation were disqualified because they had failed to disclose that one of them controlled a company at the time it was being purchased by Systems. The director who had not had the interest was disqualified for three years but Chadwick J. held that the conduct which made him unfit was an inadequate response to difficult circumstances

[6] *Secretary of State v. Bannister* [1996] 1 All E.R. 993.
[7] Company Directors Disqualification Act 1986, s.17(2).
[8] [1995] 3 W.L.R. 1.
[9] *Re Brian Sheridan Cars Ltd* [1996] 1 B.C.L.C. 327.
[10] [1989] B.C.L.C. 1.
[11] [1992] B.C.C. 557.
[12] [1997] 1 B.C.L.C. 34.

rather than a planned course of wrongdoing and that it was unlikely that he would deliberately set out to trade fraudulently. The judge did not think that the protection of the public required that he should cease to be a director of his consultancy company and also gave leave for him to be concerned in the management of two other companies provided the boards of directors were made aware of this order and the reasons for it. In relation to two other companies of which the director and his wife were the sole directors, he would only be given leave to remain on their boards if his wife were replaced by a responsible and experienced director and the outside shareholders were informed of the order and the reasons for it. In *Secretary of State v. Arif* leave to act was also dependant on business associates and banks being informed both of the disqualification order and of the terms of the leave to act.

3. Preventing directors from re-using the company name

a) Introduction

The Cork Committee recommended[13] that anyone who had been a director or concerned in the management of a company in the two years prior to an insolvent liquidation should, unless the court ordered otherwise, be personally liable for the relevant liabilities of any company which started trading within a year of that insolvency which itself became insolvent within three years. An exception would be made where the second company had a paid up share capital of £50,000 or more or was a subsidiary of a company with such a share capital. This recommendation was not accepted and section 216 of the Insolvency Act 1986 which is intended to prevent phoenix companies was not based on a specific Cork recommendation. It was introduced at a late stage in the passage of the insolvency legislation through Parliament in 1985.[14]

b) The basic provision

Section 216 applies to a person where a company has gone into insolvent liquidation[15] and the person was a director or shadow director at

---

[13] In para. 1827.
[14] See, generally, Milman [1997] J.B.L. 224.
[15] s.216(7) defines this as going into liquidation at a time when its assets are insufficient for the payment of its debts and other liabilities and the expenses of the winding up. The provision only applies where a company is in liquidation and not to administrative receiverships or administrations.

any time in the 12 months before the liquidation. It introduces the concept of a prohibited name as a name by which the insolvent company was known in that 12 months or which is so similar as to suggest an association with that company and restricts the ability of a person to whom section 216 of the Insolvency Act 1986 applies to be involved in a company or business under a prohibited name. Unless the court has given leave or the case falls in one of the three exceptions outlined below,[16] a person to whom the section applies may not for five years from the start of the liquidation be a director of or in any way involved in the promotion, formation or management of either a company or any other business known by a prohibited name. Breach is a criminal offence of strict liability.[17]

Section 217 of the Insolvency Act 1986 imposes personal liability for debts on those who contravene section 216.[18] A person will be personally responsible for all the "relevant debts" of a company if he is either involved with the management of a company in contravention of section 216 of the Insolvency Act 1986 or, as a person involved in the management of a company, he acts or is willing to act on instructions given by a person whom he knows to be in contravention of section 216. A person who has at any time acted on instructions given by a person whom he knew to be in contravention of section 216 in relation to the company will be presumed to have been so willing at any time thereafter. Liability will be joint and several with the company and any other person so liable. "Relevant debts" are those incurred by the company whilst the person was either involved in management in breach of section 216 or willing to act on the instructions of someone in breach of section 216.[19]

c) Exceptions to the basic rule[20]

The first exception applies where a company (referred to in the rules as "the successor company") acquires the whole, or substantially the

---

[16] Which, somewhat oddly, are tucked away in the Insolvency Rules 1986.

[17] The penalties for breach are contained in s.430 and Sched. 10 of the Insolvency Act 1986. In *R. v. Cole*, *The Times* July 17, 1997 the Court of Appeal held that *mens rea* was not necessary for liability under Insolvency Act 1986, s.216.

[18] This is very similar to the personal liability imposed by Company Directors Disqualification Act 1986, s.15 on a person acting in breach of a disqualification order.

[19] In *Thorne v. Silverleaf* [1994] B.C.C. 109 the plaintiff obtained judgment under s.217 against a director who had been found guilty under s.216. The Court of Appeal held that he had not waived his rights to recovery under this section even though he had allegedly aided and abetted the director and was aware of the facts relating to the offence and that those facts constituted a breach of s.216.

[20] Contained in Insolvency Rules 1986, rr. 4.228 to 4.230.

whole, of the business of an insolvent company,[21] under arrangements made by a liquidator, administrator, administrative receiver or supervisor of a company voluntary arrangement. The successor company may give notice to the insolvent company's creditors within 28 days from the completion of the arrangements telling them that the company has assumed or proposes to assume a name that is or will be prohibited under section 216 of the Insolvency Act 1986 and naming persons to whom the section applies as having been directors or shadow directors of the insolvent company whom it is proposed will be involved in the management of the successor company. If the successor company gives such a notice, any person named in the notice may act in relation to the successor company notwithstanding that he has not had leave of the court. It is therefore possible for a new company to be set up with a name otherwise prohibited and directors who would otherwise be prohibited, without the leave of the court, so long as notice is given to the creditors of the insolvent company. The creditors are not given the chance to challenge the notice or object. The only restriction on abuse is the integrity of the insolvency practitioner and the fact that where a sale to the original directors or management is contemplated, the liquidator must give notice to the creditors' committee and any creditor can apply to court in respect of the liquidator's actions.[22] This provision is intended to prevent the potential loss of value to creditors where the goodwill of a business depends on the involvement of particular managers and the continued use of an established name.

The second exception provides that where a person applies for leave of the court under section 216 of the Insolvency Act 1986 not later than seven days from the date on which the company went into liquidation he may act without leave for six weeks from the commencement of the liquidation unless the court disposes of the application for leave under section 216 earlier.[23] This exception is to deal with the situation in which the new business is already operating before the old one goes into liquidation and, in the absence of this grace period, the new business might be forced to close.

The third excepted case allows those subject to section 216 of the Insolvency Act 1986 to continue to act in relation to a company that has been known by a prohibited name for 12 months before the insolvency provided the company was not dormant during that time. The proviso is intended to prevent the incorporation of the phoenix company well

---

[21] In *Re Bonus Breaks Ltd* [1991] B.C.C. 546, Morritt J. indicated that he would be surprised if there was a requirement that liabilities of the business be transferred as well as assets.

[22] Under Insolvency Act 1986, ss.165(6) and 167(2).

[23] According to dicta in *Re Bonus Breaks* the court may extend the six-week period.

ahead of a possible liquidation. Were it not for this exception, section 216 of the Insolvency Act 1986 would give rise to problems in relation to groups of companies whose members bear similar names in the event of the insolvency of one member of the group.

d) Leave to use prohibited name

There is little reported case law on the basis on which the court decides whether or not to grant leave under section 216. The first reported case was *Re Bonus Breaks Ltd*[24] in which Morritt J. gave leave in return for undertakings that the new company's capital base was maintained and the company would not redeem any redeemable shares or purchase its own shares out of its profits for two years. It seems to have been assumed in this case that the court had to be satisfied with the prospects of the new company, thus treating applications for leave to use a prohibited name in the same way as applications for leave to act as a director whilst subject to a disqualification order.

In *Penrose v. OR*[25] Timothy Penrose and Ruth Penrose, who had been directors of Hudsons Coffee Houses Ltd which had gone into insolvent liquidation, asked for the court's leave under section 216 of the Insolvency Act 1986 to act as directors of a new company, Hudsons Coffee Houses (Holdings) Ltd. The old company had run a successful coffee house in Birmingham but had failed in an attempt to expand the business to other towns. The directors bought out the original Birmingham business but needed to be able to use the Hudson name to keep the trade brought about by guidebook entries. The new name was clearly a prohibited name within section 216. The Official Receiver did not oppose the granting of leave but the district judge in the county court took the view that he had to be satisfied with the capitalisation and management of the new company.

The appeal was heard by Chadwick J., who could only intervene if satisfied that an error of principle had occurred in the county court. In giving leave to act under section 216 of the Insolvency Act 1986, he laid down some principles for future use. He said that an application under section 216 was a different exercise from that carried out under the Company Directors Disqualification Act 1986 when a disqualified director sought leave to act. Section 216 was not intended to provide the public with general protection against the applicant acting as a company director. The mischiefs aimed at by the section were first, the risk that

---

[24] [1991] B.C.C. 546.
[25] [1996] 2 All E.R. 96 and see Robinson, 12 I.L.&P. 160.

the business of the insolvent company had been acquired at an under-value, and secondly, that creditors of the old company might be misled into believing that the new company was the same as the old. In this case, there was no risk to the new company's creditors beyond that which was permitted under the law in relation to the incorporation of limited liability companies. It was possible that these applicants were inexperienced and that the company was undercapitalised but that was a risk regarded as acceptable by the legislation. There were no other grounds on which to justify a refusal to grant leave and leave would therefore be given. If there had been evidence of unfitness such as would justify a disqualification order then it would be appropriate to refuse consent.

In *Re Lighting Electrical Contractors Ltd*[26] the court followed this more relaxed attitude and gave permission to a director of a company which had gone into insolvent liquidation to use similar names in relation to one trading company and five other dormant companies. The lack of fault on the part of the applicant for the insolvency of the original company was emphasised as was the support of its receiver and creditors. The court held that the legislation did not require the successor companies to be trading but it did refuse leave in respect of future, unidentified companies.

4. Evaluation of the provisions

The Cork Committee observed[27] that the dissatisfaction was due "not to the absence of appropriate legislation but to a failure to make use of the existing legislation" and, in the early years of the 1986 legislation, it appeared that not much had changed. There has been much public disquiet at the low level of disqualifications which have been achieved since 1986. In October 1993 the National Audit Office produced a report[28] evaluating the extent to which the current arrangements for disqualification protect the public and improve the business practices of company directors. One of its conclusions was that up to half the cases where disqualification of the director could be said to be in the public interest were not pursued by the Insolvency Service. The report found that by March 1993 only 1,700 disqualification orders had been made in response to 2,900 applications made under the 1986 Act. The report also indicated a lack of awareness amongst directors of the provisions or the existence of the Act.

---

[26] [1996] B.C.C. 950.
[27] See para. 1815.
[28] National Audit Office, *The Insolvency Service Executive Agency: Company Director Disqualification*, H.C. 907, 1993.

The position seems to be improving.[29] Since the Company Directors Disqualification Act 1986 came into force over 5,000 directors have been disqualified. Over 2,000 of these orders were made in the two years up to March 1998 which illustrates the determined efforts made by the Insolvency Service to meet criticisms directed at their earlier efforts. During 1996 the Disqualification Unit of the Insolvency Service received 4,825 reports identifying elements of unfit conduct by directors; 2,919 were from insolvency practitioners and 1,906 from official receivers in compulsory liquidations. In 1996 proceedings were issued against 1,376 directors, 1,078 applications were dealt with and 1,889 proceedings were awaiting conclusion at the end of the year. 945 disqualification orders were made in 1996 of which 686 were for five years or less.

One difficulty is the level of resources available to the Insolvency Service which frequently takes nearly the two-year period to commence proceedings. It can take up to a further four years for an order to be made, during which time the director will have been free to carry on business with limited liability. A major problem is that the system depends on the input of private sector insolvency practitioners whose main function is to maximise the assets for the creditors and who approach their public interest duties with a variety of levels of enthusiasm and commitment of time.[30]

The public perception is that there is still a problem. The Association of British Chambers of Commerce reported[31] that members regularly reported on so-called "phoenix companies" who have been made insolvent one week, yet have set up the next week having rid themselves of their debts, having acquired the stock and assets of their former company at a reduced price.

A problem which the legislation does not even address is that of directors who allow a company to run up a number of small debts and then close it down without a formal liquidation, thus avoiding investigation.

---

[29] The following information is taken from the Annual Report of the Insolvency Service for 1996 and DTI press releases of June 5, 1997 and March 18, 1998.

[30] See Wheeler (1995) 15 L.S. 283 for an interesting account of research into the attitude of insolvency practitioners to unfit conduct of directors. Rajak (ed.), *Insolvency Law Theory and Practice*, Chap. 12, contains an account from an earlier stage of the research.

[31] *Insolvency Law and Practice—A Discussion Document*, 1994.

PART V

THE CREDITORS' BATTLE FOR THE ASSETS

CHAPTER 24

INTRODUCTION TO PART V

Part V is concerned with the rights of the creditors of bankrupts and insolvent companies in liquidation. By definition, there will be insufficient available for all creditors to be paid in full. Chapter 25 explains the effect of bankruptcy and liquidation on the rights of the creditors; in particular, it will be seen that the individual rights of unsecured creditors to pursue the debtor are converted to a right to participate in the collective administration of the insolvent's assets. Secured creditors are relatively immune to the insolvency of the debtor; Chapter 29 deals with the circumstances in which the security may be challenged and it will be seen from Chapter 35 that floating charges are postponed to the preferential creditors.

The insolvency practitioner will have to identify, collect and realise the assets of the insolvent for distribution to the creditors; Chapter 26 explains the general principles relating to the availability of assets. Where the insolvent is an individual, the policy question arises of the extent to which he should be divested of assets; Chapter 27 considers the extent of the bankrupt's estate. There are particular complications in the case of the family home, which is dealt with in Chapter 27, and of the bankrupt's pension rights, dealt with in Chapter 33.[1] The insolvency practitioner will only be entitled to those assets beneficially owned by the insolvent; Chapter 28 considers the grounds on which third parties may claim to be entitled to assets in the apparent ownership of the insolvent. The insolvency practitioner may find it possible to swell the assets by clawing back property with which the insolvent has previously parted; this is dealt with in Chapter 30. In the case of a liquidation, it may be possible to make claims against those responsible for the insolvency as explained in Chapter 31. The expense of indulging in the necessary litigation may, however, prevent such claims from being a practical proposition; this is considered in Chapter 32.

Chapter 34 explains some other sources of funds available to employees and those whose claims against the insolvent have been insured.

---

[1] Which also deals with other pension topics including the extent to which any surplus in a company pension scheme may be an asset available to the liquidator.

The insolvency practitioner is under a duty to distribute the proceeds of the realisations in accordance with statute; this is explained in Chapter 35. Although the theory of contract law is that the unsecured creditors should share equally in the shortfall, it will be seen that there are categories of creditor which are treated preferentially and it has been a matter for some debate as to whether and to what extent this should be so.

CHAPTER 25

EFFECT OF LIQUIDATION OR BANKRUPTCY ON CREDITORS' RIGHTS

1. Introduction

This chapter explains the effect on a creditor's rights when a debtor becomes bankrupt or goes into liquidation; it will be seen that the individual right of the unsecured creditor to pursue the debtor, which was explained in Chapter 4, will generally come to an end and will be replaced by a right to prove in the insolvency in accordance with the rules for quantification and set-off provided by the insolvency legislation. There are likely to be some pre-insolvency methods of enforcement in progress at the onset of the bankruptcy or liquidation; the consequences of the advent of the insolvency for these are explained. The rights of some potential creditors of the insolvent will be accelerated by the insolvency so that future and contingent claims can also be dealt with in the insolvency.

2. Effect of advent of a formal insolvency

a) General principles

The debtor, once bankrupt or in liquidation, becomes subject to a collective regime in which the unsecured creditors share the available assets. This collective regime only applies to those with purely personal rights against the debtor. Where a creditor has taken security against the debtor, or otherwise obtained real rights over assets of the debtor before the insolvency, he will stand outside the collective insolvency regime to the extent of those rights.[1] The insolvency does not generally affect pre-existing rights and most vested property rights will be upheld[2] although there are certain limited circumstances in which the insolvency practitioner will be able to reclaim assets for the benefit of the creditors.[3]

---

[1] In case of a floating charge the rights are limited to an extent: see Chap. 29.

[2] The various bases on which proprietary claims may be made are examined in Chap. 28.

[3] These are examined in Chap. 30.

The right to bring or enforce individual unsecured claims against the debtor comes to an end with the onset of formal insolvency and is converted to a right to prove for the debt in the insolvency. The rationale for this was given in the early days of corporate insolvency law as maximisation of the limited assets of the insolvent through collective management of them, thus avoiding the costs involved in multiple individual actions.[4] It also has the effect of reducing harassment of the insolvent, which was one of the aims of insolvency law identified by the Cork Committee. There is some provision for the back-dating of the collectivisation to an earlier point by dint of the legislation on preferences.[5] The rules in relation to bankruptcy and the two types of liquidation are broadly the same but there are differences in detail.

b) Liquidation

The position in relation to a liquidation differs somewhat depending upon whether the liquidation is voluntary or compulsory. Where a company has gone into compulsory liquidation or a provisional liquidator has been appointed, section 130(2) of the Insolvency Act 1986 provides that no action or proceeding shall be proceeded with or commenced against the company or its property except with the leave of the court. "Action or proceeding" was held in *Re Memco Engineering Ltd*[6] to include any type of distress. In a voluntary winding up, or where a petition for compulsory liquidation has been presented but not yet adjudicated upon, there is no automatic stay but the court may on application by an interested party restrain proceedings.[7] It was held in *Re Roundwood Colliery Co*[8] that the court would exercise its power to stay in a voluntary liquidation in those circumstances in which it would not give leave under section 130(2) in a compulsory liquidation.

Under section 128 of the Insolvency Act 1986 any attachment, sequestration, distress or execution put in force against the estate or effects of the company after the commencement of a compulsory liquidation is void.[9] Section 183(1) of the Insolvency Act 1986, which applies to both types of liquidation, provides that where a creditor has issued execution against the goods or land of a company or has attached

---

[4] *Re David Lloyd* (1877) 6 Ch. D. 339.
[5] See Chap. 30.
[6] [1986] Ch. 86.
[7] Insolvency Act 1986, s.126 in the case of a compulsory winding up. In a voluntary liquidation the court has the power under Insolvency Act 1986, s.112 to exercise any power which it has in a compulsory liquidation.
[8] [1897] 1 Ch. 373.
[9] The liquidation will be deemed to have commenced on the date of the presentation of the petition on which the order was subsequently made.

any debt due to it, and the company is subsequently wound up, he is not entitled to retain the benefit of the execution or attachment against the liquidator unless he has completed the execution or attachment before the commencement of the winding up or, where the creditor has had notice of a meeting being called to consider a voluntary liquidation, before the date of that notice. Section 183(2)(c) gives the court the power to set aside the rights conferred on the liquidator by section 183(1).

In order to understand the operation of section 183 of the Insolvency Act 1986, it is necessary to identify the point at which enforcement is complete and after which the creditor will be unaffected by a subsequent liquidation. Section 183(3) provides that execution against goods will be completed by seizure and sale or by the making of a charging order; execution against land is completed by seizure, the appointment of a receiver or the making of a charging order; and attachment of a debt is completed by receipt of the debt. A person who purchases in good faith from the sheriff any goods of a company on which execution has been levied acquires a good title to them against the liquidator in all cases.[10]

Section 184 of the Insolvency Act 1986 places various duties on a sheriff[11] who has taken goods in execution of judgment. Where the sheriff is given notice of the liquidation before completion of the execution, he must on request deliver to the liquidator the goods and any money seized or recovered but the costs of the execution are a first charge on the goods or money so delivered. Where goods are sold pursuant to execution of judgment in excess of £500,[12] the sheriff charged with the execution must retain the balance of the proceeds, after deducting costs, for the 14-day period beginning with the day of sale (or of payment to avoid such sale). If within that period, the sheriff is given notice of presentation of a petition for winding up or of a meeting to consider a resolution for winding up and a liquidation follows, the proceeds shall be paid to the liquidator in priority to the claim of the execution creditor.

Although the dominant principle is that the start of a liquidation brings individual rights of enforcement to an end, it can be seen from the above that there is a discretion to allow individual action to proceed. The Court of Appeal observed recently in *Mitchell v. Buckingham International plc*[13] that the discretion is to be exercised with caution and

---

[10] Insolvency Act 1986, s.183(2)(b).

[11] Under s.184(6) the term includes any officer charged with execution of process.

[12] The amount currently prescribed by the Insolvency Proceedings (Monetary Limits Order) 1986.

[13] February 16, 1998, unreported.

only in special circumstances; the moral strength of a claim is not relevant. The courts have to decide in what circumstances they should make an exception to the collective *pari passu* rule. An argument by creditors that they could have completed enforcement in time had they not given way to the pleas of the debtor is unlikely to persuade the court. In *Re Aro*[14] the Court of Appeal held that section 183(2) gives the court the freedom to do "what is right and fair in the circumstances" and gave leave for the plaintiff to pursue a maritime claim in respect of which all the necessary steps had been taken to give the plaintiff a real right against the ship *Aro* except the service of the writ on the ship. This step had not been taken because the ship had already been arrested by another claimant and the normal practice was for further claimants to protect their position by a caveat in the Admiralty register, which the plaintiff had done. The Court of Appeal held that there was a powerful argument for leaving undisturbed this long established practice rather than sending maritime claimants the message that all claimants should go through the process of arresting the ship.

In *Re BCCI*,[15] Parker J. said that he considered that the paramount question was whether separate proceedings as opposed to the winding up process itself were the appropriate method for determining the claim. Where the proceedings have been in progress for some time and a hearing of an appeal from a refusal by the liquidator to admit the proof of debt would involve re-hearing the same issues, it may be felt appropriate to allow the case to proceed to judgment but not to allow execution of that judgment.[16] In the recent case of *Bristol & West Building Society v. Alexander and Malinek*[17] the Court was influenced by the fact that the defendants, who were solicitors facing claims of negligence and breach of contract, were insured by the Solicitors Indemnity Fund against liability. The judge referred to the principle set down in the Australian case of *ex p. Walker*[18] that leave is more likely to be granted where the defendant is insured since the intention of the legislation was not to protect insurers.

Where the creditor is claiming in respect of an obligation entered into after the start of the liquidation, permission is likely to be given to pursue the normal remedy since liquidation expenses are payable by the liquidator rather than provable in the liquidation.[19] A landlord will usually be given leave to distrain for rent due during a liquidation

---

[14] [1980] Ch. 196.
[15] [1994] 1 B.C.L.C. 419.
[16] See, *e.g. Buchler v. Chiron Corporation*, unreported, August 21, 1996.
[17] March 26, 1997, unreported.
[18] [1982] A.L.R. 423.
[19] See Chap. 35 for an explanation of the liquidation expenses principle.

provided the liquidator is positively using the premises for the purposes of the liquidation. In *Re Oak Pitts Colliery Co.*[20] it was held that it is not sufficient for the landlord to show that the liquidator had taken no steps to surrender the lease; something more than passivity is required.

c) Bankruptcy

In the case of bankruptcy, it is section 285 of the Insolvency Act 1986 which imposes restrictions on proceedings and remedies. At any time when proceedings on a bankruptcy petition are pending or an individual has been adjudged bankrupt the court may stay any action, execution or other legal process against the property or person of the debtor or bankrupt. After the making of a bankruptcy order no person who is a creditor of the bankrupt in respect of a debt provable in the bankruptcy shall have any remedy against the property or person of the bankrupt in respect of that debt or, before the discharge of the bankrupt, commence any action or other legal proceedings against the bankrupt except with the leave of the court. This is different from the position in liquidation in which all unsecured claims are subject to the same rule; in the case of a bankruptcy, any action may be stayed but only claims which are provable in bankruptcy[21] will automatically be stayed. In *Re Smith*[22], the House of Lords (holding that "legal process" included the issue of a warrant of committal for non-payment of rates) held that section 285 of the Insolvency Act 1986 was to be considered as new legislation and regard need not be had to previous authorities. In *Re Saunders*[23] it was held, refusing to follow *Re National Employees Mutual General Insurance Association*,[24] that the necessary leave may be given retrospectively. It was held that sections 130 and 285 of the Insolvency Act 1986 are sufficiently similar that case law under the one was likely to be applicable to the other.

Section 285(4) of the Insolvency Act 1986 provides that the section does not "affect the right of a secured creditor of the bankrupt to enforce his security". *Razzaq v. Pala*[25] required Lightman J. to consider whether section 285 prevented a landlord from relying on a right of re-entry. A landlord had forfeited a lease for non-payment of rent after a bankruptcy order had been made against the tenant and the court had to decide, first, whether forfeiture by re-entry was the enforcement of a security and,

---

[20] (1882) 21 Ch. D. 322.
[21] See the next section of this Chapter.
[22] [1990] 2 A.C. 215.
[23] [1997] 3 All E.R. 992.
[24] [1995] 1 B.C.L.C. 232.
[25] [1997] E.G.C.S. 75.

secondly, whether it constituted a remedy against the property of the tenant. Lightman J. held that the right of re-entry was neither a security interest[26] nor a remedy since it merely prevented the recurrence of breaches of covenant and removed a defaulting tenant from the premises. The forfeiture was, therefore, valid[27] although the court granted the tenant relief from it since the rent had been brought up to date.

Section 346 of the Insolvency Act 1986 provides that the creditor of a bankrupt is not entitled to retain the benefit of an execution or attachment, or sums paid to avoid it, unless the process has been completed or sums paid before the commencement of the bankruptcy.[28] This is a parallel provision to section 183 which was outlined above in relation to liquidation and contains a similar discretion for the court to set aside the rights conferred on the official receiver or trustee. Goods cannot be claimed from a person who has acquired them in good faith from an officer charged with an execution. Section 346(3) and (4) place the same obligations on a sheriff charged with execution as are imposed by section 184 in the case of a liquidation. Section 346(8) provides that these obligations do not apply in relation to property acquired by the bankrupt after the commencement of the bankruptcy[29] unless the sheriff had notice before the execution was completed that the property was being claimed by the trustee in bankruptcy under section 307 of the Insolvency Act 1986.

Section 347 of the Insolvency Act 1986 provides that the right to distrain for rent upon the goods and effects of an undischarged bankrupt is available against the bankrupt's estate[30] but only for six months' rent accrued due before the commencement of the bankruptcy. Landlords may not subsequently distrain against property in the bankrupt's estate after the discharge of the bankrupt. If a landlord distrains after a petition for bankruptcy has been presented and an order is subsequently made, any amount in excess of the six months' rent will be held for the bankrupt as part of his estate. Any right to distrain other than for rent is not affected by the bankruptcy order even if the right is expressed by statute to be exercisable in like manner as a right to distrain for rent.

[26] See discussion of the right of re-entry in relation to the interim order in an IVA (Chap. 9.3) and the moratorium in a company administration (Chap. 10.4). Lightman J. relied on a Court of Appeal authority, *Ezekiel v. Orakpo* [1977] 1 Q.B. 260, which was not referred to in the rescue regime cases.

[27] The judge also rejected a suggestion that the forfeiture was a knowing wrongful interference with the official receiver's performance of his duties as an officer of the court.

[28] Insolvency Act 1986, s.346(5) makes the same provision for completion of process as outlined above in relation to liquidation.

[29] See Chap. 27.4.

[30] This contrasts with the position in liquidation, where leave of the court will have to be obtained by the landlord.

3. Proving debts

a) Provable debts

On the commencement of a bankruptcy or liquidation the creditor's right to pursue the debtor to judgment in court is usually converted to a right to prove for a dividend in the distribution of the estate. The creditor will have to establish that he is claiming in respect of a debt or liability to which a company or bankrupt was subject at the start of the insolvency or which subsequently arose by reason of any obligation incurred before the insolvency.[31] "Liability" is defined as a liability to pay money or money's worth, including any liability under an enactment, any liability for breach of trust, any liability in contract, tort or bailment, and any liability arising out of an obligation to make restitution. All claims by creditors in an insolvency not specifically excluded are provable as debts against the company or bankrupt whether they are present or future, certain or contingent, ascertained or sounding only in damages.[32] Debts can therefore be proved which have arisen after the commencement of the insolvency under contracts entered into previously; for example, failure to meet rental obligations after the commencement of the insolvency gives rise to a provable debt since the obligation to pay was incurred before the insolvency even though the debt did not arise until subsequently. Damages for tort are only provable if the cause of action, which is what creates the obligation, accrued before the commencement of the insolvency. Liabilities which arise after the start of the insolvency will be expenses of the insolvency rather than provable debts.[33]

A secured creditor who is not relying solely on his security has a choice. He may value his security in his proof and prove for the balance of the debt, realise his security and prove for any deficiency or surrender his security and prove for the entire debt.[34]

In the case of a liquidation there are few debts which cannot be proved since, given that liquidation brings the company's existence to an end, there is no possibility of any debt surviving a liquidation. A

---

[31] The definitions of debt and liability are contained in Insolvency Rules 1986, r. 13.12 in relation to liquidations (the debts are those to which the company is subject at the date on which it goes into liquidation which is defined by Insolvency Act 1986, s.247(2)) and Insolvency Act 1986, s.382 in relation to bankruptcies (the debts are those to which the bankrupt is subject on the date of the order).

[32] Insolvency Rules 1986, r. 12.3, which specifies some of the excluded debts. Rule 12.3(2A) provides for the possibility of postponed debts which are not provable until all other claims in the insolvency proceedings have been paid in full with interest.

[33] See Chap. 35.

[34] Insolvency Rules 1986, rr. 4.75, 4.88 in a liquidation, rr. 6.98, 6.109 in a bankruptcy.

bankrupt, however, will survive the bankruptcy and, although the bankrupt is discharged from bankruptcy and released from most of the debts,[35] some debts do survive the bankruptcy. Some of these surviving debts may also be the subject of proof in the bankruptcy[36] but some are not provable in the bankruptcy and the creditors will only be able to take action after the discharge of the bankrupt. Although within the definition of bankruptcy debts, claims for fines imposed for an offence and obligations arising under orders made in family proceedings or under maintenance assessments under the Child Support Act 1991 are not provable and the bankrupt is not released from them on discharge. Pre-1986, the law was that arrears of maintenance in family proceedings were not provable in a bankruptcy but that an outstanding lump sum, although not released by discharge, was provable.[37]

The case of *Woodley v. Woodley*[38] reflects the current law. In this case, the court ordered a divorced husband to pay a lump sum of £60,000 to the wife; no capital could be identified but the judge was of the view that the husband had concealed the existence of assets. The husband did not pay and was made bankrupt on his own petition. The wife issued a judgment summons seeking the husband's committal to prison for wilful refusal to pay. The husband argued that the bankruptcy made it impossible to pay. The court at first instance held that the bankruptcy was no bar because the lump sum order was not a debt provable in the bankruptcy. In the Court of Appeal it was held that this view failed to take account of the fact that the assets had all vested in the trustee. The Court pointed to the possible inconsistency between sections 382 and 281 of the Insolvency Act 1986, which described a lump sum order as a bankruptcy debt but one which survived the bankruptcy, and Rule 12(3) of the Insolvency Rules 1986, which provided that the debt was not provable in the bankruptcy. When a differently constituted Court of Appeal had occasion to consider the matter again subsequently it did not accept that Rule 12.3 might be open to challenge but invited the attention of the Insolvency Rules Committee to consider restoring the former position under which a lump sum order could be proved but would not be released on the debtor's discharge. Balcombe L.J. pointed out that there was no necessary or logical link between provability of a debt and its release on discharge; it is true that there are debts which are

---

[35] The exceptions are set out in Insolvency Act 1986, s.281. See Chap. 15 above.
[36] Where the debt results from some fraud or fraudulent breach of trust to which the bankrupt was a party and, unless the court orders otherwise, damages in respect of personal injuries.
[37] See *Curtis v. Curtis* [1969] 1 W.L.R. 422.
[38] [1993] 1 F.C.R. 701 and *Woodley v. Woodley (No. 2)* [1993] Fam. Law 471. See also *Re Mordant* [1995] B.C.C. 209. Miller (1994) 10 I.L. & P. 66.

not provable and are not released but equally liability to pay damages in respect of personal injuries is provable and is not released.[39] He said: "It seems therefore that any link between provability and release on discharge is a matter of policy and I can see good policy grounds for saying that a lump sum order made in family proceedings should (like damages for personal injuries) be both provable in bankruptcy and yet not be released on discharge". If this had been the state of the law, the wife in *Woodley* would have been in a position to get the trustee to investigate the disappearance of the husband's assets.

It is understandable that periodical maintenance payments are not provable in the bankruptcy; the essence of such payments is that they are made out of current income and, in calculating the extent to which a bankrupt can be required to make over his income under an income payments order,[40] the court will not make an order which would reduce the income of the bankrupt below what appears to be necessary for meeting the reasonable domestic needs of the bankrupt and his family.

b) The rule against double proof

The rule against double proof prevents more than one proof being submitted in respect of the same debt. The most common situation of potential double proof relates to contracts of suretyship or guarantee.[41] Sureties or guarantors of debts of the insolvent have contingent claims against the insolvent in that they may be called upon to pay the principal creditor of the insolvent. If both principal creditor and guarantor were permitted to claim, the same debt might be paid twice.[42] The rule against double proof was considered recently by Robert Walker J. in *Re Polly Peck International plc*,[43] a case brought by the administrators of Polly Peck International plc for directions in connection with a scheme of arrangement which was to provide for the collection, realisation and distribution of the assets of Polly Peck International in what the judge described as "a sort of notional liquidation in advance of any actual liquidation, with a view to saving costs". The scheme provided that claims should only be admitted which would be admissible in a compulsory liquidation commencing on the date the scheme took effect. Polly Peck International plc had raised money via its wholly owned subsidiary, PPIF, which had issued £400 million of bonds and then on-lent the

---

[39] See Insolvency Act 1986, s.281(5)(a).
[40] See Chap. 27.5.
[41] It may operate in other circumstances. See, *e.g. The Liverpool (No. 2)* [1963] P. 64.
[42] See Mellish L.J. in *re Oriental Commercial Bank* (1871) 7 Ch. App 99.
[43] [1996] B.C.C. 486.

money to Polly Peck International. Polly Peck International had guaranteed repayment of the bonds to the bondholders. PPIF had gone into liquidation and the liquidator was claiming repayment of the loan from Polly Peck International, which was also facing claims from the bondholders on the guarantees. Robert Walker J. held[44] that the creditors (the bondholders) were entitled to proceed against both debtor (PPIF) and guarantor (Polly Peck), although not to receive more than was owed in total. He also observed that the guarantor could only prove in the debtor's liquidation if it had paid the creditors in full, in which case the creditors would drop out of the matter. The guarantor would not be able to claim in competition with the creditor since the guarantor's contingent claim was not regarded as an independent, free-standing debt but only as a reflection of the "real" debt.

It has been held[45] that a distinction has to be drawn between the guarantee of part of a debt and the guarantee of a whole debt subject to a maximum limit on the liability of the guarantor which is less than the amount of the guaranteed debt. In the former case, payment of the amount guaranteed entitles the guarantor to prove since he has discharged his entire liability to the creditor whereas in the latter case only the creditor may prove. The guarantee of the whole of a fluctuating debt (such as an overdraft) with a limit on the liability of the guarantor will be construed as a guarantee of part of the debt unless the guarantee contract provides otherwise.

c) Procedure for proving debts

The detailed provisions on proof of debts are contained in the Insolvency Rules.[46] In the case of a bankruptcy or compulsory liquidation, proof of debt forms requiring specified details will be sent out to every known creditor. In a voluntary liquidation debts may be proved more informally. The insolvency practitioner in any kind of insolvency may require affidavit support for the claim and if the claim is rejected in whole or in part, the insolvency practitioner must give reasons in writing to the creditor concerned. The creditor is then entitled to apply to the

---

[44] Refusing to "lift the corporate veil" and treat parent and subsidiaries companies as one entity, in which case the bondholders would have been bringing the same claim twice.

[45] See *Ellis v. Emmanuel* (1876) 1 Ex. D. 157, *Re Sass* [1896] 2 Q.B. 12, *Barclays v. TOSG* (1984) 1 B.C.C. 99,017 (in the Court of Appeal. The case went to the House of Lords (1984) 1 B.C.C. 99,081 where it was held that the debts in question were mutually exclusive and the rule against double proof did not have to be considered).

[46] Insolvency Rules 1986, rr. 4.73 to 4.94 in the case of a liquidation and 6.96 to 6.107 in the case of a bankruptcy.

court within 21 days of the date of service of the rejection for the decision to be reversed. There is no time limit for the submission of proof of debt but a creditor who has not proved his debt cannot benefit from any distribution of the assets nor vote at any meeting of creditors. Before declaring a dividend, notice must be given of the intention to do so to all known creditors who have not yet proved their debts.

d) Quantification of claims

The insolvency practitioner will estimate the value of any debt which, because it is subject to a contingency or for some other reason, does not bear a certain value and this estimated amount will be the amount provable.[47] A debt incurred or payable in a currency other than sterling will be converted into sterling at the official exchange rate prevailing on the day of the bankruptcy order or when the company went into liquidation.[48] In case of rent and other payments of a periodical nature, the creditor may prove for any amounts due and unpaid up to the date when the liquidation began or the bankruptcy order was made.[49] A creditor may prove for a debt of which payment was not yet due on the date of going into liquidation or bankruptcy[50] but the dividend payable will be adjusted for early payment.[51] Where a debt bears interest, interest in respect of the period before the start of the liquidation or bankruptcy will be provable as part of the debt. Interest up to the start of the insolvency may also be claimed in respect of a debt due by virtue of a written instrument which is payable at a certain time or where notice was served before the insolvency demanding payment and indicating an intention to charge interest from the date of the demand; in either case, the rate of interest will be that specified in section 17 of the Judgments Act 1838 on the date of the bankruptcy order or when the company went into liquidation.[52]

In quantifying the amount of the claim, the insolvency rules on set-off, which are considered in the next section, must be taken into account.

---

[47] Insolvency Rules 1986, r. 4.86 in a liquidation; Insolvency Act 1986, s.322(4) in the case of a bankruptcy.
[48] Insolvency Rules 1986, r. 4.91 (liquidation), r. 6.111 (bankruptcy).
[49] *ibid.*, r. 4.92 (liquidation), r. 6.112 (bankruptcy).
[50] *ibid.*, r. 4.94 (liquidation), r. 6.114 (bankruptcy).
[51] In accordance with the formula provided in r. 11.13.
[52] The rules on interest are contained in Insolvency Rules 1986, r. 4.93 (liquidation) and r. 6.113.

4. Mutual credit and set-off[53]

a) General

In quantifying the amount of the provable debts, the insolvency rules on set-off must be taken into account.[54] In the case of a bankruptcy, section 323 of the Insolvency Act 1986 provides as follows:

"(1) This section applies where before the commencement of the bankruptcy there have been mutual credits, mutual debts or other mutual dealings between the bankrupt and any creditor proving or claiming to prove for a bankruptcy debt.

(2) An account shall be taken of what is due from each party to the other in respect of the mutual dealings and the sums due from one party shall be set off against the sums due from the other.

(3) Sums due from the bankrupt to another party shall not be included in the account taken under subsection (2) if that other party had notice at the time they became due that a bankruptcy petition relating to the bankrupt was pending".

Similar provision is made in respect of a liquidation; rather oddly, it is tucked away in the Insolvency Rules 1986 rather than being in the main body of the Act. Rule 4.90 is to the same effect as section 323; sums due to a creditor are to be excluded if at the time they became due the creditor had notice either of a petition for a compulsory winding up or of notice calling a meeting to put the company into voluntary liquidation.

These provisions will benefit a creditor of an insolvent[55] because he will get full credit for any amounts owed to the insolvent. Were it not for the set-off rules, the creditor of an insolvent would have to make full payment of any amounts owed whilst receiving only a dividend in respect of the amount owing from the insolvent; one explanation for the

---

[53] This account draws heavily on S.R. Derham, *Set-off* (2nd ed.). See also P. Wood, *English and International Set-off*, Goode, *Principles of Corporate Insolvency* (2nd ed.), Chap. 8. In relation to employee creditors, see Pollard 11 I.L. & P. 46.

[54] These are not the same as the equitable and statutory rules of set-off which apply where the parties are not insolvent. See Derham, *Set-Off* (2nd ed.). Other forms of set-off which have taken effect before the start of the liquidation or bankruptcy may be relevant in the calculation of the indebtedness at that point.

[55] There is scope for terminological confusion in discussion of set-off since the parties involved will be both debtor and creditor. In this discussion, the term "creditor" is employed to describe the non-insolvent party unless the contrary is made clear.

development of these rules is that this was perceived as an injustice.[56] It is true that, as between the insolvent and the individual creditor, the set-off rules appear fair but the rules do have the effect of excluding some or all of the amount owing from the assets available to the creditors generally.[57]

By way of example, suppose that a bankrupt or company being wound up owed a creditor £100, that the creditor owed the insolvent £60 and that a distribution of 10 per cent would be all that the insolvency practitioner would be able to make to ordinary creditors. In the absence of set-off, the creditor would be under an obligation to pay £60 to the company and would receive £10 in the distribution; a net loss to the creditor of £50. The set-off provisions extinguish the claim against the creditor and leave him with a provable debt of £40 in respect of which he will be paid £4; a net gain of £4.[58]

The insolvency set-off provisions have been held to be mandatory and creditors are not allowed to contract out of the right.[59] The Cork Committee recommended[60] that a creditor should be allowed to renounce the right but the recommendation was not acted upon in the drafting of the legislation.

b) Circumstances in which set-off applies

The legislation requires that the creditor and the insolvent have "mutual credits, mutual debts or other mutual dealings". It is necessary to consider, first, which claims and transactions fall into the categories of credits, debts or dealings[61] and, secondly, what the requirement of mutuality imports.

Debts are claims which are both in existence and presently payable and credits, which would include debts payable at a future date, must be

---

[56] In *Stein v. Blake* [1995] 2 All E.R. 961 Lord Hoffmann said that where parties have been giving credit to each other in reliance on their ability to secure payment by withholding, it would be unjust to deprive the solvent party of this security. The origin of the rule is lost in history since, although the statutory provision only dates back to 1705, it reflects practice previous to this; it is likely that the explanation lies, at least in part, in a combination of the accounting practices of the Elizabethan commissioners in bankruptcy and the tendency of established practice to become embedded in English law.

[57] It is not a rule universally applied in other jurisdictions. See *Re BCCI SA (No. 10)* [1996] 4 All E.R. 796.

[58] The dividend percentage would not, in fact, be the same in both situations since the effect of the set-off would reduce the total quantity of assets available to be divided amongst the creditors.

[59] *National Westminster Bank v. Halesowen Presswork and Assemblies* [1972] A.C., *Stein v. Blake* [1995] 2 All E.R. 961. See the discussion in Chap. 35 below on the difficulties of contracting out of the statutory scheme of distribution.

[60] para. 1342. See Chap. 30 of the Cork Report generally on set-off.

[61] See Derham, Chap. 3.

at least likely to result in debts.[62] Dealings,[63] a category introduced into the legislation in 1869, are wider and probably include all ordinary business transactions; for example, damages claims for breach of contract, transactions which are only debateably mutual credits and debts arising after the insolvency from prior transactions. This apparently goes beyond dealings arising out of contract; in *Re DH Curtis (Builders) Ltd*[64] the cross-claims arose from the provisions of the tax legislation and it was held that the set-off provisions applied. It is necessary for a claim to be provable before set-off can apply but the fact that a claim is provable will not necessarily be enough; it seems unlikely that a claim in tort not arising out of a prior dealing would fall within the provision.[65]

Mutuality requires that the demands be between the same parties and that they be held in the same capacity, right or interest. Mutuality will be determined by reference to the beneficial, rather than the bare, legal rights of the parties.[66] The courts have recently had to consider whether an insolvent bank can set off the amounts owed by borrowers against its liability to repay sums of money deposited with it by guarantors[67] of the borrowers' obligations. In *M. S. Fashions Ltd v. BCCI*[68] the guarantor had given both a personal guarantee and a deposit and it was held that since the guarantor had incurred personal liability to the bank, there was sufficient mutuality for set-off. In *Re BCCI (No. 8)*[69] the depositors did not give a personal guarantee to the bank in addition to the deposit. The bank's liquidators wanted to know whether they should attempt to recover the whole of the loan from the principal debtors and leave the depositors to prove in the liquidation or whether they should set off the amount of the outstanding loan against the deposit and claim from the principal debtor only so much, if any, of the loan as exceeded the amount of the deposit. It was held that there was a lack of mutuality and set-off was not possible; there was no obligation due from depositor to bank in respect of which the obligation to repay could be set off. The depositors would have to prove in the liquidation[70]; Lord Hoffmann

[62] *Palmer v. Day & Sons* [1895] 2 Q.B. 618, 621.
[63] See *Peat v. Jones & Co* (1881) 8 Q.B.D. 147, *Eberle's Hotels and Restaurant Co. Ltd v. E. Jonas & Brothers* (1887) 18 Q.B.D. 459.
[64] [1978] 1 Ch. 162.
[65] See Derham 3.5.
[66] *BCCI v. Prince Fahd Bin Salaman Abdul Aziz Al-Saud* [1997] B.C.C. 63.
[67] The guarantors were the beneficial owners of the borrowing companies.
[68] [1993] Ch. 425.
[69] [1997] 4 All E.R. 568, HL, affirming the Court of Appeal's decision at [1996] 2 All E.R. 121.
[70] This produces the paradox that the bank was better off for not having taken a personal guarantee from the depositors. See Evans (1996) 17 Co. Lawyer 102 for a suggestion of how this paradox could be avoided.

observed that the sense of injustice felt by the depositors arose from the principle of separate legal personality (in that the depositors were only third parties in the eyes of the law and not in economic reality) rather than the rules of set-off.

The question has arisen as to whether there is mutuality where the cross-transactions involve different departments of the Crown. In *Re DH Curtis*[71] it was held that tax due to one department of the Crown may be set off against a repayment due from a different department. Both transactions were with the Crown and set-off can arise out of different transactions between the same parties. The Cork Committee[72] felt that this treatment of the Crown as one and indivisible conferred an unwarranted preference on it and recommended that government departments should be treated as separate entities for the purpose of set-off.[73] It also recommended that there should be no set-off between contractual and statutory obligations. These recommendations were not implemented.

Where a creditor is owed both preferential[74] and ordinary debts, the creditor would prefer to set off first against the non-preferred debt. In *Re Unit 2 Windows Ltd*,[75] Walton J. said that equity required that the rights of set-off should be exercised proportionately against each class of debt.

Set-off can only apply where the claims on each side are money demands. A proprietary claim may not be set off against a money claim.[76] A secured creditor may chose to rely entirely on the security in which case the set-off provisions are irrelevant unless there is a balance owing after enforcement. Alternatively, he may chose to surrender the security and prove for the debt, or value the security and prove for the balance. Where the creditor elects to prove on one of these bases, the provable debt can be the subject of a set-off.[77] Where the creditor has both secured and unsecured debt, he may chose to rely on the set-off as against the unsecured debt; the principle of *Re Unit 2 Windows Ltd* does not apply.

---

[71] [1978] 1 Ch. 162. This was a case on the Bankruptcy Act 1914 but would be decided in the same way under the current legislation.

[72] and the Blagden Committee before it.

[73] Cork Report paras. 306–7, 309.

[74] See Chap. 35.

[75] [1985] 1 W.L.R. 1383.

[76] *Rolls Razor Ltd v. Cox* [1967] 1 Q.B. 552 appears to be an exception in that a salesman entrusted with the company's goods was entitled to keep them by way of set-off against sums owing to him by the company. The case may be justifiable on other bases but is probably wrong on the law relating to set-off.

[77] *Re Norman Holding Co. Ltd* [1991] 1 W.L.R. 10.

c) Effect of set-off

The date which defines the accounts to be balanced is the date of the commencement of the bankruptcy[78] or of going into liquidation.[79] This means, for example, that where the insolvency practitioner sells goods after the commencement of the insolvency, the purchaser will not be able to set off his liability for the price against a provable debt owed to him.

The House of Lords in *Stein v. Blake*[80] held that the balance will be struck automatically as at that date so that the separate debts cease to exist. In this case, the parties were involved in litigation in which each had a claim against the other. Before the action came to trial the plaintiff was adjudicated bankrupt and his trustee in bankruptcy assigned to him the trustee's claims in the action in return for a share of the net proceeds recovered in the action.[81] The defendant applied to have the action dismissed, claiming that after the plaintiff had become bankrupt the plaintiff's claim and the defendant's counterclaim fell to be dealt with in the bankruptcy and until an account had been taken under section 323 of the Insolvency Act 1986 there was nothing to assign. The House of Lords held that the claims had been extinguished as separate choses in action by section 323 and replaced by a claim for the net balance. The trustee in bankruptcy could assign a claim to the net balance before that balance had been ascertained. The trustee had, therefore, been entitled to assign to the plaintiff his claim against the defendant.

A contingent liability owed by the insolvent may have a value put on it; in *Stein v. Blake* Lord Hoffmann said that "due" means treated as having been owing at the relevant date with the benefit of hindsight and, if necessary, estimation prescribed by the insolvency law. The case of *Re Charge Card*[82] concerned a company which operated a charge card scheme and assigned its receivables to a factor under an agreement that if the company went into liquidation it could be required to repurchase the debts at face value. The court had to decide whether, if a notice requiring repurchase was given after liquidation (so that at the start of the liquidation the liability to do so was merely contingent), the factor could set off the company's liability to pay the price against a debt owing by the factor to the company. Millett J. held that provided the

---

[78] The date of the order.
[79] The date of the resolution in a voluntary liquidation or of the court order; in a case involving both, it will be the earlier date.
[80] [1995] 2 All E.R. 961.
[81] See Chap. 32 on the problems faced by insolvency practitioners in funding litigation.
[82] [1988] 3 W.L.R. 764, CA, affirming [1987] Ch. 150.

contingent liability is wholly referable to a prior agreement between the parties (as was the case here), set-off between them will be possible.

There is, however, no machinery for quantifying contingent or unascertained claims of an insolvent against a creditor and such claims cannot be included in the insolvency set-off account.

d) Limitations on application of set-off

The statutory provisions substitute an earlier date for striking the account where the other party had notice of a pending petition or of a meeting to consider a resolution for winding up. This does not deal with the situation where it is quite apparent to the creditor that the debtor is unable to pay his debts; the creditor will be able to assign the debt to someone indebted to the debtor who will thereby be able to obtain the full value of the assigned debt in the course of an insolvency. The Cork Committee recognised this problem[83] and recommended a change to the rules but this has not happened.

The principle precluding a person from relying on his own wrongful act to obtain a set-off extends to fraud, breach of trust and misfeasance amounting to breach of fiduciary duty but probably not to breach of contract committed in order to benefit from set-off.[84]

e) Multiple bank accounts

Where a customer has several accounts with a bank, some in credit and some in debit, the bank may combine the accounts and proceed on the basis of the combined balance. The bank can thereby obtain the full benefit of the account in credit by setting it against the account in debit. This principle arises from the fact that there will be only one banker/customer relationship regardless of the number of accounts in existence.

---

[83] paras. 127, 307.
[84] Derham 4.7.3.

CHAPTER 26

ASSETS AVAILABLE TO THE CREDITORS: GENERAL PRINCIPLES

1. Introduction

The insolvent is likely to have a variety of assets which could be realised and the proceeds distributed to the creditors; most of these will become available to the creditors. In the case of a bankruptcy, the bankrupt's estate will fall into the custody and control of the official receiver on the making of the bankruptcy order[1] and will subsequently vest by operation of law without further formality in the trustee in bankruptcy when appointed,[2] with relation back to the start of the bankruptcy so that the trustee will be deemed to have owned the assets since the date of the bankruptcy order. There is an obligation on the bankrupt[3] to deliver up to the trustee any property of which he has possession or control and of which the trustee is required to take possession. In contrast, the assets of a company in liquidation do not normally vest in the liquidator; the liquidator takes control of them[4] as agent for the company which remains the legal owner, holding the assets on trust for the creditors.[5] This distinction means that provision has to be made in a bankruptcy in respect of assets which materialise after the vesting of the estate in the trustee[6]; in the case of a liquidation, no such provision is necessary.

A bankruptcy also involves the additional complication that the bankrupt and any dependants will need to be left sufficient assets with which to maintain themselves.[7] An obviously difficult policy issue

---

[1] Insolvency Act 1986, s.287.
[2] *ibid.*, s.306.
[3] *ibid.*, s.312.
[4] *ibid.*, s.144. The court has the power under Insolvency Act 1986, s.145 to vest property in the liquidator if necessary.
[5] If necessary, Insolvency Act 1986, s.234(2) gives the court the power to require any person to hand over to the liquidator property in his possession or control to which the company appears to be entitled.
[6] See Chap. 27.4. There is an obligation on the bankrupt to notify the trustee of any property or increased income to which he becomes entitled during the course of the bankruptcy: s.333(2).
[7] See Chap. 27.

arises of the extent to which the creditors should suffer for the needs of the bankrupt's family and vice versa. The family home and the bankrupt's pension[8] have given rise to particular problems. All the assets of a company will be distributed but there are exceptions in the case of a bankruptcy; in *Re Rae*[9] Warner J. said "The specific exceptions exist either because the property is not appropriate for distribution among the bankrupt's creditors, such as property of which he is only a trustee, or because, unlike an insolvent company, the bankrupt is a human being whose life must continue during and after insolvency".

As will be seen, the insolvency legislation has a very wide concept of the property which is available for distribution but, as indicated in the dictum of Warner J. quoted in the previous paragraph, the insolvency practitioner may only realise such beneficial interest as the insolvent holds in the assets.[10]

Some of the available assets may constitute a burden on the insolvent's estate rather than being capable of realising any distributable value. The insolvency practitioner may be able to disclaim assets which would otherwise have been available; this is considered in further detail below.

2. Property available

a) Definition of property

The term "property", as defined by section 436 of the Insolvency Act 1986, is of pivotal importance. Section 144 of the same Act provides that in a compulsory winding up the liquidator takes into his custody or under his control all the property and things in action to which the company is entitled.[11] Section 107 of the Insolvency Act 1986 provides that the company's property in a voluntary winding up shall on the winding up be applied in satisfaction of the company's liabilities. In a bankruptcy the bankrupt's estate, which vests in the trustee once appointed, comprises all property belonging to or vested in the bankrupt at the commencement of the bankruptcy and property which by virtue of the Act is treated as falling into that category.[12]

---

[8] See Chap. 33.
[9] [1995] B.C.C. 102.
[10] See below and see Chap. 28 for third party claims to beneficial interests in the assets.
[11] Insolvency Act 1986, s.143 uses the term "assets" rather than "property" in obliging the liquidator in a court winding up to secure that the assets of the company are got in, realised and distributed to the company's creditors; it seems likely that assets and property would be considered synonymous.
[12] Insolvency Act 1986, s.283. Chap. 27 explains the assets which are excluded from the bankrupt's estate.

It is, therefore, necessary to consider the definition of "property" for the purposes of the insolvency legislation. Section 436 of the Insolvency Act 1986 provides that, except in so far as the context requires, property "includes money, goods, things in action, land and every description of property wherever situated and also obligations and every description of interest, whether present or future or vested or contingent, arising out of, or incidental to, property". It is to be noted that the definition is self-referential in that it includes without definition the word "property"; Warner J. in *Re Rae*[13] said that in the insolvency context the word connoted anything which is capable of being owned and of which the ownership can be asserted or defended in legal proceedings and he pointed out that "property" as defined by section 436 is a wider concept than this. The Court of Appeal in *Bristol Airport plc v. Powdrill*[14] observed of section 436 that it "is hard to think of a wider definition of property".

This extensive but not exhaustive definition clearly encompasses interests in land (freeholds and leaseholds) and personal property, both tangible and choses in action (including documentary intangibles). Intangible property will include goodwill of a business and intellectual property such as copyrights, patents and trade marks. Choses in action consist of personal rights to claim property rather than the actual physical property itself; included in this category are debts, negotiable instruments, shares, legacies and rights of action[15] arising from torts and breaches of contract. One issue which has given rise to considerable debate is the extent to which a bankrupt's pension rights vest in the trustee in bankruptcy; this topic is considered in greater detail in Chap. 33.

The extent of the concept of property is illustrated by the case of *Re Rae*.[16] The bankrupt in this case had traded as the owner of four fishing vessels for which he held fishing licences under the Sea Fish (Conservation) Act 1967; the vessels vested in the trustee in bankruptcy but the licences did not. The effect of the bankruptcy order was to invalidate the licences but the Ministry of Agriculture and Fisheries recognised what was referred to as an "entitlement" (although this was completely at the discretion of the Ministry) in the holder, or in any person in whose favour the holder waived the entitlement, to be considered for the grant of fresh licences. That entitlement had a value, in that a practice had developed of the licence holder receiving a payment for the surrender of a licence which enabled the payer to receive a licence at the discretion

---

[13] [1995] B.C.C. 102.
[14] [1990] B.C.C. 130.
[15] See Chap. 32 on selling causes of action.
[16] [1995] B.C.C. 102.

of the Secretary of State; the issue in the case was whether the entitlement should enure for the benefit of the creditors or of the bankrupt
himself. If the entitlement were property within the Insolvency Act and
had therefore vested in the trustee, the court could order the bankrupt to
sign the necessary waiver.[17] The judge concluded that to construe the
Act as excluding the "entitlement" from the property available to the
creditors would be contrary to the purposes of the Act. He decided that
the entitlement came within the category "every description of interest"
which was wide enough to include interests not enforceable in a court
of law but nonetheless marketable and capable of being turned into
money and that this interest was incidental to the property rights in the
vessels and was, therefore, within the definition.

There are some limitations on the breadth of section 436 of the
Insolvency Act 1986. Cozens-Hardy L.J. in *Bailey v. Thurston & Co.
Ltd*[18] held that, despite the generality of the language used in the
Bankruptcy Acts, there were some contracts which could not vest in the
trustee in bankruptcy. These included contracts for purely personal
services although sums due in respect of such services which had been
rendered would vest in the trustee. In *Re Campbell*[19] it was held that the
prospect of receiving an award by the Criminal Injuries Compensation
Board did not amount to an interest in property since the definition in
section 436 could only encompass existing items (including existing
contingent and future interests).[20] In *City of London v. Brown*[21] it was
held that rights which are purely personal to the insolvent and not
capable of being realised for the benefit of the creditors will not be
included in the property which the insolvency practitioner is entitled to
disclaim. Purely personal claims of the bankrupt such as personal injury
or libel actions will not fall into the bankrupt's estate.

b) Defeasible interests

The insolvency practitioner will take property subject to any pre-
existing equities or other rights over the assets; the insolvency practitioner will, for example, be bound by the right of a seller to rescind a

---

[17] Under the power given to it by the Insolvency Act 1986, s.363 to direct the bankrupt to
assist in the administration of the estate.
[18] [1903] 1 K.B. 137 at 145.
[19] [1996] 2 All E.R. 537.
[20] It would appear that the trustee based his claim to the sum subsequently awarded on the
grounds that it was property which had vested at the start of the bankruptcy. There
would appear to have been no claim to it as after-acquired property.
[21] (1989) 22 H.L.R. 32. Insolvency Act 1986, s.283 as amended by s.117 of the Housing
Act 1988 now reflects this decision.

contract which he had been induced to enter by the fraud of the buyer.[22]

The insolvent may have held the assets on terms that insolvency would bring the interest to an end. A transfer of property upon the condition that the asset will revest if the transferee becomes insolvent is void as contrary to insolvency law[23] and also for repugnancy as such a provision is inconsistent with the outright transfer of ownership.[24] It is, however, often possible to achieve the same effect by conferring an interest which is expressed to be defeasible in the event of the transferee's insolvency. An example is the use of clauses in leases providing for re-entry on the lessee's insolvency[25]; the insolvency is treated as marking the limit of the lessee's interest rather than as imposing an invalid condition on it. The court will have jurisdiction to relieve against forfeiture under section 146 of the Law of Property Act 1925[26] within the year[27] after the commencement of the insolvency (and indefinitely if the lease is sold by the insolvency practitioner within that year) and will usually be willing to grant relief if the tenant pays the arrears and the landlord's expenses.

In *Transag Haulage Ltd v. DAF Finance plc*[28] the courts recognised the validity of a clause providing that insolvency of the lessee would determine a chattel lease and held that there was an equitable jurisdiction to relieve against forfeiture in such a case. This was a case in which receivers had taken possession of vehicles supplied to the insolvent company under hire purchase contracts which provided for termination and repossession of the vehicles in the event, *inter alia*, of the appointment of receivers. The vehicles were worth a total of about £70,000 and the remaining instalments to be paid amounted to about £14,000. The court agreed that the loss of the right to exercise the option to purchase

---

[22] *Gladstone v. Hawden* (1813) 1 M. & S. 517, *Re Eastgate* [1905] 1 K.B. 465, *Tilley v. Bourman Ltd* [1910] 1 K.B. 745, *Transag Haulage Ltd v. DAF Finance plc* [1994] 2 B.C.L.C. 88.

[23] In particular, the principle that a person is not allowed to agree with a creditor for a different distribution of his assets in an insolvency from that provided by law. See Chap. 33.3 for further discussion of this principle.

[24] *Holroyd v. Gwynne* (1809) 2 Taunt. 176, *ex p. Mackay* (1873) 8 Ch. App. 643.

[25] As early as *Roe d. Hunter v. Galliers* (1787) 2 T.R. 133 it was settled that a proviso for determination of a lease on bankruptcy would be valid. *Civil Service Co-operative Society Ltd v. Trustee of McGrigor* [1923] 2 Ch. 347 is a more recent example.

[26] See Milman and Davey, [1996] J.B.L. 541 at 546.

[27] If the lease is not sold within the year, there is no subsequent jurisdiction to relieve from forfeiture since it has been held that s.146 of the Law of Property Act 1925 ousts any non-statutory jurisdiction: *Official Custodian for Charities v. Parway Estates Development Ltd* [1985] Ch. 151.

[28] [1994] 2 B.C.L.C. 88.

at the end of the hire period was the loss of a proprietary right and held[29] that there was jurisdiction to relieve against forfeiture of an otherwise existing contingent proprietary right even where the property in question was personalty. Relief against forfeiture was granted on the condition that the outstanding instalments were paid within seven days.

In the trusts context, it was established by Lord Eldon in 1811 in *Brandon v. Robinson*[30] that a condition restraining alienation to the then equivalent of a trustee in bankruptcy could not validly be imposed on an equitable life interest but that a determinable interest was permissible: "There is no doubt that property may be given to a man until he shall become bankrupt". By the mid-nineteenth century the device had developed of adding a discretionary trust in favour of the beneficiary and his family to take effect on termination of the prior determinable interest.[31] Section 33 of the Trustee Act 1925 recognises the existence of such "protective trusts". Pension schemes use the device of the protective trust to prevent the rights of a pension scheme member becoming available to his creditors on a bankruptcy.[32] An attempt by a settlor to determine an interest by reference to his own bankruptcy will be void against the trustee in bankruptcy.

c) Recognition of pre-insolvency property rights

The onset of bankruptcy or liquidation will not generally affect property rights which have already been acquired by a third party.[33] Assets in the possession of the insolvent which are beneficially owned by third parties will not be available to the creditors and it will often transpire that the insolvent has far fewer assets than appeared to be the case. At one time, the doctrine of reputed ownership enabled creditors to claim some of the assets which appeared to belong to the insolvent; the doctrine never applied to companies and was abolished in relation to bankruptcy on the recommendation of the Cork Committee. Third party rights may arise by way of security, reservation of title or on the basis of equitable interests in property whose legal title is vested in the insolvent.[34] The value to the insolvent estate of an asset subject to a security right in favour of a third party will be any extent to which the asset is worth more than the debt it secures. Much of the case law in this area is

---

[29] Referring to the judgment of Dillon L.J. in *BICC plc v. Burndy Corporation* [1985] Ch. 232.

[30] (1811) 18 Ves. 429.

[31] See Chesterman "Family Settlements on Trust" in Rubin & Sugarman (eds), *Law, Economy and Society*.

[32] See Chap. 33.

[33] Chap. 30 examines those situations in which transfers may be defeasible.

[34] See Chaps 28 and 29.

concerned with delineating the borders between personal and proprietary claim and with determining the circumstances in which assets which might have been thought to be available to the general body of creditors are in fact the property of someone else.

It might be asked why creditors with rights *in rem* should be preferred in this way to those who hold merely personal rights against the insolvent. One argument[35] is that the ability to give security allows borrowing by those with poor credit ratings which might otherwise be impossible or only possible at very high rates of interest.[36] The upholding of security rights has been justified[37] on the basis that, if debtors were not permitted to prefer some creditors over others by conferring security, the alternative would be a complicated contractual network of priority relationships arranged between the creditors themselves. The current system achieves the same result in a simpler and cheaper fashion. Professor Goode addressed this issue several years later[38] and concluded that the bargain element is widely accepted as a proper ground for giving the secured creditor priority so long as the grant of the security does not involve an unfair preference and other creditors have notice of the security interest, so that they are not misled into thinking that the assets comprising the security are the unincumbered property of the debtor. He concluded that those who chose to lend unsecured cannot complain of their subordinate position.[39] A number of proprietary rights could come under attack on this reasoning since the formalist distinction between sale credit with retention of title and loan credit and security means that much functional security is in fact hidden from view. The rights of creditors who can base their claims on an equitable proprietary basis are also hidden from view. Furthermore, many trade creditors are unlikely to be in a position to investigate their customers and discover the existence of the secured rights[40] and involuntary creditors will have to take their debtor as they find him.

The above arguments do not address the problem that it is possible for the entirety of the assets of a corporate debtor to be secured, leaving nothing for the unsecured creditors. This has caused dissatisfaction

---

[35] See Oditah, *Legal Aspects of Receivables Financing* (1991), pp. 14–18.

[36] It is not clear that the giving of security does necessarily result in a lower rate of interest (see, *e.g.*, Goode, *Principles of Corporate Insolvency* (2nd ed.) p. 41). It is also open to debate whether the system should encourage high risk borrowing at the potential expense of the borrower's unsecured creditors.

[37] Most famously by Professors Jackson and Kronman in their much cited article at 88 Yale L.J. 1143 (1979).

[38] Goode, (1983–84) 8 Can. Bus. L.J. 53.

[39] See also Chap. 16 of Gough *Company Charges* (2nd ed.).

[40] It can be argued, though, that they are in a position to spread their risk amongst the totality of their customers and to reflect the risk in their prices.

since the advent of the floating charge in the nineteenth century. In the infamous case of *Salomon v. Salomon*,[41] Lord MacNaghten observed: "I have long thought, and I believe some of your Lordships also think, that the ordinary trade creditors of a trading company ought to have a preferential claim on the assets in liquidation in respect of debts incurred within a certain limited time before the winding up. But that is not the law at present. Everybody knows that when there is a winding up debenture holders generally step in and sweep off everything; and a great scandal it is". Preferential creditors[42] were given priority over the holders of a floating charge in 1897 but this did nothing to assist the ordinary unsecured creditor. The Cork Committee recognised that this was a cause for justifiable dissatisfaction amongst unsecured creditors. They were also concerned at the disinterest displayed and, therefore, the lack of control exercised by most unsecured creditors in the insolvency proceedings, largely because of the unlikelihood of recovering much if any of what was owing. The suggested solution of the Cork Commit-tee,[43] which has not been adopted, was that a fund equal to 10 per cent of the net moneys which would otherwise be payable to a floating chargee from the realisation of assets would be set aside and distributed *pari passu* among the ordinary unsecured creditors, subject to the overriding limitation that they would not receive a greater percentage of their debts than the debenture holder.

3. Disclaimer by insolvency practitioner

a) Right to disclaim

A trustee in bankruptcy[44] or a liquidator[45] may, by the giving of the prescribed notice, disclaim any onerous property. Onerous property is defined as any unprofitable contract and any other property which is unsaleable or not readily salcable or is such that it may give rise to a liability to pay money or perform any other onerous act.

The case law on these provisions has been largely concerned with the disclaimer of leaseholds (which may contain onerous covenants and, if the state of the market makes the rent obligations unattractive, may be unsaleable) although there has apparently also been a recent increase[46]

---

[41] [1987] A.C. 22.
[42] See Chap. 35.
[43] In para. 1539.
[44] Under Insolvency Act 1986, ss315 *et seq.*
[45] *ibid.*, ss178 *et seq.* Until 1986 liquidators needed the leave of the court to disclaim property and this should be borne in mind when reading earlier cases.
[46] In *Scmlla Properties v. Gesso Properties (BVI) Ltd* [1995] B.C.C. 793 the judge observed that he had been told that there were about 200 escheats per year.

in the disclaimer of freeholds.[47] There has been little case law relating
to the disclaimer of personal property but the statutory provisions are
not restricted to interests in land. *Re Potters Oils Ltd*[48] was a case in
which the liquidator sought to disclaim a quantity of chlorinated waste
oil which would be expensive to have removed and was potentially
hazardous; under the more restrictively worded statute then in force it
was held that the oil did not fall within the definition of property which
could be disclaimed. If a similar case arose today, the insolvency
practitioner would be able to disclaim the property. The insolvency
practitioner is only entitled to disclaim "property" within the definition
provided by section 436 so that, for example, in *City of London Corporation v. Brown*[49] it was held that the trustee could not disclaim a
statutory tenancy which was a mere personal right of irremoveability
and not "property".[50]

b) Loss of right to disclaim

The right to disclaim is not lost where the insolvency practitioner has
exercised rights of ownership in relation to the property but will be lost
if a person interested in the property has written asking whether the
insolvency practitioner will be disclaiming the property and notice of
disclaimer is not given within the next 28 days.[51] Notice of disclaimer
may only be served by a trustee in bankruptcy with the leave of the court
in respect of after-acquired property[52] or exempt property within section
308[53] where either has been claimed for the estate by the trustee.

c) Effect of disclaimer

A disclaimer will operate so as to determine the rights, interests and
liabilities of the insolvent or the insolvency practitioner in or in respect
of the disclaimed property as from the date of the disclaimer, except in
the case of leaseholds.[54] Where an insolvency practitioner proposes to
disclaim a lease, notice must be served on any underlessees or mort-
gagees claiming under the insolvent[55]; the disclaimer will not take effect

---

[47] *Re Nottingham General Cemetery Co.* [1955] 1 Ch. 683 was a case of a freehold subject
to onerous obligations since it was used as a cemetery.
[48] [1985] B.C.L.C. 203.
[49] (1990) 22 H.L.R. 32.
[50] Insolvency Act 1986, s.283(3A), inserted by Housing Act 1988, s.117(1) makes it clear
that such tenancies will not usually vest in the trustee.
[51] Insolvency Act 1986, ss178(5), 316.
[52] See Chap. 27.4.
[53] See Chap. 27.2.
[54] Insolvency Act 1986, ss178(4), 315(3).
[55] *ibid.*, ss179, 317.

until either the expiry of a 14-day period without an application being made for a vesting order or, if such an application is made, until the court directs that the disclaimer shall take place. A similar provision[56] applies to the disclaimer by a trustee in bankruptcy of any property in a dwelling house; in this case the notice has to be served on every person in occupation or claiming a right to occupy the house.

Third parties who either claim an interest in the disclaimed property or are under a liability in respect of it may apply for the vesting of the disclaimed property in, or for its delivery to, a person who is entitled to it or is under a liability in respect of it.[57] These provisions allow, for example, the vesting of a lease in an underlessee or of land in a mortgagee[58]. The court will not make an order conferring the property on a person subject to a liability in respect of it unless it would be just to do so for the purpose of compensating that person; the guarantor of obligations under a disclaimed lease might be such a person. In *Hindcastle Ltd v. Barbara Attenborough Associates Ltd*[59] the House of Lords held that the disclaimer of a lease operated to determine the lease and accelerate the reversion but, overruling previous case law to the contrary, that the wording of the legislation required the obligations of a guarantor to be treated as though the lease had continued. Lord Nicholls of Birkenhead observed in the course of his judgment that it was essential to bear in mind that the fundamental purpose of an ordinary guarantee of another's debt is that the risk of the principal debtor's insolvency should fall on the guarantor and not the creditor and that it would defeat the object of the exercise if disclaimer released the guarantor.

Any person sustaining loss or damage in consequence of the operation of a disclaimer is deemed to be a creditor in the insolvency to the extent of the loss or damage[60]; the extent of the loss may be adjusted as a consequence of a vesting order. The rights and liabilities of others will

---

[56] *ibid.*, s.318.

[57] *ibid.*, ss181, 182, 321 contain provisions relating to the terms on which the court may vest leasehold property in an underlessee or mortgagee. *Lloyd's Bank SF Nominees v. Aladdin Ltd* [1996] 1 B.C.L.C. 720 is authority that a person in occupation of premises of which he has agreed to take an assignment subject to the consent of the landlord does not have the necessary interest.

[58] *Ferris J. in Re Lee (a bankrupt), The Times*, February 24, 1998, held that conditions could be attached to the vesting order to prevent the mortgagee from getting more than was due under the mortgage. The Court could also provide for the destination of the surplus and could order that it be paid to the trustee in bankruptcy for the benefit of the creditors.

[59] [1996] 2 B.C.L.C. 234.

[60] See *Re Park Air Services Plc* [1997] 3 All E.R. 193 for a discussion of the quantification of damages payable to a landlord as a result of the disclaimer of a lease.

not be affected by the disclaimer except in so far as is necessary to release the insolvent from any liability.

The question of what happens to disclaimed property has given rise to considerable conjecture. It now seems clear that, on disclaimer, a freehold interest determines and that the Crown automatically becomes owner of the land in question on an escheat.[61] A leasehold interest will also determine and the reversion will be accelerated[62]; any sub-lease carved out of the disclaimed lease also determines but the sub-tenant's interest is deemed to continue on the terms of the disclaimed head-lease.[63] Harman J. in *Re Potters Oils Ltd*[64] felt that disclaimed chattels would be *bona vacantia* and vest in the Crown. The Treasury Solicitor, invited to consider the prospect of the Crown becoming owner of such an unwelcome chattel, was of the opinion that it would not automatically vest in the Crown but the point did not in the event have to be decided. In a number of cases, the Crown has argued against the automatic vesting of onerous freeholds or chattels in it. It would seem likely, however, that the property would vest but that the Crown could argue that its rights and liabilities should not be affected by the disclaimer even if the disclaimer caused it to become the owner of the property.

---

[61] *Scllma Properties v. Gesso Properties (BVI) Ltd* [1995] B.C.C. 793.

[62] *Hindcastle Ltd v. Barbara Attenborough Associates* [1996] 2 B.C.L.C. 234.

[63] In *Hindcastle Limited v. Barbara Attenborough Associates Limited* the House of Lords thought it likely that any problems associated with sub-leases could be solved by a vesting order in favour of the sub-tenant. See Lowe (1996) 12 I.L.&P. 148 for a discussion of the difficulties which may arise where the insolvent tenant has sub-let the property to more than one tenant.

[64] [1985] B.C.L.C. 203.

CHAPTER 27

THE EXTENT OF A BANKRUPT'S ESTATE

1. Introduction

A bankrupt's estate includes all property belonging to or vested in the bankrupt at the commencement of the bankruptcy[1] unless specifically excluded by statute; exempt assets are explained below. The bankrupt's house does not fall into the category of exempt asset but the trustee in bankruptcy may need the leave of the court to sell it. Property falls into the bankrupt estate subject to the rights of any third parties[2] unless those rights have been released.[3] Property held by the bankrupt on trust does not fall into the bankrupt's estate.[4] Assets (including income) which the bankrupt acquires in the course of the bankruptcy may also be taken into the estate, as explained below.

2. Exempt assets

The Cork Committee made the point[5] that one aim of insolvency law is to enable the bankrupt to achieve his rehabilitation as a useful and productive member of society. Certain assets necessary for this purpose are accordingly exempted from vesting in the trustee and are allowed to be retained by the bankrupt. Section 283(2) of the Insolvency Act 1986 provides that the following assets do not fall into the bankrupt's estate[6]:

> "a) such tools, books, vehicles and other items of equipment as are necessary to the bankrupt for use personally by him in his employment, business or vocation; b) such clothing, bedding, furniture,

---

[1] Insolvency Act 1986, s.283(1). The commencement of the bankruptcy will be the day on which the bankruptcy order is made: Insolvency Act 1986, s.278.

[2] Insolvency Act 1986, s.283(5).

[3] *ibid.*, s.269 or the Insolvency Rules 1986.

[4] *ibid.*, s.283(3).

[5] In para. 1096.

[6] Under Insolvency Act 1986, s.283(3A), certain protected tenancies are also excluded from the bankrupt's estate unless the trustee claims them under Insolvency Act 1986, s.308A.

household equipment and provisions as are necessary for satisfying the basic domestic needs of the bankrupt and his family."

It will be noted that vehicles only fall within the first and not the second of these categories. It may be that other members of the family can establish an arguable claim to ownership of chattels used by the family. It will often be the case that the realisable value of the chattels is not worth incurring the costs of realisation and that the bankrupt will manage to keep many of these possessions.

Under section 308 of the Insolvency Act 1986, if it appears to the trustee that the realisable value of property exempted under section 283(2) of the Insolvency Act 1986 exceeds the cost of a reasonable replacement for that property, the trustee may by notice in writing within 42 days[7] of first learning of its existence claim the property for the estate. Upon the service of the notice, the property vests in the trustee as of the date of the commencement of the bankruptcy although any purchaser of the property in good faith, for value and without notice of the bankruptcy will be protected against the claim. The trustee must provide a reasonable replacement for the claimed asset out of the funds comprised in the estate. Property will be a reasonable replacement for other property if it is reasonably adequate for meeting the needs met by the other party. *Pike v. Cork Gully*[8] is an example of this provision in operation. The trustee in bankruptcy had seized a horse box used by the bankrupt to earn about £1,000 a month. The horse box had been sold for £9,987.50. It was held that the horse box had been in the category of exempt assets and that the trustee had either to repay the net proceeds of the sale or, if less, the cost of a reasonable replacement.

3. The bankrupt's home

a) The trustee in bankruptcy's right to the home

Section 283 of the Insolvency Act 1986 does not include the home of the bankrupt among the items exempted from the estate. The trustee will acquire such beneficial interest as the bankrupt had in the home. The trustee will need to establish the extent of that beneficial interest; frequently there will be a mortgage and the bankrupt's interest will be limited to the equity of redemption. The trustee will often discover that the equity is owned jointly with a spouse or co-habitee. In many cases the interest of the trustee will be bought out either by a spouse or co-habitee remortgaging the property or a third party, such as a relative,

---

[7] The time limit is contained in Insolvency Act 1986, s.309.
[8] July 13, 1995, unreported.

producing funds. Where this is not possible, the trustee will only be able to realise the value of the property by rendering the bankrupt homeless which, if the bankrupt is occupying the property with family, is likely to involve an application to court.[9] The complexities of family property law[10] are such that the trustee in bankruptcy may find it difficult to establish who is entitled to share, and in what proportions, in the proceeds of any sale.

These difficulties may, indeed, persuade the trustee to postpone an attempt at sale, particularly if there is no great beneficial interest available for the creditors. Where the trustee cannot realise the value of a dwelling house occupied by the bankrupt, or by a spouse or former spouse, the trustee can apply to the court[11] for an order imposing a charge on the property for the benefit of the bankrupt's estate. The charge will vest in the trustee as part of the estate and the house itself will cease to form part of the estate.

b) Beneficial ownership of the home

The first issue for the trustee in bankruptcy to consider is that of who owns the property. The documentary evidence may show that the bankrupt is the sole owner of the property or it may show that the legal title to the property was conveyed to the bankrupt jointly with another, often a spouse or co-habitee. This joint ownership operates through the mechanism of a trust of land[12] and if one of the co-owners does not wish the property to be sold, a court order under section 14 of the Trusts of Land and Appointment of Trustees Act 1996[13] will be necessary before the property can be sold free of the dissentient owner's interest.

Even where the bankrupt appears to be the sole legal owner of the property, someone else may be able to establish an equitable interest in the property in which case the bankrupt will hold the legal title to the property on trust for those beneficially entitled; again, a court order under section 14 of the Trusts of Land and Appointment of Trustees Act 1996 would be necessary before the property could be sold free of the

---

[9] Under Insolvency Act 1986, ss335A, 336 or 337.

[10] Which this account can only begin to indicate. For a full explanation, see K. Gray, *Elements of Land Law* (2nd ed., 1993) and Chap. 4 of S. M.Cretney and J. M. Masson, *Principles of Family Law* (6th ed., 1997).

[11] Insolvency Act 1986, s.313.

[12] Under the Trusts of Land and Appointment of Trustees Act 1996. Previously this would have been a trust for sale under the Law of Property Act 1925.

[13] Previously Law of Property Act 1925, s.30 . The trustee in bankruptcy will be a person with "an interest in property subject to a trust of land". Where the dispute is between the original co-owners, the court will consider whether any collateral purpose of the trust is still subsisting.

beneficial interest of the unwilling seller. There has been a series of cases in which a spouse or co-habitee[14] of a sole legal owner has claimed an equitable interest in the property on the basis of an implied, resulting or constructive trust.[15] Where two people provide the purchase money jointly but the house is conveyed into the name of one of them alone, there is a rebuttable presumption that the sole legal owner holds the property on trust for both of them.[16] In principle, a similar result may be achieved by one party making an indirect financial contribution to the purchase of a house which is conveyed into the name of another provided the court can find that this was the common intention of the parties. The courts are, however, reluctant to recognise that the necessary intention to share beneficial ownership can, in the absence of express words, be inferred from anything other than the making of financial contribution to the purchase.[17]

c) Sale where the home is not owned solely by the bankrupt

An application by a trustee in bankruptcy under section 14 of the Trusts of Land and Appointment of Trustees Act 1996 is now governed by section 335A of the Insolvency Act 1986. Section 335A[18] can be traced back to the Cork Committee which concluded[19] that it would be consonant with modern social attitudes to alleviate the personal hardships of a bankrupt's dependants by allowing the court a discretion to postpone the sale of the family home.[20] The Committee considered that primary consideration should be given to the needs of any children and

---

[14] Or other claimant; *e.g.*, in *Re Sharpe (a bankrupt)* [1980] 1 W.L.R. 219 it was the bankrupt's aunt who claimed an equitable interest in the house.

[15] Proprietary estoppel, which in other circumstances may be relied on as establishing an interest in property, will be of no avail in a bankruptcy since any interest established will only date from the court declaration and will not be back-dated to the commencement of the bankruptcy.

[16] This was established in a line of cases which can be traced back to *Bull v. Bull* [1955] 1 Q.B. 234. More recent examples include *Williams and Glyn's Bank v. Boland* [1980] 3 W.L.R. 138, *City of London Building Society v. Flegg* [1988] A.C. 54 and *Tinsley v. Milligan* [1995] 1 A.C. 340.

[17] *Gissing v. Gissing* [1971] A.C. 886, *Pettitt v. Pettitt* [1970] A.C. 777, *Lloyds Bank plc v. Rosset* [1991] 1 A.C. 107.

[18] Which was added to the Insolvency Act by Schedule 3 of the Trusts of Land and Appointment of Trustees Act 1996 and replaces those parts of the original section 336 which dealt with applications under Law of Property Act 1925, s.30.

[19] In para. 1118.

[20] A contrasting attitude had earlier been adopted by the Law Commission in its report on financial provision in matrimonial proceedings (Report No. 25) which took the view that the claims of the spouse should be subordinated to those of the creditors since "marriage is a form of partnership and, on normal partnership principles, neither partner should compete with the partner's creditors".

that regard should be had to their age and other needs, avoiding emotional damage or interrupting their schooling and to the interests of the community in keeping the family together in suitable accommodation. The government response was that this was too heavily weighted against creditors and the proposal was not incorporated in the draft legislation. During the passage of the legislation through Parliament, strong pressure was brought to bear to include some measure and an inconclusive consultation process took place followed by the inclusion of provisions in the legislation at a late stage without much discussion.[21]

Section 335A provides that where a trustee makes an application under section 14 of the Trusts of Land and Appointment of Trustees Act 1996, the application is to be made to the court having jurisdiction in relation to the bankruptcy and the court shall make such order as it thinks just and reasonable having regard to:

a) the interest of the bankrupt's creditors;
b) where the application is in respect of land which includes a dwelling house which is or has been the home of the bankrupt or the bankrupt's spouse or former spouse:—
  (i) the conduct of the spouse or former spouse, so far as contributing to the bankruptcy,
  (ii) the needs and financial resources of the spouse or former spouse, and
  (iii) the needs of any children, and
c) all the circumstances of the case other than the needs of the bankrupt.

After a year from the vesting of the property in the trustee the court shall assume, unless the circumstances of the case are exceptional, that the interests of the creditors outweigh all other considerations.

The attitude likely to be taken by the courts to section 335A of the Insolvency Act 1986 is illustrated by *Re Citro*,[22] a case which was decided on the basis of previous law[23] but after the enactment of the Insolvency Act 1986. The Court of Appeal made it clear that section 336 of the Insolvency Act 1986[24] merely enacted the previous test applied by the courts. The Court pointed out that it was as well that that should be the case since the legislation only applied to spouses and not to co-habitees and it would be unfortunate if these two groups should be

---

[21] See Cretney (1991) 107 L.Q.R. 177.
[22] [1991] Ch. 142.
[23] This is because the bankruptcies in question commenced in 1985.
[24] Now s.335A and s.336.

subject to different rules.[25] A consideration of the pre-1986 case law is, therefore, necessary in order to evaluate the likely application of section 335A.

The leading case is the Court of Appeal decision in *Re Citro*.[26] In 1985 Domenico Citro and his brother, Carmine, were made bankrupt. Their only substantial assets were their shares of the beneficial interests in their matrimonial homes. One of the brothers was judicially separated from his wife and the other was living with his family. Their debts exceeded the values of the interests. The trustee applied to court for declarations as to their beneficial interests and for orders for possession and sale. Hoffmann J. held that they each had a beneficial interest in half the equity of redemption and made the requested orders; after considering the circumstances of the families and, in particular, the fact that it would not be possible to buy other accommodation in the area which would lead to schooling problems, he imposed a provision for postponement of sale in each case until the youngest child reached the age of 16. In the Court of Appeal, a delay of six months was substituted. Lord Justice Nourse considered the previous case law[27] and held that, whether or not the collateral purpose of providing a family home continued,[28] the interests of the spouse could only prevail in exceptional circumstances, "amounting to more than the ordinary consequences of debt and improvidence" which he found in these circumstances. Lord Justice Bingham regretfully agreed with this, expressing his view that a test of "exceptional circumstances" was more stringent than was warranted but conceding that Parliament "appears expressly to have approved it". Sir George Waller, the third member of the Court of Appeal, dissented; he felt that it was quite possible to argue, on the basis of the case law, that the educational difficulties which would be suffered by the children involved were sufficient to amount to the necessary exceptional circumstances.

In *Lloyds Bank v. Byrne*,[29] which was an application by a creditor who had obtained a charging order for a sale under section 30 of the Law of Property Act 1925, it was held that the same approach as that of

---

[25] s.335A applies regardless of the identity of the non-bankrupt co-owner rather than only, as previously, where the co-owner was a spouse or former spouse. The court can take into account the needs of the children but it is not clear to what extent a court may feel able to extend its regard to "all the circumstances of the case" to cover the financial needs and resources of the co-habitee where there has not been a marriage.

[26] [1991] Ch. 142.

[27] In particular, *Re Turner* [1974] 1 W.L.R. 1556, *Re Densham* [1975] 1 W.L.R. 1519, *Re Bailey* [1977] 1 W.L.R. 278, *Re Holliday* [1981] Ch. 405 (the only reported case in which a sale within a short period has not been ordered), *Re Lowrie* [1981] 3 All E.R. 353 and *Harman v. Glencross* [1986] 2 W.L.R. 637.

[28] Which, in relation to the separated brother, it did not.

[29] [1933] Fam. Law 183.

the majority in *Re Citro* would be appropriate in balancing the interests of the debtor's family and the creditor. Parker L.J. observed "there is no difference in principle between the case of a trustee in bankruptcy and that of a chargee. All the circumstances must be weighed and the court must consider whose voice should in equity prevail". In *Abbey National plc v. Moss*[30] the Court of Appeal refused to make an order for sale requested by the mortgagee of a daughter's share of a house which she held on trust for sale with her mother with the collateral purpose of providing a home for the mother alone. At first instance Cooke J. had concluded that there were no exceptional circumstances and ordered the sale. The Court of Appeal, however, held by a majority that sale should not be ordered; the distinction between this case and the earlier cases was that the collateral purpose of the trust did not require joint occupation by the joint owners. The case, together with *Re Holliday*,[31] stands out as very much the exception to the general rule that sale will be ordered within a short period once ownership vests in a creditor or trustee in bankruptcy. In *Barclays Bank v. Hendricks*,[32] a case in which an order would cause the family little real hardship, the sale was postponed to the end of the current school term. The Court of Appeal in *Bank of Baroda v. Dhillon*[33] adopted a similar approach.

d) Division of the proceeds of sale

Once it has been established who has ownership rights to the property and that the property is to be sold, the proportions in which the co-owners are entitled to share the proceeds of sale may still have to be determined.[34] The beneficial interest in a house may have been co-owned by the bankrupt and another either as joint tenants[35] or as tenants in common[36]; the bankruptcy will have the effect of severing a joint tenancy[37] so that the co-owners become tenants in common and the bankrupt's share vests in the trustee in bankruptcy. The significance of this is that if the beneficial interest had been held under a joint tenancy, the shares will be equal whereas if there had been a tenancy in common prior to the bankruptcy it will be possible that the co-owners hold the

---

[30] [1994] 1 F.L.R. 307, Hopkins (1995) 111 L.Q.R. 72.
[31] [1981] Ch. 405.
[32] [1996] 1 F.L.R. 258.
[33] October 17, 1997, unreported.
[34] The court may be asked to declare the beneficial interests under Trusts of Land and Appointment of Trustees Act 1996, s.14.
[35] Each co-owner is regarded as owning the whole interest jointly with the other co-owner so that if one of them dies the other automatically becomes sole owner of the whole.
[36] Each holds a separate share of the property.
[37] *Re Gorman (a bankrupt)* [1990] 1 All E.R. 717, *Re Palmer (dec'd)* [1994] Ch. 317.

interest in unequal shares. Where the legal title is held jointly and the conveyance sets out the beneficial interests, that will usually be conclusive.[38] In the absence of such a declaration, the court will apply similar principles to those applicable where the bankrupt is the sole legal owner. Where the contributions to the purchase price are unequal, there is a presumption that the beneficial interest is held in proportionate shares.[39]

The division of the sale proceeds may also be affected by the equity of exoneration. If a charge is given over property by joint owners in order to secure a debt of one only of them, the other owner is entitled to have the secured indebtedness discharged so far as possible out of the debtor's share of the property provided that it can be inferred from the circumstances that this was their joint intention. *Re Pittortou (a bankrupt)*[40] is an example of this principle in operation; the bankrupt's wife was entitled to require that debts incurred by her husband for his sole benefit should be treated as charged primarily on his half-share in the mortgaged property.

e) Rights of the family to remain in occupation

A spouse[41] who cannot establish either legal or equitable entitlement to the home will still have a right to remain in occupation (matrimonial home rights) under section 30 of the Family Law Act 1996. Section 336(2) of the Insolvency Act 1986 provides that where a spouse has matrimonial home rights under Part IV of the Family Law Act 1996, those rights continue to subsist notwithstanding the bankruptcy and will bind the trustee and persons deriving title from the trustee. Once a petition for bankruptcy has been presented, it will be too late to acquire matrimonial home rights. Where the spouse has rights of occupation, the trustee will have to apply under section 33 of the Family Law Act 1996 for termination of the rights. Section 336 of the Insolvency Act 1986

---

[38] *Goodman v. Gallant* [1986] 1 F.L.R. 513, CA, *Re Gorman* [1990] 1 All E.R. 717, *Harwood v. Harwood* [1991] 2 F.L.R. 274, CA, *Huntingford v. Hobbs* [1992] Fam. Law 437, CA.

[39] *Pettitt v. Pettitt* [1970] A.C. 777. The application of this is often complicated by the existence of a mortgage—see, *e.g. Spengette v. Defoe* [1992] 2 F.L.R. 388 and *Huntingford v. Hobbs* [1993] 1 F.L.R. 736. *Midland Bank v. Cooke* [1995] 2 F.L.R. 215, CA has also added to the difficulties in this area. If the bankrupt is permitted to occupy the premises on condition that he contributes to mortgage repayments or outgoings, he will not by virtue of them acquire any interest in the premises: s.338. Where one co-owner is arguing for a greater share on the basis of contribution to the improvement of a matrimonial home, the provisions of s.37 of the Matrimonial Proceedings and Property Act 1970 are declaratory of the law.

[40] [1985] 1 W.L.R. 58.

[41] But not a co-habitee.

provides that where the non-bankrupt spouse has matrimonial home rights which bind the trustee in bankruptcy, any application for an order under section 33 of the Family Law Act 1996 shall be made to the court having jurisdiction in bankruptcy and the court shall make such order as it thinks just and reasonable taking into account the same factors as apply under section 335A of the Insolvency Act 1986 to an application in respect of a trust for land.

Section 337 of the Insolvency Act 1986 is designed to give some protection to children living with the bankrupt in the situation where neither section 335A nor section 336 applies: the most likely situation will be where the bankrupt is a single parent so that there is no family member with either an interest in the property or matrimonial home rights.[42] Section 337 applies where the bankrupt is entitled to occupy a dwelling house by virtue of a beneficial estate or interest and any person under the age of 18, with whom the bankrupt had at some time occupied the dwelling house, was living with the bankrupt at the time of presentation of the petition for bankruptcy and when the bankruptcy order was made. The bankrupt is given the right not to be evicted from the house without the leave of the court or, if appropriate, the right with the leave of the court to enter and occupy the house. These rights will be treated as a charge having the priority of an equitable interest created immediately before the commencement of the bankruptcy and will be treated as if they were matrimonial home rights under the Family Law Act 1996. On an application for an order under section 33 of the Family Law Act 1996 the court shall make such order as it thinks just and reasonable having regard to the interests of the creditors, to the bankrupt's financial resources, to the needs of the children and to all the circumstances of the case other than the needs of the bankrupt. As with sections 335A and 336, after a year the court will assume, unless the circumstances of the case are exceptional, that the interest of the bankrupt's creditors outweigh all other considerations.

f) Evaluation of the rules relating to the family home[43]

It is clear that usually the most that the bankrupt's family can hope for is a delay of a year in the sale of the home. Sections 335A to 337 have clearly not achieved the change in direction recommended by the Cork Committee. Even without the restrictive interpretation which the courts have indicated will be given to the legislation, the Insolvency Act is

---

[42] See A. Clarke, *Child Law* (1991) at p. 116 for a discussion of the cases in which children will not fall within s.337.

[43] See the essays in Part II of Rajak (ed.), *Insolvency Law: Theory and Practice.*

tilted much more in favour of creditors than, for example, the homestead legislation of New Zealand and parts of Canada and the United States[44] which aims to give families security of occupation as against creditors. It has been argued that a better balance might be struck by treating the bankrupt's home as an exempt asset within section 283(2). The home would then be subject to section 308 and the trustee in bankruptcy would be entitled to claim it if the value of the property exceeded the cost of a reasonable replacement. It should also be noted that, in many cases, the bankrupt may have little or no equity of redemption in the home, the fate of which will be a matter for the mortgagee of the property and will be dealt with outside the ambit of insolvency law.

4. After-acquired assets

The trustee may, by serving a notice in writing, claim property acquired by or which devolves upon the bankrupt during the period of bankruptcy unless it is exempt property[45] or is property which may be the subject of an income payments order.[46] The notice must be served within 42 days of the day on which the acquisition by the bankrupt first came to the knowledge of the trustee. The property will vest in the trustee on service of the notice and the trustee's title will relate back to the time at which the bankrupt acquired the property. If, however, a person has acquired the property in good faith, for value and without notice of the bankruptcy or a banker has entered into a transaction in good faith and without such notice, the trustee will not have a remedy against that person or banker or anyone deriving title to property from them.

The bankrupt has a duty to inform the trustee whenever he acquires property during the period of the bankruptcy within 21 days of his becoming aware of the relevant facts.[47] The bankrupt must then keep the property for 42 days unless he has the trustee's consent in writing to dispose of it.[48] A bankrupt who is running a business may provide the trustee with a half-yearly report instead.

5. The bankrupt's income

The court may, on the application of the trustee, make an income payments order claiming for the bankrupt's estate so much of the income of the bankrupt during the period for which the order is in force

---

[44] See Gray, *Elements of Land Law* (2nd ed.), p. 604.
[45] Under Insolvency Act 1986, s.283 or any other enactment.
[46] *ibid.*, s.310.
[47] *ibid.*, s.333.
[48] Insolvency Rules 1986, r. 6.200.

as may be specified in the order.[49] Income is defined as comprising every payment in the nature of income which is from time to time made to the bankrupt or to which he from time to time becomes entitled, including any payment in respect of the carrying on of any business or in respect of any office or employment. The test of whether a payment is income is largely a matter of common sense.[50] It has been held to include payments received under a maintenance order made against the bankrupt's former spouse.[51] Section 310 of the Insolvency Act 1986 does not, unlike its predecessor provisions, apply to income whose source is property which has vested in the trustee in bankruptcy; the income is automatically that of the trustee.[52]

The court will not make an order which would have the effect of reducing the income of the bankrupt below what appears to the court to be necessary for meeting the reasonable domestic needs of the bankrupt and his family.[53] The order may require payment by either the bankrupt or by the source of the income directly to the trustee. If there is already an attachment of earnings order in force against the bankrupt, the court may discharge or vary the order when making an order. An income payments order will not usually continue to have effect after the discharge of the bankrupt.

---

[49] Insolvency Act 1986, s.310.
[50] *Affleck v. Hammond* [1912] 3 K.B. 162.
[51] *Re Landau* [1934] 1 Ch. 549, *Re Tennant's Application* [1956] 2 All E.R. 753.
[52] *Re Landau* [1997] 3 All E.R. 322, *Performing Rights Society v. Rowland* [1997] 3 All E.R. 336.
[53] This would include maintenance payments.

CHAPTER 28

ASSETS CLAIMED BY THIRD PARTIES

1. Introduction

The claim of third parties to be beneficially entitled to assets which appear to form part of the insolvent estate is the common theme of the material dealt with both by this Chapter and the next. As has been seen, only those assets to which the insolvent has a beneficial entitlement are available to the creditors so each successful proprietary claim may reduce the amount available to those who merely have personal rights against the insolvent. In many cases, however, the battle will be between competing proprietary claims and it will be clear that those who have purely personal rights will not, in any event, derive any benefit from the disputed assets. This is particularly true of corporate insolvency, where in many cases the assets would anyway be caught by a floating charge and would be unavailable to the general creditors unless and until the debenture holder had been paid off. It is, for example, frequently an administrative receiver rather than a liquidator who will be disputing a claim to be entitled to assets on the basis of retention of title.[1]

This Chapter deals with claims to absolute beneficial title to assets in respect of which the insolvent has possession or legal title; Chapter 29 deals with claims to have security rights over assets owned by the insolvent.

Before looking in more detail at the common grounds for claims to be the beneficial owner of property, it is helpful to refer briefly to the following basic concepts of property law[2]:

    a)   in order to claim a right over an asset, it is necessary to show a real right (a right "*in rem*") to it as distinct to a personal right against someone in respect of it. As has been seen,[3] personal rights will not survive the insolvency of the defendant.

---

[1] An insolvency practitioner will need funds for any litigation in which he seeks to dispute such proprietary claims. This question is considered in Chap. 32.

[2] For a more detailed exposition in relation to personal property, see Chap. 2 Goode, *Commercial Law* (2nd ed.) and, in relation to real property, Lawson and Rudden, *Introduction to the Law of Property* (2nd ed.) Chap. 5.

[3] In Chap. 25.

b) The legal title to an asset may be split from the beneficial ownership of it; where this happens the holder of the legal title will hold the property on trust for the beneficial, or equitable, owner. The historical explanation of this terminology is that the legal title is the right which would have been recognised by the courts of common law[4] (which refused to recognise divided ownership) whereas equity recognised the obligation of the legal owner to give effect to the beneficial rights which it had been intended should exist in relation to the property. Equity also treats as done that which should have been done and will give effect to an unexecuted agreement to transfer property; this enables equity to recognise interests which cannot exist at law.[5] Equitable rights attached to property bind future transferees of the property with the exception of the bona fide purchaser of the legal title without notice of the right. Where competing claimants to property only claim equitable rights, the first in time will prevail provided the equities are equal.

Where the legal and beneficial interests are vested in the same person, there will be no separate equitable interest and no scope for the application of equitable rules.

c) Concurrent ownership of property is possible either as joint tenants (that is, each holding the same interest) or as tenants in common (where each has a distinct share in the property).[6]

d) Acquisition of the legal title to property previously held by another happens by consensual transfer such as gift or sale or by operation of law on death or bankruptcy. The basic rule is that it is not possible to transfer a better title than one has[7] but there are exceptions to this.[8]

e) Transfer of title to property may be absolute or may be by way of security only in which case the transferor will have the right to reclaim the property once the secured obligation has been met. Non-possessory security rights (that is, where the giver of the security remains in possession of the assets) may be

---

[4] Until the Judicature Acts 1873–1875 the rules of common law and the rules of equity were administered as separate systems by different courts.

[5] Such as a right to future goods.

[6] See Chap. 27.3 above for further explanation of this in relation to land; the legal title to land can only be held jointly. In relation to chattels, it is possible to hold the legal title either jointly or in common.

[7] Often expressed as the "*nemo dat*" rule: "*nemo dat quod non habet*" means that no-one can give what he does not have.

[8] See Sale of Goods Act 1979, ss21–26 and the Factors Act 1889. The anachronistic exception of the bona fide purchaser in market overt contained in Sale of Goods Act 1979, s.22 has been repealed. See Chap. 16 of Goode, *Commercial Law* (2nd ed.).

granted by way of defeasible transfer of title to the property or
by a charge which acts as an encumbrance over property. It will
usually be necessary to register the security before the rights of
the mortgagee or chargee will bind third parties.

f) A proprietary claim will only succeed where the property is
identifiable. If the claim fails because the property has been
dissipated, destroyed or irrevocably commingled, the
aggrieved party will probably have a personal claim in respect
of the loss but this will not survive an insolvency. Where there
has been substitution of the original assets, the so-called tracing rules, explained in more detail below, will decide whether
or not substitute property to which there is a proprietary claim
can be identified. It can be difficult to decide whether a claim
to money is a proprietary claim which will survive an insolvency or whether it is a personal claim which would, of course,
be payable in money but which will not survive the insolvency;
this is considered further below.

Third parties may be claiming that they own, both legally and beneficially, goods in the possession of the insolvent. This may be because
they have expressly reserved title to the goods when giving possession
to the insolvent or it may be that they originally had title to the goods
and are claiming that the insolvent came into possession of the goods in
circumstances which did not defeat that title.[9] Alternatively, the claim
may be that the insolvent holds only the bare legal title to the asset and
that the equitable interest is held on trust for the third party.

The claim may be to proprietary rights (either legal or equitable) by
way of security over the assets of the insolvent; this is dealt with in the
next Chapter. Depending upon whether the value of the goods exceeds
the amount owing, this may not be a claim to the assets in their entirety;
the secured creditor will only retain the proceeds of realisation to the
extent of the secured debt.

2. Tracing property[10]

These rules on tracing property deal with the situation where the
plaintiff has established that he originally owned property which he is
no longer able to reclaim but that the defendant is in possession of
property which the plaintiff claims should be treated as a substitute. The
rules differ depending upon whether the plaintiff had legal or equitable

---

[9] *i.e.,* no exception to the *nemo dat* rule.
[10] See Goff and Jones, *The Law of Restitution* (4th ed., 1993) pp. 73–102.

title to the original property. If the defendant no longer has the property, there may still be an equitable remedy for knowing receipt of trust property or assistance in a breach of trust but this will be a personal remedy and will not survive the insolvency.[11]

The holder of the legal title to property is entitled to follow it, even where it changes its form or passes through a number of hands, provided it remains possible to identify it as replacing the original property.[12] Someone who has parted with money will almost certainly have lost his title to that particular money but where he can identify[13] that money as having been through the hands of the defendant, there will be an action for money had and received unless defendant has a defence; it seems[14] that this is a personal not a proprietary claim and therefore no use against an insolvent defendant. Although the common law can follow money from one account to another where there has been physical transfer of cash or document, apparently it is unable to do so where the transfer has taken place by electronic means.[15]

Since the common law did not recognise the rights of the equitable owner, such an owner would not be able to follow property at law and would have to trace on the basis of the equitable rules. The principle established by the Court of Appeal in *Re Diplock's Estate*[16] is that, provided there is an initial fiduciary relationship, the owner of the equitable interest in the property can trace it into the hands of anyone except a bona fide purchaser of the legal title for value and without notice.[17] Tracing will cease to be possible if the property is destroyed or dissipated or ceases to be identifiable. Equity, apparently unlike the common law, can trace into a mixed fund and, oddly, this puts the holder of an equitable interest in property into a stronger position than a legal owner since, given the absence of the necessary fiduciary relationship, a legal owner may not rely on the equitable tracing rules.

---

[11] *El Ajou v. Dollar Land Holdings plc* [1993] 3 All E.R. 717. [1994] 2 All E.R. 688, *Royal Brunei Airlines v. Tan* [1995] 3 All E.R. 97.

[12] *Lipkin Gorman (a firm) v. Karpnale Ltd* [1991] 2 A.C. 548.

[13] The common law has always had difficulty following assets if at some stage they have been mixed with other assets since it becomes impossible to identify the property physically and the common law lacks the ability to subject the mixed fund to a charge in favour of the original owner of part of it. If the mixing is done by the defendant to the action, this is not an obstacle since the cause of action is complete when the property is received. If the mixing has happened somewhere between plaintiff and defendant, the plaintiff will have a problem: *Agip (Africa) Ltd* [1989] 3 W.L.R. 1367.

[14] This is a difficult issue because it is hard to differentiate between payment of a personal remedy in money and return of money to which the plaintiff had property rights. It is only of any consequence in an insolvency. See Millett (1991) 107 L.Q.R. 71.

[15] Millett J. in *Agip (Africa) Ltd v. Jackson* [1989] 3 W.L.R. 1367 followed in *Bank Tejert v. Hong Kong and Shangai Banking Corp. (CI) Ltd* [1995] 1 Lloyd's Rep. 239.

[16] [1948] Ch. 465.

[17] See, *e.g.*, *Re Fleet Disposal Services Ltd* [1995] B.C.C. 605.

The rules on tracing into a mixed fund depend upon whether the property has been mixed with that of another innocent party or with that of the fiduciary. In the first case, the general rule is proportionate sharing, subject sometimes to "first in, first out".[18] In the second case, the general rule is proportionate sharing once any loss to the mixed fund has been borne by a fiduciary who mixed the assets in breach of trust.[19]

The exercise of a proprietary remedy depends upon the property being identifiable in the hands of the defendant. The rules applicable where a mixed fund becomes exhausted are an aspect of this; if the fund becomes exhausted at some point after the trust money has been paid into it, whether before or after the mixing, it will cease to be possible to trace the money.[20] *Bishopsgate Investment Management Ltd v. Homan*[21] is an example of this in operation. Money from pension funds belonging to the plaintiff had been wrongly transferred by Robert Maxwell into Maxwell Communication Corporation plc. The account into which the money was paid had either been or become overdrawn and it was held that this prevented the plaintiff from tracing the money.

3. Claim to be entitled to goods as purchaser[22]

The third party may be claiming to be entitled, as a purchaser from the insolvent,[23] to goods still in the possession of the insolvent. A binding contract for the purchase of chattels does not, unlike a contract to sell land, confer title on the purchaser. The purchaser may already have become the owner of the goods despite the fact that they are still in the possession of the insolvent seller since possession of and property in goods do not necessarily pass to the purchaser at the same time. Where the property in the goods has passed to the purchaser, the purchaser will be entitled to take possession of them. If the property has not passed and the insolvency practitioner decides to repudiate the contract, the purchaser will only be able to prove in the insolvency either for damages for non-delivery or for return of the purchase price. A purchaser who has not yet paid for the goods at the time of the insolvency will only suffer a loss if he has incurred expenses in making the contract with the

---

[18] *Re Diplock's Estate* [1948] Ch. 465, *Barlow Clowes International Ltd (in liquidation) v. Vaughan* [1992] 4 All E.R. 22.
[19] *Re Hallett's Estate* (1880) 13 Ch. D. 696, *Re Oatway* [1903] 2 Ch. 356, *Re Tilley's Will Trusts* [1967] 1 Ch. 1179.
[20] *Re Goldcorp Exchange Ltd* [1995] 1 A.C. 74.
[21] [1995] Ch. 211. Breslin (1995) 16 Co. Lawyer 307.
[22] See Goode, *Commercial Law* (2nd ed.) Chap. 8.
[23] See Chap. 8 of Goode, *Commercial Law*, on the passing of property under a contract for sale.

insolvent or has suffered loss due to the delay in delivery or can only obtain substitutes for more than the price asked by the insolvent seller. The purchaser who has paid for the goods in advance of their delivery and only has a personal claim will clearly lose as a result of the insolvency of the seller.

Section 17 of the Sale of Goods Act 1979 provides that property will pass when the parties intend it to and section 18 of the Sale of Goods Act 1979 provides a number of presumptions as to the intention of the parties which will apply in the absence of any contrary indication. Contrary indication may be demonstrated by the terms of the contract, the conduct of the parties or other circumstances of the case. The basic proposition of the default rules provided by section 18 of the Sale of Goods Act 1979 is that property in goods will pass at the time the contract is made provided the contract is unconditional and the goods are both specified and in a deliverable state; provision for postponement of delivery or payment, or both, is immaterial. Where something is to be done to the goods by the seller to render them specific or deliverable or to ascertain the price, property will not pass until that has been done and the buyer has notice of it.

The goods must be ascertained before title can pass; until the goods have been ascertained and appropriated to the contract, the purchaser will not be able to acquire a proprietary right.[24] Goods may be unascertained because they are sold by description only and the seller has complete freedom as to how to source the order as in *Re Goldcorp Exchange Ltd.*[25] Customers of a New Zealand company which dealt in precious metals purchased bullion for future delivery on the basis that they were purchasing gold which would be physically stored for them by the company in safekeeping as an unallocated part of the company's total stock. The company became insolvent and went into receivership under a debenture which secured by floating charge a debt exceeding the entire assets of the company. The only way in which the customers would retrieve anything from the insolvency was by demonstrating a proprietary claim to assets since there would be nothing left to meet personal claims after payment of the debenture holder. This was clearly a sale of generic goods on terms which preserved the seller's freedom to decide the source of the goods and no title to the goods could pass as a result of the contract of sale[26] until the goods had been ascertained and appropriated to the particular contracts. Lord Mustill referred to the

---

[24] Sale of Goods Act 1979, s.16.

[25] [1994] 2 All E.R. 806.

[26] The Privy Council was chiefly concerned with arguments that equitable proprietary rights had arisen outside the contract by way of trust. These arguments also ran into the difficulty that the subject matter of any trust was insufficiently identified.

"irresistible" reasoning of Atkin LJ in *Re Wait*[27] as pointing unequivocally to the conclusion that under a simple contract for the sale of unascertained goods neither legal nor equitable title can pass merely by virtue of the sale.

Goods may also be unascertained because they form part of a bulk, only some of which is to be acquired by the purchaser. Where the bulk has been reduced to the amount he has contracted for, or less, title will pass provided he is the only buyer in respect of that bulk. This principle of "ascertainment by exhaustion" was developed by the courts[28] and has been codified by the Sale of Goods (Amendment) Act 1995 which has added a third limb to rule 5 of section 18 of the Sale of Goods Act.

There may be several purchasers whose orders are to be met from a specified bulk as in *Re Staplyton Fletcher Ltd*.[29] In this case, customers of a wine merchant in administrative receivership claimed ownership of wine which they had ordered and paid for but which was stored in the wine merchant's warehouse without individual bottles being appropriated to each contract. Wine which was being stored for customers in this way was physically removed from the trading stock. The court held that the wines in the company's warehouse had been ascertained by their segregation so that the customers were tenants in common of the segregated stock. It would now be possible to reach the same conclusion by relying on the new section 20A of the Sale of Goods Act 1979 introduced by the Sale of Goods (Amendment) Act 1995. This provides that in the absence of agreement to the contrary a pre-paying buyer of goods forming part of a bulk, identified either in the contract or by subsequent agreement, becomes the owner of an undivided share in the bulk. If the buyer has paid in part only, he will receive a proportionate share and any delivery to him shall be ascribed first to the part for which he has paid. Where the aggregate of the undivided shares is more than the whole of the bulk, there will be proportionate reduction of each undivided share. This provision would not assist purchasers in the *Re Goldcorp Exchange* situation where the seller is not bound to provide the goods from an identifiable source.

Section 20B of the Sale of Goods Act 1979[30] provides that the co-owners of an undivided bulk shall be deemed to have consented to any dealing with the bulk including the delivery out of it to other

---

[27] [1927] 1 Ch. 606.
[28] *The Elafi* [1982] 1 All E.R. 208.
[29] [1994] 1 W.L.R. 1181.
[30] Also introduced by the Sale of Goods (Amendment) Act 1995.

co-owners. The Law Commissioners[31] did consider whether there should be special rules applying in the case of insolvency since this deemed consent would have the effect of preferring earlier claimants. They considered the possibility of a pro rata apportionment scheme; this would, however, involve the insolvency practitioner in the exercise of apportionment despite the fact that the insolvent seller would have no interest in the outcome. It would have been unpopular with commodity traders who would be exposed to potential liability to unknown third parties even after taking delivery of the goods. The Law Commissions decided not to recommend a separate insolvency rule; those who did not act sufficiently quickly to claim their goods would lose out to those who had acted more speedily but they would be no worse off than under the unamended law.

4. Retention of title by seller[32]

a) Development of the retention of title device

The third party may be claiming goods on the basis that they have been supplied to the insolvent under a contract containing a clause reserving title to the goods. This is clearly possible under the provisions of the Sale of Goods Act 1979 outlined above.

It has been commonplace since the nineteenth century for suppliers who provide goods on credit terms to provide that ownership of the goods will not pass until payment for the goods has been received; this form of transaction is described as a conditional sale. The hire purchase agreement[33] was devised as a more sophisticated form of seller protection since, by structuring the transaction as a contract for hire coupled with an option to purchase at the end of the hire period,[34] the seller avoided the problem of the customer being a buyer in possession able to confer title to the goods to a third party[35] and could be sure of the right to repossess the goods in the event of default. During this century, the process has been taken a stage further with the development of the finance lease under which the customer takes a lease of equipment for the length of the anticipated useful life of the asset and pays rental

---

[31] *Sale of Goods Forming Part of a Bulk* (Law Com. No. 215, Scot. Law Com. No. 145, H.C. 807, 1993).
[32] See Gerard McCormack, *Reservation of Title* (2nd ed.).
[33] *Helby v. Matthews* [1895] A.C. 471.
[34] By which time the rental payments would have amounted to the price together with a charge for the credit.
[35] *Lee v. Butler* [1893] 2 Q.B. 318 was a leading case on Factors Act 1889 s.9 which, with Sale of Goods Act 1979, s.25(1) provide the "sale by buyer in possession" exception to the *nemo dat* rule.

which will amount to the cost of the asset and of the credit; the lessor of the equipment (usually a finance house) retains purely nominal ownership but this is sufficient to allow repossession should the lessee become insolvent or otherwise default.

Retention of ownership, although designed to secure payment, is not seen by English law as a form of security since it does not involve the grant to another of rights over property. Registration as a company charge or as a bill of sale is therefore unnecessary for the device to be valid against third parties, who may be affected by rights whose existence there is no official means of discovering.[36] This very formalist distinction between sale credit and loan credit was abolished in the United States[37] some time ago and has been the subject of criticism in this country.[38]

Simple retention of title has been with us for a long time but the device has become more prominent and more complicated since the *Romalpa*[39] case, which appeared to open up the possibility of recovering not just the goods supplied but also products made with them and the proceeds of any sub-sales whenever any payment owed to the supplier was outstanding. Retention of title clauses have become more far-reaching although, as will be seen, in some cases those drafting them have been over-ambitious to counter-productive effect. Unwary draughtsmen have frequently been found to have created a registrable charge which is void for non-registration; once the buyer is conferring rights over his property on the seller, the thin dividing line between retention to title and charge will have been crossed.

b) Claims to proceeds of sub-sales

The extended retention of title clauses devised recently are attempts to provide the seller of goods with protection against the buyer's insolvency in circumstances where the goods supplied are expected to be sold on or used before the time for payment arrives. In *Romalpa* it was held that a seller who supplied on reservation of title terms, but who authorised sub-sales on condition that the buyer accounted for the proceeds of the sub-sales, had an equitable right to trace those proceeds

---

[36] See the discussion of the distinction between sale and loan credit in Chap. 2.5 above.

[37] Art. 9 of the American Uniform Commercial Code.

[38] See the report of the Crowther Committee on Consumer Credit (Cmnd 4596/1971) and Professor Diamond's *Review of Security Interests in Property* (1989). The Cork Committee felt that some provision for the registration of retention of title clauses should be made.

[39] *Aluminium Industrie Vaassen BV v. Romalpa Aluminium Ltd* [1976] 1 Lloyd's Rep. 443.

and claim proprietary rights to them, thus giving the seller priority over the holder of a floating charge in respect of the proceeds. The decision has never been over-ruled but in subsequent cases the courts have distinguished it on every similar occasion. They have held that in the cases before them the parties must be assumed to have intended that the interest in the proceeds should be by way of security only, rather than absolute, so that it amounted to an unregistered charge over the book debts arising from the sub-sales.

Mummery J. in *Compaq Computer v. Abercorn Group*[40] observed that once it was accepted that the seller's beneficial interest in the proceeds of sale was determinable on the payment of the debt, the seller was faced with the difficulty that the rights and obligations of the parties were in reality and in substance characteristic of those of the parties to a charge and not of the fiduciary relationship which would be required to give rise to the tracing rights. In *Re Weldtech Equipment Ltd*[41] Hoffmann J. considered a clause which provided that:

> "The goods remain our property until payment of the purchase price including any additional costs is effected in full and until all cheques and drafts have been cashed. This right is reserved for as long as we may have any claims against the purchaser resulting from other deliveries. With the exception of goods sold to a company for resale within the framework of their normal business operations, the customer is not entitled to sell or otherwise dispose of the goods before full payment of the purchase price. In the case of authorised resale of goods supplied by our company (in the original or a modified form or as an integral part of other deliveries) all rights to which the purchaser is entitled as a result of the contract with the third party, in particular for payment of the purchase price, are transferred to us automatically upon completion of the sale. The purchaser is obliged to advise us immediately of the resale or disposal of the equipment, stating the full address of the third party involved and the main content of the purchasing contract, in particular the terms of payment. This transfer takes place only for securing our claims against the purchaser and does not affect his payment obligations".

Hoffmann J. held that the liquidator had been correct to regard the clause as effective to preserve the title of the vendor to the equipment which was physically in the company's possession. He went on to hold that the assignment of the debts was clearly only intended to be by way

---

[40] [1991] B.C.C. 484.
[41] *ibid.* at 16.

of charge.[42] Since the clause had not been registered under section 395 of the Companies Act 1985, it was void against the liquidator.

c) Attempts to claim substitute goods

The courts have considered a number of cases in which sellers sought to rely on extended reservation of title clauses to claim ownership of goods made from or with the material supplied. The principle which can be derived from these cases is that the seller would succeed where the original material supplied remains identifiable provided that it was intended that the supplier should have absolute ownership of the substitute goods. Where the material has been mixed irrevocably with other goods, it will not be possible to identify it. *Re Andrabell Ltd*[43] was an example of the goods being mixed with others so that it was impossible to identify them. The retention of title clause in this case only reserved title until payment had been made for the particular consignment of goods; several consignments had been delivered, some paid for and some not, and it was not possible to identify the goods as coming from any particular consignment. Where goods change their identity in the course of manufacture, a new asset will have come into being to which the supplier could not have reserved title; any right claimed by the supplier over the new asset will have been granted by the purchaser and, unless it was intended to confer absolute ownership on the supplier, will be void as an unregistered security interest. In *Re Peachdart*,[44] for example, the title to leather which had been turned into handbags was lost and in *Borden (U.K.) Ltd v. Scottish Timber Products Ltd*[45] the supplier of resin which had been used to make chipboard could only claim a charge over the chipboard which, being unregistered, was void. *Hendy Lennox v. Grahame Puttick*[46] was an example of revocable mixture; the goods in question were diesel engines which had been bolted into generating sets but, since they could be unbolted, it was held that the supplier could retain the right to repossess them. In *Chaigley Farms Limited v. Crawford, Kaye & Grayshire*[47] it was held that a retention of title clause in respect of livestock sold to an abattoir was defeated by the slaughter of the animals.

---

[42] See also *Tatung (UK) Ltd v. Galex Telesure Ltd & Ors* (1989) 5 B.C.C. 325.
[43] [1984] 3 All E.R. 407.
[44] [1984] Ch. 181.
[45] [1981] Ch. 25.
[46] [1984] 1 W.L.R. 485.
[47] [1996] B.C.C. 957. The decision is queried at 13 I.L.&P. 25. The New Zealand High Court took a different view in *re Weddel (NZ) Ltd* (1996) 5 N.Z.B.I.C. 104,055, discussed by de Lacy at 13 I.L.&P. 163.

d) "All monies" clauses

The clause in *Romalpa* also provided that ownership in the material supplied would only transfer to the purchaser "when he has met all that is owing to [the supplier], no matter on what grounds". This type of so-called "all monies" clause has become commonplace and was held by the House of Lords in *Armour v. Thyssen Edelstahlwerke AG*[48] to be valid. If there was a point after the supply of the material subject to the clause at which the purchaser had paid everything owing to the supplier, the material will have vested in the purchaser then and subsequent indebtedness would not, of course, have divested the purchaser of the title. There is a problem in relation to "all monies" clauses of a potential windfall for the supplier where the purchaser has made partial payment[49]; any attempt in the wording of the clause to prevent the supplier from taking advantage of this runs the risk of turning the provision into a charge. The question of the consequences of the supplied material being worth more than the indebtedness was considered, *obiter*, by the Court of Appeal in *Clough Mill v. Martin*[50]; Sir John Donaldson M.R. said that the provision whereby the seller reserved "the right to dispose of the material until payment in full for all the material has been received" meant that the sellers could re-sell the material until they had been paid in full but that the remaining material would then become the property of the purchaser. Robert Goff L.J. suggested that repossession by the seller would follow the seller's acceptance of the buyer's repudiatory breach of contract and that the buyer would be entitled to reclaim any part of the purchase price paid for the goods on the basis of total failure of consideration. The House of Lords in the *Armour* case observed that they did not have to consider what would happen where there had been part payment of the price before repossession of the goods.

e) Successive retention of title

In *Re Highway Foods International Ltd*[51] the court had to consider the effect of a sale of meat on retention of title terms followed by a sub-sale also on retention of title terms. It was held that the sub-sale did not divest the original owner of title to the meat until the sub-purchaser either paid the purchaser or processed the meat.

---

[48] [1991] 2 A.C. 339.
[49] This is considered by Hicks in [1992] J.B.L. 398.
[50] [1985] 1 W.L.R. 111.
[51] [1995] B.C.C. 271.

f) Incorporation of the clause into the contract

In addition to the debate in any particular case as to whether the agreement amounts to a charge, there will also be the question of whether there is indeed a reservation of title provision in the contract between supplier and the insolvent. The normal contractual principles apply; the term will only be part of the contract if the purchaser had been given reasonable notice of it before or at the time of making the contract.[52] In *John Snow & Co. Ltd v. DBG Woodcroft & Co. Ltd*[53] the defendant company went into voluntary liquidation at a time when it had not paid for timber supplied to it by the plaintiff company. The plaintiff claimed to be entitled to repossess the timber on the basis of a retention of title clause reserving the property in the timber to the plaintiff until the defendant had discharged the whole of its indebtedness. The defendant argued that the terms of sale did not contain any such provision[54] since the documentation used by the plaintiff did not bring the clause sufficiently to the defendant's attention. Boreham J. held that sufficient notice had been given on the back of the plaintiff's quotation form and that retention of title clauses were not so unusual as to require "red ink" treatment. Where both purchaser and supplier have their own standard terms, the "battle of the forms" will usually be won by the last party to notify the terms before the contract is made, usually by the other party starting to perform.[55]

g) Practical effect of retention of title claims

Although a valid retention of title clause will allow the supplier to repossess the goods, this will probably be something which the supplier will attempt to avoid having to do. In practice, the use of the clause is to give the supplier a bargaining lever to extract payment from an insolvency practitioner[56] who wants to be able to use the material. The strength of the bargaining lever will probably depend on the extent to

---

[52] See any standard contract textbook on the incorporation of unsigned standard terms into a contract. This issue, which used to arise and tends to be taught largely in connection with exclusion clauses, now frequently involves arguments about whether retention of title clauses form part of a contract.

[53] [1985] B.C.L.C. 54.

[54] They also argued unsuccessfully that the provision would be void as an unregistered charge.

[55] *Butler Machine Tool Co. Ltd v. Ex-Cell-O-Corp. (England) Ltd* [1979] 1 All E.R. 965.

[56] Usually, in fact, an administrative receiver since a liquidator is not likely to carry on the business and a retention of title clause may not be enforced against an administrator.

which the insolvency practitioner needs the supplier to continue supplies. The case of *Leyland DAF Ltd v. Automotive Products*[57] is an example of this; a supplier in a monopoly position was held to be entitled to refuse to continue to supply any more parts until they were paid in full for goods which had been supplied under retention of title. *Lipe Ltd v. Leyland DAF*[58] illustrates the normal practice of insolvency practitioners which is to give a personal undertaking promising to return goods or pay their value if the clause is upheld in court; in this case, the court refused to grant the supplier an injunction preventing the insolvency practitioner from dealing with the goods.

5. Unpaid seller's rights

Section 39 of the Sale of Goods Act 1979 confers certain rights on an unpaid[59] seller of goods, notwithstanding that property may have passed to the buyer. An unpaid seller will have the right to reclaim goods which have not yet reached an insolvent purchaser despite the fact that title to the goods has passed.[60] If the seller is still in possession of the goods, he will have a lien over them in the circumstances specified in section 41 of the Sale of Goods Act 1979; the circumstances include the insolvency of the buyer.[61] The insolvency of the buyer does not bring the contract of sale to an end[62] and the seller must hold the goods available for the buyer against payment of the price unless and until the contract comes to an end. If the goods are perishable and the buyer does not pay within a reasonable time, the seller may resell the goods.[63] The seller may also resell the goods if the buyer, having been told of the seller's intention to resell, does not pay within a reasonable time.[64]

6. Equitable interests under a trust[65]

a) General

Property held by the insolvent on trust for a third party will not be available to the general creditors. In the case of bankruptcy, there is a

---

[57] (1993) B.C.C. 389.
[58] *ibid.* at 385.
[59] Defined by Sale of Goods Act 1979, s.38(1).
[60] *ibid.*, ss44–46.
[61] *ibid.*, ss41–43 set out the unpaid seller's lien in greater detail.
[62] Nor does the insolvency of the buyer since the contract may still be performed by a trustee in bankruptcy or a liquidator.
[63] Sale of Goods Act 1979, s.48.
[64] Sale of Goods Act 1979, s.48 re-enacting the common law rule that the seller may make time of the essence of the contract so that failure to pay is a repudiatory breach.
[65] See, generally, Hanbury and Martin, *Modern Equity* (15th ed.), Hayton, *Commentary and Cases on the law of trusts* (10th ed.).

specific provision to this effect in section 283(3)(a) of the Insolvency Act 1986 whereas in the case of liquidation it follows from the general principle that the creditors may only look to those assets in which the insolvent has a beneficial interest.

Readers are referred to general texts on equity, trusts and restitution for thorough discussion of this area. This text will restrict itself to a broad and somewhat simplistic indication of the circumstances in which a third party will be able to "trump" the other creditors on the basis of being beneficially entitled to property under a trust together with more detailed consideration of several cases which have arisen in the insolvency context by way of illustration.

The essence of a trust is separation of the legal title in property, which is held by the trustee, from the equitable title which vests in the beneficiary. A beneficiary under a trust has a proprietary claim to the property (provided it can be identified) or to any substitute property into which it can be traced. There does have to be identifiable property subject to the trust; a contractual obligation to establish a trust fund will not suffice to give rise to proprietary remedies.[66]

Trusts are usually categorised as express, resulting or constructive; the term "implied trust" is also used but is probably a means of establishing one of the categories of trust rather than a distinct category itself. The principles relating to express and resulting trusts are relatively clear although there is always scope for difficulty in applying those principles to any particular set of facts. The law as to the circumstances in which a constructive trust will arise is less clear; the common thread is the split of equitable from legal title in circumstances where there is no express or resulting trust but there are a number of disparate circumstances in which this will happen. Further confusion arises from the use of the description "constructive trustee" in respect of those who are personally liable for knowingly assisting in a breach of trust but against whom a proprietary claim is not necessarily possible.

Assets may be lost from a trust fund through authorised dealing by the trustee in which case the beneficiaries will have no right to reclaim them. For example, in *Space Investments Ltd v. Canadian Imperial Bank of Commerce Trust Co. (Bahamas) Ltd*[67] a trustee bank was permitted by the rules of the trust to place money on deposit with any bank, including itself. It placed trust money on deposit with itself and subsequently went into insolvent liquidation; the Privy Council held that the money had become general money of the bank, whose obligations in

---

[66] *Mac-Jordan Construction Ltd v. Brookmount Erostin Ltd* [1991] B.C.L.C. 333. A court will usually grant a mandatory injunction to require the fund to be established provided the "trustee" is not yet insolvent.

[67] [1986] 3 All E.R. 75.

relation to it were those of debtor and not of trustee. The beneficiaries were, therefore, ordinary creditors without any proprietary claim.

The vexed issue in this area is the extent to which a fiduciary relationship can co-exist with an ordinary contractual relationship. It can be argued that where a claimant has entered a transaction with the intention simply of becoming a creditor of the insolvent, there is no justification for affording him the priority of a trust interest on the basis that the debtor's behaviour has given rise to a fiduciary relationship. The Privy Council in *Re Goldcorp Exchange*[68] quoted with approval Atkin L.J. in *Re Wait*[69] on the difficulties inherent in holding that a contract gives rise to obligations of a fiduciary nature. Lord Mustill said that the essence of a fiduciary relationship is that it creates obligations of a different character from those deriving from the contract itself and went on to say: "It is possible without misuse of language to say that the customers put faith in the company, and that their trust has not been repaid. But the vocabulary is misleading; high expectations do not necessarily lead to equitable remedies".

Equitable interests arising under a trust are not registrable and are not visible to the general creditors of the insolvent trustee. Discussions[70] of whether this makes the upholding of such interests unfair to the general creditors usually conclude that the general creditors should not be able to complain of the non-availability of assets which were never in the beneficial ownership of the insolvent in the first place and that possession without title should not be seen as misleading. More doubts tend to be expressed about conferring priority in respect of assets which the beneficiary could not have acquired for himself or where the trust device appears to be being used to confer a remedy for what is fundamentally a complaint of breach of contract.

b) Express trusts

Where the insolvent is clearly a trustee under an express trust, the position will be unarguable; the property will not be available unless the insolvency practitioner can avoid the trust as a transaction intended to defeat creditors or at an undervalue.[71] Sometimes it is not clear whether

---

[68] [1994] 3 W.L.R. 199.
[69] [1927] 1 Ch. 606.
[70] See Goode 103 L.Q.R. 433, Goodhart and Jones 43 M.L.R. 489, Oakley [1995] C.L.J. 377.
[71] See Chap. 30.

or not an express trust has been created. The court will look for the so-called "three certainties" of words, subject and object. Informal language can give rise to a trust provided that the intention that the transferee of the property should not become unconditionally beneficially entitled to it is sufficiently clear.

Re Kayford Ltd[72] was an example of a case in which the court was prepared to construe the words used as having given rise to a trust. Kayford carried on a mail order business and its customers paid either fully or partially for goods when placing an order. Shortly before going into liquidation, Kayford opened a customers' trust deposit account and arranged that all money paid by customers in advance should be paid into the account and only released from it when the goods were delivered. Megarry J. decided that the money in the account was held on trust for the customers who had paid it and should not be treated as part of the general assets of the company. The judge said that the general rule is that money sent to a company as advance payment for goods would usually give rise to a merely personal claim against the company but that it was open to either sender or company to create a trust by using appropriate words in which case the obligations would become proprietary rather than contractual.

In Re Multi-Guarantee Co. Ltd,[73] a somewhat similar case, it was held that there was an insufficient manifestation of an intention to create a trust. In some cases the argument for the existence of a trust has failed because the trust property could not be clearly identified. In Re London Wine Co. (Shippers) Ltd[74] in which a company sold wine to customers which it then stored for them there was no appropriation of the wine until actual delivery.[75] The court, although apparently accepting that there had been an intention to create a trust, held that the trust failed for uncertainty of subject-matter. Even where the subject-matter has been sufficiently clearly identified, if the property is dissipated in such a way as to prevent the beneficiary from being able to trace it, there will be no possible proprietary remedy. Re Holiday Promotions (Europe) Ltd[76] is

---

[72] [1975] 1 All E.R. 604. This case has been somewhat controversial; see, e.g., Goodhart & Jones 43 M.L.R. 489 who argue strongly that it should be voidable as a preference. Prof. Goode approves; see Principles of Corporate Insolvency (2nd ed.) at p. 137 and the material cited therein at n. 74.

[73] [1987] B.C.L.C. 257.

[74] (1975) 126 N.L.J. 977.

[75] Contrast with the customers in Re Staplyton Fletcher [1994] 1 W.L.R. 1181, considered above, whose wine had been sufficiently segregated to give them legal title.

[76] [1996] 2 B.C.L.C. 618. The judge could find no intention that the monies paid should be kept apart from the general assets of the company.

an example of a recent unsuccessful attempt to claim rights under a *Re Kayford* trust.

c) Resulting trusts

A resulting trust will arise where a person transfers, or purchases property and has it conveyed, into the name of another either as sole owner or jointly with himself. In the absence of evidence of intention to give the beneficial interest to the transferee, the beneficial interest will result to him. This has been described as a presumed resulting trust.[77] An automatic resulting trust will arise where there is a transfer of property which leaves some of the equitable interest undisposed of or where the disposition fails. Since "equity abhors a beneficial vacuum",[78] the beneficial interest results back to the transferor.

This latter principle was applied in *Barclays Bank Ltd v. Quistclose Investments Ltd.*[79] Quistclose lent money to a company for the purpose of paying a dividend which had been declared. The company sent the cheque to Barclays with a request that the bank pay it into a separate account and stating that the money would only be used to pay the dividend. The company went into liquidation before the dividend could be paid. Barclays claimed to be entitled to set off the money against the company's overdraft on its other accounts but the House of Lords held that the money was impressed with a trust for repayment to Quistclose in the event of the failure of the primary trust for payment of the dividend and that Barclays had notice of this trust and was bound by it. It was held that existence of a contractual obligation to repay is not necessarily inconsistent with the existence of a trust. Lord Wilberforce looked as far back as 1819 to the case of *Toovey v. Milne*[80] for authority that money advanced for a specific purpose would not become part of the insolvent's estate.

There were similar findings in the cases of *Carreras Rothmans Ltd v. Freeman Mathews Treasure Ltd,*[81] in which payments were made to an advertising agency by a client for the specific purposes of discharging obligations to media creditors, and in *Re EVTR Ltd,*[82] in which a payment was made to a company specifically for the purchase of equipment.

---

[77] Refer back to section on the bankrupt's home in Chap. 27.
[78] *Vandervell v. IRC* [1966] Ch. 261.
[79] [1970] A.C. 567. See Millett (1985) 101 L.Q.R. 271, Rickett (1991) 107 L.Q.R. 608, Bridge (1992) 12 Ox. J.L.S. 358.
[80] (1819) 2 B. & A. 683.
[81] [1985] 1 All E.R. 155.
[82] (1987) 3 B.C.C. 389.

d) Constructive trusts

Whilst it is not possible to list precisely all the circumstances in which a constructive trust may arise, there are certain recurrent situations which have been held to give rise to such a trust. There has been an increasing tendency for creditors to seek to obtain priority by claiming a proprietary interest under a constructive trust and the principles which apply in this area are far from clear. The following propositions can be made:

i) The vendor of property who has entered into a contract[83] to sell land holds the beneficial interest on constructive trust for the purchaser.[84]

ii) A person who has acquired title to another's property by fraud or some other unconscionable act will be required to hold the property on constructive trust for the person deprived.[85]

iii) In a large number of cases, a constructive trust has been imposed on property which has been received as a result of breach of a fiduciary relationship. An example is the rule in *Keech v. Sandford*[86] under which a constructive trust will be imposed on property obtained by a trustee in his capacity as such, even if the beneficiary could not have obtained the property. This principle has been extended to agents,[87] company directors,[88] business partners[89] and others in a fiduciary relationship. The Privy Council have recently held in *Attorney-General for Hong Kong v. Reid*[90] that a fiduciary who receives a bribe holds it on constructive trust. The fiduciary was a Crown servant in Hong Kong who accepted bribes in breach of duty and used the proceeds to buy land in New Zealand. The Attorney General of Hong Kong claimed that the land belonged to the Crown. The New Zealand courts, following *Lister v. Stubbs*,[91] held that although there was a personal claim against the fiduciary it was not possible to

---

[83] Which complies with the formal requirements of the Law Reform (Miscellaneous Provisions) Act 1989.

[84] *Walsh v. Lonsdale* (1882) 21 Ch.D. 9.

[85] *Bannister v. Bannister* [1948] 2 All E.R. 133, *Binions v. Evans* [1972] Ch. 359.

[86] (1726) Sel. Cas. Ch. 61. This has been applied against directors in cases such as *Regal Hastings v. Gulliver* and *IDC v. Cooley*.

[87] *Boardman v. Phipps* [1967] 2 A.C. 46.

[88] *Cook v. Deeks* [1916] 1 A.C. 554 is one of a number of examples.

[89] *Featherstonhaugh v. Fenwick* (1810) 17 Ves. 298.

[90] [1993] A.C. 713, overruling the earlier Court of Appeal decision in *Lister v. Stubbs* (1890) 45 Ch.D. 1.

[91] (1890) 45 Ch.D. 1.

trace the money received by him into the land. The Privy Council, overruling the previous caselaw, held that the fiduciary held the bribe and any property acquired with it on constructive trust and that the Crown had an equitable interest in the land to the extent that the land had been purchased with the bribes.

iv) A person who receives property knowing[92] that the receipt is in breach of trust will hold it on constructive trust as will a person who, having received property, knowingly deals with it in breach of trust; if it is still in their possession or can be traced into substitute assets in their possession, the beneficiary will be able to claim the assets. A person who knowingly assists in a breach of trust will incur personal liability[93] but will not necessarily ever have been in possession of property to which a trust can attach.

It is less clear whether a constructive trust exists where there have been void, voidable or mistaken transactions.

Chase Manhattan Bank v. Israel–British Bank (London)[94] is a controversial case on mistaken contracts. The plaintiff New York bank as a result of a clerical error made a payment twice to another New York bank for the credit of a third English bank which subsequently became insolvent. The plaintiff claimed to be entitled to trace the second payment in equity against the insolvent bank. The applicable law was that of New York where payment under mistake of fact will give rise to a constructive trust if the payee cannot in conscience retain the money. Goulding J. observed that there would also be a constructive trust in this situation under English law. In *Westdeutsche Landesbank Girozentrale v. Islington B.C.*[95] Lord Browne-Wilkinson regarded this as incorrect although he thought the actual decision might be correct since the defendant knew of the mistake within two days of receiving payment.

There is considerable academic debate as to whether a constructive trust should be regarded as a remedy imposed by the court as a means of transferring property at that time, as is recognised to be the case in Canada and some parts of the United States, rather than a substantive institution which has been in existence since the happening of the events which gave rise to it and whose existence the court is merely declaring. There have been conflicting approaches in the recent cases of, on the

---

[92] See Gardner 112 L.Q.R. 56 on the meaning of knowledge in this context.
[93] *Royal Brunei Airlines Sdn. Bhd v. Tan* [1995] 3 W.L.R. 64 (Privy Council). See Harpum 111 L.Q.R. 545.
[94] [1980] 2 W.L.R. 202. Articles on the case include Tettenborn, [1980] C.L.J. 272.
[95] [1996] 2 W.L.R. 802.

one hand, *Attorney-General for Hong Kong v. Reid*[96] and *Lord Napier and Ettrick v. Hunter*[97] which display a discretionary approach based on the facts of the case and, on the other, *re Goldcorp Exchange Ltd*[98] in which the Privy Council seemed to be taking a more rigorous approach to the need to distinguish fiduciary obligations giving rise to ownership rights from mere contractual obligations.[99]

[96] [1994] A.C. 324.
[97] [1993] A.C. 713.
[98] [1994] 3 W.L.R. 199.
[99] See McKendrick 110 L.Q.R. 509, Oakley, [1995] C.L.J. 377.

CHAPTER 29

SECURITY RIGHTS OVER ASSETS OF THE INSOLVENT[1]

1. Introduction

Where a creditor is entitled to enforce security against assets of the debtor, that right is usually unaffected by the liquidation or bankruptcy of the debtor.[2] The exceptions are that it may be possible to invalidate the security as a preference[3] and that section 245 of the Insolvency Act 1986 contains rules, explained in detail below, under which a floating charge[4] may be invalidated. A floating chargee's rights are also postponed to those of certain other creditors.[5] The holder of a fixed charge is, therefore, in a more secure position in the event of the borrower's insolvency than is a floating chargee. There has, been a considerable amount of litigation on the issue of the distinction between the two types of charge which is considered below.

Entitlement to enforce a security depends on the security having been validly created.[6] The validity of a security has frequently been challenged on the grounds that the contract creating the security is voidable on the grounds of undue influence or misrepresentation.[7] Liquidators have sometimes argued that the security was invalid because the insolvent company lacked the capacity to enter into the security agreement or that those purporting to bind the company to the agreement lacked the authority to do so.[8] Sections 35–35A of the Companies Act 1985 now

---

[1] See, generally, Goode, *Legal Problems of Credit and Security* (2nd ed.), Gough *Company Charges* (2nd ed.), McCormack, *Registration of Company Charges*.

[2] See Chap. 4 for an explanation of how the security will be enforced.

[3] See Chap. 30.

[4] Defined in Chap. 2.4(a) and considered further below.

[5] Explained in Chap. 35 which deals with the distributional rules of insolvency law.

[6] See Chap. 23 of Goode, *Commercial Law* (2nd ed.) on the creation and attachment of security interests.

[7] See, *e.g.*, *Barclays Bank v. O'Brien* [1993] 4 All E.R. 417.

[8] *Re Introductions* [1970] Ch. 199 is one of the few cases in which the argument has worked.

prevent the validity of the security from being challenged on the basis that it is beyond the capacity of the company and, in favour of those dealing with the company in good faith, the power of the board of directors to bind the company, or authorise others to do so, is deemed to be free of limitations under the company's constitution.[9]

Entitlement to enforce security will also depend upon there having been compliance with any registration requirements[10]; nearly all consensual non-possessory[11] forms of security have registration requirements in order to perfect them against third parties.[12] Mortgages and charges given over land should be registered in accordance with the provisions of either the Land Charges Act 1972 or the Land Registration Act 1925. Mortgages given by individuals over chattels should be registered in accordance with the Bills of Sale Acts 1878–1882. In the case of a charge granted by a company, the rules governing registration have been in a state of instability for some years. The Companies Act 1989 contained a new registration regime to replace that contained in section 396 of the Companies Act 1985 but this has never been brought into effect. Under both the 1985 and 1989 provisions, and undoubtedly under whatever new provisions finally come into effect, a charge will be void against an administrator or a liquidator if it is registrable and has not been registered. The effect of non-registration is to allow the liquidator to sell the assets unencumbered by the rights of the chargee.

2. Distinction between fixed and floating charges[13]

The classic description of the difference between these two types of charge is that given by Lord Macnaghten in *Illingworth v. Houldsworth*[14]

> "A specific charge, I think, is one that without more fastens on ascertained and definite property or property capable of being

---

[9] The directors will, however, remain liable to the company for exceeding their powers.

[10] See, generally, Goode, *Commercial Law* (2nd ed.) Chap. 24 and McCormack *Registration of Company Charges*.

[11] Possession gives sufficient notice to the world of the security interest.

[12] In the case of a security interest over a debt, notice to the debtor will suffice.

[13] For discussions of the theoretical basis of the floating charge see Pennington 23 M.L.R. 630, W. J. Gough, *Company Charges* (2nd ed.) Chap. 13, Ferran [1988] C.L.J. 213, Worthington [1994] C.L.J. 81 and material cited therein.

[14] [1904] A.C. 355 at 358.

ascertained and defined[15]; a floating charge, on the other hand, is ambulatory and shifting in its nature, hovering over and so to speak floating with the property which it is intended to affect until some event occurs or some act is done which causes it to settle and fasten on the subject of the charge within its reach and grasp."

The floating charge enables a borrower to appropriate a class of assets to repayment of the debt without specifically identifying the component elements of the class. The charge only attaches specifically to items of property when the charge crystallises into a fixed charge. Until that time, the borrower may use the assets within the class as if they were unencumbered; the assets comprising the class will change in the ordinary course of business. The essence of a floating charge is that the chargor can continue to deal with the assets as if they were unencumbered; this enables a company to give security over its circulating assets. The nature of the floating charge renders it a more vulnerable form of security than a fixed charge since the lender will not be able to predict with any certainty the value of the secured assets at the time of crystallisation of the charge. In addition to the ordinary vicissitudes of trade, the charge is vulnerable to subsequent fixed charges,[16] factoring of debts,[17] assignments of property, sales and lease-back arrangements, retention of title, execution completed[18] and rights of set off[19] arising before crystallisation. A lender who has taken a floating charge will need to monitor the borrower carefully to protect the value of the security.[20] Although the lender and borrower may agree to restrict the borrower's rights to confer rights over the assets ranking above the floating chargee, it is not possible to ensure that third parties have sufficient notice of such so-called negative pledges to bind them to the chargee's rights.[21]

---

[15] It is possible to give a fixed charge over future property provided that it is sufficiently described to be identifiable when acquired:*Holroyd v. Marshall* (1862) 10 H.L.Cas. 191.

[16] *Wheatley v. Silkstone and Haigh Moor Coal Co.* (1885) 29 Ch.D. 715, *Re Castell & Brown Ltd* [1898] 1 Ch. 315.

[17] In broad terms factoring involves the sale by a company of debts (receivables) owing to it so that the company receives payment (less a discount) before the time when its customers are due to pay.

[18] *Evans v. Rival Granite Quarries* [1910] 2 K.B. 979, *Robson v. Smith* [1895] 2 Ch. 118.

[19] *Biggerstaff v. Rowatt's Wharf* [1896] 2 Ch. 93, *Rother Iron Works v. Canterbury Precision Engineers Ltd* [1974] Q.B. 1, *George Barker (Transport) Ltd v. Eynon* [1974] 1 W.L.R. 462.

[20] See Gough, *Company Charges* at p. 440 on the policy issues relating to floating charges; he argues that the floating charge should be given greater protection.

[21] Although details of the negative pledge may be registered at Companies House, registration is currently only notice to world of the existence of the charge and not of its contents.

It is only possible for a company to grant a floating charge since if an individual attempts to do so the charge will fall within the provisions of the Bills of Sale Acts (which do not apply to companies) and will be invalid unless specific details of the individual chattels subject to the charge are registered.[22]

The fact that the security relates to both current and future assets of a company does not require it to be a floating charge. It is possible to have a specific equitable charge over future property[23] provided there is agreement that the charge will attach to the property immediately on its acquisition by the debtor.[24] Although it is usual for the class of assets subject to a floating charge to fluctuate both upwards and downwards in value, it is possible to have a floating charge over a class which can only diminish in value: *Re Bond Worth*[25] is an example.

At one time it was assumed that it was not possible to take anything other than a floating charge over circulating assets. In recent years, however, the ambit of the fixed charge has been extended to cover book debts or, as they are now commonly described, receivables. In *Siebe Gorman & Co. Ltd v. Barclays Bank Ltd*[26] Slade J. held that it was possible for a fixed charge over future book debts to be granted such that the chargor was prevented from disposing of an unencumbered title to them; the essential element of a floating charge was the freedom given to the debtor company to deal with the secured assets in the ordinary course of business.[27] The words used to describe the charge are not determinative; in *Re Armagh Shoes Ltd*[28] and in *Re Brightlife Ltd*[29] charges described as fixed were held to be floating in reality. In both cases, there was held to be insufficient restriction on the company's freedom to deal with the charged assets for the charge to be fixed. *Siebe Gorman* was distinguished as a case in which the lender controlled the account into which the proceeds of the book debts would be paid. This appeared to restrict the scope of the fixed charge over receivables to charges in favour of clearing banks.

The law in this area has been taken a stage further by the Court of

---

[22] The Cork Committee recommended (para. 1569) that it should be possible for an individual to create a floating charge for business purposes.

[23] *Holroyd v. Marshall* (1862) 10 H.L.Cas. 191, *Tailby v. Official Receiver* (1888) 13 App.Cas. 523.

[24] see *Re Reis* [1904] 2 K.B. 769, *Re Lind* [1915] 2 Ch. 345, *Re Collins* [1925] Ch. 556.

[25] [1980] Ch. 228.

[26] [1979] 2 Lloyd's Rep. 142.

[27] The Cork Committee called for the *Siebe Gorman* decision to be reversed by statute but this recommendation was not accepted.

[28] [1984] B.C.L.C. 405.

[29] [1987] Ch. 22.

Appeal in *Re New Bullas Trading Ltd*[30] so that non-clearing bank lenders have almost the same access to the security as the clearing banks. The debenture in this case contained a provision described as a fixed charge over the company's present and future book debts. The agreement provided that the chargor would pay the proceeds of the book debts into a specified bank account, that the chargor would deal with the proceeds as directed by the chargee but that in the absence of directions the proceeds of the book debts were to be released from the fixed charge and be subjected to a floating charge. No directions were given by the chargee. The debenture holder stood to recover either all that it was owed or nothing depending upon whether its charge was held to be fixed or floating since the debts due to the preferential creditors exceeded the amounts which would be realised by the charged book debts. At first instance it was held that this was a floating charge over the book debts but the Court of Appeal reversed the decision and held that the book debts were subject to a fixed charge while uncollected and a floating charge on realisation. The judgment was based on the principle of freedom of contract and the clear agreement that the book debts and their proceeds were to be treated separately.

The characterisation of a charge over book debts as fixed or floating may be of great significance for the liquidator and the preferential creditors. If the charge is fixed then the book debts will be unavailable to the liquidator whereas if the charge is floating then the liquidator's expenses and the preferential creditors will take precedence.[31] The priority question will have no consequence for ordinary creditors, who will come after the chargee and the preferential creditors in whichever order they come; if, however, the charge is floating rather than fixed there is a possibility that it may be set aside under section 245 of the Insolvency Act 1986 in which case the assets subject to it will become available to the unsecured creditors.

3. Vulnerability of floating charges under section 245

There are special rules in relation to the validity of floating charges granted by companies in the period immediately preceding a liquidation

---

[30] [1994] B.C.C. 36. Professor Goode criticises the decision in 110 L.Q.R. 592. See Berg, [1995] J.B.L. 433 in reply. Both articles are critical of the Court of Appeal decision in *Re Atlantic Computer Systems plc* [1990] B.C.C. 859 for holding that charges over the rentals received by the debtor company were fixed because the property charged was specific without focusing on the fact that the debtor had freedom to deal with the rental payments. See also Worthington (1997) 113 L.Q.R. 562 for the suggestion that if the chargor has the right to remove the charged assets from the ambit of the security without recourse to the chargee, the charge must be floating and that, therefore, a charge over book debts can only be fixed if there is also a fixed charge over the proceeds.

[31] See Chap. 35.

or administration which threaten the validity of floating charges granted gratuitously. These rules are designed to prevent directors who realise that the company is in financial difficulty from taking security for the indebtedness of the company to themselves or their associates.

When the provisions were originally enacted in 1908 the period of vulnerability was only three months but it has been progressively lengthened to avoid it being possible to keep an insolvent company afloat just long enough to validate the charge. *Re William C. Leitch Brothers*[32] is an example of a case in which a director was held guilty of fraudulent trading[33] on the basis of such behaviour.

Section 245 of the Insolvency Act 1986 now provides that a floating charge created within the 12 months before the commencement of a winding up[34] or the making of an administration order in favour of a person unconnected with the company will be invalid (except to the prescribed extent) if the company is unable to pay its debts[35] at the time of creation of the charge or becomes unable to do so in consequence of the transaction under which the charge is created. A charge caught by these provisions is valid only to the extent of any cash, goods or services supplied to[36] the company, or discharge of any debt[37] of the company "at the same time as, or after, the creation of the charge". Where the charge is invalidated the lenders become ordinary unsecured creditors in respect of the loan and the assets which were alleged to be subject to the charge will become available to the unsecured creditors.[38]

Where the charge is in favour of a "connected person", it is vulnerable for two years up to the petition and it is irrelevant whether or not the company was solvent immediately after its creation. "Connected person"[39] includes directors and relatives and companies within a group.

There has been some debate as to whether "at the same time" is to be given a chronological or causal interpretation. In *Power v. Sharpe*

---

[32] [1932] 2 Ch. 71.
[33] See Chap. 31.
[34] The date of the petition or resolution whichever is earlier.
[35] Within the meaning of Insolvency Act 1986, s.123.
[36] In *Re Fairway Magazine* [1992] B.C.C. 924 it was held that money paid straight into an overdrawn bank account was not "paid to" the company within s.245(2)(a). Prentice suggests at 109 L.Q.R. 371 that the payment could have come within s.245(2)(b) as a reduction of debt.
[37] This provision is included despite the recommendation of the Cork Committee which felt (see para. 1564) that it would allow creditors to lend to discharge their earlier indebtedness and take a floating charge to secure the new loan thus securing what was previously unsecured indebtedness.
[38] Assuming there is no valid junior charge.
[39] Which is defined by Insolvency Act 1986, ss.249, 435.

Investments Ltd[40] the Court of Appeal decided that "at the same time as" meant that the new consideration had to be supplied contemporaneously with the creation of the charge; there had previously been suggestions that the words imported a requirement of causal rather than temporal connection. Any delay in executing the charge after the new value is provided will render it invalid.

Where the consideration supplied is the continuation of an overdraft facility, it can be difficult to establish to what extent the consideration is new. This issue arose in *Re Yeovil Glove*[41] in which a company went into liquidation with a bank overdraft of £67,000. The overdraft was secured by a floating charge given less than twelve months previously. Since the creation of the charge the bank had met cheques drawn by the company for £110,000 and received a similar sum for payment into the company's account. The overdraft, therefore, was at a similar level to that at the time the charge was created. The unsecured creditors attacked the charge on the basis of the predecessor provision to section 245. The court held that the bank's acts of meeting the cheques drawn by the company supplied the necessary value. The rule in *Clayton's Case*[42] was to be applied so that the sums paid into the account were to be treated as discharging the earlier indebtedness first and, therefore, the overdraft at the commencement of the liquidation was entirely secured by the charge.

4. "Charge-back" to bank

One issue which has given rise to considerable debate in this context is that of the so-called "charge" given to a bank over money deposited with it. This will arise where a bank provides financial accommodation to a customer and the customer deposits a sum of money with the bank by way of security; the deposit gives rise to a debt owing from the bank to the customer which the customer is said to charge in favour of the bank.

Re Charge Card Services[43] concerned a company, Charge Card Services Ltd, which entered into an agreement under which it factored its receivables to Commercial Credit Services Ltd (the factor). The agreement involved the company selling its debts to the factor at a discount and with a guarantee that all would be paid. The factor could require the company to repurchase the debts in certain circumstances (including the insolvent liquidation of the company). The factor had to maintain a

---

[40] [1994] 1 B.C.L.C. 111. At first instance, this case was reported as *Re Shoe Lace*.
[41] [1965] Ch. 148.
[42] (1816) 1 Mer. 572.
[43] [1987] Ch. 150.

current account which would be credited with amounts owing by the factor to the company and debited with amounts which the company owed the factor. The factor was also given the right to retain amounts as security for any claims against the company. The company went into liquidation and the liquidator disputed the factor's right to retain amounts standing to the credit of the company, arguing that it was void as an unregistered registrable charge on book debts. Millett J. said "The sum due from Commercial Credit to the company under the agreement is, of course, a book debt of the company which the company can charge to a third party. In my judgment, however, it cannot be charged in favour of Commercial Credit itself, for the simple reason that a charge in favour of a debtor of his own indebtedness to the chargor is conceptually impossible."[44] He explained this on the grounds that the benefit of a debt cannot be conveyed or assigned to or appropriated or made available to the debtor since this would result in the release of the debt: "The debtor cannot, and does not need to, resort to the creditor's claim against him in order to obtain the benefit of the security; his own liability to the creditor is automatically discharged or reduced".

Both the Court of Appeal and the House of Lords have recently considered, *obiter*, in *Re BCCI (No. 8)*[45] the question of whether this conclusion of Millett J. was correct. In this case the liquidators of BCCI sought the directions of the court in relation to the situation where BCCI had lent money to a principal debtor and had taken a deposit from another party which was charged with repayment of the loan. The charge permitted BCCI to refuse to release the deposit until the entire outstanding liabilities of the principal debtor had been repaid in full and BCCI was given the express right to use the deposit in discharge of the outstanding liabilities of the principal debtor. BCCI went into liquidation before the loan was repaid. The case was decided on the basis of the rules relating to set-off[46] but both the Court of Appeal and the House of Lords took the opportunity to express a reasoned view on the legal nature of a charge-back. In the Court of Appeal the view was expressed that a charge-back cannot create and vest in the chargee a proprietary interest in the debt which he owes to the chargor but that it takes effect as a matter of contract; the security of the "chargee" in such a case depended on the rules relating to set-off and the extent to which the contractual prohibition on assignment of the "charged" debt will bind

---

[44] A view supported by Professor Goode (see *Legal Problems of Credit and Security* (2nd ed.) pp. 124–129) but attacked by others (*e.g.* Wood, *English and International Set-Off*, Oditah [1992] J.B.L. 541).
[45] [1997] 4 All E.R. 568.
[46] See Chap. 25.4 above.

third parties.[47] In the House of Lords, however, Lord Hoffmann differed and held that a debt was property over which its owner could confer security rights in the same way that security rights could be conferred over other property; it made no difference that the beneficiary of the charge is the debtor. Lord Hoffmann indicated his agreement with the view of the Court of Appeal that designating the arrangements as a charge probably added nothing to their protection but observed "that seems to me no reason for preventing banks and their customers from creating charges over deposits if, for reasons of their own, they want to do so. The submissions to the Legal Risk Review Committee[48] make it clear that they do".

---

[47] As to which, see *Linden Gardens Trust Ltd v. Lenesta Sludge Disposals Ltd* [1994] A.C. 85.

[48] This was a committee set up in 1991 by the Bank of England to identify areas of obscurity and uncertainty in the law affecting financial markets.

CHAPTER 30

SWELLING THE ASSETS: CLAWING-BACK[1]

1. Introduction

The insolvency practitioner may be able to swell the value of the assets which were available to the creditors at the start of the insolvency by relying on claims arising from general law unrelated to the insolvency and also by bringing claims which are only available in a formal insolvency.

There may be claims which could have been brought by the insolvent, were it not for the insolvency, which can be brought by the insolvency practitioner[2] for the benefit of the creditors. These may include debts or other obligations owing to the insolvent and proprietary claims of the sort described in Chapter 28. There may also be claims arising from the circumstances leading to the insolvency. The insolvency practitioner will be looking for a defendant with "deep pockets" (or an insurer) against whom it may be possible to bring action in respect of loss caused by the insolvency; accountants, for example, have been vulnerable to such claims[3] and banks have been very wary about the possibility of incurring liability in the course of dealing with businesses in financial difficulty. Cases in which personal liability has been imposed on constructive trustees for knowing assistance with breach of trust have often arisen where the principal wrongdoer has become insolvent and the trust property has been dissipated.

There are a number of provisions under which transactions prior to the insolvency can be unscrambled.[4] Transactions intended to defeat

---

[1] See generally Fletcher, Zeigel (ed.), *Current Developments in International and Comparative Corporate Insolvency*, Chap. 12; Prentice, "Effect of insolvency on pre-liquidation transactions" in Pettet (ed.) *Company Law in Change*; Wheeler [1993] J.B.L. 256.

[2] With any necessary consent of the creditors.

[3] *Caparo Industries plc v. Dickman* [1990] 1 All E.R. 568, HL, is a prominent example.

[4] This untechnical term is used since the effect of the provisions on the transactions varies. Some transactions are rendered void but a number of them are rendered neither void nor strictly voidable but are subject to a wide discretionary power of the court to restore the previous position as far as possible.

creditors are subject to challenge[5] by anyone who has suffered in consequence, whether or not a formal insolvency is in progress. There are also a number of provisions under which prior transactions may be re-opened which are only available on a liquidation or bankruptcy or, in some cases, a company administration; the ability to pursue such claims may be a reason for putting a debtor into a formal insolvency regime. The relevant provisions, which are all[6] considered in more detail later in the chapter, are the following:

(i) transfers after the presentation of a petition for bankruptcy or winding up[7]

(ii) legal process completed after the commencement of the insolvency[8]

(iii) transactions intended to defeat creditors[9]

(iv) transfers at an undervalue immediately preceding the insolvency[10]

(v) preferences in the lead up to the insolvency[11]

(vi) extortionate credit bargains[12]

(vii) general assignment of book debts in bankruptcy.[13]

These provisions have the effect of backdating the collective *pari passu* principle in order either to prevent creditors from jumping the queue or to prevent the insolvent from gaining from having transferred assets to associates ahead of the insolvency. The Insolvency Act 1986 attempts in its definition of "associate"[14] to give a comprehensive definition of those with whom the insolvent is likely to have been dealing at less than arm's length. In relation to a liquidation, the broader concept of "connected person",[15] which includes the associates of the company, is used.

It is clear that the provisions of the insolvency legislation prevail over any property dispositions in the course of matrimonial proceedings.[16] In

---

[5] Under Insolvency Act 1986, s.423.

[6] Except for legal process completed after the start of the insolvency which has already been considered in Chap. 25.

[7] Insolvency Act 1986, s.284 (bankruptcy), s.127 (liquidation).

[8] See Chap. 25 above.

[9] Insolvency Act 1986, s.423.

[10] *ibid.*, s.339 (bankruptcy), s.238 (liquidation).

[11] *ibid.*, s.340 (bankruptcy), s.239 (liquidation).

[12] *ibid.*, s.244 (liquidation), s.343 (bankruptcy).

[13] *ibid.*, s.344.

[14] *ibid.*, s.435.

[15] *ibid.*, s.249.

[16] Matrimonial Causes Act 1973, s.39 as amended makes this clear. See Miller (1994) 10 I.L.&P. 66 for a discussion of the extent to which inter-spouse transfers should be attacked where there has been family breakdown.

Mullard v. Mullard[17] the court ordering a transfer of property in favour of a wife recognised the possibility that it might be set aside in a subsequent bankruptcy of the husband and, in view of this, made a nominal order for maintenance payments which could be revisited at a later date.

In the case of a liquidation, it may also be possible to claim a contribution from shareholders, directors and others involved in running the company; this is considered in more detail in the next Chapter.

A major factor to be taken into account by an insolvency practitioner will be the cost of any attempt to swell the assets with the inevitable risk that, if the attempt fails, the assets will have been diminished rather than increased. Consideration is given in Chapter 32 to the various means by which insolvency practitioners may seek financial assistance for an attempt to increase the assets but, in many cases, creditors may prefer not to gamble on increasing the assets.

2. Dispositions of property between petition and order

a) Circumstances in which such dispositions are void

Anyone dealing with a person or company against whom a petition for winding up or bankruptcy has been presented does so at their peril. If the court decides to make the requested bankruptcy or winding up order, any payments or dispositions of property[18] after the presentation of the petition will be void unless made with the consent of the court or subsequently ratified by the court. Section 127 of the Insolvency Act 1986 provides that any disposition of property or transfer of shares or alteration of the status of members will be void after the commencement of a winding up. The winding up will, once the order has been made, be deemed to have commenced with the presentation of the petition. Section 284 of the Insolvency Act 1986 provides for dispositions by the bankrupt to be void if made during the period beginning with the presentation of the petition and ending with the vesting of the estate in the trustee.[19] One major difference in the drafting of the two sections is that section 127 merely refers to dispositions without specifying any

---

[17] (1982) 3 F.L.R. 330.
[18] Including dispositions by a bankrupt of property which is not or would not form part of the bankrupt's estate (for example, equipment used by the bankrupt in his trade). A disposition is any act which transfers value from the insolvent to another person.
[19] There is little case law on this provision in the bankruptcy context since it was only introduced into bankruptcy law in 1986; prior to 1986 much the same effect was achieved by relating the beginning of the bankruptcy back to the first available act of bankruptcy.

particular disponor; in *Re J. Leslie Engineers*[20] the Court held that it was immaterial under section 127 whether the disposition was by the company or by a third party. Another difference is that section 127 makes no reference to the consequences of the voidness (leaving it to the general law) whereas section 284 is more specific. Guidance as to when consent will be given can be derived from the cases, most of which have arisen in the context of a compulsory liquidation[21] rather than bankruptcy.

In *Re Wiltshire Iron Co.*[22] Cairns L.J. said "this is a wholesome and necessary provision to prevent during the period which must elapse before a petition can be heard, the improper alienation and dissipation of the property of a company in extremis. But where a company actually trading, which it is in the interests of everyone to preserve and ultimately to sell as a going concern, is made the object of a winding up petition which may fail or may succeed, if it were to be supposed that transactions in the ordinary course of its current trade, bona fide entered into and completed, would be avoided, and would not in the discretion given to the court, be maintained, the result would be that the presentation of a petition, groundless or well-founded, would, *ipso facto*, paralyse the trade of the company and great injury without any counter-balance of advantage, would be done to those interested in the assets of the company". In *Re Gray's Inn Construction*[23] Buckley L.J. said that the policy of the law was to procure so far as practicable rateable payments of the unsecured creditors' claims and it was clear that the court should not validate any transaction which might result in one or more pre-liquidation creditors being paid in full at the expense of the other creditors who would only receive a dividend unless there were special circumstances making such a course desirable in the interests of the unsecured creditors as a body. Buckley L.J. observed that if it were in the interests of the creditors generally that the company's business should be carried on and this could only be achieved by paying for goods already supplied to the company, but not yet paid for, when the petition was presented the court might think fit in the exercise of its discretion to validate payment for those goods. A disposition carried out in good faith in the ordinary course of business at a time when the parties were unaware that a petition had been presented would normally be validated by the court unless there were any ground for thinking that

---

[20] [1976] 2 All E.R. 85.
[21] In the case of a voluntary liquidation, there is no "twilight period" such as that between petition and order in the case of a compulsory liquidation. The commencement of the liquidation will be the passing of the resolution.
[22] (1868) L.R. 3 Ch.App. 443.
[23] [1980] 1 W.L.R. 711. *Re S & D Wright* [1992] B.C.C. 503 also contains a set of guidelines based partly on *Re Gray's Inn Construction*.

the transaction might involve an attempt to prefer the disponee, in which case the transaction would probably not be validated. Post-liquidation dispositions for full value and transactions which increase or preserve the value of the assets could not harm the creditors.

There seem, therefore, to be two main factors to which the court will have regard: the bona fides of the transaction and whether it was in the ordinary course of business. In relation to the first issue, although ignorance of the petition will help to establish bona fides,[24] it is not necessarily fatal to the validity of the transaction that the person receiving the property or payment was aware of the presentation of the petition if he otherwise acted in good faith.[25] The transaction must also be in the ordinary course of business and, where the company has derived no benefit from it, this may be hard to establish. In *Re Clifton Place Garage Ltd*[26] it was held that good faith and legitimacy of purpose are not sufficient if the disposition was not reasonable or the company did not benefit.

An application for the court's approval or confirmation of a disposition may be made by anyone with a particular interest in the matter[27] so that either party to a transaction or proposed transaction can seek consent or ratification. The court can approve a disposition in advance; in *A. I. Levy Ltd*[28] the court permitted the company to dispose of a lease pending the hearing of the petition so that the provision contained in the lease for its forfeiture if the company were wound up should not take effect. This was followed in *Re Operator Control Cabs Ltd*[29] in which permission was given to continue to trade in the ordinary way and to dispose of assets and pay debts without needing to seek approval on each occasion; such permission is only likely to be given where it is probable that the business will be saleable in the liquidation.[30]

The case of *Re Flint*[31] is a relatively recent example of the operation of the provision in the bankruptcy context. A husband and wife married in 1969 and bought their matrimonial home as legal and beneficial joint tenants. They separated in 1986 and in 1988 the wife presented a

---

[24] *Re J. Leslie Engineers* [1976] 1 W.L.R. 292, which demonstrates that ignorance will not necessarily lead to validation of a disposition.

[25] *Re Park Ward & Co. Ltd* [1926] Ch. 828, *Re Steane's (Bournemouth) Ltd* [1950] 1 All E.R. 21.

[26] [1970] Ch. 477. Contrast *Re Civil Service and General Store Ltd* (1887) 57 L.J. Ch. 119 in which the creditor's knowledge of the petition led the court to think that the motive behind the transaction was to prefer the creditor.

[27] *Re Argentum Reductions (U.K.) Ltd* [1975] 1 All E.R. 608.

[28] [1964] Ch. 19.

[29] [1970] 3 All E.R. 657n.

[30] *Re Grays Inn Construction* [1980] 1 W.L.R. 711, *Re McGuinness Bros (U.K.) Ltd* (1987) 3 B.C.C. 571.

[31] [1993] Ch. 319.

divorce petition, giving notice of her intention to proceed with an application for ancillary relief in February 1989. In the same year the husband started a business which failed and in May 1990 one of his creditors presented a bankruptcy petition against him. On July 18, 1990 the county court made a consent order that the husband should transfer all his estate and interest in the home to the wife within 28 days. Six days later before any steps were taken to comply with the order, a bankruptcy order was made in a different county court. In December 1991 the trustee in bankruptcy obtained a declaration from the court which had made the bankruptcy order that the order providing for the transfer of the home was void against the trustee in bankruptcy under section 284 of the Insolvency Act 1986 and that the home was held by the wife and trustee in equal shares. The wife appealed, arguing first that the order was a disposition by the court not the husband and, secondly, that the court should have exercised a discretion to ratify it if the section did apply. It was held that the order was caught by the section[32] and that although there were no section 284 cases to provide guidance the guidance should look at the liquidation cases under section 127 of the Insolvency Act 1986.[33] The cases showed that the court should consider what was just and fair in all the circumstances having particular regard to good faith and honest intention. The county court had had all the financial evidence and both husband and wife knew of the impending bankruptcy at the time of transfer; the decision not to exercise the discretion was not perverse or obviously wrong and there was no basis for interfering with it.

b) Remedies available to the insolvency practitioner

Unless the court decides to validate a disposition between petition and order, the insolvency practitioner will be able to retrieve the property (or proceeds of its disposition) or payment from the transferee or payee. It will also be possible to retrieve the property (or its traceable substitute) from any subsequent transferee unless it is in or has passed through the hands of someone who received it before the commencement of the bankruptcy or liquidation in good faith, for value and without notice that the petition had been presented.

---

[32] In *Burton v. Burton* [1986] 2 F.L.R. 419, however, Butler-Sloss J. expressed the view that a property transfer order was not itself a disposition of property and that the disposition occurs when the order is carried out. Nicholls V.-C. in *Re Mordant* [1995] B.C.C. 209 pointed out the divergence between the two cases without needing to come to a conclusion of his own.

[33] It is not clear that this is correct since the two provisions are not identical and the genesis of Insolvency Act 1986, s.284 seems to lie in pre 1986 bankruptcy law.

Section 284(4) of the Insolvency Act 1986 provides that there will be no remedy against a person in respect of property or payment received before the commencement of the bankruptcy in good faith, for value and without notice that the petition had been presented. This re-enacts the pre- 1986 bankruptcy law but appears to conflict with a number of the cases on section 127 and its predecessors in the corporate context. In *Re J. Leslie Engineers*[34] a director of the insolvent company arranged matters so that a creditor of the company was paid after a petition for winding up had been presented. Part of the payment was made by a cheque drawn on the personal account of the director; a cheque for the required amount had been drawn on the company's account in favour of the director. The money ceased to be the property of the company when it was mixed with other moneys in the directors' personal account and it could not thereafter be traced to the creditor. The rest of the payment was made by drawing a cheque for £250 cash on the company's account which was subsequently converted to money orders payable to the creditor of the company. The court held that there was throughout a clearly identifiable property of the company which passed to the creditor. The court held that the payment could not be allowed to stand since it was clearly a preferential payment with the company's money and it was irrelevant that the creditor did not realise this.

In the case of an insolvent company, the liquidator may also recover the value of the property from directors or other persons who disposed of it in the company's name. There would clearly have been an action against the director in *Re J. Leslie Engineers*[35] for the disposition of the company's property both on this ground and on the basis that he was in breach of his fiduciary duty as a director.

The court is not concerned to achieve anything more than the restoration of the value of the assets which have been lost to the general creditors.[36]

It was held in *Mond v. Hammond Suddards*[37] that, since the assets are being reclaimed on the basis that the transaction was void, they will fall into any charge over that class of asset.

c) Operation of bank accounts in the "twilight period"

The transfer of money to the bank or the collection of the cheque by the bank as agent for the insolvent is arguably a disposition of property by the insolvent since it will have exchanged the cash either for a debt

[34] [1976] 2 All E.R. 85.
[35] *ibid.*
[36] *Re Gray's Inn Construction* [1980] 1 All E.R. 814.
[37] [1996] 2 B.C.L.C. 470.

owed by the bank if the account is in credit or for a reduction in its liability to the bank. Where the account is in credit and the bank is solvent, the disposition will not affect the value of the assets available to the creditors of the insolvent. If the bank is unable to meet the claim by the liquidator or trustee, there will have been a diminution in the assets available for the creditors.[38] If the account is overdrawn, there will clearly have been a disposition of property in that part of the liability to the bank will have been met and the amount available for the general creditors will have been reduced.

Withdrawals from an account in credit will clearly be dispositions of the insolvent's property. Arguably, withdrawals from an account which is overdrawn are increases in the liabilities rather than dispositions of assets[39] unless the fact of the increased overdraft has implications for the assets.[40] The Court of Appeal in *Re Gray's Inn Construction*,[41] however, held that such payments did fall within section 127.

In *Re Gray's Inn Construction*[42] the bank allowed a company to continue to use its overdrawn bank account while the hearing of the petition was pending. The Court of Appeal ruled that both payments into[43] and payments out of the account were dispositions within section 127. The Court held that the bank should have frozen the account on presentation of the petition and created a separate new account so that pre- and post-liquidation transactions could be kept separate. It held that transactions carried out before the date on which the bank should have known of the petition would stand but declined to validate those which were effected later; the liquidator was, therefore, entitled to reclaim the amounts paid in and to ignore the debts incurred. In *Re Barn Crown Ltd*[44] it was held that payments into an account in credit were not dispositions.

The withdrawal of money from the insolvent's account and the payment of money into the account of a third party will clearly be dispositions of the insolvent's property. It has been held that the further withdrawal from the account of the third party, where the money has been mixed, is not a disposal of the insolvent's property even if the

---

[38] On this basis, Professor Goode argues that payment into the account is a disposition: *Principles of Corporate Insolvency* (2nd ed.), p. 427.

[39] See Professor Goode, *Principles of Corporate Insolvency* (2nd ed.), p. 429.

[40] Such as an increase in the assets of the company subject to a floating charge securing the overdraft.

[41] [1980] 1 All E.R. 814.

[42] *ibid.*

[43] Buckley L.J. said that payments into an overdrawn account were clearly dispositions as were, in his view, payments into an account in credit.

[44] [1994] 4 All E.R. 42.

insolvent could theoretically have obtained a declaration of a charge over the mixed fund.[45]

Where a bankrupt incurs a debt to a banker by making a payment which is void under this provision, the debt is deemed for bankruptcy purposes to have been incurred before the commencement of the bankruptcy (and, therefore, a bankruptcy debt) unless the banker had notice of the bankruptcy before the debt was incurred or it is not reasonably practicable for the amount of the payment to be recovered from the person to whom it was made. The consequence of deeming the debt to be a bankruptcy debt is that the bank will be able to prove for it in the bankruptcy.

3. Transactions at an undervalue

a) Relevant provisions

Transactions which the insolvent has entered into at an undervalue are vulnerable to attack under two provisions; section 423 of the Insolvency Act 1986 which applies to transactions entered into at any time with the intention of defeating creditors and sections 238 and 339 of the Insolvency Act 1986 which apply to transactions entered into during a defined period immediately prior to the insolvency. The latter provisions avoid the need for an insolvency practitioner to prove a motive for the transfer; the more stringent rules in relation to bankruptcy reflect the fact that a company is less likely than an individual to dispose of its property at an undervalue[46] and that, where it does so, there will often be a sound commercial motive. There are various presumptions designed to make it easier for the insolvency practitioner to attack transactions with persons associated with or connected to the insolvent; these are the cases in which it is likeliest that there has been a deliberate attempt to remove assets from the reach of creditors.

b) Definition of a transaction at an undervalue

A transaction[47] will be at an undervalue for the purposes of sections 423, 238 and 339 of the Insolvency Act 1986 if the transferor receives no consideration or receives consideration the value of which in money

---

[45] *Re J. Leslie Engineers* [1976] 2 All E.R. 85.
[46] Although members of a corporate group may act like members of a family of individuals.
[47] Defined by Insolvency Act 1986, s.436 as including "a gift, agreement or arrangement".

or money's worth is significantly less than the value of the consideration provided by the debtor or receives only marriage consideration.[48]

In *Agricultural Mortgage Corp. plc v. Woodward*[49], the plaintiff had been given a charge over the farm of the first defendant who granted the second defendant a tenancy at a full market rent. The tenancy was a protected agricultural tenancy and the intention was to give the second defendant security of tenure thus reducing the value of the mortgaged land. The Court of Appeal held that this was a transaction within section 423 of the Insolvency Act 1986 since the first defendant had suffered a substantial loss in the value of his land so that the true value received by the second defendant, which included the preservation of the farm business from the creditors, was much greater than the consideration received by the first defendant. The reality of the benefit received had to be considered not merely the expressed consideration.[50]

Trustees in bankruptcy have frequently attempted to have the transfer of property from one spouse to another set aside as a transfer at an undervalue; one issue that has arisen in these cases is that of whether an agreement to take over the mortgage repayments prevents the transfer of a house from being at an undervalue. Another is the extent to which a transfer in the context of a divorce settlement is saved from being at an undervalue by an agreement to give up all other claims against the transferor. In *Re Windle*[51] the court held that where there is a substantial equity of redemption, a mere agreement to pay the mortgage cannot be valuable consideration. In *Re Abbott*,[52] which is the leading case under the old legislation,[53] a house was transferred to the wife by her husband, who was insolvent at the time although she did not know it, under a consent order as a result of a compromise of her claims for ancillary relief. The court held that relinquishing a claim to financial assistance could amount to valuable consideration. *Re Kumar*,[54] which was decided under the current provisions, concerned a transfer of a house in return for an agreement to pay the mortgage and to give up a claim to financial provision. The equity in the house was of considerable value and the consideration was clearly significantly less. The financial provision claim was worthless since the husband had no other assets and she was earning more than he. The court held that *Re Abbott* remained

---

[48] Insolvency Act 1986, ss423(1), 339(3), 238(4).
[49] [1994] B.C.C. 688, applied in *Walton v. IRC* [1996] 21 E.G. 144.
[50] See also *Barclays Bank plc v. Eustice* [1995] B.C.C. 978.
[51] [1975] 3 All E.R. 987.
[52] [1983] Ch. 45.
[53] Which only caught transfers for no consideration, not those for less than commercial value.
[54] [1993] 1 W.L.R. 224.

authority that compromise of a claim to financial provision is capable of being consideration in money or money's worth but the quantum of the value now arises for consideration and in *Re Kumar* there was an imbalance which led to the transaction being at an undervalue.

c) Transactions intended to defeat creditors: section 423

Section 423 of the Insolvency Act 1986 applies to individuals and companies and is of application whether or not there is a formal insolvency. The section allows the court to unscramble transactions entered into at an undervalue with the purpose of putting assets beyond the reach of creditors or of otherwise prejudicing the interests of such people. An application may be made by the insolvency practitioner in charge of insolvency or, with the leave of the court, by a victim of the transaction.[55]

A court faced with an application under section 423 of the Insolvency Act 1986 has to consider, first, whether the transaction was at an undervalue and, secondly, the purpose of the transaction. There is no restriction on the length of time which may have elapsed since the transaction but the longer ago it was, the more difficult it will be to establish the necessary motive.[56]

Putting assets out of the reach of a creditor or creditors must have been the purpose[57] behind the transaction, not merely the result of it. In *Royscot Spa Leasing Ltd v. Lovett*[58] it was assumed, without deciding the point, that the purpose had to be a substantial purpose rather than the dominant one; it was also held that the purpose of the transferor could not be established by a solely objective test and that it was not sufficient to establish the necessary purpose merely to show that the transfer was made to members of the transferor's family three days before summary judgment was obtained against the transferor.

Moon v. Franklin[59] is an example of a case in which an application under section 423 succeeded.[60] An accountant facing criminal charges and negligence actions decided to sell his accountancy practice. In

---

[55] Insolvency Act 1986, s.424.
[56] It is also likely to be more difficult for the court to find a remedy which does not prejudice innocent third parties.
[57] But not necessarily the sole purpose: *Chohan v. Saggar* [1992] B.C.C. 750.
[58] [1995] B.C.C. 502, CA.
[59] *The Independent*, June 22, 1990.
[60] It was not brought in the context of an insolvency but by plaintiffs bringing a claim who were concerned that assets were being transferred out of their reach.

anticipation of receiving around £68,000 for the practice, he agreed in June 1987 to pay £65,000 to his wife. She used the money to discharge the mortgage on their home, discharge a loan raised to help their son, pay £25,000 into an account in her sole name and buy a flat in the joint names of herself and her husband in August 1988. In August 1987 the matrimonial home was transferred into her sole name. The court found that the transfer of the £65,000 was a gift as was the transfer of the husband's interest in the house. As the wife's interest in the flat derived from the money originally owned by the husband he had entered into a transaction at an undervalue with respect to the flat. The court was satisfied that the payment and the transfer were transactions entered into for the purpose of putting the assets out of the reach of those taking negligence proceedings against him. The key question was his intention and it was irrelevant that the wife thought the intention was to reward her loyalty and hard work. £5,000 of the amount in her account could be shown to come from the original £23,000 and should be preserved and, pending the outcome of the proceedings, she was to be restrained from dealing with the properties.

Arbuthnot Leasing International Ltd v. Havelet Leasing Ltd[61] is an illustration of the provision in operation in the context of the corporate group. The first defendant company "Leasing" fell into arrears in making payments under its financing agreements with Arbuthnot. In April 1990, Arbuthnot entered judgment against Leasing and obtained the appointment of receivers. The receivers discovered that between December 1989 and April 1990 the business and assets of Leasing had been transferred to Finance (incorporated in 1989 with two issued £1 shares). Arbuthnot sought to reverse the transfer of Leasing's business to Finance and the court ordered that the business and assets of Finance were to be held by it on trust for Leasing. The transfer was consistent with an intention to put Leasing's assets out of Arbuthnot's reach and was at an undervalue within the meaning of section 423 of the Insolvency Act 1986.

In *Midland Bank v. Wyatt*[62] the defendant had executed a trust deed in June 1987 giving his interest in the house he had purchased jointly with his wife to his wife and two daughters in order to shelter his assets from the risk of his business failing. The court held that section 423 of the Insolvency Act 1986 did not require proof of dishonesty, merely proof that the defendant intended to avoid his creditors.

---

[61] [1990] B.C.C. 306.
[62] [1995] 1 F.L.R. 697.

d) Transactions at an undervalue within the relevant period

A trustee in bankruptcy, liquidator or administrator may apply to the court[63] for an order unscrambling transactions at an undervalue entered into during a period shortly before the insolvency referred to as "a relevant time". Identification of whether the transaction was at the relevant time involves a combination of establishing how far before the commencement of the insolvency the transaction happened and, in some cases, the state of solvency of the eventual insolvent at the time. The rules are not the same for bankruptcy as for liquidation and administration.

In the case of a bankrupt a transaction will have taken place at a relevant time if it happened in the five years before presentation of the petition on which the bankruptcy order was made provided that, if the transaction took place more than two years before the petition, it will only be at a relevant time if the bankrupt was unable to pay his debts[64] at the time or became so in consequence of the transaction.[65] Where the transaction is with an associate[66] it will be rebuttably presumed that the bankrupt was insolvent at the time; in other cases the burden of proof is on the insolvency practitioner and it may be difficult to reconstruct the financial affairs of the insolvent adequately.

In the case of a company, transactions at an undervalue are only vulnerable in the two years before the onset of the insolvency[67] and only if the company is unable to pay debts at the time or becomes so unable as a result of the transaction; a state of insolvency will be rebuttably presumed if the other party is connected with the company but in other cases the burden of proof will be on the insolvency practitioner. The court may not make an order in respect of a transaction at an undervalue entered into by a company where it is satisfied that the company entered into the transaction in good faith and for the purpose of carrying on its business and that at the time it did so there were reasonable grounds for believing that the transaction would benefit the company.

---

[63] Under Insolvency Act 1986, s.339 (bankruptcy) and Insolvency Act 1986, s.238 (liquidation, administration). This provision has only been available in corporate insolvency since 1986. Prior to its introduction, liquidators had to use ordinary company law doctrines of *ultra vires* and directors' duties to challenge transactions at an undervalue.

[64] Within the meaning of Insolvency Act 1986, s.123.

[65] *ibid.*, s.240.

[66] *ibid.*, s.435.

[67] The date of presentation of a petition for administration in the case of a company in administration or which goes into liquidation immediately upon the discharge of an administration order or, in other cases, the date of the commencement of the winding up (petition or resolution, whichever is earlier).

e) Remedies available in respect of transactions at an undervalue

The remedies available in respect of transactions subject to sections 423, 238 and 339 of the Insolvency Act 1986 are broadly identical. The court may make such order (against the insolvent or a third party) as it thinks fit for restoring the position to what it would have been if the transaction had not been entered into and for protecting the interests of persons who are victims of the transaction. There are specific examples[68] of orders the court might make but these are without prejudice to the generality of the power given to the court. Amongst the possibilities are the vesting in the applicant of property, or the proceeds of property, transferred as part of the transaction, the release of security or the payment to the applicant of benefits received from the transaction. The only limitation[69] on the order the court can make is that it cannot prejudice any interest in property which was acquired from a person other than the insolvent in good faith, for value and without notice of the relevant circumstances, or prejudice any interest deriving from such an interest and shall not require a person who received a benefit from the transaction in good faith, for value and without notice of the relevant circumstances to pay any sum unless he was a party to the transaction. In cases to which sections 238 and 339 of the Insolvency Act 1986 apply, there is a presumption of lack of good faith in respect of someone who has acquired an interest in property other than from the insolvent or who has received a benefit and, at the time of the acquisition or receipt, who had notice of the relevant circumstances and the relevant proceedings or was connected with or associated with the insolvent or the person with whom the insolvent entered the transaction.[70]

In *Chohan v. Saggar*[71] a Mr Bhambra (who was facing an action for damages for libel) transferred a house, which was subject to a legal charge in favour of Anglia Building Society, to Mrs Saggar for £50,000. On the same day the charge in favour of Anglia Building Society was discharged and a charge in favour of Chelsea Building Society was executed to secure a loan to Mrs Saggar. About a month later Mrs Saggar executed a trust deed to the effect that she held the property on trust for Mr Mallard, a business associate of Mr Bhambra. The judge, on the application of the plaintiff in the libel action, made an order under

---

[68] See Insolvency Act 1986, ss425, 241, 342.
[69] Contained in Insolvency Act 1986, ss425(2), 241(2), 342(2). It was established in *Chohan v. Sagger* [1992] B.C.C. 750 that this provision overrides the generality of Insolvency Act 1986, s.423.
[70] Insolvency Act 1986, ss241(2A), 342(2A).
[71] [1993] B.C.L.C. 661.

section 423(2) of the Insolvency Act 1986 setting aside the trust deed and declaring that Mrs Saggar held the property, subject to the charge in favour of the Chelsea Building Society, on trust for Mr Bhambra and herself. On appeal it was held that the judge had been right to set aside the trust deed rather than the transfer since to have set aside the transfer to Mrs Saggar would have prejudiced the interests of the Chelsea Building Society. An order under section 423 of the Insolvency Act 1986 must seek so far as practicable both to restore the position to what it would have been if the transaction had not been entered into and to protect the interests of the victims of the transaction. The court held that the charge in favour of the Chelsea Building Society should be debited wholly against the interest of Mrs Saggar and this would restore to the estate what had been lost by the transaction at an undervalue.

In the case of a company whose assets are subject to a crystallised floating charge, the issue arises of whether the general creditors or the debenture holder should benefit from the restored property under this provision and the provision on preference considered next. The case law has arisen in relation to preference claims and is considered in that context.

4. Preferences

a) Background

Where a company in administration or liquidation or a bankrupt has given a preference at a "relevant time" to any person, the insolvency practitioner may apply[72] to the court for an order. These provisions are designed to prevent the insolvent from enabling some of the creditors to jump the queue and obtain full repayment at a time when the collective principle of *pari passu* ought to be in operation. Where the court is persuaded that such a preference has been given it will make such order as it thinks fit for restoring the position to what it would have been if the preference had not been given. The orders which may be made are identical to those which may be made in respect of a transaction at an undervalue.

The Cork Committee were not of one mind as to the basis of the doctrine of voidable preferences. A minority proposed that the doctrine should rest purely on the consequences of the transaction[73] rather than on the intention of the debtor but the majority felt that creditors should

---

[72] Under Insolvency Act 1986, s.239 (liquidation), Insolvency Act 1986, s.340 (bankruptcy).
[73] As is the case, *e.g.*, in Australia and the United States.

be allowed to obtain payment by applying pressure on the debtor even
where this meant that they did better than other creditors in a subsequent
liquidation or bankruptcy.

b) Definition of a preference

An insolvent will have given a preference to a person if that person was
one of the insolvent's creditors or a surety or a guarantor for any
liability of the insolvent and the insolvent does anything or suffers
anything to be done which has the effect of putting that person into a
position which in the event of the insolvency will be better than the
position he would have been in if that thing had not been done. The
court will only make an order if the insolvent giving the preference was
influenced in deciding to give it by a desire to produce the effect
mentioned in the section. Such influence is presumed[74] where the
preference was given to a connected person (in the case of a company)
or an associate (in the case of a bankrupt) other than an employee.
Something done in pursuance of a court order is capable of constituting
the giving of a preference. It can be seen that there are two elements
constituting a preference; these can be referred to as "preference in
fact", which is to be determined objectively, and "preference in law",
which is to be determined subjectively with presumptions establishing
where the burden of proof lies.

Millett J. in *Re M. C. Bacon*[75] stressed that the Insolvency Act 1986
had introduced new law on preferences and that previous case law on
the old "fraudulent preference" was no longer relevant. This case
concerned the attempt of a liquidator to set aside a floating charge
created to secure the company's previously unsecured overdraft three
months before the company went into liquidation. The bank had threatened to withdraw the overdraft facility in the absence of such security
and this would have forced the company to stop trading. The judge held
that the word "desire" was to be interpreted subjectively so that the
liquidator had to establish that the debtor "positively wished" to
improve the bank's position in the event of the company's insolvent
liquidation. Since the reason for giving the security was the wish to
enable the company to continue trading rather than any wish to prefer
the bank, the floating charge was not a voidable preference. A similar
conclusion was reached in *Re Fairway Magazine Ltd*[76]; in this case a

[74] See *Weisgard v. Pilkington* [1995] B.C.C. 1, 108 and *Re Exchange Travel (Holdings)
Ltd* [1996] B.C.C. 933 for examples of cases where the directors were unable to rebut
the presumption.
[75] [1990] B.C.L.C. 324. Fletcher [1991] J.B.L. 71.
[76] [1993] B.C.L.C. 643.

company created a charge to secure a loan by a person who had guaranteed the company's overdraft but it was held not to be a preference even though part of the loan was to be used to discharge the overdraft since the purpose of the loan was to enable the company to continue trading and the lender was not willing to make the loan without the security. It has been suggested[77] that the commercially sensible result of retaining the possibility of bank lending to ailing companies could be better achieved by an effect-based test of preference coupled with a defence that the transaction was entered into in good faith and for the purpose of carrying on its business in circumstances where there were reasonable grounds for believing that the transaction would benefit the company and its unpaid creditors.

The case of *Re Ledingham-Smith*[78] is an example of a case brought by a trustee in bankruptcy. The trustee was attacking payments made to the bankrupt's accountants, who had made it clear that they would not continue to act unless their outstanding fees were met. It had been agreed that the partnership would pay a weekly sum of £5,000, first to satisfy any fees incurred in that week with the balance being used to reduce outstanding fees. Before this agreement, payment had been made by a standing order of £1,000 a month. Three months later the partnership was declared bankrupt. The judge held that original standing orders were not a preference but that the arrangements for paying at £5,000 a week were and should be repaid. Morritt J., on appeal, held that there was no preference in fact and that it was not possible to infer on the facts a desire to prefer on the part of the bankrupts. The burden was on the trustee to show that a preference had been conferred.

c) Relevant time

The court can only make an order in respect of a preference which was given at a "relevant time"[79]. If the preference is also a transaction at an undervalue, the rules about time periods for transactions at an undervalue will prevail.[80] If the preference is not also a transaction given at an undervalue, it will only be given at a relevant time if the insolvent was at that time unable to pay its debts or became so as a result of the preference; where the preference is given to a connected or associated

---

[77] By Professor Fletcher in Chap. 12, Ziegel (ed.), *Current Developments in International and Comparative Insolvency Law.*

[78] [1993] B.C.L.C. 635.

[79] Defined in Insolvency Act 1986, ss240, 341.

[80] In the case of a company, two years provided the company was insolvent at the time. In the case of an individual, five years if the individual was insolvent but two years if the individual was not insolvent at the time.

person, there will be a rebuttable presumption that the necessary state of insolvency existed. Where the preference has been given to a connected or associated person, then the relevant period is the two years before the administration, liquidation or bankruptcy. A preference given to anyone else will only be vulnerable in the six months before the insolvency.

d) Remedies

The remedies available to the court are very similar to those in relation to transactions at an undervalue.

e) Who benefits from recoveries?

Where the undertaking of a company in liquidation is subject to a floating charge and the liquidator recovers amounts paid away as transactions at an undervalue or preferences, the question arises of whether the charge bites on the recoveries or whether the recoveries are available for the unsecured creditors. In *Re Yagerphone*[81] it was held that the money in question was paid away before the crystallisation of the charge and was therefore not within the scope of the charge. It has also been argued that title to sue is vested in the liquidator on behalf of the general creditors.[82]

5. Extortionate credit bargains

Section 244 of the Insolvency Act 1986 applies where a company in liquidation or administration is, or has been, a party to a transaction for, or involving, the provision of credit to the company within the three years before the insolvency which the court decides is extortionate. A transaction will be extortionate if, having regard to the risk accepted by the person providing the credit, the terms of it required grossly exorbitant payments to be made or it otherwise grossly contravenes ordinary principles of fair dealing. The burden of proof is on those seeking to establish that a transaction was not extortionate. The court may make an order setting aside or varying such a transaction and requiring repayment or the retransfer of property. Section 343 of the Insolvency Act 1986 contains a similar provision in relation to bankruptcy.

---

[81] [1935] 1 Ch. 392, discussed in Hemsworth 13 I.L.& P. 48.
[82] This would not be a valid argument in respect to claims under Insolvency Act 1986, s.423.

6. General assignment of book debts by bankrupt

A general assignment, whether or nor by way of security, of existing or future book debts by a person engaged in any business who is subsequently adjudged bankrupt will be void under section 344 of the Insolvency Act 1986 against the trustee of the bankrupt's estate as regards book debts which were not paid before the presentation of the petition unless the assignment was registered under the Bills of Sale Act 1878.

CHAPTER 31

SWELLING THE ASSETS II: THIRD PARTY LIABILITY[1]

1. Introduction

The previous chapter considered the ability of the office-holder to swell the assets available to the creditors by clawing back into the estate assets previously transferred by the insolvent. This chapter considers the ability of the liquidator of an insolvent company to impose liability to contribute to the assets on those controlling the company whose actions have contributed to the loss of the creditors. The shareholders of a company with limited liability will only be liable to contribute to the assets available for the repayment of creditors up to the amount which they have agreed to pay for their shares. The insolvency legislation contains provisions intended to prevent those controlling businesses from unjustifiably sheltering behind the protection of limited liability. The legislation provides the liquidator with an easier method of bringing claims which were already vested in the company at the start of the liquidation where the defendants have been responsible for the management of the company.[2] The legislation also provides grounds for action against those guilty of allowing the company to continue incurring credit at a time when it should have stopped trading.[3]

There will only be any point in the liquidator bringing such an action against a defendant who has the assets to meet a successful claim. Directors who are insured against breach of duty would fall into this category. The liquidator may use the inquisitorial powers[4] to seek disclosure of existence and scope of such insurance despite the fact that the policy will usually require the policy holder and the assured not to disclose its existence.[5]

---

[1] See generally Finch "Directors duties: insolvency and the unsecured creditor" in Clarke (ed.), *Current Issues in Insolvency Law*, Cheffins, *Company Law: Theory, Structure and Operation* pp. 537 *et seq.*, Sealy in Ziegel (ed.), *Current Developments in International and Comparative Corporate Insolvency Law* Chap. 20.

[2] Insolvency Act 1936, s.212.

[3] *ibid.*, ss213,214.

[4] See Chap. 21.3(b) and 21.4(b) above.

[5] See Finch 57 M.L.R. 880. Companies Act 1985, s.310 as amended by Companies Act 1989 allows companies to fund such policies for directors.

One entity which may well have sufficient funds to meet the claims of the creditors is a solvent parent company. The doctrine of separate legal personality means that the parent company will ordinarily bear no responsibility[6] for the debts of its subsidiaries; this is seen by many as an unsatisfactory state of affairs. The situations in which the liquidator may be able to look to the parent company are considered together with some of the suggestions for reform.

The liquidator will face the same funding problems in relation to the claims discussed in this chapter as in relation to claims to claw back assets. It also has to be considered whether any sums recovered will fall into a floating charge.

2. Payments by contributories

Contributories are[7] those who are liable to contribute to the assets of a company in the event of its being wound up except for those liable on the basis of fraudulent or wrongful trading.

Section 74 of the Insolvency Act 1986 provides that when a company is wound up, every present and past member is liable to contribute to its assets to any amount sufficient for payment of its debts and liabilities and the expenses of the winding up and for the adjustment of the rights of the contributories themselves. This is subject to the major limitation that, in the case of a company limited by shares, no contribution is required from any member exceeding the amount (if any) unpaid on the shares in respect of which he is liable as a present or past member.

A past member is not liable if he has not been a member for at least a year before the liquidation or in respect of any debts or liabilities contracted after he ceased to be a member or unless the existing members are unable to satisfy the contributions required to be made by them.

A sum due to any member of the company (in his character of a member[8]) by way of dividends, profits or otherwise is not deemed to be a debt of the company payable to that member in a case of competition between himself and any other creditor not a member of the company, but any such sum may be taken into account for the purpose of the final adjustment of the rights of the contributories among themselves.[9] This means that a contributory may not set off a debt owed to him by the company against a call made on him by the liquidator.

---

[6] Unless it has given a guarantee.
[7] Insolvency Act 1986, s.79.
[8] *Soden v. British and Commonwealth Holdings plc* [1997] 4 All E.R. 353.
[9] Insolvency Act 1986, s.74(2)(f).

If a company has created a floating charge over its assets including uncalled capital, any capital called up by the liquidator will be applied to the debt secured by the floating charge in priority to the company's ordinary unsecured debts.[10]

It is rare for shares to be issued unpaid these days and these provisions are unlikely to swell the assets of the insolvent company to any extent.[11] In a compulsory liquidation the Insolvency Rules 1986[12] require the liquidator to settle a list of contributories as soon as possible after his appointment unless the court dispenses with such a list, which it will where the company is a limited one whose shares are fully paid. The liquidator must notify those who will be included on the list and they are given an opportunity to object,[13] after which the list will be conclusive against them. The liquidator will then, with the sanction of either the liquidation committee or the court, be able to make calls against the contributories. In the case of a voluntary liquidation,[14] the contributories do not have to be given notice of their inclusion on the list but have the opportunity to object when a call is made on them.

Under section 76 of the Insolvency Act 1986 the liquidator may be able to seek repayment of sums paid to a person to purchase or redeem their shares out of capital within the year before the liquidation. The directors who had signed the requisite statutory declaration of the company as to the solvency of the company under section 173(3) of the Companies Act 1985 would also be liable, jointly and severally with the ex-shareholder, for the repayment unless they had reasonable grounds for forming the opinion set out in the declaration.

3. Misfeasance applications

a) Section 212

Section 212 of the Insolvency Act 1986 applies where, in the course of winding up, it appears that a person in the designated categories has misapplied, retained or become accountable for money or property of the company or has been guilty of any misfeasance or breach of any fiduciary or other duty in relation to the company. The designated categories are those who are or have been an officer of the company or have acted as liquidator, administrator or administrative receiver of the

[10] *Re Anglo-Austrian Printing and Publishing Union* [1895] 2 Ch. 891.
[11] It is notable that nearly all the case law on this area dates from the Victorian period. *Re Apex Film Distributors Ltd* [1960] Ch. 378 is one of the few exceptions.
[12] r. 4.198.
[13] Insolvency Rules 1986, r. 4.198.
[14] *ibid.*, rr. 4.202–4.205.

company or have been otherwise involved in the promotion, formation or management of the company. The court may on the application of the official receiver, liquidator, creditor or (with the leave of the court) contributory, examine the conduct of the person and compel him to repay, restore or account for the money or property or any part of it, with interest at such rate as the court thinks just, or to contribute such sum to the company's assets by way of compensation in respect of the misfeasance or breach of fiduciary or other duty as the court thinks just.

This section provides a summary procedure for enforcing rights possessed by the company at the commencement of the liquidation; it does not provide for any new substantive rights. Defendants to a section 212 application have, in addition to any substantive defence, a possible defence under section 727 of the Companies Act 1985 which provides that an officer of the company may be relieved from liability where he has acted fairly, honestly and ought reasonably to be excused.

The duties owed by directors to their companies[15] are the duty to act with reasonable care and skill, a duty to act within their powers and a fiduciary duty to exercise those powers in good faith in the interests of the company as a whole. Whilst the company is solvent[16] it is open to members to ratify what would otherwise have been a breach of duty by the directors, thus depriving a future liquidator of a cause of action, provided that the ratification does not amount to a fraud on the minority.

b) Directors' common law duty of care

The scope of the misfeasance application was extended in 1986 so that it now includes negligence actions; company directors[17] are under an obligation to carry out their duties with reasonable care and skill. Historically, a low standard of care has been imposed on directors. In *Re City Equitable Fire and Insurance Co. Ltd*[18] it was held that the standard was a subjective one and that a director need not exhibit in performance of his duties a greater degree of skill than might reasonably be expected from a person of his knowledge and experience. It was also held that a

---

[15] Which can only be enforced by the company or by the liquidator and not by individual shareholders or creditors.

[16] But probably not when it reaches a state of near or actual insolvency since the members have an obligation to exercise their powers bona fide in the interests of the company as a whole, a concept which probably includes the creditors once the company is insolvent; see (d) below.

[17] There is no difference between the duties owed by executive and non-executive directors: *Dorchester Finance Co. Ltd v. Stebbing* [1989] B.C.L.C. 498.

[18] [1925] Ch. 407.

director is not bound to give continuous attention to the affairs of the company. Where duties may properly be left to some other official, a director is justified in trusting the official in the absence of grounds for suspicion.[19]

A director who also has a service contract with the company will be under stricter obligations since he will be expected to show the skill and care appropriate to the holding of that position and the contract is likely to impose a requirement of full time involvement in the affairs of the company. There has also been some movement recently towards imposing a stricter standard on directors *per se*; in *Re D'Jan of London Ltd*[20] Hoffmann L.J.[21] accepted that the duty of care is the objective one contained in section 214 of the Insolvency Act 1986 which is considered later in this chapter. *Re D'Jan of London Ltd* was a summons by a liquidator under section 212 against a former officer of the company whom the liquidator alleged had been negligent in completing and signing a proposal form for fire insurance with the result that the company was uninsured when a fire destroyed stock worth £174,000. It was held that the defendant was liable to compensate the company for the loss caused by his breach of duty in an amount not exceeding any unpaid dividends to which he would otherwise be entitled as an unsecured creditor. Hoffmann L.J. went on to hold that the economic reality of his 99 per cent shareholding in the company could be taken into account in exercising the discretionary power under section 727 of the Companies Act 1985 in limiting his liability to preventing his participating any further in the distribution to creditors rather than requiring him to make a contribution to the assets of the company. This was not a gross breach of duty and at the time the company was solvent so the only persons whose interests he was foreseeably putting at risk were himself and his wife.

c) Directors' breach of fiduciary duty

Directors are in a fiduciary relationship to the company. They must act in good faith in what they believe to be the best interests of the company. They must exercise their powers for the purposes for which they were given. They must not fetter their discretion as to how they act. They must not, without the consent of the company, place themselves in

---

[19] *Dovey v. Cory* [1910] A.C. 477.
[20] [1993] B.C.C. 649, Hicks 110 L.Q.R. 390.
[21] Sitting as an additional judge of the Chancery Division in the Companies Court.

a position in which their personal interests or duties to others are liable to conflict with their duties to the company.[22]

d) Directors' duty to consider interests of creditors

Directors owe their duties of care and skill and their fiduciary duties to the company. It has been suggested that once the company is no longer solvent, the interests of the company include those of the creditors. Street C.J. in the Australian case of *Kinsela v. Russell Kinsela Pty Ltd*[23] observed that, once a company is insolvent, in a practical sense the assets under the management of the directors are those of the creditors and the directors' duty to the company will extend to not prejudicing their interests. Dillon L.J. endorsed these comments in *obiter dicta* in *West Mercia Safetywear Ltd v. Dodd*[24] and Lord Templeman in *Winkworth v. Edward Baron Development Co. Ltd*[25] said that a duty was owed "by the directors to the company and to the creditors of the company to ensure that the affairs of the company are properly administered and that its property is not dissipated or exploited for the benefit of the directors themselves to the prejudice of the creditors". It seems unlikely that the suggestion that the directors might owe a duty directly to the creditors could be correct.[26] The introduction of liability for wrongful trading is likely to destroy any impetus for the further development of the line of cases suggesting that common law liability for breach of duty to the company might be imposed on the directors for failing to take the interests of the creditors into account.

e) Who is entitled to the proceeds of a section 212 application?

It seems that any sums recovered by the liquidator for breach of duty will fall into the general assets subject to any floating charge or charge over future property.[27]

---

[22] There are a vast number of cases on this area. From the recent insolvency context see, *e.g.*, *Re Welfab Engineers Ltd* [1990] B.C.C. 600 where on the facts the court held that there was no breach of duty and that, if there had been, the Companies Act 1985, s.727 defence would apply. See also *Re Purpoint* [1991] B.C.C. 121 and *Re DKG Contractors Ltd* [1990] B.C.C. 903 both of which are dealt with in greater detail in the context of wrongful trading, below.

[23] (1986) 10 A.C.L.R. 395, 401. Other Antipodean cases in which similar statements have been made are *Walker v. Wimborne* (1976) 50 A.L.J.R. 446 and *Nicholson v. Permacraft (N.Z.) Ltd* [1985] 1 N.Z.L.R. 242. See Hiley (1989) 10 Co. Lawyer 87.

[24] [1988] B.C.L.C. 250. The case actually involved fraudulent preference and misfeasance.

[25] [1986] 1 W.L.R. 1512.

[26] Toulson J. in *Yukong Lines Ltd v. Rendsburg Investments Corporation, The Times,* October 30, 1997, held that there was no duty to an individual creditor.

[27] *Re Anglo-Austrian Printing and Publishing Union* [1895] 2 Ch. 891.

4. Fraudulent trading

Section 213 of the Insolvency Act 1986 provides that if in the course of liquidation it appears that the business of the company has been carried on with intent to defraud creditors[28] of the company or of any other person or for any fraudulent purpose, the court may order anyone knowingly party to carrying on that business in that manner to make such contribution to the company's assets[29] as the court thinks proper. The court may also direct that any debt owed by the company to someone guilty of fraudulent trading will be deferred until all other debts and interest thereon has been paid by the company.[30]

Dishonesty is a necessary element of fraudulent trading.[31] In *Re William C. Leitch*[32] it was held that if a company continues to carry on business and to incur debts at a time when there is to the knowledge of the directors no reasonable prospect of the creditors ever receiving payment of those debts, it is in general a proper inference that the company is carrying on business with intent to defraud. In *Re White & Osmond (Parkstone) Ltd*[33] the court held that directors who genuinely believe that "clouds will roll away and the sunshine of prosperity shine upon them" are entitled to credit to help them over the bad time. In *R. v. Grantham*,[34] however, the Court of Appeal said the question was not whether the directors thought the company would be able to pay its way at some indeterminate time in the future but whether they thought the company in incurring further credit could pay its debts as they fell due or shortly thereafter. If they realised there was no prospect of the company being able to do this they were guilty of fraudulent trading even if they had some expectation that ultimately all debts would be

---

[28] *R. v. Smith* [1996] 2 B.C.L.C. 109 (a criminal case under Companies Act 1985, s.458) established that creditors may be potential or contingent, not merely those who could currently sue the company.

[29] Not to particular creditors. There were dicta in *Re Cyona Distributors Ltd* [1967] Ch. 889 that payment to particular creditors was possible under the previous provision but these were disapproved by Lindsay J. in *Re Esal (Commodities) Ltd* [1993] B.C.L.C. 872. *Re Cyona Distributors Ltd* held that the order could include a punitive as well as a compensatory element which is probably still the position.

[30] Insolvency Act 1986, s.215 which also provides that the court may give such other directions as it thinks proper for giving effect to the order to pay compensation. Fraudulent trading may also lead to disqualification from being concerned in the management of any company. It is also a criminal offence under Companies Act 1985, s.458.

[31] *Re Patrick & Lyon* [1933] Ch. 786. This requirement for dishonesty means that s.213 cannot apply to cases of mismanagement or undercapitalisation of subsidiaries: *Re Augustus Barnett & Son Ltd* [1986] B.C.L.C. 170 (and see 103 L.Q.R. 11).

[32] [1932] 2 Ch. 71.

[33] Referred to in *R. v. Grantham* [1984] 2 All E.R. 166. See Wheeler 1993 J.B.L. 256 at 263.

[34] [1984] 2 All E.R. 166.

paid. Liability requires active participation in the management of the company.[35] Anyone who knowingly participates in fraudulent trading may be held liable; in *Re Gerald Cooper Chemicals Ltd*[36] it was held that a creditor of a company who accepts payment of his debt out of money which he knows its directors to have obtained by fraud may be compelled personally to repay the amount. Preferring one creditor does not necessarily amount to fraudulent trading.[37]

There is a scarcity of reported cases and it was recognised by the Cork Committee as being of little assistance in swelling the assets of a company for distribution to creditors although it may well be that it assisted liquidators in achieving out-of-court settlements. The Cork Committee considered that it was unnecessary to continue to require the establishment of dishonesty, which the courts required to be established beyond reasonable doubt, before civil liability could be imposed. They recommended the imposition of liability for irresponsible trading for which a test of unreasonable conduct should apply and which they suggested should be called "wrongful trading" and they proposed abolishing civil liability for fraudulent trading. In fact, the Insolvency Act 1986 adds the provision on wrongful trading but retains civil liability for fraudulent trading. It is unlikely that liquidators will choose to bring actions for fraudulent trading since a successful wrongful trading action should be easier to achieve and will have the same consequences.

5. Wrongful trading

a) The statutory provisions

Section 214 of the Insolvency Act 1986 introduces the concept of wrongful trading[38] which imposes an objective standard of reasonable conduct in contrast to the subjective test for fraudulent trading. Wrongful trading is a purely civil matter and has no criminal aspect. Liability is imposed on directors[39] and shadow directors[40] who knew or should have realised that there was no reasonable prospect of avoiding an insolvent liquidation and failed to take every step which should have been taken to minimise loss to creditors. Liability may result either from

---

[35] *Re Maidstone Building Provisions Ltd* [1971] 3 All E.R. 363.
[36] [1978] Ch. 262.
[37] *Re Sarflax Ltd* [1979] Ch. 592.
[38] It is only referred to as such in the marginal note, the section itself does not use the phrase.
[39] Including *de facto* directors: *Re Hydrodan (Corby) Ltd* [1994] B.C.C. 161.
[40] See below.

continuing to incur liability or by dissipating assets. Insolvent liquidation in this context means a liquidation at a time when the company's assets are insufficient for the payment of its liabilities and the expenses of the winding up. A director or shadow director guilty of wrongful trading may be ordered, on the application of the liquidator, to make such contribution to the assets of the company as the court thinks fit.[41]

For the purposes of deciding what a director should have known or done, a combined objective and subjective test is to be applied. The facts which should have been known, the conclusions which should have been reached and the steps which ought to have been taken are those which would be known, reached or taken by a reasonably diligent person having both the general knowledge, skill and experience that may reasonably be expected of a person carrying out the same functions as are carried out by that director in relation to the company and the general knowledge, skill and experience that the director does have.[42] It has been held[43] that the defence provided by section 727 of the Companies Act 1985[44] is not available in wrongful trading proceedings.[45]

b) Who can be made liable?

Directors and shadow directors[46] may be made liable for wrongful trading. The definition of shadow director[47] provides that a shadow director is a person in accordance with whose directions or instructions the directors of the company are accustomed to act but that a person will not be a shadow director by reason only that the directors act on advice given by him in a professional capacity. Those who are in a position to dictate how the affairs of a company will be managed are at risk of liability for wrongful trading if they allow it to continue trading once they should realise that it is insolvent. Liquidators have sought to argue that banks and parent companies are capable of being shadow directors.

There were early suggestions that banks could incur liability where they provide credit on stringent conditions to financially troubled companies which permits them to continue trading. In *Re a Company (No.*

---

[41] Insolvency Act 1986, s.215 provides that the court may make such further directions as it thinks proper for giving effect to the order. It may also direct that debts owed by the company to the director will be deferred to other debts owed by the company.
[42] This was applied in *Re DKG Contractors Ltd* [1990] B.C.C. 903.
[43] *Re Produce Marketing Consortium Ltd* (1989) 5 B.C.C. 399.
[44] Discussed in the context of misfeasance applications, above.
[45] For a comparison of the various actions which can be brought against directors, see Wheeler [1993] J.B.L. 256.
[46] By Insolvency Act 1986, s.214(7).
[47] Insolvency Act 1986, s.251.

005009 of 1987),[48] it was argued that where a company took steps to implement recommendations in a report submitted after an investigation by the bank, the bank had become a shadow director. The court held that the argument was not obviously unsustainable and refused to strike it out. Millett J. writing extra-judicially[49] suggested that it would be reasonable for a bank to impose conditions upon its continuing support and as long as the company is allowed to make up its own mind as to whether to continue trading or go into liquidation, the bank would not be a shadow director even though company in reality had no choice but to accept the conditions. In *Re PFTZM Ltd (in liquidation)*[50] a company informed its bankers that it was unable to meet its commitments under a loan from them; it was then agreed that weekly management meetings would be attended by officers of the bank. This happened for almost two years until the company went into liquidation. The liquidators claimed that there was a prima facie case that the officers of the bank, who had attended these meetings, were shadow directors of the company. The court did not agree; the bank's officers were merely acting in defence of the bank's interests and the company did not have to accept the bank's suggestions.

There may be circumstances in which a parent company may become a shadow director of its subsidiaries. In *Re Hydrodan (Corby) Ltd,*[51] which was an application to have a section 214 application against directors of the parent company struck out, Millett J.'s judgment indicated that the courts were likely to take a restrictive view of the idea of shadow directorship and wrongful trading unless there was very clear evidence to the contrary. A parent would not be taken to be a director of its subsidiary merely because it controlled the composition of the board of directors of the subsidiary or because members of the parent board were also directors of the subsidiary or because the parent imposed budgetary or operational rules on the subsidiary or required certain decisions taken by subsidiary directors to be approved by the parent. Some direct assumption of the day-to-day running of the business would be necessary. He held that even if the parent company was a shadow director, that did not automatically make its directors shadow directors if all they had done was act as directors of the parent company by passing resolutions at meetings of its board. If the directors of the parent company, or some of them, had individually and personally given directions to the directors of the subsidiary, they could thereby have caused themselves to be shadow directors.

[48] [1989] B.C.L.C. 13.
[49] In (1991) 1 I.L.&P. 14.
[50] [1995] B.C.C. 280 (see (1995) 16 Co. Law. 313).
[51] [1994] B.C.C. 161.

d) Case law interpretation of section 214

Re Produce Marketing Consortium Ltd[52] was the first reported case on the section. It concerned two directors who had continued to run a company's fruit importing business when they ought to have known that there was no prospect of avoiding insolvent liquidation. Knox J. said that the general knowledge, skill and experience required would be much less extensive in a small company in a modest way of business, with simple accounting procedures and equipment, than in a large company with sophisticated procedures but that, nevertheless, certain minimum standards had to be attained. In particular, they should comply with the statutory obligations in relation to record keeping and the knowledge to be imputed to them would include information which would have been available had these obligations been met. The directors were held liable for continuing to trade after the time when they would have realised, had their accounting records been up to date, that the company was insolvent. Knox J. considered the approach the court should adopt in deciding on the level of contribution a director should be ordered to pay. He held that section 214 of the Insolvency Act 1986 is primarily a compensatory provision and directors should be ordered to make good the loss caused without regard to their culpability although it would be wrong to exclude entirely from consideration the degree of a director's culpability. The compensation was held to fall into the assets subject to the bank's floating charge. This led to considerable academic argument[53] that this was incorrect since the payment is the outcome of a power vested in the liquidator rather than an asset of the company; an argument which was accepted by Knox J. in *Re Ayala Holdings Ltd (No. 2)*[54] in a different context.

Apart from the *Produce Marketing* case, there have only been three other reported cases on section 214 of the Insolvency Act 1986. In *Re Purpoint Ltd*,[55] the court was faced with the difficulty of deciding, in relation to a company which had kept totally inadequate accounts, when the respondent should have realised that there was no reasonable prospect of avoiding an insolvent liquidation and how the compensation order should be calculated. It was held that the court could not direct that those creditors whose debts were incurred during the period of

---

[52] (1989) 5 B.C.C. 569.
[53] See, *e.g.*, Prentice (1990) 10 O.J.L.S. 265, Oditah [1990] L.M.C.L.Q. 205, Wheeler [1993] J.B.L. 256, Hicks (1993) 14 Co. Law. 16, 55.
[54] [1996] 1 B.C.L.C. 467.
[55] [1991] B.C.L.C. 491.

wrongful trading should be paid in priority.[56] There were also claims under section 212 of the Insolvency Act 1986 in both this case and in *Re DKG Contractors Ltd.*[57]

In *Re Purpoint* the respondent admitted in evidence that the company was unable to pay its trade debts as they fell due after December 1986; in May 1987 the company's accountants had warned him about wrongful trading. In June the respondent found a new job with a firm for which the company did a substantial amount of printing work. The company ceased trading in November 1987 and went into insolvent liquidation in May 1988. The misfeasance application related, first, to a car which had been acquired on hire purchase in April 1987 and repossessed by the finance company in November which the liquidator alleged was not needed for the purposes of the business and, secondly, to sums withdrawn in cash by the respondent and, thirdly, to transactions in June and July 1987 between the company and the firm for which the respondent was then working. The respondent was ordered to pay £12,666.79 to the liquidator under the misfeasance application in respect of the car, drawings not accounted for and work done for the firm and £353,572.15 in respect of the wrongful trading. It was held that there was no injustice in ordering payments under both sections so long as the respondent was not required to recoup more than was needed to meet the liabilities of the company as at January 1, 1987.

In *Re DKG Contractors Ltd* the respondent directors, Mr and Mrs Gibbons, had incorporated a company which the unincorporated business of Mr Gibbons supplied with services so that he became its main creditor. In the 10 months before the company went into insolvent liquidation in December 1988, £417,763 of company money found its way into the hands of Mr Gibbons. The liquidator contended, first, that it was a breach of the directors' duties to pay company money to Mr Gibbons whether or not for services rendered, particularly when the company was unable to meet its debts as they fell due; secondly, that the payments were a wrongful preference of Mr Gibbons within section 239 of the Insolvency Act 1986 and, thirdly, that the respondents were guilty of wrongful trading. The respondents argued that the payments had been made to reimburse Mr Gibbons for amounts supplied to the company and that, although he was not authorised by the articles of the company to contract with it, that the payments had been informally approved by

---

[56] See Williams 11 Co. Lawyer 222 for an argument that this prevents the section from achieving the effect of compensating with any accuracy those who suffered loss as a result of the directors behaviour.

[57] [1990] B.C.C. 903. There was also a preference under Insolvency Act 1986, s.239 in this case.

the shareholders and that they had acted honestly and reasonably and ought fairly to be excused from liability under section 727 of the Companies Act 1985. The court held, ordering the respondents to repay £417,763 to the company under section 212 of the Insolvency Act 1986, that it had been a breach of the directors' duties to make the payments when the company was of doubtful solvency. Mr Gibbons was also ordered to repay the same amount under section 239 of the Insolvency Act 1986 on the basis that the payments were a preference within section 239 of the Insolvency Act 1986. The respondents were liable for wrongful trading after end of April 1988 and were ordered to make a contribution to the company's assets equal to the amount of the trade debts incurred by the company on or after May 1, 1988. The payments made under sections 212 and 239 of the Insolvency Act 1986 were to go towards satisfying the wrongful trading liability[58] and the total liability was limited to what was necessary to pay the creditors and the costs and expenses of the liquidation. It was held that, although they had acted honestly, they had not acted reasonably and ought not to be excused.

Re Sherborne Associates Ltd,[59] the most recent case, has fuelled concerns that the wrongful trading legislation is not achieving its objectives.[60] The case was complicated by the death of one of the respondent directors but the judge appeared to be looking for some kind of moral blameworthiness as a basis for liability.

There are several explanations for the paucity of litigation on wrongful trading. A major problem is that of funding proceedings for wrongful trading, given the decision in *Re M. C. Bacon (No. 2)*[61] that a liquidator would incur personal liability for costs in an unsuccessful action. Another is that in many cases the directors in question have insufficient assets to make them worth suing. Andrew Hicks discovered in an informal survey[62] that liquidators have often managed to achieve an out of court settlement of actual or potential wrongful trading claims. It may be that the provision is having an effect on the practice of company management[63] in that those advising directors are very aware of the need to warn their clients of the consequences of wrongful trading and banks are likely to require an accountant's certificate that continued trading will not be wrongful where the company's financial situation

---

[58] cf. *Re Purpoint*. It can be seen that it is not clear how the courts should deal with the interaction of Insolvency Act 1986, ss212 and 214: see Goode, *Principles of Corporate Insolvency* (2nd ed.) pp. 461–464.

[59] [1995] B.C.C. 40. See Godfrey & Nield (1995) 11 I.L.&P.

[60] Godfrey and Nield 11 I.L.&P. 139.

[61] [1990] B.C.L.C. 607.

[62] (1993) 8 I.L.&P. 134.

[63] See Sealy, in Ziegel (ed.), *Current Developments in International and Comparative Corporate Insolvency Law*, Chap. 20.

appears fragile. The increasingly apparent lack of cases is, however, likely to undermine any deterrent effect the section might otherwise have.

6. Liability for insolvent subsidiaries[64]

Each member of a group of companies is a separate person in the eyes of the law and therefore, in the absence of a guarantee,[65] a parent company will not ordinarily be liable for the debts of its insolvent subsidiary.

Lord Justice Templeman in *Re Southard*[66] made the trenchant observation that "A parent company may spawn a number of subsidiary companies, all controlled directly or indirectly by the shareholders of the parent company. If one of the subsidiary companies, to change the metaphor, turns out to be the runt of the litter and declines into insolvency to the dismay of its creditors, the parent company and the other subsidiary companies may prosper to the joy of the shareholders without any liability for the debts of the insolvent subsidiary". As Hugh Collins says[67]: "the costs of mismanagement, the risks of undercapitalisation, or liability for hazards such as tort claims by third parties are thrown onto the creditors of the subsidiary firm, rather than being born by the economic organisation which effectively controls the productive operation".

There are sound policy reasons for upholding the principle of separate legal personality in this context since without the ability to ring-fence potential liability a successful enterprise might be reluctant, to the detriment of the general economy, to expand its activities into financially risky areas. Equally, there are situations in which creditors of the insolvent subsidiary may feel justifiably aggrieved at being unable to look to the solvent parent company.[68] In some instances, the business of the subsidiary will have been run as an integral part of the business of the parent company, with the interests of the group given priority over

---

[64] See, generally, Prentice "Group indebtedness" in Schmittoff and Wooldridge (eds), *Groups of Companies*; Muscat *The liability of the holding company for the debts of its insolvent subsidiaries*; Schulte 18 Co. Lawyer 2.

[65] Banks will frequently seek cross-guarantees from when lending to a member of a group.

[66] [1979] 1 W.L.R. 1198.

[67] (1990) 53 M.L.R. 731.

[68] The refusal of the then apparently solvent Pentos to meet the obligations of its insolvent subsidiary Athena in January 1995 led to a rash of adverse press comment. Parent companies may decide to meet the obligations for reasons of public relations.

the interests of the subsidiary.[69] The subsidiary may have been under-capitalised from the start or the parent may have contributed capital by way of debt rather than share capital so that the parent competes with the creditors in the insolvency. The group may have projected an image which gave the creditors of the subsidiary the false impression that they could look to the parent company for payment.

The Cork Committee recognised the potential for the abuse of the corporate group and observed that, even with the introduction of wrongful trading, the law would remain in an unsatisfactory state.[70] It felt unable to make definite recommendations because of the consequential effects on company law but expressed the need for reform to be considered. It identified two principal questions which arise in insolvency in relation to corporate groups: first, whether or not one or more of the companies in the group should be made liable for the external debts of the insolvent company and, secondly, how the claims of other companies in the group against the insolvent company should be treated.

The *pari passu* rule currently prevents the subordination of claims by other members of same group other than claims made by shareholders of the insolvent company in their capacity as such. In the United States the courts have an equitable jurisdiction to subordinate the claims of parent companies or other controlling shareholders against an insolvent company until the claims of the other creditors have been met.[71] The jurisdiction is discretionary and can be invoked where the conduct of the parent has been in some way unconscionable. The view of the Cork Committee[72] was that the existence of the jurisdiction had not created undue uncertainty nor had it discouraged group activity of an entrepreneurial character.

It may be possible to employ some of the provisions already discussed in this chapter and the previous chapter to impose liability on other members of the corporate group to contribute to the assets of the insolvent company. The member companies of a group are likely to be "connected persons"[73] in relation to each other, thus making it easier to establish the existence of invalid floating charges, preferences and transactions at an undervalue between them.

---

[69] Directors of a subsidiary who have given priority to the interests of other members of the corporate group will have committed a breach of their duties to the subsidiary but in many instances the parent company will be able to ratify the breach.

[70] Chap. 51 of the Cork Report.

[71] This "Deep Rock" doctrine is now contained in Bankruptcy Code, s.510(c), USCA Title 11.

[72] para. 1937.

[73] Under Insolvency Act 1986, ss249, 435.

In the event of fraudulent use of the concept of separate legal
personality, the courts will "pierce the veil of incorporation" and
impose liability on the parent company but the Court of Appeal in
Adams v. Cape Industries[74] made it clear that it is not fraudulent to
organise the corporate group so as to isolate the liabilities of one area of
operation from another.

Section 214 of the Insolvency Act 1986 would permit a statutory
"lifting of the veil" if it could be established that the parent had been
actively involved in the management of a subsidiary (and therefore a
shadow director) and had been negligent with regard to the solvency of
that company; there has yet to be a case in which a parent company has
been held to be a shadow director.

There have been suggestions that the normal rules of vicarious liability might lead to the imposition of liability on parent companies but the
case law is not encouraging.[75]

Other jurisdictions with the same basic approach to company law
have taken bolder steps to deal with this problem. Australia, for example, introduced provisions into the Australian Corporations Law[76] by the
Corporate Law Reform Act 1992 which impose liability on a holding
company for the unsecured debts of its subsidiary incurred at a time
when the subsidiary was insolvent and there were reasonable grounds
for the holding company or one or more of its directors to suspect that
to be the case. The liquidator of the subsidiary will be able to bring
proceedings against the holding company to recover compensation for
the benefit of the subsidiary's unsecured creditors. Two presumptions of
insolvency are provided to assist in proving insolvency at the relevant
time. If it can be proved that the company was insolvent at any time
during the 12 months before the start of the liquidation, it will be
presumed that it was insolvent continuously thereafter. If there has been
a failure to comply with the accounting records requirements, it must be
presumed that the company was insolvent during the period of contravention. In New Zealand, company law[77] allows the consolidation of a
group's assets in circumstances where the court considers it "just and
equitable" to do so.

At one stage, it appeared that the United Kingdom might be prompted
by Europe to consider reform. The E.C. draft ninth directive on groups
was based on the German model which draws a distinction between

---

[74] [1991] 1 All E.R. 929.
[75] (1997) 18 Co. Lawyer 138 (Grantham), *New Zealand Guardian Trust Co. Ltd v. Brooks*
[1995] 2 B.C.L.C. 242 at 245–6, *Kuwait Asia Bank E.C. v. National Mutual Life
Nominees Ltd* [1991] A.C. 187.
[76] See Stapledon 16 Co. Lawyer 152. Herzberg, in Ziegel, above, Chap. 21.
[77] New Zealand Companies Act 1955 (as amended), s.245.

contractual groups and *de facto* groups. In the former, the controlling enterprise is bound to make good the losses of subsidiaries but is allowed to induce a subsidiary to act against its own interest. In the *de facto* group, the controlling enterprise may not cause the subsidiary to act against its own interests. The draft directive is, however, unlikely to make any further progress.

CHAPTER 32

FUNDING LITIGATION BY THE INSOLVENCY PRACTITIONER

1. Introduction

A major problem faced by an insolvency practitioner in trying to swell the assets or, indeed, fight off claims which will deplete the assets is that of funding any necessary litigation. In some cases, the cost will be a first charge on the assets of the insolvent,[1] thus reducing the amount available for distribution, but in others the insolvency practitioner will become personally liable unless he can obtain an indemnity from elsewhere. It may be that, in any event, the assets provide the insolvency practitioner with insufficient resources so that he will need to find an additional source of finance. It may be possible to persuade some of the creditors to finance the litigation or to indemnify the insolvency practitioner against the costs on the basis that they will be indemnified out of the net recoveries of the action before any distribution of the recoveries is made. Where creditors might be prepared to provide funds, they may be deterred by the prospect of any proceeds of the litigation being shared with creditors who are not prepared to take the same risk.[2] The issue of whether any recovered assets will be subject to any floating charge[3] may also influence their views.

Creditors who are unwilling to risk losing more money may well refuse to provide support and may often be in a position to prevent an insolvency practitioner who could use assets in the insolvent estate from pursuing the litigation at all. A liquidator has the power to bring or defend any action or other legal proceeding in the name and on behalf

---

[1] See Chap. 35 below.
[2] See Pugh 12 I.L.&P. 167 for the suggestion that we should adopt the example set by Australian Supreme Court in *Household Financial Services Pty Ltd v. Chase Medical Centre Pty Ltd* in which proceeds of the action were paid to the creditor who had funded the litigation on basis that the recoveries were less than total of the creditor's claim and the costs of litigation. The liquidator had warned the other creditors when he was trying to obtain funding that he proposed to seek such an order.
[3] Recoveries under actions only available to the liquidator have been held not to fall into the assets subject to charge unlike the proceeds of claims brought under Insolvency Act 1986, ss.212 or 127.

of the company but will need consent to exercise the power in the case of a compulsory winding up.[4] A trustee in bankruptcy will also need the sanction of the creditors to bring, institute or defend any action or legal proceedings relating to the property comprised in the bankrupt's estate.[5]

An additional problem for office-holders in relation to insolvent companies is that if they attempt to bring an action in the name of the company they may be faced with an order for security under section 726 of the Companies Act 1985 which allows such an order to be made against a limited company which appears to be unable to pay the costs of the other side if it loses.[6] There is no equivalent provision in bankruptcy.

Obtaining outside financial support for litigation may involve obstacles presented by the doctrines of champerty and maintenance although insolvency practitioners are exempted to a large extent from the operation of these doctrines. Non-parties to the litigation who have influence over it may also be at risk of an order for costs being made against them in the event that they are unsuccessful.

2. Funding from assets under the control of the insolvency practitioner

The costs and expenses of the insolvency will be met out of the assets ahead of any other claims.[7] The Insolvency Rules 1986 provide[8] that expenses properly chargeable or incurred by the office-holder in preserving, realising or getting in any of the assets of the company or of the bankrupt are first in the general order of priority of costs. Where the office-holder has brought unsuccessful proceedings in his own name he will be liable to an order for costs but, unless he has acted improperly, will be entitled to an indemnity out of the assets.[9] An insolvency

---

[4] See Insolvency Act 1986, ss.165, 167 and Schedule II.

[5] *ibid.*, Sched. 5 Pt. I.

[6] See *Northampton Coal, Iron and Waggon Co. v. Midland Waggon Co.* (1878) 7 Ch. D. 500, *Pure Spirit Company v. Fowler* (1890) 25 Q.B.D. 235, *Aquila Design (GRB) Products Ltd v. Cornhill Insurance plc* [1988] B.C.L.C. 134 (in which the court refused to make a security order which would have forced the plaintiff company to abandon a claim with a reasonable prospect of success) and RSC, Ord. 23. Millett L.J. in *Abraham v. Thompson* [1997] 4 All E.R. 362 observed that the power had often not been exercised where it would have had the effect of stifling bona fide proceedings.

[7] See Chap. 35 below. In *Re M. C. Bacon (No. 2)* Millett J. held, relying on *Re Silver Valley Mines* (1882) 21 Ch. D. 381 and *Re Wilson Lovatt & Sons Ltd* [1977] 1 All E.R. 274 that this was a common law rather than a statutory right and that the statutory provisions merely dealt with matters of priority.

[8] r. 4.218 in liquidation, r. 6.224 in bankruptcy.

[9] *Re Wilson Lovatt & Sons Ltd* [1977] 1 All E.R. 274.

practitioner may be held personally liable for the expenses if he fails to obtain any necessary consent to pursue the litigation but retrospective authorisation for payment out of the assets may be given.[10]

In *Re M.C. Bacon Ltd (No. 2)*[11] Millett J. decided that the costs of proceedings instituted by a liquidator to challenge the validity of a charge as a voidable preference and to make the company's bank liable for wrongful trading were not expenses in realising or getting in the assets of the company. The liquidator was not, therefore, entitled to look to the assets of the company for reimbursement in priority[12] to the claims of the bank as floating chargee. Millett J. said that the proceedings were not brought by or on behalf of the company[13] nor were they brought in order to recover assets belonging to the company at the date of the winding up. He also said that the expenses of getting in the assets do not include unsuccessful attempts.

Re Berkeley Applegate (Investment consultants) Ltd (No. 2) and *(No. 3)*,[14] however, provide authority that the expenses of investigating ownership may in some cases be met from an asset which transpires not to be beneficially owned by the insolvent. This litigation concerned a company in voluntary liquidation whose business was making investments on behalf of clients on the security of first mortgages of freehold property which were taken in the company's name. Client money awaiting investment and the benefit of the mortgages were held on trust by the company for the investors. The expenses and remuneration of the liquidator were considerable and likely to greatly exceed the extent of the company's non-trust assets. The court held that, since it had jurisdiction to enforce the investors' equitable interests in the property, it would have a discretion to require an allowance to be made for costs incurred and skill and labour expended in the administration of the property. In this case, the work had been of substantial benefit to the trust property and if it had not been carried out by the liquidator would have had to be carried out by someone else at the expense of those equitably entitled to the property. The possibility of the insolvency practitioner obtaining authority in advance of incurring the cost was postulated. In *Re Biddencare Limited*[15] Hartford Fire Insurance Company had brought proceedings against Biddencare Limited in order to determine whether

[10] *Re Associated Travel Leisure and Services Ltd* [1978] 1 W.L.R. 547.
[11] [1990] B.C.L.C. 607. See Hunt 7 I.L.&P., Middleton Vol. 142, No. 6576 N.L.J. 1582. The decision has recently been doubted by the Court of Appeal in *Re Exchange Travel (Holdings) Ltd (No. 3)* [1997] 2 B.C.C. 579.
[12] Insolvency Rules 1986, r. 4.218(1)(a).
[13] The Insolvency Act 1986 provides that they are actions to be brought by the liquidator.
[14] [1989] Ch. 32 and (1989) 5 B.C.C. 803.
[15] [1994] 2 B.C.L.C. 160.

monies held in three bank accounts belonged to it or to the company which was in liquidation. The liquidators sought an order in advance that they would be entitled to their costs and expenses in dealing with a proprietary claim by a third party. It was held that such a pre-emptive costs order should not be made in hostile proceedings where there was no evidence that it would not be feasible to raise a "fighting fund" from other creditors with an interest in challenging the applicant's claim. The insolvent company in *Re Telesure Limited*[16] sold insurance policies and paid all monies received from the sale of policies into a designated insurance brokers bank account. It went into administrative receivership and subsequently into creditors' voluntary liquidation. A number of insurers claimed a proprietary interest in the insurance brokers' account. The liquidators applied for an order that the remuneration and costs incurred by them in investigating the entitlement to the insurers brokers account monies be paid out of the assets of Telesure Limited whether or not those assets belonged beneficially to the company or were held as trustees. Jacob J. held that the work of sorting out the insurance companies' claims had to be done by somebody and that even were the receivers to do it (and they were not willing at this stage to do so) the liquidators would have had to vet that operation in order to fulfil their own duties. Recourse to the funds concerned would be permitted for the purpose of investigation and at this stage there was no need for a liquidator to show that there was no prospect of obtaining a fighting fund from the creditors. The liquidators would have to return to court once their investigations were complete to obtain further directions as to the cost of any court proceedings.

3. Outside funding for litigation[17]

a) Introduction

Insolvency practitioners may be able to get a third party to provide funding for the litigation in return for a share in any recoveries from the litigation. This may be done either by selling the cause of action (which includes assigning a disputed debt for consideration) or by selling the right to share in the recoveries if the action is successful, a course which is often referred to as selling the "fruits of the action". The ancient doctrine of champerty may place obstacles in the way of the latter.

---

[16] [1997] B.C.C. 580.
[17] See Fennell 13 I.L.&P. 106.

b) Champerty and maintenance[18]

It is no longer possible to trace the origins of the doctrines of maintenance and champerty[19] but they appear to have developed to deal with weaknesses in the early court system, at a time when an independent judiciary had not yet emerged, which allowed the assignment of claims whose prospects were poor to those in a stronger position to influence the courts. In the Law Commission Report[20] which recommended its abolition as a crime, maintenance was defined as "the procurement by direct or indirect financial assistance of any person to institute or carry on or defend civil proceedings without lawful justification". The interest of the third party will amount to lawful justification if it amounts to a proprietary or genuine commercial interest, actual or contingent, in the subject matter of the litigation.[21] Champerty is an aggravated form of maintenance under which the assistance is provided in return for a share of the recoveries from the action. Although champerty and maintenance are no longer either crimes or torts, they can still be raised as grounds for invalidating an arrangement on public policy grounds.

Where a party assigns a right of action outright to a stranger in consideration for a share of any recoveries, the stranger will usually be substituted as plaintiff. If the assignment is illegal, the defendant will have a complete defence. Where the assignment is of a contingent future right to share in any recoveries in consideration for funding, the original plaintiff retains the right to sue and the assignee will usually require some say in the conduct of proceedings. It was held by Lightman J. in *Grovewood Holdings plc v. James Capel*[22] that if the assignment is champertous, the defendant can apply for the proceedings to be stayed on the grounds that they are an abuse of process.

c) General exceptions to the doctrine of champerty

It is clear that a third party with an interest in the outcome of the action may provide funding. There is, therefore, nothing objectionable in some

---

[18] See Walters 112 L.Q.R. 560.
[19] See Lord Mustill in *Giles v. Thompson* [1994] 1 A.C. 142. The judgment of Lord Justice Steyn in the Court of Appeal in *Giles v. Thompson* contains a thorough consideration of the history of the doctrine together with further references.
[20] Law Com. no. 7, 1966.
[21] See *Trendtex Trading Corporation v. Credit Suisse* [1980] Q.B. 629.
[22] [1994] 4 All E.R. 417, distinguishing *Martell v. Consett Iron Co. Ltd* [1955] 1 All E.R. 481, in which it had been held that a stay should not be granted, on the grounds that that was a case in which maintenance rather than champerty had been alleged and that since then maintenance and champerty had ceased to be crimes. Potter L.J. in *Abraham v. Thompson* [1997] 4 All E.R. 362 indicated that he preferred the reasoning in *Martell*.

or all of the creditors providing the insolvency practitioner with a "fighting fund" in respect of litigation which may swell the assets available for distribution.

There is also nothing objectionable in the legal or equitable assignment of a debt by its owner even where it was apparent at the time of the assignment that litigation would be necessary to recover it; this has quite clearly been the case since the Supreme Court of Judicature Act 1873[23] made assignable in law any debt or other legal chose in action. In *Camdex International v. Bank of Zambia*[24] the Court of Appeal held that the assignment of a debt would only be objectionable if it had maintenance or champerty as its object. It made no difference that the terms of the assignment include a provision that the assignee may account to the assignor for some of the proceeds of the litigation to recover the assigned debt; the assignee of a debt is as free as anyone else to choose what to do with the fruits of litigation. The fact that the assignee may receive more from the litigation than he has paid for the debt is also irrelevant provided a genuine commercial price has been paid for the debt. The assignment could be attacked if it could be established that in reality it was an agreement with maintenance or champerty as its object but this would have to be established by reference to evidence other than the assignment itself. In *Trendtex Trading Corp. v. Credit Suisse*[25] the House of Lords held that the assignment of a claim for breach of contract which contemplated that the assignee might sell the cause of action on to a third party manifestly "savoured of champerty" since it involved trafficking in litigation which was contrary to public policy.

Insolvency practitioners are, therefore, able to exercise the general right to assign to third parties assignable debts owed to the insolvent even where it is apparent that the third party will need to resort to litigation to enforce the debt. The insolvency practitioner cannot sell property otherwise than on the terms on which it was owned by the insolvent so it will not be possible to assign contracts which contain a prohibition on assignment. *Circuit Systems Ltd v. Zuken-Redac Ltd*[26] concerned a purported assignment to a director of the company of computer system leasing and maintenance agreements, which prohibited the assignment of any rights arising under them, and software licences which were expressed to be non-transferable. The Court of Appeal[27]

---

[23] The current provision is Law of Property Act 1925, s.136.
[24] [1996] 3 All E.R. 431.
[25] [1982] A.C. 679.
[26] [1997] 1 W.L.R. 721.
[27] Following *Linden Gardens Trust Ltd v. Lenesta Sludge Disposals Ltd* [1994] 1 A.C. 85.

upheld the decision that the agreements could not be assigned; rights to sue under the software licences were assignable since it was held that the non-transferability only related to the use of the software.

An assignment of the fruits of a prospective action for debt or breach of contract is similarly unobjectionable provided there is no interference in or control of the proceedings by the assignee.[28] Since the assignment is of future assets it will be an equitable assignment which means that the assignor has to remain a party to the proceedings. Problems may arise where the assignor agrees that the assignee will have significant control over the conduct of proceedings.

c) Insolvency exemptions from doctrine of champerty

It has been held in a line of cases going back over a century[29] that the power of a trustee in bankruptcy or liquidator[30] to sell the property comprised in the insolvent estate[31] allows the insolvency practitioner to sell a bare cause of action even where the consideration for the sale is a share of any ultimate proceeds. For example, in *Ramsey v. Hartley*,[32] a plaintiff brought proceedings in negligence against a firm of accountants and was then adjudicated bankrupt. The trustee in bankruptcy assigned the cause of action back to him on terms that if the action succeeded the bankrupt would pay 35 per cent of the net proceeds to the trustee. It was argued that such an assignment was contrary to public policy since it was unfair to the defendants to allow the action to proceed when they might if successful be unable to recover costs awarded to them. This argument was rejected by the Court of Appeal on the basis that a transaction such as this which was permitted by the bankruptcy laws could not be impeached on grounds of maintenance or champerty. In *Freightex Ltd v. International Express Co. Ltd*[33] the Court of Appeal held that there was no distinction of principle between the power of a trustee to assign to the bankrupt and the power of a liquidator to assign a chose in action to a former officer of the company. In *Bang & Olufsen v. Ton Systeme Limited*[34] the liquidator had assigned a

---

[28] *Glegg v. Bromley* [1912] 3 K.B. 474 at 484.
[29] The line of authority has been traced to *Seear v. Lawson* (1880) 15 Ch. D. 426 and *Re Park Gate Waggon Works Co.* (1881) 17 Ch. D. 234.
[30] Under Insolvency Act 1986, para. 6, Sched. 4 (liquidators), para. 9, Sched. 5 (trustees in bankruptcy) and para. 2, Sched. 1 (administrators and administrative receivers).
[31] Insolvency Act 1986, s.436 defines property as including choses in action. Actions personal to the bankrupt such as personal injury and libel claims do not vest in a trustee in bankruptcy.
[32] [1977] 1 W.L.R. 686.
[33] April 15, 1980, unreported.
[34] September 16, 1993, unreported.

company's right of action to a former director on terms that 15 per cent of any damages recovered should be paid to the liquidator for the benefit of the creditors. The plaintiff opposed the application of the director to be joined as a party. The Court of Appeal held that the plaintiff could not object on the grounds that the arrangement was champertous, given that the assignor was a liquidator.

In *Circuit Systems Ltd v. Zuken-Redac Ltd*[35] the House of Lords held that the exemption from the doctrine of champerty meant that it was unnecessary to consider whether the price paid amounted to a genuine commercial price. The insolvency practitioner must, however, assign for best price available; in *Re Edennote Limited*[36] the court set aside an assignment by the liquidator of a cause of action for a lower price than could have been obtained elsewhere.

d) Assignments still subject to the doctrine of champerty

In *Re Ayala Holdings Ltd (No. 2)*,[37] which involved claims that a disposition was void under section 127 of the Insolvency Act 1986 and that a charge was void for non-registration under section 395 of the Companies Act 1985, Knox J. held that rights of action conferred exclusively on the liquidator cannot be assigned under the statutory power of sale since they are not assets of the insolvent.[38]

Trustees in bankruptcy and liquidators have the power to transfer a beneficial interest in the fruits of the litigation in return for financing the action.[39] There is some debate about whether the statutory exemption which applies to the sale of a cause of action by the insolvency practitioner extends to the sale of a share of the fruits of the litigation.

It was held by Lightman J. in *Grovewood Holdings plc v. Capel & Co. Ltd*[40] that the exemption from the doctrine of champerty which applies to the outright sale of the cause of action, on the grounds that otherwise the statutory power of sale would have no purpose since the sale would of necessity be champertous, does not apply to an assignment of an interest in the recoveries since the statutory immunity is unnecessary. This case involved the liquidator entering into a "sponsorship arrangement" with backers under which the sponsor agreed to

---

[35] [1997] 1 W.L.R. 721.
[36] [1996] 2 B.C.L.C. 389. See Chap. 20.5(e).
[37] [1996] 1 B.C.L.C. 467.
[38] This followed the decision in *Re M.C. Bacon (No. 2)* that claims which could only be brought by the liquidator were not property of the company.
[39] See *Grovewood Holdings plc v. Capel & Co. Ltd* [1994] 4 All E.R. 417 and cases cited therein.
[40] [1994] 4 All E.R. 417.

continue the action in the name of the company[41] with the assistance of the liquidator. It was envisaged by the agreement that the sponsors might sell on part of their rights under the agreement in return for a contribution to the funding. The liquidator's solicitors agreed to defer charging costs to the sponsor until the outcome of the litigation. It was agreed that if the litigation was successful the recoveries would be applied first in meeting costs and that the balance would be shared equally between the sponsor and the company in liquidation. The sponsors agreed to meet the costs if the recoveries were insufficient. The liquidation committee approved the arrangement. Lightman J. held that if the assignment of the potential recoveries was unobjectionable, as in *Glegg v. Bromley*,[42] the insolvency practitioner would need no immunity and, if the assignment was objectionable as including a provision for the financing of litigation, he could see no reason for extending the statutory immunity to cover it. The agreement appeared to be objectionable on two particular grounds. In the first place it was improper for the liquidator to surrender his fiduciary power to control proceedings commenced in the name of the company. Secondly, the fact that the agreement envisaged the sponsor selling part of its rights was objectionable. The agreement was clearly champertous and he granted a stay of the proceedings on the basis that they constituted an abuse of process.

There has been conflicting Court of Appeal dicta as to whether the approach of Lightman J. was correct. Simon Brown L.J. in *Circuit Systems Ltd v. Zuken-Redac Ltd*[43] observed, *obiter*, of the *Grovewood* case: "the decision was the necessity for the statutory exemption applicable in the case of sales of bare causes of action does not extend to sales of the fruits of litigation; these remain subject to the full force and effect of the law of maintenance". *Re Oasis Merchandising*,[44] which was a case in which a liquidator wished to pursue the directors of the company for wrongful trading, involved consideration of both the assignment of fruits of the action and the extent of the statutory power of the liquidator. The liquidator entered into an agreement which provided that the proceedings would be in the name of the liquidator but that the assignee, an organisation specialising in the funding of litigation, would be in control of the proceedings and would be reimbursed for any expenditure from any recoveries with any balance being divided. Peter Gibson J. in the Court of Appeal said that the question of loss of

---

[41] The sponsors were extremely concerned to remain anonymous which probably explains why an outright sale of the cause of action which would then proceed in their name was not possible.

[42] [1912] 3 K.B. 474.

[43] [1997] 1 W.L.R. 721.

[44] [1995] 2 B.C.L.C. 493 (Robert Walker J.), [1997] 1 All E.R. 1009, CA.

control over the proceedings was relevant to the propriety of the liquidator's act in entering into the agreement: "As a matter of policy we think there is much to be said for allowing a liquidator to sell the fruits of an action provided that it does not give the purchaser the right to influence the course of, or interfere with the liquidator's conduct of, the proceedings." The actual basis of the Court of Appeal decision was that the liquidator had no power under paragraph 6 of Schedule 4 to assign the fruits of a section 214 action since property assignable under that paragraph did not include property which arose in the future and which was recoverable only by the liquidator and then held by him on the statutory trust for distribution. It was also held that since section 214 of the Insolvency Act 1986 had a public or penal element, the court was entitled to expect to have the assistance of the liquidator so that even a partial loss of control by the liquidator of the litigation was objectionable. The Court of Appeal also dismissed an argument that the liquidator could rely on the statutory power in paragraph 13 of Schedule 4 "to do all such other things as may be necessary for winding up the company's affairs and distributing its assets", holding that the power was limited to what was necessary and that it was a general power which did not authorise the carrying out of illegal acts. Furthermore, given that the liquidator had now managed to negotiate a conditional fee arrangement[45] with a firm of solicitors, it could not be said that the champertous agreement was the only way of funding the action.

It would appear, therefore, to be impossible for a liquidator to assign either the cause of action or the fruits of the action in respect of claims for fraudulent or wrongful trading or to set aside a transfer at an undervalue or a preference. It is possible that an agreement which gives the funder any degree of control over the litigation will be found to be champertous. The courts seem to have signalled a clear preference that office-holders negotiate conditional fee agreements with their legal advisers.

e) Assignment to legally aided assignee

In a number of cases the object of the assignment of the cause of action to an individual has been to enable the individual to pursue the action with the benefit of legal aid which would not be available to the company or the trustee in bankruptcy. The assignment to an individual by a liquidator also avoids the problem of the company being ordered to give security for costs.

[45] See below.

In *Norglen Limited v. Reeds Rains Prudential Limited*[46] a cause of action had been assigned to directors of the company. At first instance it had been held that this was a sham to enable the action to be continued by individuals at the expense of the Legal Aid board and to avoid security for cost being imposed. The Court of Appeal held[47] that the legal aid aspect should not invalidate the assignment since it was something the liquidator had the power to do. This was followed by the Court of Appeal in *Circuit Systems Ltd v. Zuken-Redac Ltd*.[48] The House of Lords has upheld the Court of Appeal decisions in both cases,[49] holding that the question of whether an assignment was an abuse of legal aid was a matter for the Legal Aid Board.

The House of Lords in *Stein v. Blake*[50] had previously upheld the assignment of by a trustee in bankruptcy of a cause of action back to the bankrupt in return for a share in the realisations in a situation where it was anticipated that bankrupt would get legal aid. Lord Hoffmann referred to the suggestion that there were policy reasons for taking a restrictive view of assignments of causes of action by insolvency practitioners to individuals but observed that "the problems can be said to arise not so much from the law of insolvency as from the insoluble difficulties of operating a system of legal aid and costs which is fair to both plaintiffs and defendants. Mr Blake is in no worse position now than he was before the bankruptcy when Mr Stein was suing him with legal aid (although this would not have been the case if the plaintiff had been a company). Mr Blake's complaint is that the bankruptcy has brought him no relief. But whether it should seems to me a matter for Parliament to decide".

Parliament has, in fact, intervened to an extent to limit the practice of assigning causes of action to those likely to obtain a legal aid certificate which would guarantee both funding and probably immunity from liability for the other side's costs. The Legal Aid authorities now have the power to refuse a certificate to a person who is an assignee where the assignment was entered into "with a view" to allowing the action to be commenced or continued with the benefit of legal aid.[51]

---

[46] [1996] B.C.C. 532.
[47] Following *Eurocross Sales Ltd v. Cornhill Insurance plc* [1995] 1 W.L.R. 1517 and distinguishing *Advanced Technology Ltd v. Crow Valley Products Limited* [1993] B.C.L.C. 723.
[48] [1997] 1 W.L.R. 721.
[49] [1998] 1 All E.R. 218.
[50] [1995] 2 All E.R. 961.
[51] Civil Legal Aid (General) Regulations 1996 inserting Reg. 33A into the 1989 Regulations.

f) Third party costs order[52]

The court has jurisdiction to make an order for costs against a non-party to the litigation where the interests of justice so require.[53] There is a risk that an insolvency practitioner who retains control over litigation or a funder who acquires control might be liable to such an order. A number of costs applications have also been made in relation to directors of insolvent companies who have caused the companies to bring unsuccessful actions. The Court of Appeal indicated in *Taylor v. Pace Developments Ltd*[54] that, although such orders were not impossible, in the absence of bad faith on the part of the director such an order would usually be an impermissible breach of the principle of limited liability.

It would appear, from *Metalloy Supplies Ltd v. MA (U.K.) Ltd*,[55] that similar principles will apply to liquidators. The defendants applied for an order that the liquidator personally pay the cost of the action, which had been discontinued when the company were ordered to make a payment of security for costs. The defendants argued that the liquidator had known that the plaintiff had insufficient funds to cover the cost of the trial. At first instance, it was held that the liquidator was liable for the costs from the date on which the defendants had served a defence. The Court of Appeal, allowing the appeal, held that the jurisdiction to order a liquidator as a non-party to proceedings brought by the insolvent company to pay costs personally would only be exercised in exceptional circumstances where there had been impropriety on the part of the liquidator. In most such cases, the Court observed, the defendant would be protected by the ability to apply for security for costs.[56]

Third party funders of litigation might be at greater risk of an order for costs although in *Condliffe v. Hislop*[57] the Court of Appeal held that the mere fact of lending money to a plaintiff to fund litigation ought not to lead to a risk of liability. In *Cooper v. Maxwell*[58] a mother who funded

---

[52] See Passmore, 1997 N.L.J., pp. 1465, 1521, 1554.

[53] Supreme Court Act 1981, s.51(1) as interpreted by the House of Lords in *Aiden Shipping Co. Limited v. Interbulk Limited* [1986] A.C. 965. There is no power to make an order for security of costs in advance against a third party funder: *CT Bowring & Co. (Insurance) Ltd v. Corsi Partners* [1994] 2 Lloyd's Rep. 567 and in *Abraham v. Thompson* [1997] 4 All E.R. 362 the Court of Appeal refused to stay an action on the grounds that it was being maintained by a third party which would not accept liability for costs; the proper course was to seek a costs order after the event.

[54] [1991] B.C.C. 406.

[55] [1997] 1 All E.R. 418.

[56] See *Eastglen Ltd v. Grafton* [1996] 2 B.C.L.C. 279.

[57] [1996] 1 W.L.R. 753.

[58] March 20, 1992, unreported, CA, quoted in *Murphy v. Young & Co.'s Brewery* [1997] 1 All E.R. 518.

her bankrupt son's unsuccessful appeal to the Court of Appeal was held not to be personally liable for the costs. This case appears to reflect the general view, although in *Thistleton v. Hendricks*,[59] a similar case, the mother was ordered to contribute towards the successful defendant's costs. The judge was influenced to make the order by the fact that the son was the plaintiff (in the *Maxwell* case the son was the defendant at first instance) and that the defendant was a private individual.

4. Conditional fee orders

Since 1995[60] solicitors have been able to enter into conditional fee agreements for insolvency work[61]; previously such arrangements were champertous. This can be coupled with insurance against the liability to pay the defendants' costs if the action is unsuccessful.

---

[59] (1992) 32 Con. L.R. 123.
[60] Conditional Fee Agreements Order 1995 (S.I. 1995 No. 1674) and the Conditional Fee Agreements Regulations 1995 (S.I. 1995 No. 1675) made under the Courts and Legal Services Act 1990.
[61] See 12 I.L.&P. 163 for a model of such an agreement.

CHAPTER 33

INTRODUCTION TO PENSIONS ISSUES

1. Introduction

A vast amount of wealth is tied up in pension schemes, so it is not surprising that on an insolvency, the insolvency practitioner may need to consider whether a pension scheme with which the insolvent is associated might be a source of funds to meet the insolvent's liabilities. In the case of a bankruptcy, the trustee in bankruptcy may seek to realise the value of the bankrupt's pension rights, whether or not they are already payable, for the benefit of the creditors. A pension cannot be mortgaged or charged and may well be the only unencumbered asset of any value possessed by the bankrupt. The underlying policy issues here are very much the same as in relation to the bankrupt's family house; there is obviously a tension between the interests of the bankrupt's dependants and those of the creditors. Whilst the immediate reaction of many would be that a bankrupt's pension should be protected, it has to be remembered that where a bankrupt has been paying money into a private pension scheme, he may have been able to shelter assets which would otherwise be available for his creditors. In the case of a liquidation, the insolvent company may have set up a pension scheme for its employees: the issue here is the extent to which the liquidator is entitled to any surplus in the pension fund once the obligations to the members of the scheme have been met.

2. Types of pension scheme

There are two main types of private pension scheme: occupational pension schemes set up by employers for the benefit of their employees and personal pension schemes. There are also public sector pension schemes but these are usually governed by their own detailed statutory provisions.

An occupational pension scheme is usually set up under a trust and legal ownership of the scheme's assets will be vested in the trustees of the scheme. The trust deed and rules will give a member various rights to pension and lump sum benefits on retirement and death. Members, as beneficiaries of the trust, have the right to require the trustees to administer the scheme in accordance with the rules. It is common for the employing company to act as trustee; the company may have both fiduciary powers under the scheme and powers which it can exercise in a beneficial capacity. Pension scheme members may be either active (that is still in employment and accruing entitlement to benefits) or deferred (no longer in employment but whose pensions are not yet payable) or pensioners, whose pensions have already commenced.

A personal pension scheme is a contractual arrangement between the individual and a pension provider under which the individual makes contributions to the scheme in return for the promised benefits.

Both types of scheme may be contracted out of the state earnings related pension scheme. In return for a reduction in national insurance payments the scheme will provide a guaranteed minimum pension or a protected rights fund depending on the type of scheme.

3. The bankrupt's pension entitlement[1]

a) General

The bankrupt may already be in receipt of a pension or he may have a future right[2] to pension and lump sum benefits on retirement or death, often with a right to call for early payment of the sums. It will be seen that the consequences of a bankruptcy will depend to an extent[3] on the precise mechanism through which the pension is provided. This is partly because the provisions of the Pensions Act 1995 only apply to occupational pension schemes. The other main difference arises from the operation of the general principle of trust law that a settlor may not settle his property on a trust arising in the event of his bankruptcy since this is seen as a fraud on the bankruptcy laws; in the case of an occupational pension scheme, it is the employer who is in the position of a settlor, whereas in a private pension scheme it is the member himself in the position of the settlor.

b) Attempts to prevent pension rights from vesting in the trustee in bankruptcy

Most pension schemes contain provisions prohibiting assignment of the policy and there have been attempts to argue that this prevents the

---

[1] See Greenstreet 11 I.L.&P. 133, 168 and 13 I.L.&P. 101; Simmons 13 I.L.&P. 98; Lowe 13 I.L.&P. 14.

[2] Either an equitable right as a beneficiary under an occupational pension scheme or a contractual right under a private pensions scheme. In either event this will be a chose in action and therefore "property" within Insolvency Act 1986, s.436.

[3] Many would say to a larger extent than justifiable.

pension rights from vesting in the trustee in bankruptcy. In *Re Landau*[4] Ferris J. held that the vesting in the trustee of assets by operation of law was not the same as assignment and therefore a clause prohibiting assignment was ineffective to prevent such vesting. It would prevent the trustee from assigning the policy.

Occupational pension schemes usually contain forfeiture clauses under which the bankruptcy of a member will cause his rights to be forfeited to the trustees who will then hold them on discretionary trusts for a class of beneficiaries including the member and his dependants. Where such a clause works, it prevents there from being an asset to vest in the trustee; the trustees of the pension scheme will usually exercise their discretion to pay the pension to the bankrupt's dependants until discharge and to the bankrupt thereafter. Despite some debate as to the effect of such clauses[5], the Pensions Act 1995 contains statutory recognition that pension benefits in occupational schemes can be forfeited on bankruptcy. The forfeiture device probably cannot be used in the case of a personal pension scheme since it would be tantamount to the member settling his assets on protective trust in the event of his bankruptcy.

The Pensions Act 1995, which implements the recommendations of the Goode Committee[6] set up to review pension law in the wake of the Maxwell scandal, will prevent entitlement to both an existing pension and accrued right to future pension payments under an occupational pension scheme from forming part of the bankrupt's estate. An income payments order will still be obtainable except in respect of any guaranteed minimum pension or protected rights pension where pension rights are not forfeited.

It is clear that a member of a personal pension scheme is vulnerable to bankruptcy except in respect of any guaranteed minimum pension or protected rights pension. Under the Bankruptcy Act 1914 the position was that the pension would have to be claimed by the trustee by way of income payment order when it came to be paid and that this would give the court a discretion to order that the bankrupt should retain part of it. The wording of the 1986 Insolvency Act is somewhat different and gave rise to debate as to whether the pension rights would vest automatically or whether an income payments order would still be required. This point has been settled recently in the case of *Re Landau*. Mr Landau, the bankrupt, had effected a pension policy in 1982 which provided for the

---

[4] [1997] 3 All E.R. 322.

[5] See *Re The Trusts of the Scientific Investment Pension Plan, The Times,* March 5, 1998 for a pre-Pensions Act 1995 case on the point.

[6] The Report of the Pension Law Review Committee, 1993, Cmnd 2342 recommended that future pension rights (as distinct from pension payments) should not be treated as bankruptcy assets and that forfeiture clauses should be allowed.

payment of an annuity to him provided he survived to his seventieth birthday on February 9, 1999 and a lump sum payment if he died earlier. The policy allowed Mr Landau the right to alter the date when the annuity would become payable to any date between his sixtieth and seventy-fifth birthdays (with concomitant alteration to the amount payable). It also allowed him to require payment of a capital sum by way of premium under an approved annuity contract to be issued by another institution. He could also require a lump sum instead of a limited part of the annuity and could amend the terms of payment in certain other ways including relinquishing part of the annuity in exchange for an annuity payable to his widow. Apart from these specific provisions, the policy could not be surrendered and no annuity could be assigned or commuted. In 1989 Mr Landau converted the policy into a fully paid policy under which no further premiums were payable. He also stipulated that the annuity would become payable on his sixty-fifth birthday in 1994.

Mr Landau was declared bankrupt on May 3, 1990 with liabilities in excess of £250,000. He was discharged from bankruptcy on May 3, 1993. In February 1994 Mr Landau sought to obtain the benefits obtainable under the policy. The trustee in bankruptcy did not initially object to the annual pension being paid but did seek payment of the lump sum payable on commutation of part of the annuity to be paid to him as trustee. Mr Landau did not accept this and eventually the trustee contended that he was entitled to both the sum and the annuity and that he, not Mr Landau, should be treated as the annuitant. The basis for this contention was that the policy had vested in him under section 306 of the Insolvency Act 1986 as property in the ownership of the bankrupt at the start of the bankruptcy, an argument with which Ferris J. agreed. Ferris J. held that section 310 of the Insolvency Act 1986, under which the trustee can apply for an income payments order, is not relevant where the property has already vested under section 306.

The consequence of this is that the pension rights under a private pension scheme will vest automatically in the trustee in bankruptcy and will remain so vested, even after discharge of the bankrupt, unless disclaimed by the trustee or, perhaps, re-assigned to the bankrupt in return for suitable payment. It is often likely to be the case, particularly where the bankrupt is young, that the costs of keeping the bankruptcy open will outweigh any potential gain to the creditors.[7] Similarly, although in theory the decision opens the way to the re-opening[8] of old bankruptcies in order to recover the value of pensions which have

---

[7] And, therefore, the trustee will be able to close the bankruptcy under Insolvency Act 1986, s.330(1).

[8] Under Insolvency Act 1986, s.300(8).

subsequently become payable, the costs problem may prove insuperable.

c) Excessive contributions

There might be scope for the application of sections 339 and 423 of the Insolvency Act 1986; the problem is likely to be that the member will have received adequate consideration in the form of additional benefits under the scheme. Section 95[9] of the Pensions Act 1995 provides (by inserting a new section 342A into the Insolvency Act 1986) in respect of an occupational pension scheme that the trustee in bankruptcy will be able (whether or not the scheme contains a forfeiture clause) to obtain an order to recover any "excessive" contributions made to such a scheme if the court is satisfied the making of such contributions unfairly prejudiced the bankrupt's creditors. The order could be in respect of employer's contributions if the individual had agreed to forgo salary in return for increased contributions to the pension scheme. The purpose of the order would be to restore the position to what it would have been if the excessive contributions had not been made. In deciding whether contributions were excessive the court has to have regard in particular to the following:

  i) whether any of the contributions were made for the purpose of putting assets beyond the reach of creditors;
  ii) whether the amount of contributions made during the relevant period (the five years preceding bankruptcy) was excessive in view of the individual's circumstances when they were made;
  iii) whether the level of benefits provided by the scheme together with benefits under any other occupational pension scheme to which the individual was likely to be entitled is excessive in all the circumstances of the case.

4. Contributions shortfall

Contributions collected by the company and not handed over to the trustees of the pension scheme before the insolvency are almost certainly trust assets and not assets of the company, especially where the contributions can be identified as a separate fund. Claims can be made against the National Insurance Fund for at least some of the missing contributions.[10]

[9] Not yet in force.
[10] Pensions Schemes Act 1993.

5. Occupational pension fund surpluses[11]

a) Establishing whether there is a surplus

A liquidator of a company with an occupational pension scheme will need to establish whether it will have a surplus when it is wound up. The benefit entitlements of members under the scheme will be secured by transferring them to another scheme or by purchasing annuities in their own names. The costs of the winding up of the scheme are likely to reduce any apparent surplus considerably: a scheme which appears to have a surplus on a going-concern basis may well actually be in deficit on a winding up of the scheme. Where there is a deficit, this will be a debt provable in the liquidation against the company. In calculating the amounts required to meet liabilities to members, the statutory requirement[12] for prescribed index linked increases in pension benefits must be taken into account.

b) Exercise of powers in relation to a surplus

The liquidator steps into the shoes of the company and, therefore, into its rights in relation to the pension scheme. The courts have held,[13] as a matter of general trust law, that a liquidator may not exercise a power to distribute a surplus on a wind up vested in the company in a fiduciary capacity because of the potential conflict between the duty to the beneficiaries under the scheme and the duty to the creditors in the liquidation. The Pension Schemes Act 1993[14] now requires that all such fiduciary powers must be exercised by an independent trustee; it is the duty of an insolvency practitioner to ensure that there is such an independent trustee in place. The courts have given some guidance as to the factors to be taken into consideration; these include the source of the surplus, the needs of the members of the scheme and the financial position of the employer. Over-funding of the scheme at the expense of the creditors would be a relevant factor.[15]

c) Entitlement to any surplus[16]

The liquidator will need to consult the trust documents under which the scheme is set up in order to identify what may happen to any surplus. In

---

[11] Moffat (1993) 56 M.L.R. 471, Greenstreet 12 I.L.&P. 35, 78.
[12] Pension Schemes Act 1993, s.108.
[13] In *Mettoy Pension Trustees Ltd v. Evans* [1991] 2 All E.R. 513 and *Re William Makin & Son Ltd* [1993] O.P.L.R 171.
[14] ss119–122.
[15] *Thrells (1974) Pension Scheme v. Lomas* [1992] O.P.L.R. 21.
[16] Nobles (1987) 16 I.L.J. 164, (1990) 19 I.L.J. 204, [1992] J.B.L. 261.

a few cases there is a mandatory obligation to repay any surplus to the company in which case the creditors will receive all the surplus.[17]

In most cases there will be either an obligation or a discretion (which may be exercisable by the trustees, sometimes with the consent of the company, or by the company) to provide the maximum possible increase (within Inland Revenue rules) to the benefits of the members from the surplus. Where this discretion is vested in the company, it will be exercised by the independent trustee. The position in relation to a power of veto by the company is not clear; it is possible that the company might be held to hold the veto in a fiduciary capacity but it seems more likely that it would be held in a beneficial capacity and that the only limitation on its exercise by the liquidator would be the duty to exercise it in good faith by giving genuine consideration to whether or not it should be exercised.

In some cases the scheme makes provision for increase in benefits but is silent as to the destination of any remaining surplus; unless it is very clear that the company should not benefit (in which case the surplus goes to the Crown as *bona vacantia*), the common law position is that it is likely that any surplus will pass to the company under a resulting trust.[18] Section 77 of the Pensions Act 1995 provides that surplus will be repaid to the employers in respect of the schemes to which it applies.

In any case in which a surplus from the pension fund is to go to the company in liquidation, it is vital that the pension scheme is wound up first.

---

[17] The surplus will be subject to 40% tax under ICTA 1988, s.601.
[18] *Re Richards & Wallington Group Pension Scheme* [1990] 1 W.L.R. 1511.

CHAPTER 34

OTHER SOURCES OF FUNDS FOR CREDITORS

1. Insured liabilities of the insolvent

If an insolvent[1] has insured against liabilities which it has incurred to a third party, either before or after the insolvency, the third party can compel the insurance company to pay the insurance money directly to him under the Third Parties (Rights Against Insurers) Act 1930. Some liabilities against insurance companies only arise when the insured has paid out on the claim; if the insured goes into liquidation or bankruptcy before paying the third party, there will be no right capable of being transferred to the third party.[2]

This right does not arise until the existence and amount of the liability has been established[3]. This can give rise to problems where an insolvent company is dissolved without the liability having been established, as happened in *Bradley v. Eagle Star Insurance Co. Ltd.*[4] The court has the power under section 651 of the Companies Act 1985 to declare the dissolution void and revivify the company but only if an application is made within two years of the date of dissolution.

There will be no protection for the third party if the insurance company has already paid the insolvent insured; in that case the insurance moneys form part of the general assets and the third party will be an ordinary creditor in the insolvency.

It is not possible to contract out of the provisions of the Third Parties (Rights Against Insurers) Act 1930 nor for the insured and insurer to come to any arrangement after the start of the insolvency which would defeat or affect the rights of the third party.

---

[1] In this context, this includes a bankrupt, a debtor who has made an arrangement or composition with creditors and a company in liquidation, administration, administrative receiver or party to a company voluntary arrangement.
[2] *The Fanti* and *The Padre Island* [1991] 2 A.C. 1.
[3] See *Re Greenfield, Jackson v. Debtors*, January 19, 1998, unreported.
[4] [1989] B.C.L.C. 469. See also *Post Office v. Norwich Fire Insurance Society Ltd* [1967] 2 Q.B. 363.

2. Claims of employees against the National Insurance Fund

a) Background

Certain payments owing to the employees of an insolvent employer are guaranteed by the state and will be met out of the National Insurance Fund. This is a requirement of the E.C. Directive on Insolvency Protection.[5]

If payment is made to an employee, the Department of Employment becomes subrogated to his rights against the employer.[6] A recent report by the National Audit Office[7] concluded that if the Redundancy Payments Service were to be a more active creditor it could recover a higher proportion of the payments of around £240 million each year that it makes to employees who have become redundant on the insolvency of their employers.

b) Categories of guaranteed payments

i) Redundancy payments.[8] These are guaranteed[9] both where the employer is formally insolvent and where the employee has taken all reasonable steps (other than legal proceedings to enforce an industrial tribunal decision) to recover the payment, and the employer has refused or failed to pay. This will include the situation where the employer has so few assets that no-one has thought it worth incurring the expense of a formal insolvency.

ii) Statutory maternity pay is guaranteed[10] in the same way as redundancy pay.

iii) Other payments guaranteed on a formal insolvency are set out in section 184 of the Employment Rights Act 1996. The requirements for these payments are more complicated than

---

[5] Dir. 80/987. It is not entirely clear that this Directive has been correctly implemented: see Hepple & Byre (1989) 18 I.L.J. 129. It was the failure of the Italian government properly to implement this directive which led to the landmark decision of *Francovich v. Italian Republic* [1992] I.R.L.R. 84 in which the European Court of Justice held that a claim could in some circumstances be brought against a government by an individual who has suffered as a result of the failure in implementation.

[6] See Chap. 35.5 for discussion of the view of the Cork Committee on this.

[7] Published on October 17, 1996.

[8] Under Employment Rights Act 1996, s.135.

[9] *ibid.*, s.166.

[10] Under reg. 7 of the Statutory Maternity Pay Regulations 1986.

for redundancy and maternity payments and are considered below.

c) Payments guaranteed under section 184 of the Employment Rights Act 1996

Before a payment will be made out of the Fund, the Department of Employment must be satisfied of the following four elements.

i) the debt claimed is within the categories specified by section 184 of the Employment Rights Act 1996. These are, broadly: remuneration[11] due during the eight weeks prior to the commencement of the insolvency; notice moneys for the statutory periods of notice[12]; holiday pay; and unfair dismissal basic awards. The calculation of the gross amount[13] of any periodic payment guaranteed by the Fund is subject to a statutory maximum currently[14] set at £220 per week. If the employee owes money to the employer, the set-off provisions will apply.[15]

ii) the employer is formally insolvent, as defined in section 183.[16] If this is not the case, the employees may have to seek a winding up or bankruptcy themselves in order to take advantage of the guarantee provision.[17] The employer will not be insolvent for these purposes on the basis that a receiver has been appointed pursuant to a fixed charge.[18] Where the employer is a partnership, the section has been construed as requiring that all the partners be individually bankrupt before the employer will be treated as insolvent.[19]

iii) the employment of the employee has been terminated; and

---

[11] Defined to include protective awards (see Chap. 12.2(f) above).

[12] Set out in Employment Rights Act 1996, s.86.

[13] Which will be subject to deduction for mitigation: *Westwood v. Secretary of State for Employment* [1984] I.R.L.R. 209. In *Secretary of State for Employment v. Cooper* [1987] I.C.R. 766 the Employment Appeal Tribunal held that the payment made from the Fund should be reduced by an amount equivalent to the basic rate of income tax. See *Secretary of State for Employment v. Wilson* [1996] I.R.L.R. 334 for a recent case on this area in the context of unemployment benefit.

[14] Since April 1998. See below for whether this complies with E.C. law.

[15] *Secretary of State v. Wilson* [1996] I.R.L.R. 330. See Chap. 25.4.

[16] In the case of a corporate employer: liquidation, administration, administrative receivership and company voluntary arrangement. In the case of an individual: bankruptcy, composition or arrangement with creditors, deceased insolvent.

[17] *Pollard v. Teako* [1967] 2 I.T.R 357, *Re Eloc Electro-Optieck and Communicatie BV* [1981] 2 ALL E.R. 1111.

[18] *Secretary of State v. Stone* [1994] I.C.R. 761 (fixed charge over book debts).

[19] *Secretary of State v. Forde* [1997] I.R.L.R. 387.

iv) the debt was due on the appropriate date. The appropriate date[20] is, in relation to arrears of pay and holiday pay, the date on which the employer became insolvent, as defined by section 183 of the Employment Rights Act 1996. In relation to protective awards under section 189 of the Trade Union and Labour Relations (Consolidation) Act 1992 and basic awards of compensation for unfair dismissal, the appropriate date is the latest of the date on which the employer became insolvent, the date of the termination of the employee's employment, and the date on which the award was made. In relation to any other guaranteed payment, it is the later of the date on which the employer became insolvent and the date of termination of the employee's employment.

d) The statutory ceiling

In *Potter v. Secretary of State for Employment*[21] the Court of Appeal left open the question of whether the statutory weekly ceiling on the amount to be claimed by any employee is in accordance with the social objective of the Insolvency Directive. In the Employment Appeal Tribunal it had been held that the ceiling could be justified as avoiding the payment of sums going beyond the protection aimed at by the Insolvency Directive, which expressly permitted a ceiling provided it was consistent with the social objective of the Directive. In the Court of Appeal it was decided that protective awards, the subject matter of the claim, did not fall within the Insolvency Directive so they did not have to decide the point. They did, however, point out that attention had been drawn to the increasing disparity between the average level of earnings in the United Kingdom and the ceiling; they said that in other circumstances they might have thought it right to refer a question to the European Court of Justice for guidance as to the circumstances to be taken into account in considering the validity of a ceiling.

e) Complaints against the Fund

An employee may complain to an industrial tribunal that the Fund has paid too little.[22] Such application must be presented within three months of the Department's decision; there is no right to complain of an

---

[20] Employment Rights Act 1996, s.185.
[21] [1997] I.R.L.R. 2.
[22] Employment Rights Act 1996, s.188.

unreasonable delay in the Department reaching a decision. If the complaint is proved the tribunal will make a declaration as to the amount due but does not actually order payment.

e) Controlling shareholders[23]

Until recently no distinction has been made between ordinary employees and those who are also controlling shareholders of an insolvent company. The Employment Appeal Tribunal in *Buchan v. Secretary of State for Employment*[24] then held that a controlling shareholder is not an employee for the purposes of the employment protection legislation since it would be inconsistent with the purpose of the legislation to extend protection to a person who cannot be dismissed from his position in a company without his agreement. Subsequently, the Court of Session in *Fleming v. Secretary of State for Trade and Industry*[25] held that there was no rule of law that a controlling shareholder could not be an employee for these purposes. They noted in particular that in *Buchan* reliance had been placed on the proposition that a controlling shareholder could prevent his dismissal and queried how that would apply where the dismissal had been effected by the liquidator.[26]

---

[23] See Tolmie (1997) 113 L.Q.R. 536.
[24] [1997] I.R.L.R. 80.
[25] [1997] I.R.L.R. 682 on appeal from the Scottish EAT, upholding a finding that the shareholder was not an employee on the facts of the case.
[26] In *Secretary of State v. Bottril*, January 12, 1998, unreported, the EAT concluded on the facts of the case that the shareholder was an employee.

CHAPTER 35

DISTRIBUTION OF THE AVAILABLE ASSETS

1. Introduction

Once the liquidator or trustee in bankruptcy has identified and realised the assets which are available to the creditors of the insolvent, the question arises as to the manner and order of distribution. As has been seen, a basic principle of insolvency law since Tudor times is that of rateable or "*pari passu*" distribution of the assets. In reality, the recognition of pre-existing proprietary rights explained in the foregoing chapters is likely to mean that in many cases the unsecured creditors are participating rateably in very little.[1] Although the ordinary creditors share the available assets equally, the expenses of the insolvency and the preferential creditors must be paid before any assets become available to them.[2] The ordinary creditors are a residual class comprising all creditors not specifically designated as preferential or deferred. Post-insolvency interest on preferential and ordinary debts will only be paid if there are funds left after payment of the ordinary creditors. Finally, there is a category of deferred or postponed debts. Each category of debts has to be paid in full before the next category of creditors is entitled to receive anything and where there is insufficient to pay all members of a category fully, the amounts paid will be reduced rateably.

Secured creditors will often alter the order of priority amongst themselves by mutual agreement and this has led to some conundrums of priority where floating charges and preferential creditors are involved. Those who will be unsecured creditors in the event of an insolvency may also wish to agree amongst themselves that distribution will be other than *pari passu*. They will face the same difficulty as those who wish to contract out of the statutory set-off scheme in that the court is

---

[1] See Oditah (1992) L.Q.R. 459 on the impact of proprietary claims.
[2] The provisions on priority of payment are found in Insolvency Act 1986, s.328 (bankruptcy), Insolvency Act, s.107 (voluntary winding up) and Insolvency Rules 1986, r. 4.181 (compulsory winding up). The rules on set off considered in Chap. 25.4 above also have the effect of bestowing a preference on those creditors able to take advantage of them.

likely to hold that such an agreement is of no effect, although recently the courts have showed some relaxation of the rule in this context.

This Chapter considers each category of creditor in turn, starting at the top of the order of priority. It concludes by considering the extent to which unsecured creditors may contract out of the statutory scheme.

2. Manner of distribution

The statutory provisions about the manner of distribution to the creditors are the same in bankruptcy and liquidation. In relation to bankruptcy the rules are contained in the Insolvency Act 1986[3]; identical provisions relating to liquidation are to be found in the Insolvency Rules.[4] Part 11 of the Insolvency Rules contains additional provisions about the declaration and payment of dividends which apply to both winding up and bankruptcy.

Whenever the office-holder has sufficient funds in hand he shall,[5] subject to the retention of sums necessary to meet the expenses of the insolvency, declare and distribute dividends amongst the creditors in respect of the debts which they have proved. He must give notice of his intention to declare and distribute a dividend to all creditors whose addresses are known to him and who have not proved their debts; unless he has already invited creditors by public advertisement to prove their debts, he must publicly advertise the intention to declare a dividend. The notices will specify a last date for proving which must not be less than 21 days from the notice; the dividend will usually be declared within four months from that date. Where he has declared a dividend, he shall give details of it to all those who have proved their debts.

In the calculation and distribution of a dividend the office-holder shall make provision for any debts which appear to him to be due to persons who live at a distance and have not yet been able to establish a proof. He must also provide for any debts which are the subject of claims which have not yet been determined and for disputed proofs and claims. A creditor who has not proved his debt before the declaration of a dividend is not entitled to disturb that dividend but when he has proved the debt, he will be entitled to be paid, out of any money for the time being available for the payment of any further dividend, any dividend

---

[3] Insolvency Act 1986, ss324, 325, 326, 330.
[4] Insolvency Rules 1986, rr. 4.180, 4.182, 4.183, 4.184, 4.186.
[5] By Insolvency Act 1986, s.324, Insolvency Rules 1986, r. 4.180.

which he has failed to receive before further dividends are paid to other creditors. No action lies against the office-holder for a dividend but if he refuses to pay a dividend the court may, if it thinks fit, order him to pay it and also to pay, out of his own money, interest on the dividend and the costs of the proceedings in which the order to pay is made.

If there is property which cannot be readily or advantageously sold, the office-holder may obtain the permission of the creditors' committee to distribute the property itself according to its value.[6] Permission must relate to a particular proposed exercise of the power in question. If the office-holder has acted in a case of urgency to distribute the property *in specie*, the court or the creditors' committee may ratify his act for the purpose of enabling him to recoup his expenses provided he seeks ratification without undue delay.

Where the office-holder has realised all the estate or so much of it as he thinks can be realised without needlessly protracting the insolvency, he shall give notice of his intention to declare a final dividend or that no dividend, or further dividend, will be declared.[7] The notice shall require claims to be established by the final date specified in the notice. After the final date, which may be delayed by the court on the application of any person, the office-holder shall defray any outstanding expenses out of the estate and declare and distribute any final dividend without regard to any claims which have not already been proved.

Sections 334 and 335 of the Insolvency Act 1986 make provision for the situation where a bankruptcy order is made against an undischarged bankrupt. Once the trustee in the first bankruptcy has notice of the petition for the second bankruptcy, any subsequent distribution out of property acquired as after-acquired property or by virtue of an income payments order in the first bankruptcy will be void unless made with the consent of the court or subsequently ratified by the court. After-acquired property (and its proceeds) and the proceeds of income payments orders held by the first trustee at the commencement of the second bankruptcy will fall into the estate for the purposes of that bankruptcy. The expenses of the first trustee in relation to property which has fallen into the estate in the second bankruptcy will be a first charge on that estate. The creditors of the earlier bankruptcy will not be creditors in respect of the same debts in the later bankruptcy but the first trustee may prove in the later bankruptcy for the unsatisfied balance of the debts, interest payable on that balance and any unpaid expenses of the earlier bankruptcy; the

[6] Insolvency Act 1986, s.326, Insolvency Rules 1986, r. 4.183.
[7] *ibid.*, s.330, Insolvency Rules 1986, r. 4.186.

claims will be deferred to the debts and interest provable in the later bankruptcy.

3. Expenses and post-insolvency creditors[8]

As explained above, the office-holder will retain sums to meet the expenses of the insolvency before making distributions to the creditors. Expenses are payable in full by the office-holder out of the available assets rather than provable in the insolvency. The court will usually permit a post-insolvency creditor to take individual action such as levying of distress against the insolvent.

Section 328 of the Insolvency Act 1986, which sets out the order of priority of debts in a bankruptcy, provides that the preferential debts will be postponed to the expenses of the bankruptcy but will be paid in priority to other debts. This has the effect of placing the expenses of the bankruptcy at the top of the order of distribution. The Insolvency Rules 1986[9] set out the order of priority of the expenses. The issue of the expenses of a bankruptcy does not seem to have generated the same volume of litigation as has been the case in the context of liquidation.

The provisions of the Insolvency Act 1986 relevant to liquidations date back to the Companies Act 1862 which themselves reflected previous case law on the subject.[10] Section 115 of the Insolvency Act 1986 provides that all expenses properly incurred in the winding up, including the remuneration of the liquidator, are payable out of the company's assets in priority to all other claims. In relation to compulsory liquidation, the Insolvency Act 1986[11] provides that the court may, in the event of the assets being insufficient to satisfy the liabilities, make an order as to the payment out of the assets of the expenses incurred in the winding up in such order of priority as the court thinks just.[12] The Insolvency Rules 1986[13] set out the general order of priority of payment of the expenses of liquidation; it is to be noted that each category is to

---

[8] Insolvency Act 1986, s.115 (voluntary winding up); Insolvency Rules 1986, r. 4.180(1) (compulsory winding up); Insolvency Act 1986, s.324 (bankruptcy).

[9] r. 6.224.

[10] See, generally, Moss and Segal [1997] C.F.I.L.R. 1 on the history of the liquidation expenses principle.

[11] s.156.

[12] Under Insolvency Act 1986, s.112 the court has the same power in relation to a voluntary liquidation. In *Webb v. Whiffin* (1872) L.R. 5 H.L. 711, it was suggested that the absence of a direction that the expenses of a compulsory liquidation should come out of the company's assets was because it was assumed that the court did not need such an instruction.

[13] rr. 4.218, 4.219. An order of priority was first provided in 1890.

be paid in full before anything is paid to the next and that the remuneration of the liquidator comes towards the bottom of the list.[14] First in the order of priority are the expenses properly incurred in preserving, realising or getting in any of the assets of the company which reflects the common law view that the other expenses could only be paid out of the assets net of the costs of realisation.[15] The Insolvency Rules 1986 expressly provide[16] that this order of priority is subject to the power of the court under section 156 of the Insolvency Act 1986 to order how the expenses are to be met where the assets are insufficient to satisfy the liabilities. It is also provided[17] that nothing in the Rules affects the power of any court in proceedings by or against the company to order costs to be paid by the company or the liquidator. It will be seen that the statutory provisions do not confer an absolute right of priority on the expenses of the liquidation since the court is given an ultimate discretion. Millett J. in *Re M. C. Bacon*[18] observed that section 115 of the Insolvency Act 1986 was concerned with priority of payment out of the assets; it assumed that the expenses would be payable out of the assets but did not so provide. In *Re Atlantic Computers* the Court of Appeal[19] observed that the so-called "liquidation expenses" principle is a statement of how, in general, the court will exercise its discretion.

The right of those claiming to be entitled to priority as creditors in relation to an expense of the liquidation can, therefore, be seen to derive from common law rather than statute. The judges have also developed the law as to what is to be regarded as an expense of the liquidation for these purposes. Debts and liabilities arising in the course of the liquidation as a result of contracts entered into by the liquidator on behalf of the company clearly fall into this category; the position with regard to contracts and leases which the liquidator has continued has given rise to more difficulty. Where the leased property has been used or contractual performance accepted for the purposes or convenience of the winding up, the rent or payment has been held to be an expense of the winding

---

[14] Items ahead of the liquidator's own remuneration include the fees of the official receiver, the costs of the petition, costs in connection with any provisional liquidation, certain costs in connection with the preparation of the statement of affairs and disbursements, including the allowable expenses of the liquidation committee. Necessary disbursements were held in *Re Mesco Properties Ltd* [1980] 1 W.L.R. 96 to include tax on any post-liquidation profits.
[15] *Re London Metallurgical* [1895] 1 Ch. 758.
[16] r. 4.220.
[17] Insolvency Rules 1986, r. 4.220(2).
[18] [1990] B.C.L.C. 607.
[19] In deciding that the "liquidation expenses" principle does not apply in an administration (see Chap. 10).

up.[20] In *Re ABC Coupler & Engineering Co.*[21] Plowman J. observed that "it appears that, apart from the question of some special equity . . . the test of liability for payment in full of rent accrued since the winding up is whether the liquidator has retained possession 'for the convenience of the winding up' and that whether he has done so or not depends upon his purpose in retaining possession". A distinction has to be drawn between active "preservation" of property and mere retention as a result of inaction.[22]

The costs of unsuccessful litigation undertaken by the liquidator in connection with the assets of the company[23] will usually[24] fall within the category of an expense of the litigation.[25]

Preservation of the assets may require payment by the insolvency practitioner of a pre-insolvency debt, for example to avoid forfeiture of a lease or distress; in this case, payment will be an expense of the insolvency. Public utility suppliers are no longer permitted to make payment of amounts owing in respect of pre-insolvency services a condition of continuing to supply[26]; the suppliers would have to prove as ordinary creditors for such payments. Such suppliers may, however, require a personal guarantee from the insolvency practitioner in respect of payment for services supplied during the insolvency; the insolvency practitioner would be entitled to an indemnity from the assets.

One question which has yet to be answered is the status of liability under the environment protection legislation[27]; it is not clear whether post-insolvency remedial work would be an expense of the insolvency.

In some cases there may be successive insolvency practitioners. The Insolvency Rules 1986[28] provide that where a compulsory winding up follows immediately on a voluntary winding up, the remuneration of the voluntary liquidator and the costs and expenses of the voluntary liquidation allowed by the court will rank with the first category of expenses in

---

[20] See *Re Lundy Granite Co.* (1871) L.R. 6 Ch. App. 462, *Re Oak Pitts Colliery Co.* (1882) 21 Ch. D. 322, *Re ABC Coupler & Engineering Co.* [1970] 1 W.L.R. 702, *Re Downer* [1974] 1 W.L.R. 1460, *Nolton Business Centres Ltd* [1996] 1 B.C.L.C. 400 (on apportionment as between pre- and post-liquidation rates).

[21] [1970] 1 W.L.R. 702.

[22] *Re Linda Marie* [1989] B.C.L.C. 46.

[23] Note the discussion in Chap. 32 above.

[24] In exceptional cases, costs may be awarded personally against the liquidator: *Re Wilson Lovatt & Sons Ltd* [1977] 1 All E.R. 274.

[25] *Re London Metallurgical* [1895] 1 Ch. 758, *Re London Drapery Stores* [1898] 2 Ch. 684 (it makes no difference that the litigation started before the liquidation), *Re Pacific Coast Syndicate Ltd* [1913] 2 Ch. 26, *Re Movitex Ltd* [1990] B.C.C. 491.

[26] s.233, enacted in response to criticism by the Cork Committee (Chap. 33).

[27] Environmental Protection Act 1990, Environment Act 1995. See the discussion by Professor Goode in *Principles of Corporate Insolvency* (2nd ed.) p. 162.

[28] r. 4.129.

the compulsory liquidation. In *Re Tony Rowse NMC Ltd*[29] the court said that it would usually allow costs unless there was a good reason otherwise. In that case, the liquidator appointed in the voluntary liquidation had speedily given work which was not really necessary to an associate despite the fact that he knew the creditors were likely to seek a compulsory liquidation; the costs of the work were disallowed. In *Merrygold v. Horton*[30] the court held that, where there were insufficient assets to meet the expenses of successive liquidators of a company in creditors' voluntary liquidation, their claims should abate rateably.

The Insolvency Rules 1986[31] also provide for the priority of expenses where there are successive bankruptcies.

4. Pre-preferential bankruptcy debts

Under section 348 of the Insolvency Act 1986 apprentices or articled clerks articled to the bankrupt may recover, ahead of the distribution of the estate, such part of any premium which was paid as the trustee thinks fit if their articles are discharged.[32] If the bankrupt was an officer of a Friendly Society, the trustees have a first right against his estate in respect of any money or property in his possession at the time of his being adjudicated bankrupt.[33] The funeral expenses of a deceased insolvent are also pre-preferential.[34]

5. Preferential creditors

a) Background history

Employees have had a statutory preferential claim to payment of certain sums owing to them since the Bankruptcy Act 1825 and, before this, it is likely that they were treated as expenses of the insolvency as a matter of practice. Crown preference at common law is also of great antiquity. It was first given statutory expression in the insolvency legislation in the Bankruptcy Act 1849 in relation to assessed taxes; local rates were also given statutory preferential status at the same time. It was held in *Food Controller v. Clark*[35] that the statutory provisions were exhaustive of Crown preference in the distribution of an insolvent's assets.

[29] [1996] 2 B.C.L.C. 225.
[30] *The Times*, July 11, 1997.
[31] rr. 6.225–6.228.
[32] This is also guaranteed out of the National Insurance Fund.
[33] Friendly Societies Act 1974, s.59.
[34] Art. 4(2) of the Administration of Insolvent Estates of Deceased Persons Order 1986.
[35] [1923] A.C. 647.

By the time of the Cork Report the categories of Crown preferential debt had expanded greatly.[36] The Cork Committee[37] received a considerable amount of critical comment on the existence of preferential debts and recommended major changes. The current legislation incorporates their recommendation that Crown preference should only be retained for taxes collected by insolvents rather than for those assessed on them; the rationale for retaining the preference for collected taxes is that it would be wrong for statutory provisions enacted for the more convenient collection of revenue to enure to the benefit of private creditors.

The provisions of the Insolvency Act 1986 conferring preferential status on the categories of debt set out in Schedule 6 are section 328 in relation to bankruptcy and section 175 in relation to liquidation.

b) "Relevant date"

The preferential debts are all defined by reference to "the relevant date". This is itself defined[38] as follows:

i) in relation to a compulsory winding up, the earliest out of the dates of an administration order[39] immediately preceding the winding up, a resolution for voluntary liquidation, the appointment of a provisional liquidator or the making of the winding up order;

ii) in relation to a voluntary winding up, the date of the resolution for winding up;

iii) in relation to a bankruptcy, the date of the bankruptcy order unless an interim receiver was appointed between the presentation of the petition and the making of the order, in which case the relevant date will be the date of that appointment;

iv) in relation to a company in receivership, the date of the appointment of the receiver;

v) in relation to an individual voluntary arrangement, the date of the interim order;

---

[36] See the list at para. 1402.
[37] See Chap. 32 of the Report.
[38] By s.387.
[39] There is no parallel provision in relation to an administration preceding a voluntary liquidation: *Re Powerstore (Trading) Ltd* [1998] 1 All E.R. 121. Those who had preferential debts at the start of the administration are likely to be unhappy if it is followed by a voluntary liquidation rather than a compulsory liquidation or a company voluntary arrangement both of which will protect their interests.

vi) in relation to a company voluntary arrangement, the date of approval of the arrangement or, if the company is in administration, the date of the making of the administration order.

c) Categories of preferential debt

There are six categories of preferential debt set out in the Act,[40] which all rank *pari passu* amongst themselves so that, if there is insufficient to pay all the preferential claims, each preferential creditor will receive the same proportion of what is owing as the others. The categories of preferential debt are as follows:

i) sums due to the Inland Revenue on account of deductions of income tax from emoluments paid during the 12 months before the relevant date. These deductions are those which the debtor was liable to make under the pay as you earn (PAYE) provisions of the Income and Corporation Taxes Act 1988 less the amount of the repayments of income tax which the debtor was liable to make during that period.

ii) Debts due to Customs and Excise in respect of Value Added Tax and insurance premium tax referable to the period of the six months before the relevant date, car tax and various gaming taxes which became due during the 12 months before the relevant date and excise duty on beer which became due during the six months before the relevant date.

iii) Class 1 and Class 2 social security contributions which became due from the debtor in the 12 months before the relevant date and up to one year's Class 4 contributions due to the Inland Revenue.

iv) Contributions to occupational pension schemes and state scheme premiums owed by the debtor to which Schedule 4 of the Pension Schemes Act 1993 applies.

v) Remuneration[41] owed to current or past employees in respect of the four months before the relevant date up to the limit prescribed by the Secretary of State which is currently £800 per claimant. Accrued holiday remuneration in respect of any period of employment before the relevant date, to a person whose employment by the debtor has been terminated,

---

[40] s.386 and Sched. 6.
[41] As defined in Sched. 6, para. 13. This includes wages or salary whether for time or for piece work or by way of commission. It also includes a number of other payments to which employees may be entitled under the employment protection and collective labour law legislation.

whether before, on or after that date. Amounts due under the Reserve Force (Safeguard of Employment) Act 1985 in respect of a default before the relevant date in obligations under that Act.

vi) Sums due at the relevant date in respect of levies on the production of coal and steel referred to in the ECSC Treaty.

d) Subrogation

Where sums have been advanced to pay remuneration or holiday pay, which would otherwise have been preferential payments, that loan becomes a preferential debt.[42] The Cork Committee observed[43] that the subrogated and preferential claims of banks and others who had advanced money for the purpose of paying wages were of far greater significance than the claims by the employees. Prior to 1986, this right of subrogation only existed in relation to corporate insolvency. The Committee was satisfied that the difference in treatment as between bankruptcy and liquidation could not be supported but was divided as to whether this right of subrogation should be retained at all, acknowledging the argument that it sometimes encouraged banks to continue to support non-viable businesses. The majority of the Committee were persuaded by the argument that the banks might refuse to make the necessary loans were they to be denied this preferential status and that this might lead to the closure of viable businesses which might otherwise have continued trading. They did suggest that any repayments by the insolvent during the four month period should be set against the money advanced to pay the wages rather than against earlier advances; this suggestion was not accepted.

Where employees are owed amounts which both carry preferential status and are guaranteed, they will generally recover more of what is owed (since the monetary limit on guaranteed payments is higher) more quickly by claiming against the National Insurance Fund than from proving in the insolvency proceedings. The only circumstances in which an employee is likely to prove for preferential debts will be where the claim is for sums due for periods outside the Fund limits (eight weeks) or where the employee is still employed by the insolvent employer. If the employees have made claims on the National Insurance Fund, the Secretary of State will be subrogated to their claims including any priority in respect of preferential debts. The Cork Committee suggested,

---

[42] Insolvency Act 1986, Sched. 6, para. 11. *Re Primrose (Builders) Ltd* [1950] Ch. 561, *Re Rampgill Mill Ltd* [1967] Ch. 1138, *Re E. J. Morel (1934) Ltd* [1962] Ch. 21, *Re James R. Rutherford & Sons Ltd* [1964] 3 All E.R. 137.

[43] At para. 1436.

in a recommendation which was not accepted, that employees' claims should be dealt with through the state guarantee system and removed from the category of preferential debt so that the subrogated claim of the Department of Employment would be as an ordinary creditor. The Committee said[44] that "we would emphasise that the priority accorded to employees in an insolvency is a social measure, intended to alleviate special financial hardship, and that in modern times the cost of meeting such social needs ought properly to be borne by the community".

d) Preferential debts and distress for rent

Where a landlord or other person has distrained on the goods of an insolvent within the three months before a compulsory liquidation or bankruptcy, preferential debts are charged on the goods distrained and the proceeds of selling them if the company's unencumbered assets are insufficient to satisfy the preferential debts in full.[45] In the case of a bankruptcy the charge is over distrained goods recovered in respect of the six months' rent due before the bankruptcy rather than over goods in respect of an earlier period which will already have fallen into the bankrupt's estate under section 347(2) of the Insolvency Act 1986. The distrainor is subrogated to the rights of the company's preferential creditors to the extent that their claims are satisfied out of the distrained goods or the proceeds of sale.

This does not apply in a voluntary liquidation[46] in respect of which the only limitation is that the court may order that distress shall not be levied or completed after passing of winding up resolution.[47] The court will usually interfere where the landlord tries to distrain after the liquidation has commenced in respect of arrears which have arisen before the commencement of the liquidation.

6. Preferential debts and floating charges

The holders of floating charges have been postponed to preferential creditors since 1897. The current provision is section 175(2)(b) of the Insolvency Act 1986 which provides that preferential debts, so far as the assets of the company available for payment of general creditors are insufficient to meet them, have priority over the claims of holders of

---

[44] At para. 1435.
[45] s.176 (liquidation), s.347(3) (bankruptcy) of the Insolvency Act 1986.
[46] *Herbert Berry Associates Ltd v. IRC* [1978] 1 All E.R. 161.
[47] *Re Roundwood Colliery Co.* [1897] 1 Ch. 373. The liquidator has the power to apply to the court for such an order under section 112 of the Insolvency Act 1986.

debentures secured by, or holders of, any floating charge[48] created by the company, and shall be paid out of property subject to that charge.

Creditors secured by a floating charge are entitled to an indemnity from the general assets of the company; this will have no relevance where the floating charge is over the entire undertaking. If a floating charge crystallises before the company goes into liquidation as a result of the appointment of a receiver, claimants in respect of debts which would be preferential on a liquidation at that date have priority for payment out of the assets subject to the charge.[49] If the company then goes into liquidation, another set of preferential claims will arise in respect of that later relevant date. Where a liquidation precedes a receivership, the only set of preferential claims will be that arising at the start of the liquidation.

If a floating charge crystallises on a company going into liquidation, the expenses of the liquidation will be payable out of the assets comprised in the charge in priority to the amount secured by the charge.[50] This is because the preferential creditors are themselves postponed to the expenses.

In certain circumstances, problems of circularity of priority can give rise to difficulty in deciding the order of payment. This happens where a floating charge has priority over a subsequent fixed charge which in turn has priority over the preferential debts. In *Re Woodroffes (Musical Instruments) Ltd*[51] it was held that the floating chargee should be treated as subrogated to the rights of the fixed chargee to the extent of the sum secured by the floating charge so that the floating chargee obtained priority over preferential creditors in right of the fixed charge. In *Re Portbase Clothing Ltd*[52] Chadwick J. disputed the correctness of this analysis and preferred instead to follow the Australian case of *Waters v. Widdows*[53] in which it was held that, as a matter of statutory policy, the fixed chargee by subordinating his claim to that of the floating chargee also subordinated them to the preferential creditors.

The question of what happens when a receiver is appointed under a floating charge which is subordinate to another floating charge has been considered above.[54]

---

[48] Defined by the Insolvency Act 1986, s.251 as a charge which, as created, was a floating charge. The question of whether and, if so, when the charge crystallised is not, therefore, relevant.

[49] Insolvency Act 1986, s.40. See Chap. 6.5(c) above.

[50] *Re Barleycorn Enterprises Ltd* [1970] Ch. 465.

[51] [1986] Ch. 366.

[52] [1993] Ch. 388.

[53] [1984] V.R. 503.

[54] See Chap. 6.5(c).

7. Ordinary creditors

The ordinary creditors are a residual category of creditors in that they encompass all those who have not been specifically allocated to some other category of creditor.

8. Post insolvency interest[55]

Interest will be payable on debts proved in the insolvency at the official rate of interest.[56] Interest on both preferential and ordinary debts will be paid out of any surplus remaining after payment of the ordinary creditors. Interest will rank equally, irrespective of the status of the debt on which it is payable.

9. Deferred creditors[57]

A number of provisions have the effect of deferring the claims of those who have been involved in an insolvent business at less than arm's length. If money is advanced in return for payments contingent on or varying with the profits of the business by a lender who does not thereby become a partner in the business, that lender is postponed to all the other creditors in the event of the borrower's insolvency.[58] If a company is under an obligation to repurchase or redeem shares at the start of a liquidation, those claims are postponed to all other debts and liabilities of the company except those due to members in their character as such.[59] Sums due to a member in his character as member may not be claimed in competition with any other creditor who is not a member of the company.[60] The House of Lords has held[61] that sums due to a member in his character as a member were restricted to those sums falling due under and by virtue of the statutory contract contained in section 14 of the Companies Act 1985; a member having a cause of action independent of the statutory contract will be in the same position as other creditors. Sums owed to those found liable for fraudulent or

---

[55] Insolvency Act 1986, s 189 (liquidation), Insolvency Act 1986, s.328 (bankruptcy).
[56] The greater of the rate specified in s.17 of the Judgments Act 1838 on the day on which the insolvency regime started and the rate applicable to the debt apart from the insolvency.
[57] Insolvency Rules 1986, r. 12.3(2A).
[58] Partnership Act 1890, ss2(3), 3.
[59] Companies Act 1985, s.178.
[60] Insolvency Act 1986, s.74.
[61] *Soden v. British Commonwealth Holdings* [1997] 4 All E.R. 353. The shareholder was claiming damages for negligent misrepresentation which had induced the purchase of the shares; this was held not to be owed in its character as a member.

wrongful trading may also be deferred to other claims against the company.[62] As noted above,[63] English law has not developed a doctrine of equitable subordination as has happened in the United States.

A similar principle of deferring the claims of those closely associated with the insolvent can be seen in the provision of bankruptcy law which defers loans by spouses. Section 329 of the Insolvency Act 1986 provides that bankruptcy debts[64] owed in respect of credit provided by a person who was the bankrupt's spouse at the commencement of the bankruptcy[65] will rank in priority after the ordinary debts and interest on the preferential and ordinary debts.

10. Attempts to contract out of the statutory scheme[66]

The *pari passu* principle is mandatory and strikes down agreements which have as their effect an unequal distribution (except as provided for by the law) amongst the ordinary creditors on an insolvency.[67] Agreements may seek to achieve this effect by excluding or altering the set-off rules which would otherwise apply or by subordinating the right of a debtor or debtors to be paid *pari passu* with the other ordinary creditors. There has been more success with the latter category of agreement than the former.

National Westminster Bank Ltd v. Halesowen Presswork & Assemblies Ltd[68] is a leading case in this area. This was a case in which it had been agreed during attempts to rescue an ailing company that the company's overdrawn account should be frozen and that a new account would be opened which would remain in credit; the bank would not set the two accounts off against each other. The company subsequently went into liquidation and the House of Lords held that an agreement of this sort could not operate to exclude the rules on set-off contained in the insolvency legislation. These were rules of public policy for the orderly administration of the assets of an insolvent rather than private rights which creditors would be free to alter. The only way to have achieved the desired result would have been to open the second account with a different bank.

A set-off agreement which provides for set-off in circumstances not provided for by the insolvency legislation will be equally ineffective;

---

[62] Insolvency Act 1986, s.215(4).
[63] Chap. 31.6.
[64] And interest on them since the start of the bankruptcy.
[65] Their status at the time the credit was provided is irrelevant.
[66] See Wood, *The Law of Subordinated Debt*; Chap. 40 of Gough, *Company Charges*; Oditah (1992) 108 L.Q.R. 459; Nolan [1995] J.B.L. 485.
[67] *ex p. Mackay* (1873) 8 Ch. App. 643.
[68] [1972] A.C. 785.

those with claims against the company must be paid *pari passu* and the quantum of the claim is to be established in accordance with the legislation. An example was the case of *British Eagle International Air Lines Ltd v. Compagnie Nationale Air France.*[69] The International Air Transport Association ("IATA") had set up a clearing house system for the monthly settlement of debits and credits arising as between members. A balance would be struck between the total sum owing to a particular member in respect of services supplied by it for all other members and the total owing by that member in respect of services supplied by all other members. The House of Lords said that debits and credits cleared through the system before the commencement of a liquidation would bind the liquidator of a member but that the liquidator could recover uncleared credits owing to the company and that members with uncleared debits against the company would each have to prove for them. Each member could set off the sums owing to it individually by the company against its individual indebtedness to the company.

The Cork Committee recommended[70] that a creditor should be permitted to agree in advance to waive his right to invoke set off; the recommendation was not accepted. It has, however, been held, in *Re Maxwell Communications Corp. (No. 2)*,[71] that a subordination agreement, in which a creditor agrees to subordinate his claim to that of others, will be effective. Vinelott J. held that the principle for which the *Halesowen* case is authority only prevented one creditor from gaining an advantage over another and that a subordination agreement does not have that effect. It has also been pointed out[72] that creditors are expressly permitted[73] to assign a right of dividend in a liquidation to other creditors; it would be strange if the agreement pursuant to which such an assignment were made were to be held void.

---

[69] [1975] 1 W.L.R. 758.
[70] At para. 306.
[71] [1994] 1 B.C.L.C. 1.
[72] Goode, *Principles of Corporate Insolvency* (2nd ed.), p. 146.
[73] By Insolvency Rules 1986, r. 11.11(1).

PART VI

AN INTRODUCTION TO ISSUES OF CROSS-BORDER INSOLVENCY

CHAPTER 36

AN INTRODUCTION TO CROSS-BORDER ISSUES

1. Introduction

Many insolvencies (particularly, and increasingly, corporate insolvencies) have international aspects to them in that either the assets or the creditors, or both, are in more than one jurisdiction. Whilst the most efficient and, therefore, asset-maximising approach would be for the insolvency to be dealt with in one set of proceedings with universal effect, there are tremendous problems in achieving such an outcome. The insolvency laws of the various jurisdictions differ considerably both in matters of principle and matters of detail so that the outcome for any particular creditor may be significantly different depending upon which set of rules determines his claim. Jurisdictions also adopt different approaches to the question of what sort of connection with the jurisdiction the parties to litigation there should have. These problems raise huge difficulties in deciding who should control the proceedings and what rules should be applied. A couple of examples from recent global insolvencies serve to demonstrate the nature of the issues which may arise.

Re BCCI (No. 10)[1] is an example of the how two systems may have fundamentally different distributional rules. Liquidations were being conducted in England and in Luxembourg, with the English liquidation ancillary to the main one. The English liquidators wished to transfer the funds at their disposal to the foreign liquidators to facilitate world wide distribution. Luxembourg law does not recognise the right to set-off provided by insolvency law in the United Kingdom. The court held that the liquidators would have to retain sufficient funds to satisfy those creditors in the English liquidation who would have benefited from rights of set-off.

The simultaneous administration in the United Kingdom and Chapter 11 Bankruptcy in the United States of Maxwell Communication Corporation threw into sharp relief the many differences between the two systems, both of principle and of detail. The agreement arrived at with

---

[1] [1996] B.C.C. 980. See Fletcher [1997] J.B.L. 471.

creditors in both jurisdictions had to cope with numerous differences of detail between the requirements of the English scheme of arrangement and the U.S. plan of reorganisation. For example, Chapter 11 debars new creditors from coming forward and claiming in an insolvency after a fixed date whereas English law allows creditors to catch up with distributions which they have missed. Chapter 11 converts claims into dollars at the time of filing whereas English law converts claims into sterling at the start of the scheme. United States priority and English preferential creditors are defined differently. Under Chapter 11, creditors can vote by post and approval needs a two-thirds majority whereas in England they must vote at the meeting and the required majority is three-quarters. A major difference in principle was encountered by the administrators in their attempt to set aside various payments made to creditors immediately prior to the administration which had the effect of putting those creditors in a better position than the other unsecured creditors.[2] As has been seen,[3] English law requires that the insolvency practitioner establish that the company was influenced by the desire to prefer in making the payments whereas under the United States Bankruptcy Code the question of intention is irrelevant.

This chapter will consider briefly[4] the issues of English jurisdiction over insolvencies with a foreign aspect to them, English recognition of overseas insolvencies and attempts at achieving international co-operation.

2. The jurisdiction of English courts[5]

a) Insolvent foreign individual

A bankruptcy petition may not be presented to the court[6] unless the debtor is domiciled[7] in England and Wales or is personally present in the jurisdiction on the day when the petition is presented or has at any time in the three years ending on that day been ordinarily resident,[8] has had

---

[2] See Fletcher [1997] J.B.L. 476.
[3] See Chap. 30 above.
[4] For greater detail on this area, see Fletcher, *The Law of Insolvency*, Pt. III, Smart. *Cross-border Insolvency*. Ziegel (ed.), *Current Developments in Comparative and International Corporate Insolvency*. Rajak, *Insolvency Law: Theory and Practice*, Pt. IV.
[5] The Brussels Convention on the Jurisdiction and Enforcement of Judgments (implemented by the Civil Jurisdiction and Judgments Act 1982) does not apply to insolvencies.
[6] Insolvency Act 1986, s.264.
[7] See Dicey and Morris, *The Conflict of Laws* (12th ed.), Chap. 7.
[8] *Re Bright* (1903) 19 T.L.R. 203.

a place of residence or has carried on business[9] in the jurisdiction. Where the debtor is normally absent from the jurisdiction it may prove difficult to serve a statutory demand.

An individual can only be adjudicated bankrupt if he owes debts recognised by English law. If he has been discharged from the debts as a result of proceedings in another jurisdiction and that discharge is recognised by English law, he will not be a debtor. English courts will only recognise the discharge if it was granted in the country whose law is the proper law of the obligation or is recognised by that law. In *Gibbs v. La Société Industrielle*,[10] for example, the English courts refused to recognise discharge of a debt granted by the French courts where they considered that the proper law of the obligation was English. The individual will also not be a debtor for the purposes of being made bankrupt if the debt is based on a foreign judgment not recognised in this country.

The court's jurisdiction to make a bankruptcy order is discretionary so even where the above requirements are met, the court may still decide that it would be more appropriate for insolvency proceedings to take place elsewhere. In practice, the courts will refuse to make an order if the debtor has no assets in the jurisdiction.[11] It is no obstacle to the making of an order that concurrent proceedings are pending abroad or that the debtor has already been adjudicated bankrupt abroad.

b) Insolvent foreign company

The nationality of a company is determined by the place of its incorporation. Any company incorporated in England and Wales will be treated as a domestic company subject to liquidation under Part IV of the Insolvency Act regardless of where its business is carried out.

A company which was incorporated abroad may be wound up under Part V of the Insolvency Act 1986 as an unregistered company[12] on the basis that it is dissolved, or has ceased to carry on business, or is carrying on business only for the purpose of winding up its affairs or is unable to pay its debts or where the court is of the opinion that it is just and equitable that it should be wound up. Given that English law recognises the dissolution of a company under the laws of its country of incorporation, this means that strictly there is nothing left to be wound up and that the English assets of the dissolved company will have

---

[9] See *Theophile v. Solicitor General* [1950] A.C. 186, *Re Bird* [1962] 2 All E.R. 406, *Re Brauch* [1978] Ch. 316, *Re a debtor* [1992] Ch. 554.
[10] (1890) 25 Q.B.D. 399.
[11] Smart [1989] J.B.L. 126.
[12] Insolvency Act 1986, s.221(5).

passed to the Crown as *bona vacantia*. The courts have adopted the approach that in such a case the dissolved foreign company is deemed to be revived in order to undergo winding up in this country[13]; the Crown's title to the goods is treated as defeasible on such a revival.[14]

Section 225 of the Insolvency Act 1986 provides specifically that an overseas company carrying on business in Great Britain may be wound up here even though it has been dissolved under the laws of its country of incorporation.[15]

There is no statutory explanation of when the courts should exercise their wide jurisdiction and order a winding up; the relevant principles have to be extracted from the case law. There will have to be some connection with this jurisdiction before the court will agree to make an order.[16] The company need not have a place of business here[17] but there will usually need to be either assets of the company within the jurisdiction or one or more persons concerned with the distribution of the assets over whom jurisdiction is exercisable.[18] The assets may be of any nature so that a claim against an insurer[19] or some right of action maintainable here with a reasonable possibility of success[20] will suffice. The assets need not be distributable by the liquidator to the creditors; it will suffice that a claim may be made against a third party such as an insurer under the Third Parties (Rights Against Insurers) Act 1930 or, by an employee, against the National Insurance Fund. In *International Westminster Bank v. Okeanos*[21] the court went further and held that it was not even necessary that there should be assets in the jurisdiction; it was enough that there was a sufficiently close connection with the jurisdiction established by the debtor borrowing money here together with an absence of any more suitable forum in which proceedings could be maintained and some prospect of benefit to the creditors.[22] A similar conclusion was reached by Harman J. in *ex p. Nycklen Finance Co. Ltd.*[23]

---

[13] *Russian and English Bank v. Baring Bros* [1936] A.C. 405.

[14] *ibid.*, also *Re Azoff-Don Commercial Bank* [1954] 1 Ch. 315, *Re Banque Industrielle de Moscou* [1952] 1 Ch. 919.

[15] This was added to the legislation in 1929 but in fact adds little to the common law position which the courts have arrived at in relation to the predecessors of Insolvency Act 1986, s.221(5).

[16] *Re Real Estate Development Co.* [1991] B.C.L.C. 210 is an example of a case in which the court refused to make an order on the basis that there was insufficient connection with the jurisdiction.

[17] *Banque des Marchands de Moscou v. Kindersley* [1951] 1 Ch. 112, CA.

[18] *Re Compania Merabello San Nicholas SA* [1973] 1 Ch. 75.

[19] *ibid.*

[20] *Re Eloc Electro-Optieck and Communicatie BV* [1981] 2 All E.R. 1111.

[21] [1988] Ch. 210.

[22] From a wrongful trading action.

[23] [1991] B.C.L.C. 539.

The court may decide to stay proceedings in this country on the basis that foreign proceedings constitute a more appropriate forum. It may also make a winding up order with object of conducting an ancillary winding up, as in *Re Federal Bank of Australia*.[24] An ancillary liquidation involves the application of the rules of English insolvency law to the realisation of the English assets and the assembling of a list of English creditors.

There is no jurisdiction to make an administration order against a foreign company but in *Re Dallhold Estates*[25] such an order was made in response to a request by a foreign court under section 426 of the Insolvency Act 1986.[26]

c) Entitlement of foreign claimants

The English court will give equal effect to claims by foreign creditors with the exception of claims by foreign states to enforce tax debts.[27]

d) Assets of the insolvent abroad

English adjudication purports to have universal application regardless of the location of the property. In relation to property outside the jurisdiction, the insolvency practitioner will have to submit a claim under local law and will be dependent on the local courts recognising the English ruling and his authority.[28] Under a general rule of private international law, the courts of one country will not enforce a foreign judgment or order which is in substance an order for the payment of foreign taxes. Courts tend to be readier to allow access to the debtor's movable property than to the immovable property. The insolvent will be under a duty to assist in the recovery of the property.

e) Creditor pursuing insolvent in another jurisdiction

Where an insolvent has assets in another jurisdiction, it would be possible for a creditor to seek redress there in a way which could cause him to obtain a greater percentage of what was owing to him than

---

[24] (1893) 62 L.J. Ch. 561.
[25] [1992] B.C.C. 394.
[26] See below.
[27] *Taylor v. Government of India* [1955] A.C. 491.
[28] *Re Maudslay, Sons and Field* [1900] 1 Ch. 602.

obtained by other creditors.[29] This would be contrary to the *pari passu* rule and the courts will do what they can to prevent this happening. There is no objection to creditors enforcing overseas security rights against the insolvent.[30]

The English courts have no power to compel a foreign court to abandon proceedings[31] although it may agree to do so.[32] However, a creditor who is subject to the jurisdiction of the English courts can be restrained from bringing or continuing any proceedings abroad in the courts' inherent power to restrain foreign proceedings.[33] If the creditor is not subject to the *"in personam"* jurisdiction of the English courts nothing can be done unless and until the creditor seeks to prove in the English insolvency. A creditor seeking to prove in the English insolvency can be compelled to bring sums recovered abroad into the common fund for the benefit of creditors generally under the hotchpot rule. In *Banco de Portugal v. Waddell*[34] the appellants, who had received a dividend in Portugal, sought to prove in the English bankruptcy. The House of Lords held that they could only receive a dividend after all the other creditors had received an amount equal to the dividend they had received in the Portuguese proceedings.

3. Recognition of foreign proceedings by English courts

As a matter of common law, the English courts will recognise bankruptcy proceedings in the country of domicile of a bankrupt and also in other situations where the bankrupt was properly subject to the jurisdiction of the courts of the country in which he was made bankrupt. Where the bankruptcy is recognised, the trustee will acquire title to moveable property in England and court may allow the sale of immovable property for benefit of creditors.

The court will recognise liquidations where they are conducted or recognised by the country of incorporation of the insolvent company,

---

[29] See, *e.g.*, the factual background to *Re Buckingham International plc*, *The Times*, November 20, 1997, in which judgment creditors of an English company noticed that assets of the debtor included debts due in the USA, obtained an order in Florida recognising the English debt and sought to garnish the debts. In this case the U.S. court granted the English liquidator a stay and, in effect, referred the case to the English court for decision.

[30] *Re Oriental Inland Steam Co.* (1874) L.R. 9 Ch. App. 557.

[31] *Re Vocalion (Foreign) Ltd* [1932] 2 Ch. 196.

[32] *Re BCCI (No. 10)* [1996] B.C.C. 980.

[33] *Bank of Tokyo v. Karoon* [1987] 1 A.C. 45, *S. N. Industrielle Aerospatiale v. Lee Kui Jak* [1987] A.C. 871, *Re Maxwell Communications Corporation plc (No. 2)* [1992] B.C.C. 757.

[34] (1880) 5 App. Cas. 161.

where the company has submitted to the jurisdiction of the foreign court[35] or where the company has carried on business within the foreign jurisdiction.

Insolvency proceedings will not be recognised where they are offensive to English public policy or are in breach of natural justice. Insolvency proceedings which amount to nothing more than an attempt to enforce the criminal or taxation laws of another country will not be recognised.[36] The courts will refuse to assist a foreign court where the English creditors will be unfairly discriminated against in the foreign proceedings; this was demonstrated in *Felixstowe Dock and Railway Co. v. USL Inc.*[37] USL, which was a United States shipping company incorporated in Delaware which carried on business in many countries including England, was in Chapter 11 Bankruptcy.[38] The New York court had issued an order purporting to be a worldwide restraint on legal action against USL. The plaintiffs proceeded to seek, and obtain, *Mareva* injunctions in England preventing USL from removing its assets from the jurisdiction. Hirst J. refused USL's application to have the injunctions set aside and the assets repatriated to the United States on a number of bases. Amongst the factors contributing to his decision was the intention of USL to withdraw from the European market so that it was unlikely that the English creditors would benefit from the worldwide reorganisation. In the course of his judgment he observed that the usual practice was to regard the courts of the place of incorporation as the principal forum for controlling a winding up of a company but that in so far as the company had assets in England it would be normal to carry out an ancillary winding up in England in accordance with English rules. He held that the assets should remain in England pending distribution in an ancillary winding up.

If a foreign liquidation is recognised, the liquidator will have authority to deal with assets in England unless there is an ancillary English winding up taking place. Claims to assets in England will still be subject to any existing rights of creditors under English law. In *Galbraith v. Grimshaw*[39] the House of Lords held that a judgment creditor who had commenced garnishee proceedings in England in order to satisfy a judgment obtained against his debtor in Scotland was not to be deprived of the fruits of this attachment by reason of the judgment debtor's subsequently becoming subject to sequestration in Scotland.

---

[35] *Re International Power Industries NV* [1985] B.C.L.C. 128.
[36] See *Government of India v. Taylor* [1955] A.C. 491, *Peter Buchanan v. McVey* [1955] A.C. 516, *Re State of Norway's Application (Nos 1 and 2)* [1989] 1 All E.R. 745.
[37] [1989] Q.B. 360.
[38] This is not a liquidation but similar recognition issues arise.
[39] [1910] A.C. 508.

4. International co-operation

a) International conventions

The ideal would be for agreement to be reached between the various jurisdictions on a set of rules allowing insolvency proceedings to be opened in one jurisdiction only and for all issues arising in the insolvency to be governed by one set of rules. Despite attempts at obtaining such international agreement going back into the nineteenth century,[40] little has so far been achieved.[41]

Two multilateral conventions of particular interest to the United Kingdom exist although neither is yet in force. One is the Istanbul Convention of 1990 prepared by the Council of Europe. The other is the E.C. Convention on Insolvency Proceedings of 1995; this has been signed by 14 of the 15 Members. The fifteenth, the United Kingdom, refused to do so because of a decision to suspend co-operation in E.C. matters in connection with the dispute over BSE in British beef. The time for signature of the convention has now expired and all 15 Members will need to give fresh agreement before it can come into force. Both conventions provide for a main bankruptcy to be opened in the state with the main connection with the insolvent and allow for secondary proceedings to be opened in other states in which the insolvent has an establishment. The E.C. Convention also makes provision for the applicable law[42]; amongst its provisions is a statement that the opening of the main proceedings will not affect rights *in rem* over assets of the debtor situated within another Member State.

The International Bar Association and the United Nations Commission on International Trade Law ("UNCITRAL") have also been working on model codes for international insolvencies.

b) Judicial co-operation

Section 426(4) of the Insolvency Act 1986 provides that the courts having jurisdiction in relation to insolvency law in any part of the United Kingdom shall assist the courts (not the office-holder) having the corresponding jurisdiction in any other part of the United Kingdom or

---

[40] See Graham, *Currrent Legal Problems* 1989.
[41] See Prior, in Rajak (ed.), *Insolvency Law: Theory and Práctice*, Chap. 14, for a survey of the insolvency treaties in existence at the beginning of the 1990s. He identified three main multilateral treaties between the Nordic countries, a group of South American countries and a group of Central American countries.
[42] Usually the state of incorporation.

any relevant country or territory. This latter category is defined[43] to denote the Channel Islands, the Isle of Man and any country or territory designated for the purposes of this section by the Secretary of State by order made by statutory instrument.[44] Examples of co-operation under the provision are *Re Dallhold Estates (U.K.) Pty Ltd*,[45] in which Chadwick J. made an administration order pursuant to a letter of request from the Australian Federal Court, and *Re BCCI (No. 2)*[46] in which declarations under sections 213, 214 and 238 of the Insolvency Act 1986 were made at the request of the Grand Court of the Cayman Islands. In *Re Focus Insurance Co. Ltd*,[47] however, the court refused to make an order for the assistance of foreign liquidators in the recovery of English assets where the relief sought could be obtained by the English trustee in bankruptcy. The Court of Appeal has recently had its first opportunity to consider the operation of section 426 of the Insolvency Act 1986 in *Hughes v. Hannover Ruckversicherungs-Aktiengesellschaft*.[48] It confirmed that the wording of section 426(5), which empowers the court to apply the insolvency law "applicable by either court in relation to comparable matters falling within its jurisdiction", gives the court a jurisdiction that it might not otherwise have had.[49] The English court may use all its general powers and jurisdiction whether or not conferred on them by virtue of "insolvency law" as defined in section 426(10) of the Insolvency Act 1986. Where the court is being asked to apply a measure of insolvency law, it should grant the assistance provided it may properly do so; where the assistance requested is a measure not having its source in insolvency law, the court has a greater degree of discretion.

English courts have also been willing to co-operate with the courts and office-holders of other jurisdictions where section 426 of the Insolvency Act 1986 is not applicable. The simultaneous administration order proceedings in England and Chapter 11 on bankruptcy in the United States of Maxwell Communications Corp. plc are much cited as an example of what can be achieved by judicial co-operation.[50] *Barclays*

---

[43] By Insolvency Act 1986, s.426(10).

[44] S.I. 1986 No. 2123, S.I. 1996 No. 253. The vast majority of countries designated are Commonwealth members. The United States is not designated despite the fact that s.304 of its bankruptcy code allows assistance in the other direction.

[45] [1992] B.C.C. 394.

[46] [1992] B.C.C. 715.

[47] [1996] B.C.C. 659.

[48] [1997] 1 B.C.L.C. See Fletcher [1997] J.B.L. 480.

[49] Such as the ability of the court in *Re Dallhold* to make an administration order in respect of a foreign company.

[50] See Chap. 25, Ziegel (ed.), *Current Developments in Comparative and International Corporate Insolvency Law*.

Bank v. Homan[51] involved an application by the plaintiff for the court to prevent the administrator from taking proceedings in the United States to set aside certain payments.[52] Hoffmann J. refused to grant an injunction, observing that it could serve no purpose except to antagonise the United States court and prejudice co-operation. He said that if the U.S. judge did not think there was sufficient connection with the U.S. jurisdiction, she would dismiss the action and, if she thought otherwise, the action would be allowed to go ahead despite any injunction.

[51] [1992] B.C.C. 757.
[52] See above in the introductory section of this chapter.

INDEX